MR.
ASSOCIATED
PRESS

The History of Communication

Robert W. McChesney and John C. Nerone, editors

A list of books in the series appears at the end of this book.

MR. ASSOCIATED PRESS

KENT COOPER
AND THE
TWENTIETH-CENTURY
WORLD OF NEWS

Gene Allen

UNIVERSITY OF ILLINOIS PRESS
Urbana, Chicago, and Springfield

Library of Congress Cataloging-in-Publication Data
Names: Allen, Gene, 1952– author.
Title: Mr. Associated Press : Kent Cooper and the
    twentieth-century world of news / Gene Allen.
Description: Urbana : University of Illinois Press, [2023]
    | Series: The history of communication | Includes
    bibliographical references and index.
Identifiers: LCCN 2022059018 (print) | LCCN 2022059019
    (ebook) | ISBN 9780252045103 (cloth) | ISBN
    9780252087233 (paperback) | ISBN 9780252054471
    (ebook)
Subjects: LCSH: Cooper, Kent, 1880–1965. | Journalists—
    United States—Biography. | Associated Press. |
    Journalism—United States—History—20th century.
Classification: LCC PN4874.C685 A45 2023 (print) | LCC
    PN4874.C685 (ebook) | DDC 070.92 [B]—dc23/
    eng/20230130
LC record available at https://lccn.loc.gov/2022059018
LC ebook record available at https://lccn.loc.gov/
    2022059019

For Erika

Contents

Acknowledgments

It is a pleasure to acknowledge the assistance I've received from many people and institutions in researching and writing this book. The research generally was supported by a grant from the Social Science and Humanities Research Council of Canada. An Everett Helm Visiting Fellowship at Indiana University supported a research trip to the Lilly Library, where Kent Cooper's personal papers are held. An appointment as Velma Rogers Research Chair in the School of Journalism at Toronto Metropolitan University from 2015 to 2018 provided time to write.

I'm grateful to archivists at several repositories. Valerie Komor, corporate archivist at Associated Press, has been a kind and thoughtful supporter of this project from the beginning. Valerie and her colleague Francesca Pitaro have been unfailingly helpful in assisting my navigation through their voluminous collection, the most important of many consulted for this history. In London, the late John Entwisle, corporate archivist at Thomson Reuters and a friend to many news-agency researchers, facilitated my access to the Reuters and Roderick Jones collections; his successor, Rory Carruthers, is carrying on in the same spirit. Staff at the Lilly Library were kind, helpful, and efficient during my research trip there, and archivists at many other repositories have gone out of their way to provide assistance.

Among academic colleagues, I'm grateful to John Nerone for his initial and continuing interest in this project and for his thoughtful comments on an earlier draft of the manuscript. Dave Nord gave me valuable advice about the Cooper and Roy Howard material at Indiana University. Heidi Tworek and Michael Stamm generously commented on specific sections of the manuscript. I'm also grateful to members of the Communication History division, International Communication Association, for their responses to several papers reporting on the research in progress. Reviewers for the University of Illinois Press were generous with their attention and constructive in their suggestions; any remaining shortcomings are, of course, entirely my responsibility. Eleanor Patterson, Jennifer Harker, and Elena Maria Egawhary efficiently tracked down relevant archival material in repositories that I was unable to visit in person.

Danny Nasset of the University of Illinois Press has been a patient and encouraging supporter of this project and has given me much useful advice. Jill Hughes's careful copyediting improved the manuscript, and Judy Davis ably compiled the index.

My greatest debt, and the one that gives me the greatest pleasure to acknowledge, is to Erika Ritter. Erika strongly encouraged me to take on this daunting project in the first place. Her support has never wavered, and I've relied on her good advice throughout. For these, and for many other reasons, this book is affectionately dedicated to her.

MR.
ASSOCIATED
PRESS

1

"Fitting Himself for the Newspaper Profession"

On February 3, 1965, at 1:30 p.m. New York time, the international wire network of the Associated Press (AP) news agency fell silent. In AP's hectic central newsroom in Rockefeller Center, the clatter of teletype machines stopped. The flow of news to and from the agency's major bureaus in the United States and abroad—Chicago, Los Angeles, Moscow, London, Tokyo, and scores of other places—came to a halt. In thousands of newsrooms and radio stations across the United States and around the world, AP printers stopped as well.

The constant flow of news through this "vast, intricately reticulated" network was AP's lifeblood, its reason for existence.[1] Shutting down the network—even for one minute, as on this occasion—was not done lightly. The unaccustomed silence, AP's equivalent of a twenty-one-gun salute, marked the funeral of Kent Cooper. As AP's general manager and executive director from 1925 to 1951 (and a senior executive for fifteen years before that), Cooper led the company through a series of transformations: in a radical restructuring of the international news system; in how AP conceived of, and presented, news; in embracing, and sometimes resisting, new and disruptive journalistic technologies; in how it managed (and at times mismanaged) the tensions between AP's self-interest and its journalistic mission; in how it dealt with governments in the United States and around the world; and in how it struggled to maintain its preeminence in a highly competitive U.S. journalistic marketplace—all within a one member, one vote system of governance that presented unusual challenges. Cooper did none of these things single-handedly, but the priorities he set and the causes he championed shaped every aspect of AP's evolution in the first half of the twentieth century. Cooper's era was a time when print journalism in the United States enjoyed unparalleled cultural authority, a solid economic foundation, and robustly growing audiences, and AP was "the chief single source of news for the American press."[2] Its standards regarding what was newsworthy and how news should be presented, stressing factual accuracy and impartiality, were widely accepted as the embodiment of journalistic objectivity and reliability. Cooper's years at AP also coincided with the high tide of growing U.S. international influence in the twentieth century, and he contributed to that growth in important ways. In championing AP's expansion into Latin America, Europe, and Asia, he shaped the way that news flowed around the world. By mid-century, AP was well on its way to becoming the world's dominant news agency, giving rise to questions about American power and dominance in international communications that continue to be raised today.[3]

In an editorial marking Cooper's death, the *New York Times*—a paper whose representatives on AP's board of directors had a long, often supportive, and sometimes contentious relationship with him—described Cooper as "almost unknown to most Americans" and yet "one of their great educators . . . a communicator—anonymous but entirely beneficial—to the world."[4] This assessment was not entirely correct. Cooper was indeed hardly a household name, but practically every newspaper editor in the United States knew him by name—or by his initials, "K. C."—and many had strong opinions about him one way or another. At times, especially in the middle to late 1940s, he actively sought a more public role—first in what he termed a "crusade" to bring American-style press freedom (or at least American-style news) to every country in the world and then, in a related campaign, to prevent AP from supplying its news to the U.S. State Department's Voice of America broadcasts.[5] He wrote (or cowrote) four books, all calculated to enhance AP's, and his own, reputation. Cooper was nothing if not highly aware and protective of his public and professional image.

For all that, though, the *Times* was correct in saying that most Americans had never heard of Cooper, and except for specialists in the history of journalism and communication, his name is not widely recognized today. But for more than twenty-five years in the middle decades of the twentieth century, Cooper's judgments about what kind of news AP should cover and how it should be covered, and his views about the proper place of American journalism outside the United States, conditioned the way that millions of Americans—and, eventually, hundreds of millions more in other countries—learned about what was going on in their nations and elsewhere in the world. As the *Times* observed, between 1925 and 1948 Cooper "in a very real sense *was* the Associated Press." When anyone thought of AP during those years, "you thought of Mr. Cooper. And when you thought of Mr. Cooper you thought of the A.P. The identification was complete and compelling."[6] He ran AP as a "one-man show," usually (though not invariably) persuading the board of directors to go along with whatever he wanted to pursue.[7] Cooper, in short, was a much more significant figure in the history of the twentieth century than the limited public knowledge of his life and work might suggest.

Many of the issues that Cooper grappled with remain relevant today. Some involve journalism's most basic claim: that it provides a reliable, factual account of happenings in the world. The notion of objectivity has faced critical scrutiny for decades, sometimes by journalists and sometimes by their critics.[8] In the United States, outlets like Fox News now embrace overt political bias, presenting it as a corrective to an illusory impartiality that actually masks liberal bias and spreading dangerous falsehoods in the service of ideology.[9] But for Cooper and his AP colleagues, objectivity was an unquestioned value. What did objectivity, and the related idea of impartiality, mean to him? AP news, Cooper insisted, was truthful and unbiased. How did he understand those values and put them into effect? Cooper often asserted with pride that AP was independent and free of outside influence. But independent of whom? For Cooper, it was a matter of independence from government influence and from the overt political agendas of individual AP publishers, even while he vigorously defended private ownership as the essential and only foundation for truthful journalism.

Cooper was also in charge of AP's health as a business, and here too versions of the questions he faced are often heard today: Does competition produce better journalism or a race to the bottom? To what extent is news a form of entertainment? How do new technologies affect established journalistic practices? Should they be embraced—and if so, at what cost—or resisted, and if so, how? Can journalism have a public service role and an imperative to succeed in the market at the same time? The assault on journalism as an "enemy of the people" and on fact-based discourse generally by former U.S. president Donald Trump, along with the devastation of long-established journalistic business models, make these questions particularly urgent.

At 1:31 p.m. on February 3, 1965, teletype machines in the Rockefeller Center newsroom, in AP bureaus everywhere, and in newsrooms around the world started up again, hammering out news copy at sixty words a minute.

*   *   *

Kent Cooper was born on March 22, 1880, in Columbus, Indiana, a town of forty-eight hundred people some forty-five miles south of Indianapolis. In a memoir published almost eighty years later, Cooper remembered it as "a quiet, God-fearing community in which life flowed sweetly without any of the alarms such as those which arise from the present-day global turmoil."[10] His father, George W. Cooper, had just completed a two-year term as mayor and was then serving as city attorney. In 1888 the senior Cooper was elected to Congress as a Democrat and served three terms. Cooper's mother, the former Sina Green, was also unusually accomplished; she was one of the first women to attend and graduate from Indiana University and the only woman in George Cooper's class, where the two met. Kent was their fourth child; he had three older sisters.

Kent Cooper's name first appeared in print when he was nine years old. During a Sunday school picnic, Kent went into the Driftwood River with friends, got in over his head, and (as the *Indianapolis Journal* reported) "would have drowned but for the timely assistance of a gentleman who happened along at the critical moment."[11] He was pulled unconscious from the river and resuscitated. Two years later, a reporter for the *Louisville (KY) Courier-Journal* recounted that Kent had dug up a trove of old Spanish, Mexican, Italian, and American silver coins on his uncle's farm near Bloomington, Indiana.[12] "Even at that age I was fascinated with what he wrote," Cooper recalled in his autobiography. "It was about me!"[13] One of Cooper's first decisions as general manager of the Associated Press more than thirty years later was to make room in the report for more human-interest stories; these early appearances in print might have planted a germ of that idea.

As the son of a prominent family, with an active social life, Cooper appeared often in the pages of the *Columbus (IN) Evening Republican* during his teenage years. He began working for the paper on summer vacations at the age of eleven—first in the printing shop and then recording the arrivals and departures of railway travelers.[14] In a typical news item, sixteen-year-old Kent was one of a "party of fun-loving young folks" who "tendered a merry surprise" to two young visitors from nearby Shelbyville in the mid-summer of 1896.[15] In 1897 he spoke for the junior class at commencement exercises at Central High School, and other brief items recorded his accomplishments as a musician and performer.[16] Since bylines were extremely rare in American newspapers before around 1920, there is no way of knowing who actually wrote these reports. It's possible, though, that Cooper may have written some of them himself as he took on greater responsibilities at the *Evening Republican*; in 1898, when the paper's city editor suddenly resigned, it was seventeen-year-old Cooper who "cover[ed] the local field" that day.[17]

George Cooper's political career widened Kent's horizons. During the six years that he represented Indiana's Fifth District in Congress, the family, including Kent, spent two winters in Washington, D.C. Vigorous partisanship was still the norm in American journalism at the time, though this was beginning to change. Indianapolis, the closest big city to Columbus, exemplified the broader trends, with one pro-Republican paper (the *Indianapolis Journal*), one Democratic organ (the *Indianapolis State Sentinel*), and one adopting a neutral, impartial approach (the *Indianapolis News*.)[18] In 1892, as the senior Cooper pursued explosive allegations of corruption in Washington against the federal commissioner of pensions, the *Journal* denounced him as an "insectiferous demagogue," while the loyal *Sentinel* assured its readers that their representative "completely exonerate[d] himself" of counter-charges that his office was enmeshed in corrupt practices of its own.[19] Years later, Kent Cooper stressed political impartiality as a key characteristic of AP news. The "vituperative, pyrotechnic, brilliant partisan journalism" of the nineteenth century was "picturesque, but . . . it was not service," he wrote. The crucial thing was "accuracy of statement, and without bias." Now "both sides to a controversy, political, social or religious . . . have access to the news columns. . . . People of opposite views can read the same paper."[20] He might have had the one-sided attacks on and defense of his father in mind as he wrote these words.

Kent was an enthusiastic supporter of his father's political career. At the age of twelve he organized a "Cooper Club," whose members "paraded and campaigned in the towns of the congressional district, accompanied by their own band."[21] By the time Kent was sixteen, however—after his father's congressional defeat in 1894—his political affiliation had changed. A few days after the 1896 presidential election, in which William McKinley soundly defeated William Jennings Bryan, Kent was among a group of "Republican friends" treated to an oyster supper by a group of young Democrats in settlement of a pre-election wager.[22] "In every direction the noble countenance of William McKinley greeted the eye," the *Evening Republican* reported. Souvenirs included "dollars for the ladies tied with ribbon and inscribed 'in gold we trust and in silver we bust.'" During his long AP career, Cooper generally kept his own political preferences to himself and repeatedly stressed the importance of impartiality in AP news coverage. In the extensive collections of the AP Corporate Archives, none of the correspondence to or from Cooper mentions his personal political beliefs— though in an AP oral history interview conducted in the 1980s, Alan Gould, who worked closely with Cooper for decades, described him as a "strong Republican, a card-carrying qualified Roosevelt-hater."[23] Other sources confirm that Cooper's political leaning, however carefully he may have limited its expression, was distinctly Republican,[24] and this apparently began at an early age.

Around this time, Cooper decided on a career: he wanted to be a journalist. In September 1898, he left Columbus to attend Indiana University "with a view to fitting himself for the newspaper profession, for which he has a natural inclination."[25] But early in Cooper's second year, his father's health, which had been deteriorating for years, became a critical problem. After undergoing an operation for tuberculosis in the fall of 1899, the elder Cooper died on November 27, at the age of forty-eight. One of his final acts was to ask a friend—the former publisher of the *Indianapolis News*, who was starting a new newspaper, the *Press*—to find a job for his son.[26] Kent left university and began work as a reporter for the *Indianapolis Press* in December 1899, earning twelve dollars a week; by 1903 he was covering the police beat for the *Indianapolis Sun* and became city editor soon afterward. At the time of his mother's death—at the age of fifty-three, on Christmas Eve 1904—the rival *Indianapolis Star* described him as a "well-known newspaper man."[27]

Near the end of 1903, Cooper had his first involvement with a news agency, the kind of institution that would occupy almost the next fifty years of his life. The *Sun* was a client of the Scripps-McRae news agency, which provided regional, national, and international news, mainly to newspapers in the midwestern and western United States.[28] The telegraph operator who transcribed agency dispatches coming into the newsroom by Morse code—and who occasionally transmitted noteworthy Indianapolis stories out onto the network—sat near Cooper's desk. News agencies like Scripps-McRae (and the Associated Press and many others) came into existence after it became apparent in the midnineteenth century that the telegraph allowed tremendous efficiencies in the distribution of fresh news. Instead of waiting for out-of-town newspapers to arrive in the mail, or with travelers, and reprinting the regional, national, and international news they contained, local editors could receive news from distant places almost instantaneously. The much higher costs of telegraphic news (clipping news from other papers cost essentially nothing) were mitigated by the fact that one telegraphic report could be distributed to many recipients at once, as long as they were on the same telegraphic circuit, and the costs shared among them. News agencies organized the collection and distribution of telegraphic news, and by 1900 they were the indispensable infrastructure of daily journalism. When Cooper sent a one-hundred-word local news story to Scripps-McRae's Chicago bureau, he became its de facto Indianapolis correspondent.[29]

After becoming a semi-regular Scripps-McRae contributor, Cooper proposed that for ten dollars a week he would sign up ten additional clients for the agency among small Indiana papers that did not already subscribe, providing a five-hundred-word daily news package. Within six months, Cooper had signed up enough new clients to guarantee him fifteen dollars a week, and he then re-signed from the *Sun* to work full-time for Scripps-McRae. Until 1920, Cooper was mainly a specialist in news distribution and in news agency management and strategy rather than a reporter or editor; his full-time newspaper employment in Indianapolis lasted a little less than four years. But editing and filing a daily news report for Scripps-McRae clients certainly required the exercise of journalistic skills. Much of his work involved selling the news service to clients, maintaining those relationships, and organizing distribution channels, but the journalistic functions of selection, editing, and emphasis—deciding which stories would be sent each day and in what order, editing each story to a suitable length within the overall five-hundred-word limit, and meeting deadlines—were equally important.

Now in his mid-twenties, Cooper increasingly demonstrated ambition and a willingness to go his own way. When Scripps-McRae turned down his request for a raise in 1905, he quit and set up a small agency of his own to serve his existing clients. Cooper was one of five directors, along with the former private secretary of the outgoing Republican state governor.[30] Cooper was active at the time in local Republican circles, serving as a delegate at the state party's Indianapolis convention in 1904.[31]

Organizing a supply of news for his agency's clients brought Cooper, for the first time, into contact with the long-established and dominant Associated Press. In April 1905, he asked AP whether it would allow one of its members, the *Chicago News*, to exchange news with his organization.[32] He realized that this was against AP's rules—exclusivity, both of AP news provided to its members and of members' local news supplied back to AP, was the foundation of AP's structure, and for decades after 1910 Cooper spent much of his time protecting this exclusivity. But since another AP member in Chicago already exchanged news with Scripps-McRae, Cooper wondered if a similar arrangement could be made with the *News*. There is no record of a response to this inquiry. A year later Cooper was hired back by Scripps-McRae and spent the next several years with Scripps and its successor, United Press (UP), first as manager of the Indianapolis bureau and then as a traveling sales agent throughout the middle western and mid-central states.[33]

Cooper's advancement was based on a relatively new method of distributing news to small newspaper clients: the telephone. He negotiated special press rates with the Bell system's Indiana subsidiary, allowing small-scale "pony" clients on a common telephone circuit to receive more news than could be sent by telegraph for the same cost.[34] When this proved to be a success, attracting more clients, he was asked to expand his efforts to the larger multi-state area. Bell had received inquiries about distributing news by telephone as early as 1880, and in general, the transmission of information had been migrating from telegraph to telephone for more than twenty years by the time Cooper got involved.[35] But he may have been the first to apply it to news agency operations in a systematic way. By 1910, however, after several years of near-constant travel on a budget of two dollars a day for meals and accommodation, Cooper decided to leave UP and once again go into business on his own.

Cooper married in 1905. His wife, the former Daisy McBride, was the daughter of Robert McBride, a former Indiana Supreme Court judge who was then a prominent lawyer in Indianapolis. This was Daisy's second marriage.[36] It is not clear whether she was widowed or divorced; in any case, she had two children and was ten years older than Cooper. The Cooper-McBride wedding was a low-key affair, held at the bride's parents' house in Indianapolis, with only members of their immediate families attending.[37] For a single woman in her mid-thirties with two children, the ambitious, twenty-five-year-old Cooper, from a respectable family and with decent prospects if not wealthy, might have seemed a good and possibly providential match. Cooper's own reasons are harder to understand. If he married for love, one might expect him to have said something about this first, fifteen-year-long marriage in his autobiography. In fact, Daisy Cooper is not mentioned anywhere in it or in any of his other writings. He may have seen marriage to the daughter of a prominent Indianapolis lawyer as socially, and perhaps financially, advantageous. No evidence has come to light that could answer these questions definitively, as is the case with many other aspects of Cooper's personal life. In February 1908, Daisy gave birth to a daughter, Jane, Cooper's only direct descendant.[38]

After leaving United Press, Cooper traveled to New York in the fall of 1910. His plan was to establish a company to distribute news by telephone throughout the United States to small newspapers served by all three national news agencies: Associated Press, United Press, and the Hearst-owned International News Service. He first discussed the plan with Charles H. Wilson, the general manager of AT&T, who suggested that Cooper present the idea to Melville Stone, the venerable general manager of AP.[39]

Stone had been AP's general manager since 1893, when he played a pivotal role in establishing its primacy among American agencies by securing exclusive U.S. rights to the international news provided by the dominant cartel of Reuters, the French agency Havas, and the German agency Wolff. Since the 1850s, these three had divided up the world among themselves for the collection, interchange, and distribution of telegraphic news—roughly paralleling the expansion of their respective nations' territorial empires.[40] By securing exclusive rights to the cartel's news, Stone gave AP a decisive advantage in a life-or-death struggle with a competing agency (confusingly called United Press, though it had no connection to the Scripps-backed agency established in 1907).[41] In exchange, AP gave the cartel exclusive rights to distribute its U.S. domestic news in most parts of the world; its own news distribution activities were strictly confined to North America, Central America, and the Caribbean. Many of the powerful publishers who had gone through the 1893 struggle with Stone were still members of its board of directors—notably, Victor Lawson of the *Chicago Daily News*, Frank Noyes of the *Washington Star* (who became AP's president in 1900), and Adolph Ochs of the *New York Times*. Although a special committee appointed by the board of directors had recently investigated, then decisively rejected, charges that Stone was "controlled absolutely" by Standard Oil,[42] no one doubted that Stone's forging of AP's alliance with the cartel had been essential to its continued success.

Compared to the organizations Cooper had been involved with until 1910, AP was a colossus, the dominant U.S. news agency for more than a decade, with a truly national reach.[43] Unlike its competitors, it was a nonprofit cooperative jointly owned by its newspaper members. All members were required to provide their own news exclusively to AP before publication, which gave it tremendous strength in U.S. domestic newsgathering. AP was dominated by well-established morning newspapers that generally served more affluent readers and was considered a conservative, though not overtly Republican, institution;[44] its political coverage, in fact, was carefully neutral to the point of dullness. When it came to labor disputes, however, AP was sharply criticized for favoring the rights of property. Upton Sinclair—not, admittedly, a neutral observer—denounced it in his book *The Brass Check* as a "reactionary organization" and "leading agency of capitalist repression."[45] It also fiercely protected the interests of local members by giving many of them an effective veto over the admission of new competitors, leading to charges (and, on a few occasions, adverse court rulings) that it was monopolistic. This also contributed to the growth of competing agencies serving newspapers that could not obtain AP's news service, especially E. W. Scripps's United Press Association.

Stone was one of four men—the others were Noyes, who remained AP's president during much of Cooper's tenure as general manager; Noyes's immediate successor, Robert McLean; and Roderick Jones, the managing director of Reuters—with whom Cooper had intense, important (and sometimes difficult) relationships. Stone cast a long shadow over Cooper's career at AP—in the role of counselor, he continued to exercise considerable influence even after Cooper became general manager in 1925—and Cooper's account of their first meeting is revealing in several respects. First, while Cooper devoted several pages to this encounter in his autobiography, Stone did not mention Cooper at all in his own memoir or in any other published work. (Almost forty years later, Cooper lamented that he had never been "Stone's white-hired boy."[46]) Cooper's account also emphasizes how old-fashioned he found AP: "The place was not even pleasantly antique—it reeked of old age."[47] Cooper always considered himself a modernizer as AP's chief executive, and his first impression was that there was much modernization to be done.

Cooper depicted himself as being quite unwilling, at first, to work for AP, practically insulting Stone by telling him that the agency Stone had led for almost twenty years was "moribund." But Stone was concerned about losing small-town AP members to the cheaper method of distributing news that Cooper had developed and was impressed by Cooper's knowledge of distribution channels. When Cooper explained, apparently off the cuff, why it would be cheaper to provide news by telephone to the AP member in Burlington, Vermont, from Albany, New York, rather than from AP's main New England bureau in Boston—he had memorized the distances involved—Stone offered him a job on the spot. After some hesitation, Cooper accepted because he thought AP would offer better chances of advancement than United Press: "I thought I might go further . . . than I could at the United Press[,] where there were several competent young men with high ambitions." One of those ambitious young men was Roy Howard, three years younger than Cooper, whom Cooper had come to know when they both worked for newspapers in Indianapolis. Their careers were to be entwined in remarkable ways for many years. By 1910 Howard was general news manager of United Press and became its president two years later. By contrast, Cooper wrote, AP's men were "elderly. I had seen few young AP men anywhere."[48]

Cooper reported for work at AP headquarters, in the newly created position of traveling inspector, on December 5, 1910, beginning an association that lasted for more than forty years and eventually made him the most influential newsman in the world. Stone was not there to greet his new employee. After waiting in his anteroom for three hours, Cooper was told the general manager was en route to Chicago that day.[49]

2

Apprenticeship and Ascent

Cooper's first years at Associated Press were deeply frustrating. In his role as AP's first traveling inspector, he visited every AP bureau in the United States and almost one thousand member newspapers over a period of two years, covering some two hundred thousand miles.[1] His main assignment was to sign up smaller newspapers for a limited "pony" service delivered by telephone, as he had done in Indiana.[2] In the course of his travels, Cooper also determined that substantial savings could be made in telegraph charges, which, along with telegraphers' wages, accounted for more than 75 percent of AP's expenses.[3] His proposed remedy was to encourage competition between Western Union—which until then had almost all of AP's telegraphic business, in a sometimes collusive symbiosis that had been crucial to AP's nineteenth-century growth[4]—and other telegraph companies. But when Cooper presented this idea to Stone, arguing that it could save AP one hundred thousand dollars a year and turn an annual fifty-thousand-dollar deficit into a surplus, no action was taken. Cooper negotiated a contract that would drastically reduce the cost of AP's connections between Denver and El Paso, but his letter to Stone seeking authorization to proceed remained unanswered until he returned to New York three weeks later. Stone's explanation was that many problems solved themselves if ignored for several weeks.[5]

A year after Cooper joined AP, a member of the board of directors, V. S. McClatchy of the *Sacramento (CA) Bee*, noticed him sitting at his desk outside

Stone's office and asked what his job was. Cooper explained his position, adding that he didn't plan to remain with AP and citing the failure to adopt his plan to reduce telegraph costs as one reason. McClatchy then introduced Cooper to Adolph Ochs, publisher of the *New York Times* and one of AP's most influential directors. At noon on a Sunday, Cooper and McClatchy met Ochs in the second-floor library of his house on West Seventy-Fifth Street, where he listened with interest but some incredulity to Cooper's account of the inefficiency of Stone's office. Ochs then raised the issue with Stone, with the result that Cooper was authorized to go ahead with the cost-saving plan. Years later, Ochs looked back on this first meeting with "great satisfaction. . . . I then discovered your exceptional qualities of mind and heart; and I take the flattering unction to my soul that I know a good thing when I see it."[6] AP's president, Frank Noyes, reportedly saw this as something of a conspiracy behind Stone's back—which it was—but did not criticize Cooper, believing that his "force and desire and eagerness" were crucial to AP's success.[7] When the predicted savings were realized, Cooper was appointed superintendent of the traffic department in February 1912, with responsibility for all of AP's wires.[8]

McClatchy and Ochs also supported Cooper's proposal to revamp AP's administrative structure. As things stood, it was highly decentralized—individual bureau chiefs and correspondents hired and supervised their local telegraph operators, and four regional superintendents had extensive authority in many areas. Cooper argued that it made no sense for him to be in charge of the physical wires as head of the traffic department but not the operators (of whom AP employed more than one thousand by the 1920s).[9] More broadly, he wanted AP to adopt a structure like that of AT&T, which had separate head office divisions for commercial services, plant, and traffic.[10] In AP's case the divisions would be news, traffic, and finance. Although Cooper at this point had virtually no experience in managing a large organization, it seems as though he almost instinctively gravitated to the kind of multidivisional corporate structure that Alfred D. Chandler identified as characteristic of modernizing American business.[11] This plan was adopted in the fall of 1912, with Cooper becoming chief of the newly centralized traffic department.[12] He continued to make improvements in the traffic operation, experimenting with teletype machines to replace Morse operators in 1914 (over the objections of AP's assistant general manager, Frederick Roy Martin[13]) and establishing for the first time a cross-country telegraphic circuit—covering twenty-six thousand miles and connecting almost five hundred telegraph operators simultaneously—for AP's coverage of the 1916

World Series. Thomas Edison, relying on one of the organic metaphors that seemed inescapable when discussing telegraphic networks, congratulated AP on the achievement: "Uncle Sam has now a real arterial system and it is never going to harden."[14]

Cooper also had a sympathetic, if paternalistic, interest in the welfare of AP employees. Unlike the publishers—business owners—who made up the board of directors, Cooper was an employee for his entire AP career. While quite capable of acting peremptorily and arbitrarily toward the AP staffers who worked for him, Cooper was relatively open to approaching questions of benefits and working conditions from the employees' perspective. (This openness caused him serious problems when AP editorial employees attempted to unionize in the 1930s.[15]) His support of a pension plan for AP employees, despite opposition from directors who feared it would establish an unwelcome precedent for their own newspapers' employees, was one example of this. Cooper also began the practice—later introduced to the editorial department after he became general manager—of asking each telegrapher to fill out a personal questionnaire, suggest how AP's wire operations could be improved, and state his personal ambitions within AP. Throughout his career, Cooper saw himself as the kind of manager who established close individual relationships with and even inspired his employees. Many responded with loyalty and affection, but this was far from a universal reaction; after Cooper's death, the *New York Times* observed that AP staffers "either liked Mr. Cooper with all [their] heart, or the opposite. There was never any middle ground."[16]

By now, Cooper had overcome his early reservations about AP. Early in 1916, Roy Howard—now president of AP's main competitor, United Press—tried to hire him away: "For some time I have been after your services and partnership and Mr. Stone's goat. I think I have the one and I expect to get the other."[17] When Cooper hesitated, Howard told him that staying at AP was a gamble—based on the hope that he might succeed Stone as general manager—"rather than a cinch" meaning assurance of promotion and higher pay at UP.[18] Eventually Cooper decided to remain at AP, even though "I believe that financially speaking I am giving up the greatest opportunity that will ever come to me."[19] Howard accepted the decision gracefully: "If we can't have you in our organization, nothing would suit us better than to see you at the head of the other one. . . . You are the one man in the other organization who appreciates the uselessness and the waste of energy in much of the so-called 'competition' between the U.P. and the A.P."[20] In fact, while Cooper and Howard remained personally friendly over the next thirty-five years, competition with United Press—whose emergence as a serious rival coincided with Cooper's arrival at AP—proved to be one of the biggest and most enduring challenges he faced.[21]

While Stone never treated his subordinate with much warmth, Cooper's powerful allies on the board of directors went out of their way to praise him publicly. In a speech to AP's annual luncheon in 1918—the high point of its annual meeting, attended by hundreds of members and usually all the directors, and covered extensively in the trade press and elsewhere—Ochs singled out Cooper as someone who rose from the ranks and "has done wonders."[22] Recognition of Cooper's accomplishments went along with growing concern about Stone's ability to meet the demands of his position. In April 1918, McClatchy complained to Ochs that Stone had not responded to an inquiry from the "Federal Intelligence Bureau" (he probably meant "Bureau of Investigation") about a speech he had delivered that questioned whether German troops had carried out atrocities in Belgium. McClatchy was less concerned about the substance of Stone's remarks than the administrative shortcomings the incident revealed, something an internal review committee had identified years earlier: "This is one of many letters which because of his condition of health and mind have received no attention.... None of us wish to hurt Mr. Stone's feelings but we can not afford to sacrifice the organization."[23] If Cooper expected that Stone would not remain long as general manager, there were good reasons to think so.

*   *   *

AP's expansion into South America beginning in 1918 is rightly seen as a major turning point in its history, and Cooper was at the center of these events. Until then, he was entirely occupied with AP's domestic operations in the United States; the South American venture was the first time he became involved in the gathering and delivery of news outside the United States, which became a major focus of his career for the next thirty years. Under its contract with the Reuters-Havas-Wolff cartel, AP was allowed to supply its news only to newspapers in the United States, Canada, Mexico, Central America, the islands of the Caribbean, the Philippines, and Hawaii.[24] South America was part of the extensive territory reserved to the French agency Havas (along with Italy, Spain, Portugal, and Switzerland), while Reuters had exclusive rights in the British Empire (except Canada) and colonies, along with Egypt, Turkey, Japan, and China; and the German agency Wolff had exclusive rights until 1914 in Scandinavia, Holland, the Balkans, and the Slavic countries, including Russia.[25]

The way that Cooper became aware of these territorial restrictions and de-cided that AP should be released from them has taken on something of the char-acter of an origin myth. His version of the story is related in two books—*Barri-ers Down*, a 1942 account of how AP (and he) reshaped the international news system, and his autobiography, published in 1959—in numerous AP in-house publications, and in contemporary press accounts. In *Barriers Down*, Cooper describes the arrival of a cable from *La Nación* of Buenos Aires in September 1914, asking AP to provide it with German war communiqués, as a seminal de-velopment that eventually turned AP "against the great monopoly of European proprietary news agencies" and led to "the greatest crusade of newspaperdom ... in which [AP] waged a struggle not only for its freedom but for the freedom of international news exchange by all those who were under any restrictions in any country."[26] Much as Cooper stressed these idealistic motives in retrospect, at the time they played a relatively minor role in AP's expansion into South America. The main impetus (and a great deal of practical assistance) came from the U.S. government; AP's strategic and competitive interests were involved as well.

It was not surprising that South America was the first major international market to be targeted for AP expansion. For almost a century, the United States government and business had considered the continent to be firmly within the American sphere of influence.[27] Argentina was a particular source of concern for the State Department during World War I because of its insistence on neutral-ity and German influence on its politics.[28] One significant irritant was a pro-German news service that took the name La Prensa Asociada—the Spanish translation of "Associated Press." Cooper never explained the nature of German control of Prensa Asociada, but since 1908 South America had been a particular target of several German government-organized and government-supported international news services that were intended to disseminate its point of view, "subvert the influence of Reuters and Havas," and "influence neutral countries."[29] In the winter of 1916, Frank Polk, the assistant U.S. secretary of state, urged AP to send its own news to South America and discredit Prensa Asociada. AP resisted the pressure for almost two years before (in Melville Stone's words) "yield[ing] to the importunities of the United States Government."[30] A related concern was that Havas, in sending AP's American news to South America—as it was entitled to do under the cartel contract—presented a generally unfavor-able view of the United States as a country plagued by "race riots and suffering through railroad accidents, tornadoes, floods, and criminals."[31]

While the U.S. government's geopolitical concerns were the main reason for AP's actions, commercial and strategic motives had an important secondary role. The path that AP eventually followed in South America was shaped by interconnected and shifting currents of competition in a dynamic and unstable market for international news. On the one hand, Havas, AP, United Press, and other distant news providers competed with one another to bring international news into South America; and on the other, two powerful newspapers, *La Prensa* and *La Nación*, competed with each other (and with their news agency suppliers) to control its distribution within the continent.

Buenos Aires—a vibrant and wealthy newspaper market that was the most highly developed in Latin America—was the key locale. *La Prensa* was its largest and most successful paper, with daily circulation of around 150,000 in 1910 and 250,000 in 1927.[32] *La Nación*, its chief competitor, appealed to a somewhat narrower elite audience but still had a circulation of 210,000 by the mid-1930s. Both newspapers already redistributed some of the news they collected to other South American papers and had ambitions to do more. Under the cartel structure, *La Nación* depended on Havas for most of its international news. This became problematic during the war when Havas, which was heavily subsidized by the French government, refused to distribute German war communiqués, leaving its subscribers to depend entirely on Allied accounts of the war's progress.[33] The situation was different for *La Prensa*. It had been receiving a secondhand version of the AP news report (including the international news that AP received from the cartel) for years through a somewhat murky arrangement with the *New York Herald* and the Central and South American (C&SA) cable company, which provided the cable connection between New York and South America. This service consisted largely of AP news that had been published in the *Herald*, so sending it onward was a violation of AP rules.[34] But the news was sent after publication, and AP took no action to stop it. A full-time representative of *La Prensa*, based in New York, compiled the report. It was not only delivered to *La Prensa* but also sold to sixteen or seventeen other South American newspapers along the cable route.[35] *La Prensa* did not need AP news to overcome the omissions and selective bias of Havas when war broke out in 1914.

AP, which considered the Havas-Reuters contract sacrosanct, was initially unwilling to supply news to *La Nación*. Its chief competitor, United Press—which, not being a member of the cartel, could sell its news anywhere—was not. Taking advantage of reduced press rates between New York and Buenos

Aires (a result of U.S. government pressure on the C&SA cable company), and with the personal encouragement of President Woodrow Wilson, Roy Howard of UP signed a contract with *La Nación* in 1916.[36] Combining the international and U.S. news supplied by UP with international news from other sources, *La Nación* then sold a service to newspapers in Uruguay, Paraguay, and Chile.[37]

While AP initially ignored *La Nación*'s 1914 request for service (according to Cooper, this was the first time he learned about the restrictive cartel contract), the State Department was persistent. In a meeting attended by Stone, Noyes, Secretary of State Robert Lansing, Charles Houssaye of Havas, and French ambassador Jean Jules Jusserand in the spring of 1918, Havas was flatly told that AP "must have a free hand" in South America. Lansing "put it up pretty bluntly to the French Ambassador and Houssaye that . . . there has been an historical governmental policy, a Pan-American policy here, and that the French people must be sympathetic with that."[38] Before his trips to South America in 1918 and 1919, Cooper had several discussions with Woodrow Wilson's chief adviser, Col. Edward House, and carried a letter of introduction from Lansing.[39] One of the first things Cooper did after his initial voyage, before reporting to the board, was to brief House "in accord with your wish that I advise you."[40]

Many of the major themes that marked AP's debates over international expansion for the next thirty years arose for the first time in board of directors' discussions of South America in the spring of 1918. Although the word "imperialism" was never used, a sharp exchange between Stone and several directors raised the basic issue of whether the arrival of an American news agency in other countries would be welcomed or not. Stone, for one, doubted that South American publishers would automatically flock to a U.S. news service. The United States, he observed, had a long history "of the invasion of other countries. They have a right, a perfect right to suspect us." Noyes forcefully rejected this view, calling Stone "pessimistic and oratorical to the highest degree." John Rathom, publisher of the *Providence (RI) Journal*, took a benign view of the connection between economic and political-cultural ties: U.S. firms were spending millions of dollars to promote trade with South America, "and with the increase of this traffic will come much more close relations."[41] Cooper reported later that his conversations with South American publishers about the prospect of joining AP focused strictly on journalism; there had been no discussion "of the desirability of the connections on account of 'trade relations' or 'Pan-Americanism.'"[42] But that was certainly not true of the board's discussions nor of the U.S. government's wishes.

Questions of propaganda and government subsidies also had a prominent place in the discussion. Although AP responded to direct U.S. government pressure and took advantage of several kinds of practical assistance in its South American expansion, the agency prided itself on refusing to accept direct subsidies. Stone rejected Lansing's suggestion that AP should deliver what was essentially a propaganda service—or at least a strongly pro-American service—to Buenos Aires.[43] When it came to Havas, Noyes told the board that he and Stone were certain it received subsidies to disseminate the French government's point of view.[44] The refusal to provide German war communiqués to *La Nación* was a direct result of this pro-French bias. As was often the case, questions of what constituted a proper approach to journalism were tangled up with the search for competitive advantage; after AP began sending its news directly to South America in 1919, another objection to French government subsidies was that they allowed Havas to offer unrealistically low rates to smaller South American newspapers, underselling AP.

AP's directors and executives were united in condemning government subsidies and news in the service of propaganda but deeply divided about what this meant for the broader relationship with Reuters and Havas, both controlled to some extent by their respective governments.[45] Stone insisted that AP had no choice but to work cooperatively with Havas in South America and should not push too hard in the negotiations; if AP insisted on a free hand, Houssaye warned, Havas would abandon it and turn to United Press.[46] Beyond that, AP relied almost exclusively on Havas for coverage of France, Italy, and Spain through its alliance with the national agencies of those countries. In Noyes's view, breaking AP's connection with Reuters and Havas would be "the most foolish thing the Lord ever permitted grown men to do. . . . As long as the British people put up with that kind of agency, and as long as the French people put up with that kind of agency, we have got to get the news from the agency that collects the news."[47] Other directors, including Ochs and Oswald Villard of the *New York Evening Post*, disagreed. Ochs denounced Reuters, Havas, and Wolff as organizations "whose main object"—unlike the nonprofit AP—"is to make money, and they are willing to take government money, and you cannot compete with them on fair terms, because you are not that kind of an organization."[48] Villard added, presciently, that it might take twenty-five or fifty years before AP could go out on its own, "but that is the thing you have to work to." In fact, it took about fifteen years for AP to break with the cartel, with Cooper strongly on the Ochs-Villard side of the debate but Noyes remaining loyal to Stone's legacy for many years.

In the spring of 1918, the board sent Cooper to South America to assess the situation and make recommendations about how to proceed. It also gave notice to Havas and Reuters that AP's contract with the cartel would not be renewed when it expired on December 31, setting the stage for a renegotiation in which AP's demand for freedom of action in South America would be the central issue.[49] Although Cooper was junior to Stone and to Martin, he was chosen for this crucial assignment because Noyes wanted someone who supported AP expansion in South America to make the trip.[50]

When Cooper arrived in Buenos Aires, he found that Howard was already there.[51] Howard had spent the last several months trying to sign up additional clients throughout the continent, but these efforts angered La Nación, which canceled its UP contract after Howard made an agreement to sell news to papers in Rio de Janeiro that La Nación was already supplying.[52] For the next several months, Howard and Cooper shadowed each other around the continent, "each not disclosing to the other what he was actually doing."[53] Cooper reported later that Howard was waiting for AP to make a mistake by alienating La Prensa, which Howard hoped to sign for UP after losing La Nación.[54] Eventually the paper's publisher, Ezequiel Paz, accepted Cooper's offer of Associated Press membership instead, telling him of the decision while Howard waited in an adjoining room.[55]

Under a preliminary agreement, La Prensa's representative in New York was to send between three thousand and four thousand words a day to Buenos Aires, about three-quarters of which was AP material.[56] AP received no payment but was permitted to station its own representative in La Prensa's newsroom, a useful post for reporting South American news back to New York. Havas consented to this new arrangement but also claimed the right to sell to other South American papers the AP news delivered to La Prensa—as La Prensa also hoped to do on its own account. This would be a very attractive proposition for Havas, sparing it from any transmission costs between New York and Buenos Aires and greatly strengthening its position against United Press. As Martin, the assistant general manager, complained, AP could be left in the position of providing a wonderful news service for nothing, only to see "La Prensa and Havas competing for its sale through South America."[57]

Cooper presented characteristically forceful recommendations to the board when he returned to New York in September. The discussion to date had been mainly about AP supplying its news to South American papers, but Cooper emphasized the importance of providing better coverage of South American news for AP members in the United States, in competition with UP. His view of international newsgathering was that AP should establish the same kind of system abroad as existed in the United States. For U.S. domestic news, one of AP's greatest strengths was its cooperative structure, which obliged every member to deliver its local and regional news to AP as soon as it was received—and, crucially, before publication. This meant that, for example, a report of a major fire in Chicago that broke out after the last editions of Chicago afternoon newspapers had appeared on the streets could be sent on AP's wires before the story was published in the next morning's Chicago dailies. This allowed AP morning papers across the country to publish the news at the same time as it appeared in Chicago. If AP had to wait until the Chicago papers published the story before sending a rewritten version out on the wires, the news would be twenty-four hours old by the time other AP morning paper members could print it. In the intense struggle with UP, sending a story even a few minutes before a competitor was considered a tremendous advantage, so it was no wonder that Cooper put so much weight on this persistent advantage provided by AP's membership rules.

While Havas had the exclusive right to sell the cartel's news in South America, coverage of the continent that it provided back to the cartel was, in Cooper's words, "just a little better than nothing." It was not that Havas's newspaper clients, from whom it would normally receive the news, provided inadequate coverage—the best of them had their own correspondents throughout the continent and spent substantial sums on telegraph and cable news. But Havas had no access to their news until after it was published, which meant that "morning paper news there becomes evening paper news here, and evening paper news there is not available until morning newspaper time."[58]

For Cooper, the delivery of South American news to U.S. newspapers was inseparable from AP's plans to distribute news there. AP already had a strong reputation in South America—not surprising, since much of what Havas sent was AP material, as was the case with the long-standing *New York Herald*/C&SA cable company service. Many newspapers were willing to become AP members and provide their own news before publication in return, Cooper reported. (A key aspect of AP's nonprofit, cooperative structure was that it did not sell news but provided it only to members, who were admitted under strict regulations and paid fees based on their circulation.) At the stroke of a pen, AP membership would solve the problems of both distributing AP news in South America and receiving better, faster coverage from the continent.

Cooper's main recommendation, therefore, was that AP should admit South American newspapers, including both *La Prensa* and *La Nación*, as members and deliver news to them directly, not through Havas—a major change in the cartel's basic method of operation. This would also help to promote U.S. interests and counter German influence, considerations of great importance to the U.S. government. As AP members, South American papers would "actively proceed to discredit the Hun organization that has stolen our name." Furthermore, members had to abide by AP's highly prescriptive and detailed bylaws, strengthening AP's hand in its relations with the two powerful Buenos Aires newspapers: "There must be some equality created as between the papers that are to be served, and each should understand that it is being served by The Associated Press and not by the Buenos Aires papers."[59]

This was largely, then, a matter of strengthening AP's position, both in providing news to South America—against Havas, the Buenos Aires publishers, Prensa Asociada, and United Press—and in supplying news to its domestic members, against UP. Beyond this, Cooper and senior AP directors also insisted that their actions would guarantee or improve the quality of journalism. AP's purpose in going into South America was not to make as much money as possible, Noyes asserted, but to develop an independent, nonprofit cooperative owned by newspapers as in the United States and as AP had successfully encouraged in Canada.[60] Ochs stressed that South American newspapers should not be dictated to but should be able to select the Associated Press news that they wished to print just as U.S. newspapers did: "We shall be assured that their service from the United States is a decent, impartial service, and not pro-French, and they [Havas] can send all the pro-French service which they want to."[61]

Cooper's recommendation was unanimously endorsed by the board, and he was instructed to return to South America to negotiate and sign contracts.[62] First, however, a permanent agreement had to be reached allowing AP to operate independently throughout a continent that was still, contractually speaking, Havas territory. While Cooper and AP directors spoke of a free hand in South America, the eventual agreement with Havas restricted its freedom in several ways. AP could sign independent contracts to deliver news to South American newspapers, but Havas was to be compensated fully for any business that it lost in Argentina, Brazil, Uruguay, or Paraguay as a result.[63] Havas could continue to send AP's foreign and U.S. news directly from New York to South American newspapers that refused to become AP members, competing with those that did join the association.[64] As long as AP was unwilling to risk its overall relationship with the cartel, there were real limits to the degree of independence it could achieve.

Imperfect though it was, the agreement with Havas meant that on his return to South America, Cooper could begin signing up new members for AP. With U.S. government encouragement, the C&SA cable company had agreed to abandon its connection with the *New York Herald* and work directly with AP.[65] When the *Herald* service was canceled, some sixteen newspapers along the cable route to Buenos Aires faced the prospect of seeing their relatively inexpensive supply of international news cut off entirely.[66] AP essentially replaced this service: "Every paper that had been taking the news report from [the cable company] came into The Associated Press."[67] AP's striking success in enlisting members in South America—twenty-five newspapers when its service officially began on January 1, 1919—rested mainly on the network that *La Prensa* and the C&SA company had already established.

La Prensa and *La Nación* were among the new members. There was initially some doubt about whether both would join AP in view of their competitive relationship, and this doubt was well founded: six months after joining AP, *La Prensa* signed a contract with United Press for a special supplementary service.[68] Soon afterward, *La Prensa* threatened to resign if it could not have the AP service exclusively in Buenos Aires.[69] When AP refused, *La Prensa* made good on the threat and signed up for UP's full world news service. While expansion into South America served the interests of U.S. news agencies and the U.S. government, the commercially powerful newspapers of Buenos Aires exercised a great deal of control over the process.

The loss of *La Prensa* had important consequences for AP. Among other things, *La Prensa* wanted extensive coverage of Spain and Italy, the countries of origin for many Argentine citizens, and was willing to pay for it. At one point, *La Prensa* was paying UP more than half a million dollars a year, which UP used to expand and strengthen its European news bureaus.[70] Roy Howard described the split with *La Nación* as "the best thing that ever happened" to UP's foreign service.[71] Until its expropriation by the Peronist regime in 1951, *La Prensa* remained United Press's largest single client.

The triumphs of 1918 and 1919, enthusiastically documented by Cooper, and in which he played so prominent a role, appeared less impressive in hindsight. By 1925 about half the new South American members had left AP, and *La Nación* proved to be a disappointing partner.[72] In 1931 AP's South American operation had declined to such an extent that it was an open question whether it would continue. In the words of Lloyd Stratton, who was in charge of all of AP's international operations for many years, AP then "suffered the further indignity" of turning over its South American service to Havas, the very situation from which it had struggled so hard to extricate itself thirteen years earlier. AP resumed its own service in 1935, but in general the South American venture—crucially important though it was in setting AP's sights on markets outside the United States and in setting a precedent for challenging the cartel's territorial restrictions—left a mixed legacy. In a wide-ranging review of AP's Latin American experience forty years after Cooper's initial triumph, Stratton concluded that it remained the only part of the world where AP's news service did not pay its way.[73]

*   *   *

After returning to New York in the spring of 1919, Cooper left again almost immediately—this time for Europe, to study AP's system of news transmission.[74] His success in South America had impressed the board, and now he turned his attention to AP's overall relations with the ruling partners of the cartel, Reuters and Havas. When Cooper arrived in Paris, negotiations for the postwar peace settlement were under way, and according to his autobiography this was the moment when he first conceived of his "crusade" to provide "true, unbiased news" to the whole world—a crusade that would involve, among other things, press freedom in every country, free exchange of news internationally, and, as a corollary, AP's ability to operate anywhere outside the United States, free of the cartel's territorial restrictions. While watching the victorious Allied armies parade under the Arc de Triomphe, Cooper wrote, he wondered what had made the soldiers of so many nations "come from all corners of the world for one purpose, and that was to kill!" The cause, he concluded, was government propaganda distributed by government-controlled or -subsidized cartel news agencies, which "made them believe they had reason to hate."[75]

This focus on propaganda became one of the foundations of Cooper's approach to the international news system, although it was frequently overshadowed by more immediate competitive concerns.[76] His solution was to end the restrictions that allowed government-influenced cartel agencies to maintain their dominant position and to establish an AP world news service so that people everywhere "could read truthful news." One step toward this goal would be to include a clause guaranteeing press freedom and free international news exchange in the peace treaties. The idea that the United States should offer moral leadership to the world (especially to the corrupted nations of Old Europe) was a long-standing element of its approach to foreign policy and international trade, one that Cooper evidently shared.[77] And in consistently urging that binding international agreements should prevent other nations from interfering with this vision—a position he advocated for the following thirty years—Cooper was aligned with those who sought to restructure the post-imperial, postwar world in a way that allowed maximum freedom for U.S. business interests.[78] Nothing came of this effort in 1919, however. When Cooper asked Col. Edward House—also in Paris in his capacity as Woodrow Wilson's adviser—about the possibility of guaranteeing press freedom in postwar settlements, he was told that the matter had been settled privately.[79] Cooper realized only later that this meant more power for Reuters and Havas.

The end of the war brought significant changes in the way the cartel was organized and operated, but none of these made Reuters and Havas any more likely to grant AP greater freedom of action. Postwar territorial realignment—Wolff's territory was now limited to Germany, leaving the Scandinavian, Central European, and Balkan areas that it formerly controlled to be divided among Reuters and Havas—and the creation of new European nation-states meant substantial reorganization of the news agency system, since most agencies (other than multinationals like Reuters, Havas, and United Press) operated on a national basis. Havas and Reuters faced an urgent task in reconstituting their network of subsidiary European agencies, a process that took almost five years and represented a major strategic effort for both.[80] Since newspapers in many of the post-conflict states could not afford to pay for international news services themselves, Reuters and Havas allied themselves with what were in many cases government-controlled national press agencies of one kind or another. In Heidi Tworek's words, the new structure of European agencies, known as the *Agences alliées*, "prioritized an agency's access to official and national news, which generally meant cooperation with government-owned or government-influenced agencies."[81] Although quasi-democratic, the new alliance was dominated by Reuters and Havas. There was nothing new about governments controlling or influencing news agencies, but government-subsidized or -controlled agencies were a central part of the postwar news structure that Reuters and Havas created and depended on.

Although Cooper had been sent to Europe in his capacity as traffic chief primarily to find ways of speeding up the delivery of AP's foreign news, he interpreted the assignment broadly and ended up examining the overall operations of both Havas and Reuters.[82] Either because he knew his audience (since Stone's commitment to the agency relationship was absolute), or because the "crusade" referred to in *Barriers Down* and his autobiography did not take shape in his own mind until later, Cooper's recommendations were intended to improve AP's relationship with Havas and Reuters, not to displace them.

He identified different problems in AP's relations with each agency but proposed the same solution for both. Havas distributed advertising as well as news and had powerful political connections, both of which it deployed to keep provincial papers in a dependent position. The mixing of news and advertising was wholly inconsistent with what Cooper considered the proper approach to agency news (as practiced by AP): nonprofit, cooperative, and unconnected with any other kind of business. Provincial papers in France were in revolt against Havas, Cooper reported, and had formed their own cooperative news exchange alliance. UP hoped to establish its own connection with the alliance, partly by emphasizing AP's ties to Havas. Since AP could not exchange news directly with French newspapers, it was cut off from important sources of news and was relatively unknown in France, unlike UP, whose dispatches frequently appeared with credit in important Paris dailies.

For all that, though, Cooper concluded that Havas still had "more and better news than any other French agency." AP should therefore maintain its connection until a better alternative was available, and in the meantime, much could be done to improve the relationship. He recommended that AP be allowed to exchange news directly with any newspaper or with any cooperative organized, like itself, on a nonprofit basis, as well as with Havas's subsidiary agencies in Italy, Spain, Belgium, and elsewhere. Beyond that, Havas and its subsidiaries would retain the exclusive right to distribute AP news in their territories.

The situation with Reuters in Britain was different in many ways, but here too Cooper saw free exchange of news between AP and local newspapers as the solution to several problems. Reuters did not cover British domestic news (unlike Havas in France) but provided international news to the London dailies and to the Press Association (PA), a cooperative of British provincial papers that did cover domestic news. Cooper had no concern about the international news provided by Reuters, but AP was facing a critical problem, largely of its own making, with the supply of news from Britain. Until recently, AP had simply rewritten British news stories after they were published in the London newspapers, as Reuters and other news agencies did. However, in the wake of the 1918 ruling of the U.S. Supreme Court that William Randolph Hearst's International News Service (INS) had misappropriated AP news, AP abandoned its previous practice of reprinting published news unless the newspaper gave consent.[83] In London only one national daily agreed to allow AP's rewriting of its news to continue, with the result that every day Cooper saw good stories in the other London newspapers that AP could not use. Nor did the Press Association's coverage of British domestic news make up for what had been lost. Under an informal arrangement with Reuters, AP received the sheets containing PA news after Reuters had finished with them. This was typically between one and four hours after the PA sheets left its office, by which time the news had already appeared in the latest editions of the London newspapers. This allowed United Press, not constrained by the AP versus INS ruling, to rewrite and transmit British news to its U.S. clients as quickly as AP could. With AP having "no worth-while method of getting the news of the British Isles" beyond the efforts of its own small London staff, further assistance from Reuters was necessary.[84]

Cooper arranged to meet Sir Roderick Jones, Reuters' managing director and majority shareholder, while he was in London. Their first in-person encounter, on July 25, 1919, marked the beginning of a deeply uncomfortable, often antagonistic relationship that would play out over more than thirty years, with important implications for the evolution of the international news system. The two were about the same age—Jones was born in 1877, Cooper three years later—and both had spent most of their working lives in news agencies. Yet there was none of the generational or journalistic fellow feeling that might have been expected. Part of the reason had to do with status, of which Jones was highly conscious. The historian of Reuters describes Jones as someone who, to camouflage his own modest origins (his father was a hat salesman in Manchester, and Jones himself never attended university), "overcompensated by acting too emphatically as if he came from a 'good' family and received a 'good' education" and "dressed with excessive correctness."[85] He also was very focused on making money and had acted as head of cable and wireless propaganda for the British government during the war, making him a practically ideal foil for Cooper's insistence on a nonprofit ethos for news agencies and rejection of any overt connection with government propaganda. As managing director, a member, and soon to be chairman of the board of directors and majority shareholder, Jones was at the very summit of the Reuters hierarchy and was known for treating subordinates dismissively. When Cooper, merely chief of the traffic department of what Reuters still considered a subordinate agency, arrived in Jones's office bearing a letter of introduction from Stone, "his attitude appeared to be one of wonderment that I had called upon him," Cooper recalled later.[86] By Cooper's account, he made the mistake of trying to enlist Jones as a collaborator in "the cause of freedom of the press and freedom of news exchange," a proposal that was met with chilly silence. This awkward encounter set the pattern for all their subsequent interactions. Reuters' chief editor speculated years later that Cooper was never entirely comfortable with Jones because he felt that Jones was "patronizing him and . . . did not really regard him as a 'gentleman.'"[87] At the end of his long career, on receiving an invitation to be the featured speaker at Reuters' high-profile one-hundredth-anniversary celebration in 1951—ten years after Jones had left his position at Reuters—one of Cooper's first questions was "Is Jones coming to the banquet?"[88]

No sign of this tension appeared in the account of their meeting that Cooper delivered to Stone when he returned to New York, however. Cooper reported that he had reminded Jones that AP's access to the local news of all its U.S. members before publication was also valuable to Reuters. However, since Reuters did not have prepublication access to the local news of its British clients, the exchange was unequal. The solution was to allow AP to make news exchange contracts with individual British newspapers, but, as in France, this was prohibited by the existing contract. Jones hesitated but eventually offered to seek permission for AP to use the London newspapers' published news at least. (In fact, Jones's temporizing on this issue continued for years, eventually becoming a major irritant.) Jones had a bigger worry—that AP might want to sell its news in Britain and Europe in competition with the cartel—but was reassured by Cooper's insistence that AP's only goal in Europe was to obtain a better and faster supply of news for its U.S. members.[89] Cooper may not have had the idea of selling AP news in Britain and Europe in mind in 1919, but he did soon afterward, and this became the biggest source of tension between AP and the cartel agencies over the next fifteen years.

As with Havas, Cooper recommended that AP should have the right to exchange news directly with any of Reuters' client newspapers in the British Isles, with any nonprofit cooperative (a clear reference to the Press Association), and with any of the northern European agencies allied with Reuters. The subsidiary agencies of Havas and Reuters in Spain, Italy, Belgium, Holland, and elsewhere were deeply dissatisfied, wanting to "throw off the yoke and deal directly with the press of other countries":

> Governments everywhere have tasted the fruits of propaganda by news dissemination. Privately owned agencies are standing by to get what they can get, and the press of their own countries look on contemptuously. While nations and peoples are seeking liberty, the agencies are actually tightening the cords . . . of domination of the press. . . . The agencies may be under a dark cloud and by reputation of association The Associated Press may go with them.[90]

For the time being, however, news exchange agreements with French and British newspapers would allow AP to improve its news supply dramatically while maintaining its connection to the cartel for as long as it seemed desirable. This was hardly a ringing endorsement of the Reuters-Havas connection but was typical of Cooper's approach throughout the 1920s: an often scathing critique of Havas's and Reuters' shortcomings, combined with a recommendation of limited, practical reforms (which nonetheless required substantial revisions of their contracts with AP). This remained Cooper's approach as long as Melville Stone's commitment to the agency relationship—and, after Stone's departure, Frank Noyes's commitment to his legacy—continued to define AP's attitude. It was a sensible plan. A frontal assault on the cartel relationship would never have succeeded at the time; in the meantime, Cooper's repeated enumeration of problems and his urging of what appeared to be limited and reasonable changes was likely to yield satisfactory results no matter how things turned out. If Reuters and Havas accepted AP's demands, there would be practical improvements, the contracts would increasingly be seen as malleable, and the stage would be set for the next round of demands. If the cartel agencies resisted change, traditionalist directors like Noyes would eventually begin to share Cooper's frustrations—as other powerful directors like Ochs already did. On rereading this memorandum almost forty years later, Cooper described it as "the first gun I fired in written form against the antiquated agency relationship." Sooner or later, his long game would achieve its desired result.

* * *

Cooper's wife, Daisy, died of pneumonia in January 1920, at the age of forty-nine.[91] Her illness lasted for three weeks; her mother, who had come from Indianapolis, was present in the Cooper home in Brooklyn when she died.[92] Of Daisy's two children from her previous marriage, her daughter was now married and her son, Robert, lived in Brooklyn. Jane Cooper, the only child of Kent and Daisy's marriage, was almost twelve years old. In reply to a letter of condolence from Col. Edward House, Cooper wrote that he was "just beginning to recover from the bewilderment of it all. . . . That you remembered me in the time of sorrow is a real help in clearing away the clouds."[93] Eight months later, he remarried. Cooper's marriage to Marian Frances Rothwell lasted for nineteen years, ending in divorce in 1939.[94]

* * *

Coming so soon after the successful move into South America, Cooper's European trip in 1919 signaled clearly that he was rising in the AP organization. It came as no surprise, then, when he was appointed assistant general manager in April 1920, two months after his wife's death.[95] Martin—now acting general manager, with Cooper his "immediate aide"—was given the top position on a permanent basis in April 1921.[96] Stone retained the title of counselor, kept his large office at AP headquarters, and remained a forceful presence and an influential voice at directors meetings until his death in 1929.

Martin's years as general manager (1921–1925) constituted in retrospect a kind of interregnum and were for Cooper "the trying years" of his life.[97] Robert McLean of the *Philadelphia Bulletin,* a board member during this period (and eventually AP's president), recalled later that the board fired Martin because he was so indecisive.[98] As a result, Noyes, publisher of the *Washington Star,* had to spend a great deal of time in New York in an effort to "prevent complete stagnation." Even at the time of Martin's appointment there were misgivings: Noyes confessed to Stone that he was not certain whether Martin had "all the qualifications we hoped for when we invited him to assume his present position." On the other hand, he wrote:

> I have been greatly impressed with Cooper's initiative and general grasp and the spirit that has forced him into a more and more responsible relation to the management. I recognize that his very unfamiliarity with the reasons for many of our practices handicaps him and that a further intellectual and

cultural development is very desirable but I think I never knew a man who developed faster and on broader lines than he has.[99]

Martin was no supporter of Cooper, however, and his ascendancy once again left Cooper raising the possibility of leaving AP. But once again, a direct appeal to Ochs brought reassurance. "I am a little disturbed by the suggestion you make about leaving the service of the Associated Press," Ochs wrote to Cooper in October 1921. "Please do not come to any such decision until you have a talk with me on the subject. The Associated Press cannot spare you, and I think the Association should make it satisfactory and attractive for you to remain in the service."[100] With the support of Noyes and Ochs, and through them the opportunity to submit his views directly to the board, Cooper presented an image of vigor and clarity of purpose that contrasted sharply with Martin's unenergetic leadership.

In January 1922 Cooper presented to the board a report on AP's international connections that was much more uncompromising than his earlier memorandum to Stone.[101] AP, he asserted, was in a much stronger position vis-à-vis Reuters and Havas than many AP executives and directors believed. The attitude "that they are doing us a great favor unselfishly to continue relations" might have been understandable in 1900, when the cartel agencies supplied 90 percent of AP's international news. Now, however, AP provided 90 percent of its own international news, yet it still paid the same fee to the cartel as in 1900. Meanwhile, since the European agencies did nothing to prevent AP's competitors from "stealing" their news after publication, "they never give us an exclusive story of spontaneous origin. . . . If we wish exclusive news we must get it ourselves."

Anticipating the rejoinder that AP was relatively unimportant to Reuters, Havas, and their subsidiary agencies because their client newspapers printed little U.S. news, Cooper made a radical observation. AP's greatest value to the cartel agencies "is not based on what we do but what we DON'T do"—selling AP's own U.S. and international news in the Far East, Australia, and elsewhere, in competition with Reuters. AP news had been received very favorably in South America, and the response in other countries would be similar. While Cooper continued to assure Reuters and Havas that the desire to make connections with newspapers in their territories was strictly intended to provide a better supply of news for its U.S. members, the idea that AP might distribute its news around the world in a systematic way was unprecedented. For now, Cooper presented the idea only to persuade his colleagues and superiors that AP was in a better negotiating position than they thought, not as a concrete plan of action. But this would very soon change.

Cooper rejected the whole extraterritorial basis of the cartel system, which gave Reuters and Havas exclusive news distribution rights in large areas around the world:

> [Havas] in the end must be restricted to its own country. . . . Ultimately we shall have to come to that with any agency: that in a foreign land, foreign to them and foreign to us, we must be on an even keel and let the excellence of the news reports determine the matter. . . . If this means ultimately breaking with the agencies, I have no fear of it whatever.[102]

In Cooper's vision, the international news system should be a federation of strictly national agencies, with each having equal rights to exchange news of its national territory for the national news of every other agency. If allowed to deal directly with agencies like Stefani (Italy) and Fabra (Spain) rather than through Havas, AP could make its own selection of Italian and Spanish news, rather than relying on Havas's choices, and demand assurances that Stefani and Fabra were not also supplying their news to United Press. Each agency would have the exclusive right to distribute in its own national territory the news it received from allies, with one crucial exception: a foreign agency (like AP) could exchange news directly with local newspapers in other countries if this yielded better and faster news coverage than could be obtained by working through the national agency. Cooper was clearly thinking of the situation in London, where Reuters did not provide prepublication access to the news of its clients or allow AP to make its own exchange arrangements with them. In general, news would be exchanged among agencies or with individual newspapers with no fee paid by either party, but Cooper also spelled out a few revealing exceptions to this regime of national equality. Canada, for example—which had established a cooperative national news agency in 1917 that was modeled on and directly inspired by AP—"is by nature dependent primarily upon The Associated Press in the United States," which justified a payment to AP. Similarly, Holland was "naturally dependent" on Reuters, justifying payment to Reuters in that case as well. Cooper imagined a definite hierarchy in which some national agencies (including, of course, AP) were more equal than others. He also suggested how the "natural" connections that should govern the relations among agencies could be identified: "International communication facilities, racial ties and common interests are the natural bonds of union in news exchange. To deny the right of one agency to meet a demand for its news due to these bonds is like sweeping back the tide." If the demand for international news in any country could not be met by the authorized local agency, outside competitors—a clear reference to United Press—would step in. "So it was in South America," Cooper wrote, and—anticipating the next international market on which AP would set its sights—"so it is or will be in the Orient."[103]

Cooper put heavy emphasis on the threat to AP from United Press. UP had not only developed connections with newspapers and agencies in France, Japan, Australia, South America, and Britain during the war,[104] but it had also established a subsidiary, British United Press, to sell its news to British newspapers in 1923. AP had no plans to transmit American news on its own at present but might be driven to it if Reuters failed to take full advantage of its AP connection in countries like Japan, China, and Australia, thereby allowing UP to exploit the opportunity. This formula provided the basic rationale for AP's international activities over the next fifteen years. The intention was not to break AP's connection with Reuters and Havas as a matter of principle, or to expand for expansion's sake, but to prevent UP from gaining a major competitive advantage. Cooper also doubted that the fee AP paid to Reuters and Havas was still justified in view of the value of the U.S. news that AP provided. Every aspect of AP's relations with the cartel was increasingly open to question.

3

"Very Much the Boss"

In the first decade of his Associated Press career, Cooper concentrated primarily on news transmission and, after 1918, AP's international strategy. But he had little to do with its main and most important business: the daily news report provided to approximately one thousand U.S. member newspapers. That situation changed dramatically in the early 1920s. As he aggressively pursued the general manager's position, Cooper set out a new, more market-oriented vision for AP journalism—one designed to meet competition from United Press and International News Service for space in AP member newspapers and ultimately for their readers and revenue. Once he got the job, Cooper staked out positions on fundamental journalistic issues that were coming to the fore in the 1920s: journalism's legitimacy and democratic purpose; the possibility of objectivity in an era of propaganda, or of independence at a time of growing corporate control; monopoly or meaningful competition; information versus entertainment; and the nature of the public interest. His prominence as a public defender of U.S. journalistic standards would increase significantly in the coming decades.

*   *   *

In the winter of 1922, Cooper visited AP members across the country while traveling to the Pacific Coast. The result of his conversations was a long memorandum to Frederick Roy Martin that raised serious questions about the adequacy of AP's news service and made wide-ranging recommendations for improvement.[1] The report—presented immediately to the board of directors— was, in all but name, an application for the general manager's job. As with most of Cooper's manifestos over the years, it fairly burst with a sense of urgency. Expansion plans by the Scripps and Hearst newspaper chains—each of which controlled its own news agency and therefore competed directly with AP—were deeply concerning. Meanwhile, UP and INS stories were displacing AP copy in member newspapers to a startling extent.

AP prided itself on the accuracy and neutrality of its news report, and Cooper was adamant about its superiority to the Scripps-controlled United Press and Hearst's INS, asserting that their journalism was "the antithesis of what the A.P. stands for." Despite this claim, many AP members were paying for UP and INS services, providing funds that Scripps and Hearst could then use to buy or establish newspapers in competition with those same AP members. Meanwhile, AP's bylaws imposed severe restrictions, especially by limiting members' hours of publication (a way of controlling local competition between morning and afternoon newspapers). Hearst or Scripps papers that were not AP members faced no such restrictions; they could publish whenever they liked, attracting additional readers at their AP competitors' expense. Neither competing agency existed when the AP bylaws were drawn up twenty years earlier, and Cooper suggested the bylaws should now be revised—usually a highly controversial proceeding, since changes that benefited some members typically hurt others.

If AP's reporting was more accurate and more reliable than that of its competitors—a basic tenet of its self-image and the key to its reputation—the rejection of AP material in favor of UP or INS stories constituted a grave problem. Many members complained that their agency had "a monotonously routine way of saying things." The solution might lie in encouraging more individuality of style: "If our writers adhere to any rules other than good English and statement of the facts, there is some monotony in our report." Appealing to readers was a moral obligation, which meant that facts must be attractively presented. Only by doing this could AP news "'get by' the jaded telegraph editor of the big paper. . . . Like it or not, many telegraph editors prefer an inaccurate story attractively written to an accurate story unattractively written." Some journalistic professionals might have low standards but had to be catered to nonetheless.

A stodgy, formulaic writing style was not the only problem. As matters stood, AP did not cover stories—about celebrities, for example—that it considered advertising. But for Cooper, an exaggerated fear of falling victim to public relations stunts "censors and kills really interesting news." AP should, therefore, broaden the range of stories that it covered, as many newspapers had already done.[2] "Newspaper readers are interested in people," he wrote. "They read of neighbors whom they know, and of prominent people of whom they have heard." What sense did it make to write stories about the operatic soprano Mary Garden but not Charlie Chaplin? AP should cover movies, theater, and other forms of popular culture. The same was true of human-interest stories; even if they were not important news, AP's members wanted them, and everyone in the organization had to understand their value: "If one man fails to file a story of a millionairess marrying a poor factory hand because that man understands such a story is not properly A.P. stuff, such an error of news judgment ought to be generally made known to other employees." AP should not adopt a flippant style or approach but must "respond to the changed conditions of the newspaper business." Although AP was itself a nonprofit cooperative, this was fundamentally a market orientation to news: readers attracted advertisers, livelier and more varied news attracted readers, and the agency that provided such news attracted publishers and fended off competitors.

In terms of international coverage, Cooper proposed an expansion of AP's staff in Manila, Shanghai, and Canton and repeated his demand for direct exchange of news with newspapers in foreign countries. For the first time, he also recommended that AP's foreign news operation should be financially self-sustaining, which implied payment of fees by the newspapers or agencies with which AP exchanged news. The gulf between what AP was seeking and what Reuters and Havas might be convinced to concede was growing ever wider.

There is no record of how Martin or Stone, whose leadership was clearly being criticized, responded to this report. But Martin and Cooper were already seriously at loggerheads. In the spring of 1924, Cooper told Frank Noyes, AP's president, that he was once again thinking of leaving AP.[3] As Noyes recounted to Adolph Ochs, Martin was "very willing for [Cooper] to go elsewhere, as Martin apparently thought there was not sufficient work for all of them"—a view entirely at odds with the board's highly favorable opinion of Cooper. Cooper made a more damning complaint to Noyes: he could no longer accept Martin's criticism of Noyes, but taking a stand against this would make his position untenable. While AP directorships were unpaid positions, Noyes as president had been receiving an annual payment of ten thousand dollars since 1914 in recognition of the "necessary demands put upon him by reason of the constant growth of the association" (and perhaps in tacit acknowledgment of growing concerns about Stone's management).[4] Cooper reported that Martin was sharply critical of the board for making the payment and of Noyes for accepting it, and that Martin resented what he characterized as Noyes's "over-activities" in AP business. Martin consistently tried to foment tension between Cooper and Jackson S. Elliott, an AP veteran who as general superintendent was responsible for the day-to-day news operation.[5] Cooper "made clear the low estimation in which he holds Martin's ability and knowledge of the affairs of the organization." If Noyes retired as president, Cooper would leave AP—"he would not go on with Martin without the support I had given him."[6] As he had done with great success in 1911, Cooper did not hesitate to take his complaints directly to the top. Noyes then asked Elliott if he had ever heard any criticism of the ten-thousand-dollar payment, to which he replied, "Never, except from Mr. Martin." Elliott also confirmed "that Martin had endeavored to keep him and Cooper antagonistic and that this course generally was very harmful to the esprit de corps of the organization." If Noyes reported Cooper's and Elliott's criticism to Martin, it would be difficult for them to continue as Martin's subordinates, but neither should "the present condition of smoldering antagonisms" be allowed to continue.

After Noyes discussed the situation with Ochs, it was decided that Martin's tenure as general manager must end. Not quite a year later came the public announcement that he was leaving AP to pursue other, unspecified business connections.[7] Cooper, whose ambition to succeed Martin had been evident for several years, was appointed the new general manager on April 18, 1925.[8] An article in the *New York Times* that obviously reflected Ochs's views made much of Cooper's rise from a modest starting point, showing that "the old road of progress to the top from the bottom by individual merit is still open."[9] Betraying some anxiety on this point, the article referred several times to Cooper's news background. While he had spent most of his early years at AP dealing with traffic questions, "he was and is fundamentally a news man," and after becoming assistant general manager in 1920, he "devoted himself to the news work of the organization." (Cooper himself observed in his autobiography that he had spent the previous twenty years "expediting delivery of news but not writing it, not even having authority to say what kind of news should be sought or how it should be written."[10])

While Cooper never worked as a front-line reporter or editor at AP, developing its organizational and technical infrastructure was an important journalistic function. Even in its nineteenth-century origins, the Associated Press flourished because it established a system to manage the complex, highly time-sensitive flows that were its stock in trade—not just electrical flows through its telegraphic network but especially the constant flow of news copy based on journalistic decisions that linked the head office in New York, divisional points, and bureaus in the United States and, increasingly, around the world.[11] At every point, decisions had to be coordinated not only about what to cover and how to cover it but also—taking into account the limits of the transmission network's capacity—what news to send, how much, with what priority, and to which locations. All of this was done in a context where poor decisions and even brief delays caused significant competitive embarrassment for AP's members and for the whole organization. It was not such a radical departure, then, that someone like Cooper, who had made his name on the more explicitly organizational and technological side of AP's operations, and who had a clear aptitude for strategic thinking, should become its chief executive. And as his 1922 memorandum clearly showed, he had many ideas about how the news report should change, ideas he would now have the authority to put into effect.

In a brief statement to the board, Cooper accepted his new role with "due humility and a deep sense of responsibility."[12] He also emphasized that he had risen from a modest position, working with AP editors, correspondents, telegraph operators, and superintendents, and vowed that "their interests shall be of deep concern, for it is from them and the members and the spirit engendered in them that a greater and yet greater Associated Press shall arise." Of the man he was replacing, Cooper said only that he wished Martin every success, offering a lukewarm assurance that "always the latchstring will be out for him here." To Melville Stone, who continued in his influential role of counselor, "I need say little, because I am sure he understands my feelings." His warmest words were reserved for Noyes, who along with Ochs and McClatchy had been his champions: "To Mr. Noyes I give salutations of a lieutenant to his captain." In the coming years, Cooper's relationship with Noyes would largely determine how much he could achieve of the ambitious agenda for change he had laid out and how quickly he could achieve it.

Cooper now faced a delicate balancing act. On one hand, the board of directors had promoted him with the explicit expectation that AP would quickly make up for lost time in rejuvenating its journalistic practices and its news report. But he had to find a way of doing so that did not appear to be a repudiation of Melville Stone. For the generation of AP directors who established the agency in its modern form in 1893, including Noyes and Ochs, Stone was their contemporary, the hero of AP's fight for independence, and the public embodiment of its journalistic self-image. The news report that Stone had super-vised for almost thirty years was presented, above all, as *accurate*: sober, factual, and unbiased. (Byron Price, whom Cooper appointed as Washington bureau chief and who was eventually seen as Cooper's likeliest successor, considered AP's news "colorless and stodgy."[13]) In the increasingly sharp competition with UP and INS, AP insisted that its rivals' more engaging style and less restrictive conception of what counted as news came at the cost of factual unreliability. So when Cooper set out to put his own stamp on AP's reporting, he made it a priority to assert its claim of being the one truly authoritative U.S. news agency. In that spirit, he urged all members shortly after his promotion to ensure that every AP story was explicitly credited to the agency because its name was "in-tended to be a synonym for accuracy"[14]—a clear statement of what, almost a century later, would be described as an exercise in branding.

By 1925 journalism in the United States had become big business. Metro-politan papers like the *Chicago Tribune* were huge, often vertically integrated operations, printing hundreds of thousands of advertising-laden copies a day.[15] The massive high-speed presses that made this consumer-based model of jour-nalism possible and the imposing purpose-built towers that housed them re-quired heavy capital spending and presented steep barriers to entry.[16] Mean-while, the number of newspapers had begun a slow decline from its pre–World War I peak (even as total daily circulation continued to rise), and chains like those owned by Hearst and Scripps accounted for a growing proportion of all dailies.[17] Attracting the largest possible number of readers—women as well as men, immigrants as well as the native-born, working-class as well as middle- and upper-class readers—was the key feature of this industrial-era journalism. That meant offering many different kinds of content besides general and politi-cal news: sports, business, entertainment, recipes, games and puzzles, fashion, and emotive human-interest stories.[18]

The changes that Cooper introduced to AP's journalism were all intended to provide more of the kinds of content that industrial newspapers wanted. In the opening words of his "Creed" published in AP's *Service Bulletin* soon after his appointment, Cooper promised a new emphasis on human interest.[19] Noth-ing is so fascinating, he wrote, "as the true day by day story of humanity. Man, what he feels, what he does, what he says: his fears, his hopes, his aspirations. And, as truth is stranger than fiction, nothing can be more engrossing than the truthful portrayal of life itself." News stories solidly based on facts, Cooper ar-gued, "need never be colorless or dull." This approach was entirely consistent with AP's traditions and did not indicate that AP was in any way mimicking its competitors, always portrayed as being willing to sacrifice accuracy: "The head of another press association once said that it was always proper to qualify the news with color. This I deny. Artificiality and superficiality in news writing not only are unnecessary, but ultimately must have a baneful influence on the reader." In this critique, AP's nonprofit character was presented as a bulwark against the excesses of its profit-seeking "commercial" competitors. Yet by electing to fight UP and INS on the ground they had already staked out, AP was itself embracing a more market-oriented approach to journalism.

The changes Cooper was introducing—a livelier writing style; the use of photographs; more coverage of sports, entertainment, and science; and more state and regional news—did not amount to "a destructive modernism . . . [but] a constructive modernism based upon and cemented to the organization's fundamentals." Ultimately, the main aim of journalism was to reach the largest possible number of readers, and to accomplish this the AP news report must include "light and curious things" as well as serious news.[20] Readers were no longer mainly businessmen, politicians, or professional men. Women were "better readers of general news than men, [but] do not generally immerse themselves in news of business and state." Years later, Cooper underscored the economic importance of female readers: "A man may bring the newspaper home, but the woman keeps it there. . . . You have to make women read every page of a paper, or they never see all the ads!"[21]

Human interest, broadly defined, was at the center of a reporter's work: "He"—although Cooper also expanded the employment of female reporters,[22] they remained rare exceptions to the masculine norm—"sees mankind in all his moods . . . in misfortune and in fortune." This line of argument provided an answer to some critics of the press. There were publishers, he acknowledged, whose only interest was making money. But for the reporter or editor immersed in day-to-day news work, "contact with the joys and sorrows of the poor and rich brings him, altogether subconsciously, to a broad conception of and interest in humanity." Even if the publisher's only motive was profit, a newspaper's success depended on the staff's "idealism brought into being through varied contact with the woes and happiness of man."[23] In this way, a fundamentally commercialized type of journalism also served the broad public interest.

Cooper also spelled out his view of journalistic objectivity, presenting it as the foundation of AP's approach.[24] Although scholars disagree about when exactly objectivity emerged as a taken-for-granted journalistic standard (and about exactly what it meant), invoking some version of objectivity was certainly well-established by the 1920s. For Cooper, objectivity essentially meant impartiality, primarily as between the two main American political parties—a decisive rejection of the highly partisan journalism that had characterized much of the U.S. press for most of the nineteenth century—but also between the proponents of any contentious issue that had opposing sides.

AP's founders, he wrote, came of age in the era of overt partisanship but eventually realized that the news they collectively received by telegraph had to be accurate and free of bias. Since they had widely varying views on politics and other issues, only a news report that was truthful and politically neutral could be acceptable to all of them. The news system should never be under the control of one man—a clear dig at the Scripps-owned UP and the Hearst-owned INS—but "in the control of all who engaged to publish it," as was the case with the cooperatively owned AP. The principle that news and opinion were entirely distinct spread across the United States, and the unwritten journalistic code was that the views of both sides of any controversy should be fairly represented. As a result, "People of opposite views can read the same paper." This had a reassuring corollary for the industrial organization of newspaper publishing, since it meant that a single newspaper could serve a community just as well as two or three. Consolidation and the resulting loss of local competition were not causes for concern; newspapers may be fewer, but those that remained were bigger and better.

For Cooper, the accurate, unbiased news that newspapers provided through AP was crucial to the functioning of American democracy: "If a man gets his facts straight he will think straight, and if he thinks straight he will build and not destroy ... he will function as an honest useful citizen." This was a version of the Progressive faith that was in the ascendant when Cooper began his career: the rational, independent (and white male) citizen, free of partisan constraints, needed only honest information in order to chart an enlightened course. Cooper did not acknowledge the postwar debate about whether, in a world marked by growing and perhaps insurmountable complexity, this optimistic formula was realistic.[25]

Cooper often spoke of truthfulness as another essential characteristic of AP news. He did not think of truth in a philosophical sense—as in Walter Lippmann's argument that truth was not the same as news but operated to "bring to light the hidden facts"[26]—but primarily as a synonym for factual accuracy. He also understood truth as being in opposition to propaganda, widely believed to have exercised a malign influence on wartime public opinion in the United States and other combatant nations.[27]

At the same time as Cooper was presenting this account in public, he reinforced other aspects of objectivity—and of AP's traditional practices—internally, insisting in a memorandum to be read and initialed by all staff that every news report must be clearly attributed to named sources. Some AP journalists had "permitted their zealousness for speed to sacrifice our traditional aim for reliability" by sending unconfirmed reports. Speed was important, but "we can and must conserve accuracy," and anyone violating this policy would be held to account.[28]

Reliance on anonymous sources presented particular problems. In 1917 one of AP's assistant general managers had (in the words of Byron Price) "incredibly" argued against AP's Washington bureau writing a story about the notorious Zimmerman telegram—in which Germany sought to induce Mexico to declare war against the United States—because the State Department made it available to AP only on the condition that the source not be identified.[29] Cooper later described this as an example of AP being used as a vehicle for pro-war government propaganda,[30] but more than a year after he took charge, another AP story showed its Washington coverage being manipulated in a similar way. Without identifying a source, the story claimed that "the spectre of Mexican-fostered Bolshevist hegemony intervening between the United States and the Panama Canal has thrust itself into American-Mexico relations."[31] It later emerged that the source was the undersecretary of state, who had called representatives of AP, UP, and INS into his office and—as had happened with the Zimmerman telegram—made them promise not to quote him by name. UP and INS refused to publish the story, but AP did, opening it up to criticism that it had made itself a vehicle for "inspired propaganda." Cooper's defense of the decision was lukewarm at best; he said only that the story came to AP "in the usual course of newsgathering in Washington from sources which it has a right to expect are well informed and correctly represent the view of the government."[32]

While Cooper stressed some well-established aspects of objectivity, he also favored the use of bylines, which until then AP did not allow—acknowledging the individuality of reporters was a sharp departure from its tradition of impersonal news. A few months after his promotion, Cooper authorized publication of a first-person account by AP reporter John Bouman of the hardships he experienced while following the attempt to rescue Arctic explorer Roald Amundsen.[33] Soon afterward, he approved a more general use of bylines in AP's Latin American service in response to urgent requests from South American members.[34] The urgency most likely reflected concerns about competition with other agencies that did use bylines—which were, among other things, a marketing tool. A key condition was that nothing should change in what was actually written, and there was no excuse for writers using the first-person pronoun. Nine months later the board of directors approved the use of bylines in the general news service, but only for exceptional stories.[35]

The abandonment of long-established orthodoxy did not go entirely smoothly. In 1930 Jackson Elliott had a stern message for writers who "abuse the privilege" of bylines by treating the opinions of sources as if they were facts.[36] For example, if an AP reporter wrote that a public official "believed" something—as opposed to stating in time-honored fashion that the official had made such-and-such a statement—readers might see this as a judgment by AP itself, "which has no opinions or beliefs and which does not consider itself justified in . . . taking any position on public matters." Cooper, however, contradicted this directive a few months later. He complained to Price, the newly appointed Washington bureau chief, about a story in which President Herbert Hoover "was described . . . as highly pleased" that employers were not reducing wage rates in response to the depression, and adding, "It was said that Mr. Hoover was deeply appreciative" and that "Mr. Hoover, it was added, will continue to advocate" keeping wages at existing levels.[37] AP reporters in these circumstances should state what they knew and not be unduly concerned about attribution:

> When we know what we are talking about in a case like this I see no reason to get behind numerous "it was saids," "it was added," and other plainly discernible camouflage. Either what we described as gossip was true or it was not true. If it was true, we should have eliminated the identification of it as gossip. If it was not true, we should not have carried it at all.[38]

The reporter should simply have written, on his own authority, that Hoover was highly pleased. This departure from AP's traditional requirement that reporters avoid anything that looked like a personal opinion was made without fanfare or publicity.

Another manifestation of the new approach was a series of interviews with celebrity athletes, including golf champions Bobby Jones and Walter Hagen and tennis stars Helen Wills, Bill Tilden, and Suzanne Lenglen.[39] Cooper proudly told AP director Robert McLean that these interviews could have been sold to privately owned feature syndicates for thousands of dollars, with half the proceeds going to the interview subjects, but no one asked for payment: "Each responded enthusiastically to my personal request." Cooper enjoyed associating with celebrities; Jones in particular was his golf partner on several occasions.[40]

One celebrity interview in the summer of 1926 made a particularly big splash. It was conducted by Bruce Barton—principal of the prominent advertising firm Barton, Durstine & Osborn, a popular writer of inspirational editorials for *Every Week* magazine, and frequent golf partner of Cooper's—with the no-toriously reticent president Calvin Coolidge.[41] Barton had served Coolidge as a public relations strategist for years, played a key role in his 1924 presidential campaign, and had written several favorable magazine articles about him, but there is no indication that AP or Cooper considered this close relationship a problem.[42] This was the first time during Coolidge's presidency that he al-lowed himself to be quoted directly. For regular Washington correspondents, Coolidge's statements in press conferences had to be paraphrased and attributed to an unnamed "White House spokesman," and they understandably protested over this high-profile breaking of the rules they had to observe.[43] AP's widely published account of how the interview came about was flatly misleading. It was described as the result of a casual conversation between Coolidge and Barton at Coolidge's holiday camp in the Adirondacks, which proved to be "such an interesting revelation of the human side of the chief executive" that Barton per-suaded him to allow direct quotation. In fact, Cooper had carefully arranged the interview in advance, speaking at length to Coolidge in person and persuading him to participate by promising that it would "adequately portray for the first time the sterling human side of a man who has been too deeply engrossed in matters of transcendent importance to give the public time to know him in any other way than as the nation's chief executive." A stenographer was hired to be present for Barton's subsequent and ostensibly spontaneous conversation.[44] As Kerry Buckley has written, the published interview was "a sensational public relations coup." It received front-page play in many newspapers, and Cooper was so pleased with the results that he made Barton an honorary member of the AP staff.[45]

Relying almost entirely on long direct quotations, the interview did indeed show Coolidge's human side; as a critic in H. L. Mencken's *American Mercury* observed, "One sought in vain to learn his views on any public question, but found with delight that he strongly endorsed marriage and motherhood."[46] Reaction from AP members was mixed. The *Albuquerque (NM) Journal* hailed it as a "triumph . . . an unusual departure from the regular news policy of the Associated Press, but in line with the progressive policy of Kent Cooper."[47] A firmly Democratic paper, the *Louisville (KY) Courier-Journal*, described the interview as "unexampled 'propaganda'" issued in the middle of a congressional election campaign.[48] *Editor & Publisher*, a trade publication that normally treated the industry it covered gently, suggested that the exclusive interview, with its implication that AP had received favorable treatment from the White House in obtaining it, put the agency "in a rather embarrassing position if the Secretary of State or his fifty-seventh assistant wants a special favor for a political measure. The character of the Associated Press, like that of Caesar's wife, should be above suspicion."[49]

Many AP members applauded the wide-ranging changes that Cooper introduced. The telegraph editor of the *Milwaukee (WI) Journal* concluded that within a few months of Cooper's promotion, AP copy had augmented its traditional reputation for reliability by being "'interesting,' 'clear' and 'readable.' . . . It has indeed been a pleasure to handle A.P. copy the last month."[50] AP was providing many of the soft news stories that previously were available only from its competitors, making extra payment unnecessary. J. H. Zerbey Jr. of the *Pottsville (PA) Evening Republican* astonished his fellow Pennsylvania members in November 1925 by renouncing the critical stance toward AP that he and his father had previously always adopted after a recent talk with Cooper in New York had shown him the AP in a new light. Not only was he now in favor of expanding AP's facilities in the state, but he also believed the proposed extra spending of $110 a week was not enough to bring the desired results.[51]

There were critics of the changes as well. Noyes complained at one point about "jazzing" of the news report.[52] An AP account of a lawsuit described one woman involved in the case as an "an infamous bootlegging queen," which struck Noyes as recklessly risking a libel suit for the sake of "an utterly unnecessary story." Cooper was quick to agree. Noyes's letter confirmed "a feeling I have had for several weeks. . . . I have warned the general editors and am preparing a note to send out generally."[53] The *American Mercury* commented sardonically on the changes in AP's writing style and type of coverage. By 1927, AP had become more flowery than INS and included more human-interest angles in its stories than United Press.[54]

The introduction of a supplementary feature service in January 1927 was immediately controversial. It was offered at extra cost to compete against Scripps's Newspaper Enterprise Association and Hearst's King Features Syndicate (among others). These provided illustrated features, comic strips, and other non-news materials that were increasingly essential to the mass audience form of journalism.[55] Although Ochs shared the expectation that Cooper would bring in new approaches as general manager, he sharply criticized the feature service. When Cooper reported to the board of directors that it was essentially paying its own way after three months in operation, Ochs denounced it as "a bad thing" for AP:[56] "A good deal of this stuff in our office is looked upon as the vilest rubbish, and it is discrediting [AP] in our office and raising a question frequently about where the news is coming from." Ochs was especially concerned about the practice of modifying datelines—which specified where and when each story had been filed—to give the impression that stories sent by mail were more recent than they actually were.[57] He also objected to what he saw as the frivolity of many features, citing one recent story about women using flyswatters to improve their figures. Cooper replied that most AP members wanted the lighter material the feature service provided, asking "how far in a practical world The Associated Press can continue in existence and be aloof from modern ethical newspaper standards. . . . I have tried to arrive at a median line which is still a respectable line and still an honest line, in order to give publishers who pay big money for this service something that will permit it to endure."[58] Where the AP report was disappearing from member papers five years ago, it had now "practically displaced all other services." Ochs acknowledged that opinions differed about the value of soft features: "We really and truly have got to meet competition and . . . a great many of our members attach more importance to the features than they do to the news." But he suggested that both dates and the AP logotype should be left off feature material, which was eventually done.

Other members were unhappy as well. While most state meetings more or less embraced the new service, several New England members complained that attention to features was interfering with regular news coverage.[59] Cooper firmly denied the charge.[60] If the feature service "is a good thing for the institution it must be a good thing for you, if for no other reason than that it is insurance against the rapacious demands of feature syndicates." He told Noyes that he realized there would be opposition to new initiatives, but AP had to choose between "standing still . . . or modestly endeavoring to make it a little more complete effort." The phrase was telling: Cooper's inclination was to provide extra services whenever he thought AP could do so more economically than the members could do on their own, including by purchase from affiliates of UP or INS.

The hiring of a few female reporters into an institution where almost all the reporters and editors were men was another innovation, intended to produce more stories that would attract women. Liz Watts has carefully documented the AP careers of eight women hired between 1926 and 1931.[61] They were mostly limited to reporting stories directly involving women—for example, two recently hired employees of AP's Washington bureau, Martha Dalrymple and Mary Bainbridge Hayden, were sent to the Democratic and Republican political conventions in 1928 specifically to cover the role of women at both events. They went on to cover parts of the presidential campaigns of Al Smith and Herbert Hoover, focusing on the candidates' wives. This approach was repeated in 1932, with the much more newsworthy Eleanor Roosevelt eventually being covered by AP staffer Lorena Hickok, with whom she developed an increasingly close friendship. Meanwhile, female reporters based in Washington concentrated on the busy social life of the capital, the small number of female members of the House of Representatives, the activities of national women's organizations such as the Daughters of the American Revolution and League of Women Voters, and the progress of legislation considered of particular interest to women. Foreign news editor Charles Stephenson Smith noted in 1928 that women "in considerable numbers" had begun working for AP during World War I to replace men who had joined the U.S. armed forces.[62] Smith also observed that women held senior positions as secretary to Cooper (Sally Gibbs, who became his third wife in 1942) and Elliott, jobs that were previously held by men and required "an expert knowledge of news problems the world over."

Despite his concerns about the feature service, Ochs lavishly praised Cooper at AP's 1927 annual meeting as "able, courageous, resourceful, energetic and genial," and disclosed that Cooper had received "innumerable tempting offers" that would have more than doubled his AP salary.[63] In private, however, Ochs continued to criticize Cooper—on one occasion for what he saw as excessive self-promotion. Cooper had ordered that AP's interview with Bill Tilden must be accompanied by a statement that Tilden had agreed to be interviewed in response to Cooper's personal request, which prompted Ochs to complain to Noyes, "I do not think that the names of staff should be published except where it is absolutely necessary, and do not appreciate the importance of a statement that a particular item was secured at the request of the General Manager."[64] Noyes agreed and forwarded Ochs's note to Cooper, saying "I do not want Kent to feel that I am the only one who tries to check him [but] I hesitate to discourage any initiative on his part. I think he has developed some really good stories though."[65]

Reuters' bureau chief in New York—for whom keeping an eye on AP was a major part of his assignment—reported to Roderick Jones soon after Cooper's promotion that he was "very much the Boss now and evidently Noyes is giving him a very free hand and complete control."[66] Noyes did indeed strongly support Cooper's wide-ranging reforms—this was, after all, why he was made general manager in the first place. Soon after Cooper's promotion, Noyes defended him when Stone complained that Cooper was improperly trespassing on prerogatives that properly belonged to the directors in trying to convince members to limit the geographical extent of their exclusive local AP franchises.[67] In fact, Noyes replied, he had strongly encouraged Cooper to take these steps and was immensely gratified by the results. The message that Cooper was now fully in charge—subject to Noyes's direction and criticism when he considered it necessary, a direction that Cooper invariably deferred to—was clear.

By all accounts, the feature service—which provided expanded coverage of business, science, labor, agriculture, fashion, politics, aviation, radio, movies, art, drama, and music, and eventually included cartoons, comic strips, daily serials, home decoration features, a crossword puzzle, daily columns on health and sports, and a children's column[68]—was a great success. By 1929 four-fifths of members were subscribers, and Cooper urged the staff to apply the feature service's approach to general news as well.[69] With every story, editors and correspondents should ask themselves, "How can this story be presented most effectively? How can a bright, touching, inspiring or humorous spot be placed in the report while observing all the tenets of good taste and maintaining the reputation for accuracy which The Associated Press has so carefully preserved?"[70] The emphasis on making news entertaining as well as informative was by now a settled feature of Cooper's leadership.

If anyone still had doubts about whether Cooper's ascendancy was permanent, AP's annual meeting in 1930 would have put them to rest. The annual luncheon was the high point of AP's calendar, concluding with a speech directed to the hundreds of members in attendance. The main speaker that year was U.S. secretary of state Henry Stimson, speaking by radio from London; Cooper followed Stimson's address at the podium.[71] His speech, mostly a vigorous defense of the changes he had championed, illuminated some important underlying beliefs about how journalism should operate in the United States and about AP's role. Before an audience of fellow journalists, he vigorously denounced AP's critics.[72] All, he said, have "a selfish complex," wanting AP "to exclude everything except that which is compatible with their own mental composure or which furthers their own selfish interests." Partisans of any cause found it inconceivable that AP could be impartial between interests that were "liberal, conservative, wet, dry, Catholic, Protestant, Republican, Democrat, pro-labor, capitalistic, &c." Cooper acknowledged that members of the board of directors might have their own political leanings but insisted that "they would not try to impose their partisan views upon my administration of the news report . . . nor could they." Furthermore, Cooper had never given any member of the staff any indication of his own political views "if I have any." Critics might say that AP news was dry or poorly written, but if anyone charged that it had had an ax to grind on behalf of any particular party or interest, "deal with him . . . as you would with any liar." It was a strong restatement of impartiality, a central element in the classical definition of objectivity.

Cooper's analysis of newspaper publishing as an industry underlay his decision to include features and other forms of soft news in the AP service. Here again, outside critics were misinformed and short sighted. AP's chief role was to provide "news of interest to every class [in order to] aid you in forever extending your newspaper circulation." This made it possible to simultaneously serve the public and bring profits to publishers—there was no conflict between the two goals. (As Richard Kaplan has argued, the assertion that twentieth-century journalism—highly profitable and increasingly oligopolistic—served the general public interest was "a fundamentally reformulated claim of legitimacy" as overt partisanship waned.[73]) Cooper was unconcerned about consolidation of ownership. In an ideal world, there might be a wide range of newspapers in each community so that every group of readers could get "exclusively just what it wanted to read." But this was financially impossible; in most localities, one or two papers had to try to satisfy everyone. In these circumstances, the chief obligation of each newspaper was to print "really essential information; news that substantially represents the political and economic trend of the times." Fortunately, this had always been AP's basic approach, and it was now providing more news of this kind than ever before.

But while everyone understood the importance of serious news, the "highly intellectual layman" often objected to human-interest stories. These great intelligences lacked "sympathetic understanding of their fellow-men." Here Cooper was invoking the anti-intellectualism that has often characterized popular journalism. If AP did not provide both kinds of news, its competitors would fill the void. Meanwhile, by adopting this catholic approach, AP was "welding the people into true brotherhood and mutual understanding" while "enlarging the horizon of the reader [and] lifting him out of his provincialism." Cooper's list of the top ten news events in 1930 showed what this approach meant in practice: they included Arctic exploration, the first East-West transatlantic airplane flight, Bobby Jones winning four major golf tournaments, Mohandas Gandhi's campaign of civil disobedience in India, the birth of Charles Lindbergh's baby, a penitentiary fire in which more than three hundred inmates died, drought in the American West, the discovery of the planet Pluto, the return of King Carol to the Romanian throne, and the destruction of the British dirigible R-101. Two stories of major international importance—the signing of the London naval treaty by representatives of Britain, Japan, France, Italy, and the United States, and the adoption of a revised scheme of German reparations arising from World War I—were not included because they lacked the "alluring spontaneous element" that Cooper considered an essential aspect of the biggest news events.[74]

Cooper went to great lengths to show that his approach had the approval of Melville Stone (who had died a year earlier). He recalled how, during a rail trip he and Stone took in 1915, Stone established an easy rapport with a group of railway workers during an unexpected delay—sharing their chewing tobacco and regaling them with humorous stories—and later had a serious discussion of politics with a former Canadian prime minister who was also a passenger on the train. The two conversations, Cooper told Stone, reflected his hope that the AP news report would be "at home and welcome in both such circles as he had been welcome that night."[75] He and Stone then talked for hours about Cooper's ideas, ending with Stone's declaration that "if I were a younger man I might try your idea as an experiment." When Cooper took over as general manager, Stone "was not unhappy to see me cautiously strike out" in the direction they had discussed. "Not unhappy" was scarcely a ringing endorsement but was apparently the closest thing to a laying on of hands that could credibly be claimed.

Although many members urged AP to keep going in the direction Cooper had established,[76] the New York Times remained skeptical of some Cooper-era reporting practices. At one point Ochs complained about the description of the late senator Thaddeus Caraway as a "firebrand Democrat whose tongue was a lash."[77] Replying on behalf of Cooper—who had been ordered by his oculist to rest his eyes for several days—Elliott argued that such colorful phrases were not "hostile references but . . . truthful descriptions."[78] He acknowledged that in the past this would not have been permitted, but AP was not serving its members if it excluded proper color. At the moment, several South Dakota members were considering leaving AP for United Press, whose political coverage "is more picturesque and better suited to newspapers in a region inclined toward progressivism." But the argument based on competitive necessity did not mollify the Times; a few months later, managing editor Edwin "Jimmy" James wrote sardonically to Ochs about "the nice, conservative, dignified, old A.P.!" citing lurid coverage of a sensational murder trial in Honolulu that included phrases like "white spark of fury" and "tear drenched story."[79] Finding an approach that satisfied both large-circulation papers in highly differentiated markets—where, for example, the *Times* could succeed with a restrained and austere approach to news[80]—and papers in smaller markets that wanted a more general appeal was a continuing challenge.

Despite such criticism, Cooper's supporters on the board of directors were pleased with AP's direction after five years of his leadership. His value was underscored by a lucrative job offer in 1930 from David Sarnoff, the chairman of NBC—an offer that reflected Cooper's favorable attitude toward radio in general (unlike many AP directors and members) and NBC in particular, as well as his close personal friendship with NBC's president, M. H. "Deac" Aylesworth.[81] Cooper turned down the offer, telling Sarnoff that he realized he was giving up the prospect of "unusually remunerative and congenial work which has a great future."[82] He did not expect any further financial recognition from AP:

> But I began something here that is not finished. I have free swing to continue it. A lot of young men who are devoting the best years of their lives are counting on me to continue. Having gotten up a blind alley financially myself I at least want to see the undertaking here succeed.[83]

Cooper then forwarded the correspondence to Ochs, observing disingenuously that even if Ochs was not much concerned about whether he would accept the offer, "you have a deep personal interest in my future and my work."[84] As Cooper no doubt expected, Ochs responded with great warmth:

> I realize you are making a great personal sacrifice. . . . You are ably and admirably occupying one of the most important and useful positions in America. The preservation of the ideals of the Associated Press and their practical and efficient application is a job worthy of the greatest talent, and there is no greater opportunity for public service. I congratulate you that you can disregard the "flesh pots" and dedicate your life to a noble enterprise which is deeply impressed with a public interest.[85]

Ochs wanted to discuss European expansion, the focus of Cooper's current efforts, soon: "There are great possibilities there." There was a more immediate result as well: the board of directors decided to take out a $250,000 life insurance policy in Cooper's name (worth about $3.9 million in 2020) and pay the annual premium of almost $14,000.[86] In a 1978 newsletter for AP retirees, Ben Bassett, AP's foreign news editor from 1948 to 1973, described it as an annuity, "in effect pay deferred until retirement."[87] Thanks to the NBC offer, Cooper's financial prospects at AP had improved considerably.

*   *   *

In parallel with changes in the news service, Cooper's reorganization of AP's administration was rapid and far-reaching. The effect was to centralize authority in his hands to an unprecedented degree. In Cooper's obituary in 1965, the *New York Times* commented that he had run AP as a "one-man show," and the organizational changes he introduced within a few years of taking over as general manager made this possible.

The biggest change was the virtual elimination of formerly powerful regional superintendents, who had once been responsible for all aspects of AP's operations within large territories. The centralization of traffic responsibilities that Cooper engineered in 1912 had gone partway in this direction;[88] now he was in a position to do the same with the news service as a whole. The main elements of the plan were laid out in February 1928.[89] Thirty-eight bureau chiefs and correspondents in "strategic centers" were to report directly to Cooper from now on instead of to the regional superintendents. All correspondence about editorial personnel was to go directly to Cooper, with no copies to anyone else. If there was any doubt about whom to consult, all inquiries should be addressed to Cooper in the first instance.

Strategic correspondents were instructed to take over almost all management of relations with AP member newspapers in their respective territories from the superintendents.[90] The main goals were to counter efforts by UP and INS to create dissatisfaction about the AP news report, solicit suggestions for the expansion of AP's activities, and sign up new subscribers for the feature and news photo services. If a correspondent was not successful in selling additional AP services, "it will naturally have to go against him in an appraisal of his value." A year after the new system was established, Cooper reported that it had brought quicker action on administrative matters, more direct contact between members and the general manager, faster collection and distribution of news, and more opportunities for a larger number of employees, who now had the chance to demonstrate their ability and "stand or fall on the results."

Cooper's conclusion that the new approach had no disadvantages would have been sharply disputed by the long-serving regional superintendents, who were stripped of many responsibilities. Edgar Cutter, the Chicago-based superintendent of the central region and a veteran with forty-four years of AP employment, protested bitterly about this "humiliation." Cooper's suggestion that he should concentrate on selling the AP photo service was "a matter of reduction, plainly tending toward elimination and the giving up of my title, earned after years of service which you admit has been of high grade."[91] He had no intention of resigning and could not believe that the AP board of directors ever imagined "dropping loyal men within a few years of retirement." According to L. C. Probert, who had recently resigned as Washington superintendent—Cooper had earlier identified him as one of the "high salaried men" whom he would like to do without—the only happy superintendent was Paul Cowles, based in San Francisco, who was "so far away they can't get at him."[92] When another long-serving AP veteran, general news editor "Matty" White, resigned in 1931, Bernard Rickatson-Hatt, a gossipy visitor from Reuters to AP's New York newsroom, reported to Roderick Jones that this reflected "very discreditably upon K.C.: 'Matty' White is as much adored by every man on the A.P. as K.C. is detested (at least by the majority). . . . The fact of the matter is that, as senior A.P. man once said to me, M.A.W. was 'too much of a gentleman to be around K.C.'"[93] Rickatson-Hatt had a generally skeptical view of Cooper, especially at a time when relations between Reuters and AP were increasingly strained,[94] but by 1931 it would not have been a surprise to anyone that Noyes's and Ochs's highly favorable opinion of Cooper was not universally shared within AP.

*   *   *

While the economic climate for AP was favorable during the first several years of Cooper's tenure, the 1929 economic crash and subsequent depression brought sharp reductions in newspaper revenue and growing demands for cost-cutting. Early in 1932, AP announced that as part of the revision of assessments carried out every ten years, members would receive any reductions to which they were entitled, but increases would be deferred indefinitely. About half of AP's leased-wire members received rebates, an annual revenue loss of around three hundred thousand dollars.[95] Cooper tried to prevent any further reductions, but demands for relief continued. Shortly before the 1932 annual meeting, a group of Alabama AP publishers called for immediate across-the-board reductions, even if the news service had to be curtailed as a result, and threatened to withdraw from AP if their demands were not met.[96] Cooper complained that many requests of this kind came from AP members who had signed long-term contracts with UP and

> now find that the opposition will not reduce its price, so they make a demand on The Associated Press to do so. . . . I see no reason why the salaries of loyal Associated Press men should be cut in order to reduce assessments

of members who take the opposition service for which they will have to pay in full and thus further enrich the employes [*sic*] of the opposition service and its owners.[97]

Cutting AP services to members would be a false economy, since they would probably have to compensate by purchasing additional UP or INS services at greater cost.

At the 1932 annual meeting, the board strongly defended its actions to date. The reduction of three hundred thousand dollars already imposed, in addition to loss of foreign and domestic revenue because of service cancelation, had required "economies . . . in every direction."[98] Thanks in large part to Cooper's efficient management, there had been tremendous improvements over the past twenty years in the cost and capacity of AP's leased wires, saving members millions of dollars. Further cost reductions, including salary cuts, were being considered, but the most efficient AP writers and editors were already paid substantially less than their counterparts in rival agencies. In an interview with *Editor & Publisher*, Noyes stressed that a "complete news service [was] essential to newspapers and to the public," that there was no evidence of a decline in readers' demand for news, and that when economic conditions improved, there would be rapid progress in the further development of AP's news service.[99] For Cooper, the fact that circulation remained stable showed that "newspapers have established themselves as a necessity. . . . A complete supply of intelligence [is] more necessary in times of depression, perhaps, than in a prosperous era. To dig themselves out of depression people must think, and they cannot think unless they are reliably informed."[100] The board's determination to maintain the news service and make no further assessment reductions was received with general approbation, according to *Editor & Publisher*.

But the board changed course the day after the annual meeting, ordering executive salaries (including Cooper's) to be cut by 10 percent and leaving it to Cooper to decide on other salary cuts and cost reductions. Cooper subsequently advised members that two major elements of the assessment were to be reduced by between 10 and 20 percent. All editorial and administrative salaries were cut by at least 10 percent (not to be restored until 1937).[101] Cooper told the news editors and strategic correspondents who reported to him that he had resisted pressure to cut salaries for eighteen months, but now this had to be done so that AP members would retain their confidence "in you and the management."[102] His memorandum was to be read by every editorial employee: "The acceptance of this by you and each of the men with whom you [work] will be the test of your and their real allegiance to what I believe to be the finest work in which men are engaging today and which, therefore, is worthy of any sacrifice that may be necessary to maintain it." The 10 percent salary cut—more for those who were identified as poor performers—would, he hoped, "tide us over until better times when those who show the right spirit today will be warmly appreciated and rewarded." It was vintage Cooper: warm expressions of solidarity and even affection, an invitation to enter the charmed circle of those in his confidence, and not-so-thinly-veiled hints of repercussions for those who failed to respond enthusiastically. (Among the less enthusiastic was Byron Price, who complained that efforts to improve the writing of AP journalists ultimately failed because "AP was getting what a meager salary scale was paying for."[103])

Although the speed of the board's retreat from its January policy of targeted reductions and no salary cuts was striking, the continuing collapse of newspapers' advertising revenue made it unlikely that the pressure for more substantial cost relief could have been resisted indefinitely. In July, Cooper recommended to Noyes that rates charged to the smallest members should be rolled back to their 1912 level: "We are losing pony papers uncomfortably fast," with six giving notice of withdrawal in the past several days alone.[104] By March 1933, AP was collecting approximately $2 million less from its members annually than in 1931, an overall reduction of around 20 percent.[105] Just as AP was poised to begin a major expansion of its international newsgathering and news distribution operations,[106] this reduction in revenue sharply limited what could be accomplished until the end of the decade.

Even while Cooper recognized that the situation was an emergency, he worried about the competitive implications.[107] For example, if wire facilities for the general news report were reduced enough to allow a 25 percent cut in overall assessments, AP's transmission network would end up being inferior to that of United Press. Meanwhile, more than thirty-five members who were now paying less for AP news used the savings to subscribe to UP as well.[108] Cooper genuinely saw the rivalry with UP as a struggle for survival, setting the stage for much sharper forms of conflict.

4

The Opposition

Soon after Cooper was confirmed as AP's general manager in the spring of 1925, Roy Howard—no longer directly in charge of United Press but, as head of Scripps-Howard newspapers, its biggest customer—warned his successor to prepare for a serious new challenge. Until recently, he would have said that Hearst's INS was UP's most worrisome competitor, but no longer:

> Make no mistake about it, Cooper is going to work a tremendous improvement in [the AP] service. In fact he has already done so. . . . Never in the past twenty-five years I have been conversant with its efforts has A.P. shown the life, the originality, the enterprise, and the go-out-and-get-'em spirit in the handling of its news report as it has evidenced in the past fortnight.

Cooper knew for a year that he was going to be in charge and had been making plans. He was going to "encourage original thinking . . . as it has not been encouraged in the entire history of the A.P."[1]

Howard's letter set out what was and would remain one of the central preoccupations of Cooper's career: competition between AP and UP. Since UP's founding in 1907, it had expanded rapidly, selling its service to newspapers—many in the Scripps-McRae and later the Scripps-Howard chain, but others as well—that could not obtain AP's news service because many AP members had the effective right to veto any new franchises in their localities. With its colorful and sometimes sensational approach, celebrity interviews, and lively sports coverage, UP anticipated many of the reforms that Cooper was to introduce after 1925, sometimes luring members away from AP entirely or becoming a supplementary service for papers that were already AP members. By 1925 it had more than one thousand newspapers in the United States and around the world as customers.[2]

Exclusive arrangements—a central feature of national and international news distribution generally—set the context in which the competition between AP and UP played out.[3] In AP's domestic news operation, all members were required to provide their local news exclusively to AP; in addition, some two hundred of twelve hundred members had the effective right to veto the admission of any new, directly competing members in their localities.[4] These protests could be overridden only by a vote of four-fifths of all AP members, in practice an insurmountable hurdle. The control of its members' local news was a huge competitive advantage for AP; as Cooper once said, it was as if AP had eighty thousand journalists covering the news of the United States on its behalf.[5] Internationally, the cartel led by Reuters and Havas provided news to and received news from national agencies around the world in a complex structure of exclusive relationships. AP was the beneficiary of the international system of exclusivity in one respect—in that AP and no competing agency had the right to use the cartel's news in North and Central America (and, after 1918, in South America)—but the same system also prevented it from selling its own news or exchanging it with partners anywhere outside its limited assigned territory.

For the executives who ran AP, as opposed to the local publishers who comprised its membership, exclusivity had another great disadvantage: it provided substantial and continuing competitive opportunities to United Press. Shortly before Cooper became general manager, one of his major assignments was to convince several AP members to reduce the territorial scope of their protest rights, which in some cases extended sixty miles beyond the city of publication in all directions.[6] His task was to convince them to accept a ten-mile radius instead, and in this he was largely successful despite the obvious benefit of having a larger rather than a smaller exclusive territory. For Cooper, the weakening of local exclusivity was essential to AP's well-being; otherwise, "its service, in competition with press association rivals which had strengthened themselves numerically and financially because of [AP's] exclusiveness, would have been prohibitive as to cost and incompetent as against its press association opposition."[7] One persistent problem caused by local exclusivity was that many members with afternoon memberships were forced to patronize one of AP's competitors because they were denied the use of AP material for their Sunday editions. These, like all Sunday newspapers, were published early in the day—which allowed the existing morning newspaper members to exercise their protest rights. As of 1927 about fifty AP members were taking the UP service for this reason alone.[8]

Within a few months of Cooper's promotion, Howard's warnings about AP's new direction became more forceful. AP was preparing an offensive against UP, taking aim directly at its journalistic values: "You have got to be on your guard against an attack on the accuracy of your report and you are going to have a real problem in meeting that as it is dirty and insidious propaganda and practically forces you into a defensive attitude."[9] Howard was less concerned about attacks on UP as privately owned and profit-making, unlike the cooperatively owned, nonprofit AP: "Neither Noyes, Ochs nor Cooper has dared to intimate that the U.P. has been crooked, has dealt in propaganda or has been used by its 'private owners.'"[10] Meanwhile, AP was highly vulnerable to criticism on account of its own system of governance. Where any UP client could cancel the service if it was considered unsatisfactory for any reason (although many were bound by long-term contracts), the typical AP member was in a much worse situation: AP's nominal structure of giving every member an equal voice in major decisions was belied by the fact that a few large newspapers—"a carefully selected oligarchy"—had disproportionate weight in electing the board of directors:[11] "Couple this up with the would-be monopolistic ambitions of the A.P. and I believe that in six months you can have them so damned busy covering up to protect their own crookedness that they will be glad to drop their gas attack on the private ownership of the U.P."[12]

While the wide-ranging attack on UP that Howard predicted did not materialize, Cooper did take steps in the summer and fall of 1925 to limit inroads by UP and INS. In a circular to all members, Cooper acknowledged that they were frequently solicited by salesmen for UP and INS, while AP, "having nothing to *sell*, does not employ salesmen."[13] But it would be a mistake to conclude from this that AP did not want its members to sign up for additional services such as features. In fact, AP could meet its members' needs "better and usually more economically than any other agency." On another front, Cooper vigorously pursued all reports of UP using news that it had improperly obtained from AP members. Ever since the U.S. Supreme Court ruled in 1918 that INS could not reprint AP material, AP had strongly defended the quasi-property right that the ruling conferred. It was in this spirit that Cooper sent his UP counterpart, Karl Bickel, a list of all AP members so that UP would not be able to plead ignorance if it took any news to which it was not entitled.[14] He also complained to Hearst executives that, despite assurances to the contrary, INS salesmen were soliciting members to leave AP and take their service instead, leading to the recent loss of five members.[15] Meanwhile, Cooper's deputy Jackson Elliott continued to send notices to all superintendents and correspondents disputing UP and INS claims that they had beaten AP on one story or another—claims that were otherwise effective ammunition for UP and INS salesmen.[16]

In this tense competitive atmosphere, any error in news coverage or other failing on AP's part was quickly exploited by its rivals. One such incident happened in May 1926 when an AP member in Florida mixed up two men named Osborne, one (George) a former warden of the New Jersey penitentiary and the other (Thomas) a former warden of Sing Sing and prominent prison reform advocate. The result was that when George Osborne died, AP named *Thomas* Osborne as the deceased man. A correction was sent fourteen minutes later, but the telegraph editor of the *Boston Herald* failed to notice it and the inaccurate report was published. To make matters worse, the editor of the *Herald* wrote an editorial blaming AP for the mistake, which was promptly copied and widely distributed by UP salesmen.[17] Cooper protested to Howard and Bickel, and one of his letters ended up in the hands of UP's pugnacious business manager and later president, Hugh Baillie.[18] Baillie mocked Cooper's complaints in a circular sent to all UP business representatives and bureau managers: "Cooper accused us of sending out 'propaganda' . . . and seemed to feel that we were being rather unclubby. I am sorry we hurt Kent's feelings." In fact, just around the same time, "the Old Lady's foot slipped again"—"Old Lady" being a sarcastic nickname for AP—with an erroneous report that Charles Ponzi, originator of the swindle that bears his name, was in New Hampshire when he was not.[19] This was not a huge error, Baillie acknowledged, but merited attention "because it emanates from an organization which pretends to be infallible." This "may come in handy sometime when you are talking to rapidly dwindling number of deluded editors who believe that the A.P. . . . is somehow immune from mistakes."

In his explanations to the board of directors about the Osborne incident—a clear indication of how seriously attacks on AP's accuracy were taken—Cooper raised an awkward question: many board members were UP subscribers themselves, which made it difficult to argue that ordinary members should not strengthen AP's chief competitor by subscribing to UP.[20] Cooper insisted that he did not object to UP's existence, because he wanted AP to have competition—but competition of the clean and honorable kind, a standard that UP did not meet when it refused to withdraw its propaganda about the Osborne incident despite being told that the *Herald* editorial blaming AP was in error. Whatever the theoretical merits of competition may have been—besides keeping AP on its journalistic toes, the existence of UP and INS meant that newspapers excluded from AP membership had other options for news service, thus mitigating the anti-monopoly critique—Cooper repeatedly made clear in practice that he would much prefer it if no AP members subscribed to UP. Any revenue that went to UP allowed it to expand its news report, making it an ever more formidable competitor. But Cooper's repeated exhortations to AP members to show loyalty to the cooperative of which they were the joint owners were never as effective as he hoped, because in competitive local newspaper markets, publishers saw having something extra by way of UP, INS, or another independent service as a way of differentiating themselves from their AP-only rivals. Despite frequent browbeating by Cooper, Noyes, and Ochs, eight out of fifteen board members were subscribers to UP or INS (and in some cases, both) at the end of 1926.

Around the same time, in what *Editor & Publisher* described as "the most remarkable series of newspaper sales and mergers of recent years," Scripps-Howard—in effect the newspaper publishing arm of the Scripps-owned United Press—bought four newspapers in Denver, Knoxville, and Memphis.[21] Scripps-Howard was now the owner of twenty-five newspapers, making it the largest single-owner newspaper chain in the world. The worrisome development from AP's perspective was that three of the four papers involved were AP members. When Scripps-Howard refused to accept the requirement that they provide their local news exclusively to AP, the newspapers' AP news service was canceled.[22] For Ochs, Scripps's action in buying AP newspapers and then "contemptuously withdraw[ing] them from the A.P. is a menace to honest journalism, and to purity, impartiality and fairness in reporting current news."[23] As the head of INS told William Randolph Hearst, this defiant attitude showed the Scripps organization's confidence that any paper with UP service could do without AP—a strong argument for UP salesmen to exploit.[24]

UP's challenge went well beyond this, however. AP executive Norris Huse warned Cooper that Scripps-Howard had launched a "deliberate war" against AP.[25] According to reports Huse had received, Scripps representatives were saying that AP was "'capitalistic' and 'Republican'; and that 'the public can only get an untrammeled news service'" through United Press. The Scripps chain, focusing on afternoon newspapers with many working-class readers, had a left-of-center, pro-labor orientation ("to make a hero of the laboring man, right or wrong," in the words of Huse's informant), while AP was dominated by powerful morning newspapers that typically had a wealthier, more conservative readership and, in the words of Byron Price, wanted a "safe" news service.[26] At the same time, Scripps representatives were telling advertisers that the newspapers they represented had changed from a radical to a "safe and sane" attitude, as shown by their recent withdrawal of support from the Progressive (Republican) senator Robert La Follette Jr. Huse argued that AP member newspapers should launch a counter campaign to convince national advertisers that AP was "outstandingly supreme" and that any advertising placed in an AP paper "is in good company and will sell more goods." He also suggested that members speak to advertisers about the dangers of a press association owned by one person who "ardently favored a La Follette, or any other man for president." Cooper expressed similar views about AP's privately owned rivals. In a draft letter to President Calvin Coolidge's secretary that he ultimately did not send, Cooper objected strenuously to Coolidge's plan to address a meeting of UP subscribers in 1927 but not the AP annual meeting: "The greatest menace to a free press today is the possibility of its main news source, the press association, coming under the control of a single individual. If the public does not know the difference the President does. Should he contribute to the deception?"[27]

Jackson Elliott was equally worried about the Scripps/UP developments. "In my humble opinion, we cannot go on under present conditions," he told Cooper in November 1926. A Virginia member who had recently met Karl Bickel of United Press reported that Bickel was exultant, predicting that all AP members would soon be signing up with UP and that AP was "gasping."[28] AP "suffer[s] all the disadvantages that go with ironclad rules" restricting members' use of its news, especially the time of day when it could be published. UP, in contrast, imposed no restrictions on when its news could be published, which led to AP's rules being criticized by its own members. If AP members would not operate in accordance with the bylaws, the rules would have to be changed "so that we can compete with the United Press on business principles."

William Cowles, a member of the board of directors and publisher of the *Spokane (WA) Spokesman-Review*, reported that the situation in the Rocky Mountain region was critical. A growing number of members were signing long-term contracts with UP and other agencies, "destroying their own ability, or rather inclination" to support the expansion of AP services. The board should simply develop an improved (and more costly) service for the whole region "and then drive it through."[29] Cooper was sympathetic, but the board would incur lasting enmity if members were forced to pay for "something that they say they do not want." With so many members of the board subscribing to UP or INS, it was hard to argue that ordinary members should be forced to take additional AP services as a way of fighting UP.[30]

At a board meeting in January 1927, Cooper reported that the number of AP members subscribing to UP had increased to around 200 from 150 a year earlier, comprising one-third of UP's clients in the United States.[31] Noyes concluded that the real danger came from AP members who, "without any absolute necessity for it and largely with a view of monopolizing the news of their territory," were supporting AP's chief competitor. Members had to be convinced "that it is their duty to stop slaughtering The Associated Press," to which Ochs added "and how far we are responsible for that condition."[32] The normally restrained Noyes gave in to frustration: "What more can I say than I have said in the Board? . . . What can Mr. Ochs say more . . . ?" It was "discouraging beyond words . . . to feel that behind our backs the men who are running this organization are sticking a knife in this organization." Whenever the question of supporting UP was raised with an ordinary AP member, Cowles added, the reply was: "So many members of the Board are taking these services; why shouldn't we?" Cooper reported that UP salesmen brought copies of board members' newspapers with them when making calls, pointing out their use of UP material and saying, "This man is a member of the Board. Look what he thinks of the United Press."[33]

That spring, Cooper's successor as chief of the traffic department presented a comprehensive report on the state of news agency competition.[34] Of 1,926 U.S. newspapers that used a news service, about 60 percent were AP members, just over one-third used UP services, and one in six used INS or its Universal affiliate. More than one-fifth of AP members subscribed to either UP or INS. Various reasons were given: waiting for an existing contract to end; afternoon newspapers' need for a Sunday morning news service; forestalling local competition (although UP and INS did not offer exclusive local franchises, both issued "asset-value contracts" that had a similar effect); the need for a supplementary service; the requirement for a Hearst news service subscription in order to obtain other Hearst features (such as comic strips) or Hearst ownership of the newspaper in question; or the "colorful and interpretive style" of the competing agencies.

Individual members fleshed out these reasons in an illuminating way. The *San Diego Union* initially subscribed to INS years ago when threatened with local

competition and was still doing so: "We believe that so long as we subscribe
... the possibility of other newspapers coming into our territory is reduced
to a minimum."[35] Jack Wright of the *San Jose (CA) Evening News* complained
that AP's news service seemed designed mainly for morning newspapers.[36] The
complete UP report arrived by 3 p.m.—an ideal time for the late edition of an
afternoon paper—while AP's report was complete at midnight, equally good
for a morning newspaper but often stale or outdated by the next afternoon.
Furthermore, Wright said, "We like the colorfulness and dash with which the
United Press stuff is written." Several members commented on the changes to
AP's news coverage and writing style that Cooper had championed, in a context that made the competitive motives behind these changes crystal clear. The
Miami Herald had signed up for additional services because they provided a
variety of material that "aided us in meeting all competition."[37] Now, however,
AP was providing many of the same features that others offered. The telegraph
editor of the *Indianapolis News* considered UP's foreign news coverage particularly strong, but for U.S. domestic news "there is of course no comparison" to
AP.[38] Here, too, AP's "short human interest stories of late have been much valued. There are not enough of them to change the character of the service, but
enough to salt the salad." Cooper's reforms were appreciated but not enough
by themselves to prevent the inroads made by UP and INS.

Several embarrassing errors by AP staff in covering high-profile international
stories in the spring and summer of 1927 gave UP further grounds for gleeful
criticism. A series of false flashes was sent out about the flight of the airplane
Columbia from New York to Berlin, barely two weeks after Charles Lindbergh
completed the first transatlantic flight. An employee of the *New York Times* drew
up a grim account of the journalistic debacle for Adolph Ochs:

> June 7 2:00 a.m.—AP flashed "Columbia sighted at Berlin"
> 2:35 a.m.—AP flashed "Kill" on the above
> 3:45 a.m.—AP flashed "Columbia lands in Berlin 8:35"
> 3:45 (Followed above instantly) "Kill it"—"Kill it"
> 5:00 a.m.—Hearst and U.P. announcement of landing picked up by The
> Times
> 5:30 a.m.—AP announced arrival but gave wrong place
> 5:57 a.m.—AP made correction[39]

A circular to all UP bureaus and sales representatives cited AP's "utter demor-
alization" over the parade of errors, taking direct aim at the reputation that AP

cultivated so carefully: "The stable old sheets which have always depended upon the A.P. and boasted of its accuracy are vitally hurt, and they have a tremendous need right now for United Press."[40] After a further embarrassing AP error about a transatlantic flight by U.S. Navy commander Richard Byrd, Cooper apologized profusely to Noyes for the high-profile failings.[41] In the case of the *Columbia*, overzealous AP telegraph operators in London who had prepared bulletins in advance and released them without consulting the bureau chief were blamed for sending multiple false reports. This practice had been going on for years, Cooper reported, "and so far as I know, this is the first time anything has gone wrong." But on the strength of this experience, Cooper ordered that it never be done again. The practice was not completely stopped, however; in 1935 a similar mistake in sending a preplanned bulletin led to one of the most embarrassing errors in AP's history.[42]

AP's alliance with the Reuters-Havas-Wolff cartel provided more ammunition for UP's criticism. In 1927 Cooper attended a meeting in Warsaw of the Reuters and Havas–affiliated *Agences alliées*—which Howard described as "all the European government controlled and subsidized news agencies":

> These agencies, almost without exception, the propaganda distributors of their respective governments . . . have been convicted repeatedly of dealing in tainted and doctored news. They are all allied with and furnish most of the European and Asiatic news dispatches of the A.P. Thoroughly conscious of the disreputable company with which it is associated, the A.P. is exceedingly touchy about any reference to its dependence upon these propaganda agencies. I believe that Cooper would be glad to be free from the entire outfit, but to cut loose would require too much courage and initiative.[43]

Cooper essentially agreed, at least in private, telling Noyes that these "so called agencies are nothing at all but press bureau departments of governments."[44]

UP coverage of the Warsaw meeting noted that AP had been elected to membership in the association of allied agencies, which the Polish foreign minister saluted as "organs which supplement the ministries of foreign affairs," responsible for "communicating to the public the intentions of your governments."[45] The story went on to observe pointedly that UP, which now operated in thirteen European countries, "has no connection directly or indirectly with any of the so-called 'allied agencies.'" Unfortunately, it appeared that no Scripps-Howard papers had used the item, just at a time when AP, "due to internal dissensions, to its unsound and uneconomic organization . . . [and] its rapidly increasing inaccuracy and irresponsibility . . . is stumbling and staggering as in no previous time in its history."[46]

Early in 1929, UP began making major inroads among AP members in Washington state using high-pressure, and, in AP's eyes, deceptive sales practices. As the Seattle correspondent explained, UP had frightened five smaller AP members into buying a service "which all of them admit they neither need nor want."[47] The method was simple and effective: advance agents would arrive in a town, making "what purported to be a 'survey' for a [new] Scripps paper." A UP salesman would then approach the AP member, tell him that a competing paper was about to begin publishing, and offer an exclusive contract for UP material. The promise of exclusivity was based on what were called accrued asset-value contracts.[48] These provided that if a new subscriber signed up for UP's news service in a place where an existing client was already established, the newcomer would have to pay at least 50 percent more than the established client. An existing client that had subscribed to UP for five years would receive the extra sum directly, with the rebate increasing for every additional year the contract had been in force. This was not only a virtually insurmountable obstacle for any would-be competitor but also a powerful incentive to be the first UP client in any city or town with more than one newspaper. Paul Cowles, the regional superintendent, warned Cooper that if UP could stampede Washington state members "by practically blackmailing them to take their service," the same thing could happen elsewhere.[49] AP's legal counsel, William Cannon, advised the board of directors that UP's asset-value contract probably constituted a violation of the Clayton Antitrust Act but was not certain a prosecution would be successful.[50] In view of AP's own vulnerability to prosecution for antitrust violations,[51] legal action against UP on these grounds would have been presumptuous, if not downright dangerous.

Despite competition that AP considered a severe threat to its well-being and frequent complaints that UP was stealing AP members' news—complaints that led Cooper to urge AP's lawyers to seek an injunction against UP for violating the 1918 Supreme Court ruling[52]—Cooper's direct relationship with senior UP executives was complex and variable. The tone of his personal dealings with Howard and Karl Bickel varied widely, from cold anger over Hugh Baillie's mocking circulars and evident frustration about other irritants, to cooperation where it seemed mutually advantageous, to what appeared at times like friendliness. A similar pattern emerged later in AP's and Cooper's relationship with Reuters as well, and for similar reasons. Agency-to-agency interactions often took place at multiple sites and at different levels more or less simultaneously.

Cooper was quite consistent in wanting to reduce—and, if possible, elimi-nate—public disparagement of UP by AP and vice versa. At a board meeting in October 1927, Ochs urged Cooper to tell AP members how UP "fake[s] and how they distort and take chances with the news. . . . We do know or believe that they are unreliable and untrustworthy."[53] Cooper strongly resisted Ochs's suggestion, arguing that UP "would just be tickled to death" if AP made a practice of draw-ing attention to its failings: "They have so many faults themselves that they try to cover up some of their own faults by calling attention to ours, and we could get down in the gutter with them." Cooper told AP's Pacific region superintendent that AP—unlike UP—should not send out "brag sheets" boasting about its news triumphs over competitors: "It is the old story if when a dog bites a man it is not news but when a man bites a dog it is news. It is taken for granted that The Associ-ated Press will be first and the United Press will be second. As long as we can keep our members in that state of mind we will be all right."[54] In a subsequent letter to "My dear Kent," Bickel gently chided Cooper about an AP story that mentioned an error committed by UP.[55] "Is it your idea to establish this as a regular practice?" Bickel asked. "It was dropped some years ago by agreement, I think because we recognized we both had ten fingers and that a lot of pointing could be done on all sides. . . . I'm much more interested in building up than tearing down, and I think you are too." Cooper congratulated Bickel a few months later after he issued a stern warning to UP staff not to use any material from AP papers without explicit permission, further evidence of "the fine relationship between us, to which I want to contribute when it comes my turn."[56]

A cooperative approach brought other benefits as well. When Scripps-How-ard bought the *Buffalo (NY) Times* in 1929, Cooper and Howard worked out an agreement allowing the paper to continue as an AP member despite Scripps's high-profile insistence two years earlier that it could never accept AP's claim to exclusive use of the paper's local news. The written exchanges on this tricky question were kept deliberately vague. Ultimately, Howard noted with satis-faction that "we got through the whole Buffalo situation without giving any publicity" to the question of whether the *Times* would continue to use AP, and he endorsed Cooper's view that "the least said the better."[57] The exact nature of their agreement was not spelled out, but the extreme discretion exercised on both sides suggests it involved concessions that would have been controversial if made public—probably an informal agreement by Cooper not to insist on strict fulfillment of the requirement that the *Times* provide all of its local news exclusively to AP, in exchange for the new Scripps paper maintaining its AP membership and using AP copy in the Buffalo market. When Scripps-Howard purchased the *New York World* in 1931, it retained the paper's AP membership, a status it shared with six others among the twenty-three Scripps-Howard properties.[58] But once again Cooper feared that the newly renamed *World-Telegram* might resign from AP if it insisted on enforcing the prohibition against members' supplying their news to UP.[59] The same problem arose with several other AP members that had contracts to provide news to UP or INS. Cooper also wanted to avoid too much public scrutiny of AP's highly restrictive rules. "I don't know what the courts might do with that [exclusivity] section of the bylaws under the present trend of court decisions," he told Noyes, anticipating by almost a decade the antitrust suit that the Justice Department launched against AP in 1942.[60] For all these reasons, the solution was simply not to enforce the bylaws in these cases while saying nothing about it publicly.

Despite these instances of cooperation, competition remained the dominant feature of AP's relationship with UP. This was not surprising, because any gains that UP made were essentially at AP's expense.[61] W. F. Brooks, who was in charge of relations with members, reported to Cooper in 1934 that fifteen AP members added UP service that year, nine renewed UP contracts, and ten more dropped or intended to drop AP entirely in favor of UP, while only two members canceled their UP service.[62] The likelihood of AP adding new members to offset the UP gains, meanwhile, was severely limited by the protest rights that allowed every AP member effectively to prevent the admission of new members. William Cowles warned Cooper that AP "stands a big chance of being destroyed as a result of this boring from within by the United Press. . . . The more customers the United Press finds among the members of the Associated Press, the more difficult it will be to make a fight."[63] UP's strength in international news added to AP's concerns.[64] By 1930 UP had 1,276 clients around the world, while AP had 1,280 members; five years later, Jackson Elliott warned that UP would soon "be able truthfully to proclaim a larger clientele than we have membership."[65]

* * *

Hearst's International News Service had fewer subscribers than UP and to that extent was less of a competitive threat. But the Hearst organization also owned more AP member newspapers than anyone else, was expanding rapidly—between 1921 and 1924, Hearst purchased or started twelve newspapers, most in large cities[66]—and was aggressive in seeking changes to AP's rules to serve its interests.

As a bitter fight in 1924 about the entry of new members in Baltimore and Rochester, New York, showed, many AP members viewed Hearst—seen as unpatriotic, immoral, and politically opportunistic[67]—with great suspicion. Newspapers that had recently come under Hearst ownership exercised their protest rights to bar Frank Gannett's *Rochester (NY) Times-Union* and Paul Patterson's *Evening Sun* in Baltimore from membership. Although the board of directors supported both applications, the protests could be overridden only by a vote of four-fifths of members attending the annual meeting. This led to a heated debate at the 1924 meeting, with charges that Hearst's *Baltimore News*—previously "one of the great evening Associated Press papers"—was playing down its AP affiliation as much as possible and playing up INS and other Hearst services. Hearst general counsel William de Ford replied that Hearst's ownership of twelve AP newspapers made him deeply interested in AP's welfare. John Lyons, general manager of the *News*, added that for those with local protest rights, "your A.P. membership has a very definite value" by virtue of its exclusivity, and if the *News* couldn't count on that value, neither could others. If a competitor was granted AP membership over a protest, "would you think that your business was injured or that your property rights would be impaired?" De Ford asked. "Of course you would." (Department of Justice prosecutors leading the antitrust case against AP in the 1940s would have been interested to see these statements, contradicting, as they did, AP's claim at the time that the protest right was not intended to eliminate local competition.[68]) Ochs argued that the provision for a vote by four-fifths of the membership to override a protest was a way of convincing the public that AP was not a monopoly. This was a major theme among AP's critics: a few years earlier, Upton Sinclair denounced it as "the most powerful and most sinister monopoly in America."[69]

The debate had a political dimension too, as Hearst-owned newspapers had been proponents for decades of "virulent populist trustbusting, anti-big-business, anti-capital rhetoric."[70] Although Hearst began to move toward orthodox big-business Republicanism in the 1920s, this process was far from complete, and many conservative AP members considered him a dangerous radical. The distrust was clearly borne out by the vote on the *Sun*'s and *Times-Union*'s applications: of the 534 members who cast ballots, 423 voted to override Hearst's protest, just four votes short of the four-fifths majority required.

The tensions that had been building up between Hearst and the AP board of directors came to a head in 1926 and 1927, just as competition with UP was reaching its peak. Two closely related aspects of AP's organizational structure—one that allowed a relatively small number of members to exercise disproportionate influence in elections to the board of directors and another that gave some, but by no means all, the right to exclude new local competition—were involved. In 1900 AP moved from Chicago to New York to take advantage of New York's more forgiving incorporation laws after the Illinois Supreme Court declared its system of locally exclusive franchises an illegal restraint of trade. In the reorganization, big-city members that had an ownership share in the Illinois corporation were permitted to purchase bonds that allowed each to cast up to forty extra votes for board candidates (as compared to a single vote for non-bondholding members, the great majority). The result, as intended, was that long-serving representatives of major newspapers continued to dominate the board.[71] The fact that fewer than one-fifth of members had protest rights was another legacy of the Illinois corporation, whose wealthiest original members could veto the admission to AP membership of any new competitor within a radius of sixty miles. They—but not subsequent arrivals—were given broadly similar exclusionary rights in the 1900 reorganization.[72]

At AP's 1926 annual meeting a further attempt was made to admit the *Rochester Times-Union*, but the Hearst organization continued to assert its protest rights, and once again Gannett's supporters fell just short of the four-fifths majority needed.[73] During the debate, a frustrated Ochs challenged the Hearst organization's attempt to present itself as acting in the interests of ordinary AP members. Ochs observed that through its own bondholdings the Hearst organization could cast 640 votes for directors, leaving the impression that Hearst, in the words of his representative John Francis Neylan, "desired to enjoy with other minority members of The Associated Press some special privilege."[74] This was not an effective attack, however, because the accusation was readily turned back on Ochs and his board colleagues, most of whom were also bondholders. In fact, the board was highly vulnerable to being depicted as a self-perpetuating oligarchy. Powerful members like Noyes, Ochs, and (until his death in 1925) Victor Lawson of the *Chicago Daily News*—all with central roles in the historic AP reorganizations in 1893 and 1900—had served without interruption for decades.

In June 1926, Neylan, who was publisher of the Hearst-owned *San Francisco Call-Pilot* and increasingly acted as the face of all the Hearst interests in AP, fired the opening salvo in what became a two-year-long struggle over AP's system of governance. In an open letter to AP members, he drew attention to Ochs's comment about the Hearst bondholding, and to the fact that only two hundred

AP members had protest rights while one thousand did not.[75] Hearst was prepared to give up his bondholdings if others did the same, giving all members an equal voice in the election of directors. Neylan also proposed that local protest rights should be extended to all AP newspapers that had been members for five years, giving them "an invaluable protection—an insurance against competition . . . the only real tangible thing about your Associated Press membership that could give it asset value on your books."[76] This was a direct challenge, both to the board members as individuals—since almost all owned bonds and had local protest rights—and to the system of big-paper dominance that had been in place since 1900.

Neylan's proposals struck a chord. Henry Allen of the *Wichita (KS) Beacon* told Cooper that the unequal distribution of voting power "is responsible for a feeling at every election time that the ordinary member of the Associated Press hasn't much to say about his government."[77] James Thompson of the *New Orleans Item-Tribune* "always had something of the feeling of the poor boy at a frolic when it comes to voting for directors. . . . I suppose other people around the country feel the same way."[78]

In response to Neylan's demands, a subcommittee of the board was charged with finding a way to broaden the distribution of bonds. When the system was established in 1893, the group reported, bonds were allocated according to the size and importance of each newspaper, as measured by the assessment it paid.[79] Other newspapers of comparable size and importance subsequently became members, but because the amount of bonds issued was limited, they did not get equal holdings. This was something that could and should be remedied. Absolute equality, however, in the sense of equal weight for each member regardless of size, was impossible:

> [AP] cannot fall into the hands of an unscrupulous majority based on a distribution of control absolutely democratic or, on the other hand, fall into the hands of an unscrupulous minority based on an organization in which the control might be acquired by a few large owners of more than one newspaper. . . . There is as much danger from complete democracy as a principle of organization, as there is from a complete monopoly, or any principle of organization which partakes more of one than the other.[80]

The reference to "large owners of more than one newspaper" seemed specifically aimed at Hearst. The committee recommended that new bonds should be issued in proportion to the assessment that each newspaper paid so that larger newspapers collectively would still dominate board elections. The differences in size were substantial, and it was essential for this to be reflected in any reform. About 30 percent of AP members paid assessments of less than fifty dollars a week, another one-third paid between fifty and one hundred dollars, and the rest paid more than one hundred dollars. This latter group provided three-quarters of AP's total revenue despite making up a little more than one-third of the membership. The sixty-one largest members comprised just 5 percent of the membership but contributed almost 30 percent of total revenue.

While it seemed likely that the bondholding system could be adjusted without too much difficulty, the board was initially reluctant to expand protest rights. The reason for hesitation was simple and compelling: if more newspapers were prevented from obtaining AP's news service through the protest right, UP and INS had more potential customers. In supporting Gannett and Patterson in Rochester and Baltimore, the board had already made clear that it did not see established protest rights as sacrosanct. It took a further, pointed step in October 1926 by admitting a direct competitor of Hearst's *San Antonio (TX) Light* as a member, setting the stage for an increasingly sharp confrontation between the board and the organization that owned its largest single group of member newspapers.

J. H. Zerbey Jr., publisher of the *Pottsville (PA) Morning Paper* and *Evening Republican,* gave Cooper the first warning about a new dimension of the Hearst campaign.[81] In January 1927 a man named Culver arrived at the newspaper's office, saying he was from Associated Press.[82] Zerbey was suspicious, however; he "knew of no Culver with the Associated Press. . . . Culver could not tell me who the general manager preceding Mr. Cooper had been . . . and he did not have a list of Associated Press members." Culver eventually admitted that he was not an AP employee but went on to ask the publisher to sign a proxy pledging to support Hearst at the next annual meeting, which Zerbey refused to do. This marked the beginning of an extensive and highly organized campaign: Hearst had assigned about thirty members of his staff in Chicago to solicit proxies in different sections of the country.[83] AP members in Ohio, Illinois, Indiana, Florida, Arkansas, New England, Kentucky, Kansas, Missouri, Colorado, Wisconsin, and other states in the Southwest and Northwest were visited by Hearst representatives soliciting proxies.[84] While Cooper insisted publicly that he had nothing to do with issues of membership and governance, he coordinated AP's counter campaign to persuade those who had signed proxies to revoke them and support the board of directors instead.[85] In his own appeal to members, Noyes stressed the gains that AP's competitors would make if protest rights were extended: "No action could be more for the benefit of the privately owned news services, including Mr. Hearst's."[86] But while AP's institutional interests pushed it toward limiting protest rights, members' desire to forestall local competition pushed them strongly in the opposite direction.

At the annual meeting three weeks later, the board chose cooperation rather than confrontation. Noyes, Ochs, and McLean had already agreed that more members should be given the opportunity to purchase bonds but only in proportion to their assessments. Neylan and two other leaders of Hearst's proxy campaign were appointed to a new committee to work out the details, along with Noyes, Ochs, and McLean.[87] Neylan was so pleased with the result that he asked Hearst to send a letter to all of his editors stating that after years of misunderstanding, the Hearst-AP relationship was now on a basis of "mutual confidence and helpfulness" and warning against any further violations of AP rules.[88] Cooper played an important role behind the scenes in bringing the two sides together. In his part of a mutually flattering exchange a year later, Neylan told Cooper it was fortunate that they had met, because "the attitude and activities of some of your principal associates were not such as to inspire confidence. . . . Had it not been for yourself there probably would have been open warfare disastrous to the interests of everybody."[89] At the 1928 annual meeting, it was agreed that every member should have the right to purchase at least four bonds as well as two more for each twenty-five-dollar increment in the paper's weekly assessment beyond fifty dollars. It was emphatically not a system of one member, one vote, but one that gave every member "the right to cast votes for directors upon the basis of the amount that he contributes."[90]

While the bondholding question stimulated much discussion and debate, extending the right of protest to every member of more than five years' standing—ultimately a more significant decision—was adopted almost as an afterthought.[91] The U.S. government's antitrust suit against AP in the 1940s would certainly have unfolded much differently if protest rights had remained restricted. One immediate result, as predicted, was to attract additional subscribers to United Press in places where new AP franchises were no longer available.[92] But the peaceful resolution of the bondholding and protest rights questions brought a "new entente cordiale between Hearst and The Associated Press," which lasted until Neylan led the next Hearst-inspired proxy campaign against AP's directors and management in 1935.[93]

5

International Ambitions

The reorganization of AP's domestic news service was only one of the major tasks that Cooper faced after becoming general manager. AP's relations with the Reuters-Havas cartel—on which AP relied for its international news from many parts of the world—presented an even greater challenge, one that had to be faced almost immediately. United Press was making rapid progress in its foreign news operation, both in gathering news abroad for its U.S. clients and, crucially, in selling its U.S. and international news to a growing number of clients around the world, and any delay in AP's response would only allow the gap between them to widen.

AP had known for years about UP's success in international markets, but except for the 1918 expansion into South America, little was done about it, especially in Europe. In the final months of Frederick Roy Martin's tenure, Jackson Elliott warned that UP was establishing connections with all the most important European newspapers.[1] With UP's news appearing regularly in major publications, it got the benefit of becoming increasingly well known and gained a further advantage by enlisting correspondents from client newspapers who provided up-to-the-minute news to UP and its U.S. customers. AP's allies in Europe, meanwhile, were "asleep as to the possibilities of doing something to strengthen themselves and us and to the dangers of their present course." Their practice of waiting until news was published in local newspapers before forwarding it to AP gave its rival an important edge in terms of timeliness.

Cooper had already expressed serious reservations about AP's reliance on Reuters, Havas, and their affiliated agencies for international news, and about the restrictions that the cartel imposed on AP's ability to distribute its own news outside North and (more recently) South America.[2] Reuters was aware of Cooper's views about the increasing value of AP news to Reuters and the other members of the cartel but dismissed them. Even before Cooper became general manager, Roderick Jones warned his New York bureau chief not to "encourage the A.P. notion, of which perhaps Mr. Kent Cooper is the chief protagonist . . . that the A.P. are all efficient and all sufficient and that Reuters, however good and respectable they may be, really play a secondary and rather inferior role."[3] A few months after Cooper's appointment, Jones welcomed his proposed visit to London, which would provide an opportunity to "enlighten him considerably about news conditions in Europe and in the Far East. . . . Especially do I want him to appreciate, what I am sure at present he does not appreciate, the part Reuters play in Europe, in the Empire, and in the Far East."[4] Reuters' relationship with the new general manager would not "ever be way it ought to be until some straight talking has cleared the air."[5]

In Jones's view, the evidence that Reuters was much more valuable to AP than vice versa was clear. While Reuters used only 250 words of AP news from New York on a typical day, AP depended heavily on Reuters for coverage of the British Parliament and British domestic news through Reuters' close affiliate and its eventual owner, the Press Association. AP covered most of Europe itself by this point, but "from Gibraltar onwards Reuter is practically their only source of information" for coverage of Egypt, India, South Africa, Australia, and the Far East (although AP also maintained correspondents at various points in China).[6] These, Jones loftily concluded, were "the kind of facts and arguments to which sooner or later we may prevail upon Mr. Kent Cooper and some of his colleagues to give adequate weight."[7]

AP's attitude to Reuters, by contrast, was complicated by the fact that Noyes and Cooper had sharply differing opinions. Noyes considered Jones a personal friend (Jones and his wife had spent two weeks at Noyes's summer residence in Maine in 1923, which Jones later described as "a fragrant memory that will never fade"[8]), trusted him personally, and saw a continuing friendly connection to Reuters, even if aspects of it had to be renegotiated, as integral to AP's future. Cooper distrusted and disliked Jones personally and saw Reuters as the main barrier to AP's development. He also believed that Jones was motivated primarily by greed, increasing charges to the smaller allied agencies and through them to their newspaper clients to an unreasonable extent, arousing their hostility and providing an opening for United Press.[9] Jones—Reuters' largest shareholder until its recent sale to the Press Association, which made him very rich—"was seeking a fortune, and he obtained it." As a result of their widely diverging views, Cooper wanted to move faster and with fewer compromises at every turn of the complex AP-Reuters negotiations that began in 1926, while Noyes consistently urged him to proceed more cautiously. Although Ochs and other influential directors also supported a bolder approach, Cooper ultimately deferred to Noyes while doing everything he could to draw attention to—and, if possible, to sharpen—points of tension between the two agencies.

So it was that as AP prepared for the first renegotiation of the overall cartel contract in more than a decade, it seemed as if the real negotiations were taking place between Noyes and Cooper as much as between AP and Reuters. In January 1926, Cooper told Noyes that he was inclined to say nothing about AP's relationship with the cartel agencies because "you told me that you felt I am hostile to them." This was not so, "but I am interested in a constructive program that will bring the connection to a point of some value to us for what we pay them, to say nothing of the tremendous values that we give to them." This value arose not only from the news that AP provided to Reuters and its partners but also from "the enormous benefit to them in what we don't do in their fields compared to what we could do but which of course we never will do"—that is, to bypass the cartel and its allies and sell news directly to their newspaper clients.[10] For the next several years, AP insisted that its efforts to loosen the cartel restrictions were intended only to improve the supply of foreign news for its U.S. members and not to compete with the cartel agencies in their own assigned territories. Despite his insistence that AP would never do such a thing, however, Cooper had already been thinking about it for several years.

After exchanging ideas about the terms of the new contract and AP's negotiating strategy all through the spring and summer of 1926, Noyes and Cooper eventually agreed on an approach very similar to what Cooper had recommended in 1922.[11] Smaller agencies should be able to make their main connection with any agency that they chose (such as AP), thus challenging the exclusive and extraterritorial rights that Reuters and Havas enjoyed around the world.[12] A direct relationship with subsidiary agencies such as Fabra of Spain or Stefani of Italy would allow AP to put pressure on them to speed up their delivery of domestic news. As matters stood, Fabra's news service to Spanish newspapers was wholly inadequate, creating an opening that UP had already exploited.[13] Cooper also urged that all contracting agencies should be required to emulate AP by obtaining the news of their local newspapers before publication.[14] In addition, his draft contract stipulated that any agency (like AP) would be allowed to exchange news directly with newspapers in another agency's home territory (like Britain) if this was necessary in order to obtain their news "more efficiently, more comprehensively or more economically" than the local agency was able to do—a response to the frustrating lack of progress in obtaining access to British domestic news through Reuters.[15] No profit was to be made from these exchanges, a provision intended to ease concerns that Reuters, Havas, or other agencies might have about AP's motives. None of these contract proposals was considered essential, however; Noyes would not consider breaking with Reuters under any circumstances, regardless of how Jones responded to any proposed changes.[16]

By August, Cooper had concluded that a new Reuters agreement along the lines he and Noyes agreed on would be a long step in the right direction. On almost all the issues at stake, Cooper's proposals reflected changes that Noyes had wanted to see for years:

> My only caution is that—as you know—I really value our connection with Reuters and even more so since its amalgamation with the Press Association. I would not be especially concerned if we were obliged to come to a break with the others but a break with Reuter would cause me very serious misgiving. I am certain, however, that this feeling is also deep with Sir Roderick and I know of no reason why we should not insist on a just settlement of our relations.[17]

Jones already knew that AP wanted to abolish the annual fee of sixteen thousand dollars that it paid for cartel news (in addition to providing its own U.S. domestic news) and that it wanted direct access to the news of Reuters' newspaper clients.[18] The only potential sticking point, in Noyes's view, was AP's desire to establish direct relations with smaller agencies in Reuters' and Havas's exclusive territories. The really crucial countries for AP, in Noyes's view, were China and Japan, where he had traveled extensively in 1922 to assess AP's prospects;[19] any subsidiary agency in one of these territories that wanted to make its main contract with AP should be free to do so. Cooper agreed. AP's geographical position and the implications of this for transmission costs "stops us from any practical dissemination in any territory in which we do not now disseminate, with the possible exception of Japan."[20] (By this point Cooper had already had extensive discussions about this possibility with the managing director of the Japanese news agency served by Reuters.[21])

Jones and Cooper signed the new agreement in New York in October 1926.[22] Unlike the existing four-party contract, it was an agreement between AP and Reuters only—to be carried out "in conjunction with" Havas and Wolff if possible or without them if not. Reuters' subsidiary agencies were forbidden from providing their news to any other agency besides AP, an attempt to limit the inroads that United Press was making in Europe and elsewhere. The fee that AP had been paying since 1893 was eliminated, subject to agreement by Havas and Wolff.

The contract also gave AP something it had been seeking for years: the right to supply news directly to any newspaper client of Reuters in the British Isles in exchange for its local and domestic news. However, in a substantial departure from Cooper's initial proposal, the news supplied to AP under this arrangement was deemed to be worth just half the value of what AP provided in exchange. The remaining half was to be covered by a cash payment from the newspaper, which AP would then hand over to Reuters, making the proposition much less appealing to British newspapers. Reuters maintained the exclusive right to sell news provided by the cartel and any of its affiliates in a very extensive territory: beyond the British Isles, it included Holland, Egypt, India, the Straits Settlements (Malaysia and Singapore), the Far East (Japan and China), South Africa, Australia, New Zealand, and all other parts of the British Empire except Canada. The sole modification to this list was that AP would be allowed "free entry" into Japan to serve Reuters' ally there (the Japanese news agency Nippon Shimbun Rengo, previously known as Kokusai). If Rengo replaced any of its Reuters news with material from AP, however, Reuters was to be reimbursed in full for any lost revenue. As with the question of news exchange with British newspapers (and as had happened with Havas in AP's earlier expansion into South America), AP's wish to encroach on what was previously jealously guarded as exclusive territory was granted, but on terms that sharply reduced the concession's value. Jones told the Reuters directors that AP's entry into Japan would be good for Reuters because it would help counteract UP's activities there. (UP already had an alliance with another Japanese news agency, Nippon Dempo, and was also competing with Reuters in China.) The new contract "would practically mean a defensive and offensive alliance between Reuters and AP." Cooperation, combined with limits on AP's independent activities, could serve Reuters' interests well.

The remaining question was whether Havas and Wolff would accept the terms of the new AP-Reuters agreement. In May 1927 Cooper traveled to London, where he, Jones, André Meynot of Havas, and Heinrich Mantler of Wolff began negotiations, leading to the signing of a new four-party agreement in Geneva in August.[23] Back in New York, a triumphant Cooper told the board of directors that at times the discussion was "acrimonious . . . very heated," complicated by the fact that Jones had been instructed by his board of directors to revise some of the terms agreed to in New York a year earlier.[24] The crucial clause allowing AP to provide its news to newspapers in other agencies' territory was circumscribed in several ways: the relevant cartel agency (Reuters or Havas) had to be consulted before AP could even raise the possibility with any individual newspaper; the service could be only supplementary to the main news service provided by the cartel agency and must follow the fundamental principle that the ruling agency had "the first claim to and the exclusive rights of" the news of its partners; and half of the fee charged was to be paid to the cartel agency. This, Cooper confessed, "emasculates the thing I had in mind . . . but it came to the point of breaking up the negotiations for me to insist on the text that we agreed on here last year." It was, however, "a great advance over the present [contract], which does not recognize any rights whatever." AP was now free to increase the distribution of its news "in Paris or Berlin or England." As Ochs observed, this would allow AP to provide its European news to newspapers in the United Kingdom as it passed through London, without having to bear the costs of transmission to New York and back, and would also allow AP news to be sold to European newspapers, "meeting that competition which the United Press is offering us over there and by which they are making so much reputation for themselves in Europe." But the board remained divided in some respects, with Noyes cautioning that the goal was merely to improve the supply of foreign news to AP's U.S. members, not to find new sources of revenue.

This was the most significant contract revision since Melville Stone had signed the original agreement with Reuters, Havas, and Wolff in 1893. While previously AP's contract had been subsidiary to the main, tripartite, cartel agreement, now it was one of four equal parties. Elimination of the fee was another acknowledgment of AP's equal status. AP's right to sell news to Rengo in Japan was kept out of the main agreement because Jones "did not like to admit to the other two . . . that there had been any indication of a weaning away of Reuters territory." This provision was spelled out in a separate and secret AP-Reuters side agreement under which AP would reimburse Reuters for any lost revenue, and any news that AP supplied to Rengo would also be available to Reuters for distribution elsewhere in its Far Eastern territories.[25] All negotiations between AP and Rengo had to be based on explicit recognition that Japan was Reuters' exclusive territory and were to be carried out in London with Reuters as an intermediary, with AP promising to inform Reuters about any arrangements it made with Rengo or individual Japanese newspapers. (Cooper's deviation from these terms was the immediate cause of the AP-Reuters split in 1933.[26]) For Cooper, it was just a matter of time before changes in trans-Pacific transmission rates set the stage for AP—or anther U.S. agency—to supplant Reuters entirely in Japan. As matters stood, Reuters was paying fourteen cents a word to send news to Japan, substantially less than the rate currently available to AP. But if AP could send news to Japan for five cents a word, "it would be to Reuters' interest to step aside. The Japanese agencies or newspapers could better afford to buy Reuters out of their rights in Japan and avail themselves of a five-cent cable rate from America."

* * *

In the years after Noyes's reconnaissance trip to China and Japan in 1922, United Press made significant headway in supplying international news to clients in those countries in competition with Reuters and in providing Chinese and Japanese news to its clients in the United States and Europe.[27] UP's partner in Japan was the Nippon Dempo agency, the chief competitor of Reuters' and AP's ally, Kokusai (later renamed Rengo). Kokusai was not primarily a newsgathering agency, as AP's Tokyo bureau chief Victor Eubank explained to Cooper in 1925. It was owned by bankers, financiers, and big-business proprietors, and its main purpose was to provide them with commercial news and stock and commodity quotations from abroad.[28] Beyond this, it imported a very good European news report from Reuters. But Kokusai's exclusive contract to distribute Reuters news in Japan was expensive and did not bring in the expected revenue. Meanwhile, Nippon Dempo had money, numerous leased wires, better connections with Japanese newspapers, and better news coverage than Kokusai: "Consequently at any time we [AP] may be beaten" on Japanese news.[29] More broadly, Cooper should understand that the term "news agency" meant something different in Japan than in North America. All four existing organizations "depend for their livelihood upon everything except news. All of them operate commercial bureaus or advertising agencies, are subsidized by business concerns, the government or otherwise. The idea of news, as we understand the word, is secondary."

Yukichi Iwanaga, who became the first Japanese managing director of Kokusai in 1924,[30] made the development of a closer relationship with AP one of his top priorities over the next ten years, in part by reorganizing Kokusai along lines that were more consistent with Cooper's ideas of what a news agency should be. But even as Iwanaga embraced what Cooper, Ochs, and others frequently described as the ideal of a nonprofit, cooperative news agency, he was also, in Tomoko Akami's words, "driven by his strong sense of mission as one of the [Japanese] national/imperial elite."[31] After 1920, Kokusai was heavily subsidized by the Japanese foreign ministry, and it was the vice minister of foreign affairs who convinced Iwanaga to take the managing director's job four years later.[32] Iwanaga had been a schoolmate of, and occasionally advised, the future prime minister, Konoe Fumimaro; he was also a protégé of Goto Shimpei, who held positions as foreign minister and deputy prime minister. From 1911 to 1917, Iwanaga was a stationmaster for the Japanese-owned railway and a colonial administrator in Manchuria (the region of northeastern China where Japan exercised informal control after its victory in the Russo-Japanese War of 1904–1905), later becoming secretary to Shimpei as railway minister. The Reuters contract prevented Kokusai from distributing Japanese news—or, through its connection with a separate, secretly government-controlled agency, propaganda—in China, then in the throes of a long civil war. In Akami's words, Iwanaga's efforts to win autonomy from Reuters so that Japanese-controlled news could be distributed in China and elsewhere in Asia "both resulted from, and contributed to, the Japanese military aggression in China, and then beyond China."[33] At the same time, Iwanaga genuinely believed that Kokusai should be restructured on AP-like lines. In his view, a cooperative structure, the independence it brought, and the resulting reputation for providing reliable news would allow Kokusai to serve the nation's interests more effectively.[34]

In the late summer of 1925, soon after he and Cooper assumed their new positions, Iwanaga came to New York to meet his American counterpart. It was a significant encounter: the character of Cooper's personal relationships with the heads of other agencies—either positive (as with J.F.B. Livesay of Canadian Press and, in the early 1940s, William John Haley of Reuters) or negative (as with Roderick Jones)—had a great deal to do with how institutional agency-to-agency relationships developed. In the case of Iwanaga, it was the beginning of what Cooper later described as "a friendship which, because of our mutual adherence to the principle of a free press and freedom of international news without governmental control, lasted until Iwanaga's death."[35] Urging Cooper to keep their discussions confidential, Iwanaga said he wanted to be free to have direct relations with any of Reuters' allies, specifically AP.[36] He also wanted AP to support Kokusai's wishes for greater autonomy in its own dealings with Reuters, and perhaps even to promote the idea. Noyes was skeptical, complaining that by not taking his concerns directly to Roderick Jones, Iwanaga was putting AP in the position of initiating a change in its relationship with Reuters.[37] But for Cooper, Iwanaga's plan was entirely in keeping with what he wanted to achieve ever since he first analyzed the international news agency system in 1919, and it deserved AP's support accordingly. "I can understand Mr. Iwanaga's timidity . . . after the experience he has had with Reuter," he replied. "If [AP] did not welcome the suggestion and see it through effectively, the infant cooperative agency in Japan might be at a disadvantage in making a new contract with Reuter. . . . If The Associated Press were determined in the matter, Mr. Iwanaga would be equally determined."[38]

Iwanaga's plan to reorganize Kokusai as a nonprofit cooperative, owned by major Japanese newspapers—inspired by, if not an exact copy of, AP's structure—was equally pleasing to Cooper. The new organization was to be called Nippon Shimbun Rengo (Associated Press of Japan).[39] Rengo was much more closely held than AP, with the eight largest Japanese newspapers owning it outright, and it would not, at least at first, gather and exchange Japanese domestic news—one of the main things AP wanted from its ally.[40] (Rengo's member newspapers would provide their news of the "Japanese Empire" to its allies, however.[41]) One major difference between Rengo and AP was that the Japanese agency received a monthly subsidy from the Foreign Office of 12,000 yen (the equivalent of about $5,600 in U.S. currency) to help meet the heavy costs of the Reuters contract, Eubank reported. As part of this agreement, Rengo was to end the employment of all foreigners, meaning that AP "will have to deal altogether with Japanese who are paid to put over Japanese propaganda in every way possible." Rengo also took over the government-sponsored Toho agency, which distributed what Akami describes as Japanese "news propaganda" in China.[42] (Iwanaga told Cooper that this only involved bringing Toho's news from China into Japan and not vice versa, but this may have been an attempt to avoid mentioning news distribution activities in China that violated Reuters' exclusive rights. Both Rengo and its successor, Domei, also denied as a matter of policy that they received subsidies in order to preserve their reputation for independence.[43]) Rengo eventually received annual sums ranging between 330,000 and 570,000 yen—between 20 and 50 percent of its overall budget—before it was forcibly incorporated into the Domei agency in 1935, and this was primarily to support its international distribution of news, publicity, and propaganda.[44]

Cooper, in short, knew perfectly well that Rengo received substantial government subsidies (even if he may not have known their full extent) connected to Japanese propaganda activities, failings of a kind that often led him to denounce other agencies. What was different about Rengo, then? Most importantly, AP needed an ally in Japan to compete with the United Press–Nippon Dempo combination, and Rengo was the only possible candidate. In addition, Cooper had established a personal friendship with Iwanaga, whose desire for greater independence from Reuters corresponded to one of Cooper's central strategic goals. Despite the many substantial differences between the structures of the newspaper industry in Japan and the United States, Rengo was at least a kind of newspaper-owned nonprofit cooperative, and that too was something Cooper genuinely valued. (He also acknowledged at least some of the differences, arguing that Rengo was "no worse off" than AP had been in its own, conflicted, formative years.[45])

Iwanaga and Cooper wanted to establish a direct AP-Rengo relationship without causing a breach with Reuters, which meant this had to be done with Reuters' consent. Reuters, for its part, understood clearly what its American and Japanese allies wanted. William Turner, Reuters' Far Eastern manager, told Jones that Iwanaga hated the idea of having to make its arrangements with AP through Reuters, but it was "of almost supreme importance to Reuters" to insist on this point.[46] Jones recognized that American agencies had a geographical advantage in sending at least their domestic news to Japan but also stressed "the notorious desire of the Americans," including AP, to replace British news services—seen as "pro-British and un-American (if not worse) and there[fore] harmful to American interests."[47] While the terms of the new contract allowed AP to say it was free to serve Japan, "it safeguards absolutely our revenue and generally places us in a pretty strong position."

The provision that AP had to consult Reuters about every aspect of its relationship with Rengo was something Cooper accepted—for now—with equanimity. "We would not think of dealing with the Japanese question seriously without due notice and consultation with Reuters," he told Noyes.[48] AP was "in a fine strategic position either to help Rengo in its relations with Reuters or to do something directly ourselves after notifying Reuters." Six years later, however, it was a dispute over Japan and Rengo that led to a decisive break between Reuters and AP.

*   *   *

The first decade of Cooper's efforts to expand AP's international presence was an era of growing fascism and authoritarianism in Italy, Spain, Germany, and Japan. AP's, and Cooper's, general policy was not to challenge the political system of any country in which it operated. This applied in Communist Russia, where AP had a news exchange agreement with the Soviet news agency TASS and its predecessor Rosta since 1925 as much as in Fascist Italy,[49] where Benito Mussolini took power in 1922, or Germany under Nazi rule after 1933. The basic argument, as AP's long-serving Berlin bureau chief Louis Lochner wrote in his memoir, was that while correspondents of individual newspapers could afford to stand on principle and risk expulsion, a news agency correspondent could not: the newspaper whose own special correspondent was expelled could count on the news agency reporter remaining to provide whatever coverage could still be obtained. Despite "the sense of outrage which seized us at what we saw and learned, and to which we could give but imperfect expression in our dispatches, any one of which might lead to our deportation, . . . our orders from our bosses were to tell no untruth, but to report only as much of the truth, without distorting the picture, as would enable us to remain at our posts."[50] This was not a simple position to be in. AP's resident correspondents in Rome and Berlin were accused, at the time and subsequently, of at least soft-pedalling, and at worst ignoring or seeming to justify the abuses and crimes of the Nazi and Fascist regimes. As Harold Ickes, then Franklin Delano Roosevelt's secretary of the interior, wrote to Noyes in 1941, when Nazi armies occupied most of Europe but the United States had not yet entered the war—and AP's correspondent remained in Berlin—"I sometimes wonder whether we would not be better off without dispatches from that country if the alternative is to be fed daily doses of arsenical propaganda."[51] Broad ethical questions of this kind were rarely raised in Cooper's correspondence or in discussions of the board of directors. (One notable exception was Ochs's observation in 1932 that censorship in Italy and Spain was due to "the complacency of Havas and Reuters and others who do not want to be in disfavor with them." If the agencies threatened to stop sending news entirely if any of it was stopped, "I think they could do it."[52]) Instead, the correspondence between Cooper and his European bureau chiefs emphasized practical problems of day-to-day journalism: how to cope with and, as far as possible, work around censorship; how to manage relations with and get good news coverage from ostensibly allied national news agencies that increasingly came under explicit political direction; and, always, how best to compete with United Press.

A few months after Cooper became general manager, AP's long-serving Rome correspondent, Salvatore Cortesi, sent him a detailed account of the Fascist takeover of AP's ostensible ally, the Stefani agency, two years earlier.[53] Cortesi, an Italian citizen, had been AP's full-time correspondent since 1903 and also served Reuters.[54] In his study of the U.S. response to Mussolini, which was largely favorable (during the 1920s, at least), John Diggins describes Cortesi as an "avid supporter of the Fascist regime."[55] According to George Seldes, who was expelled as Rome correspondent for the *Chicago Tribune* in 1925 after reporting on the Fascist-inspired murder of the Socialist politician Giacomo Matteotti and who later became a prominent critic of the U.S. press in general, Cortesi "loved Fascism, hated the Opposition, and . . . refused even to read the Opposition press, let alone send out Opposition views" and had done "Fascist propaganda a greater service than all paid agents."[56] Percy Winner, who worked in AP's Rome bureau under Cortesi, told Seldes that AP "backed up everything pro-Fascist of Salvatore Cortesi's to the hilt. . . . The AP says as a basic maxim that the government in power must be assumed to be right. . . . AP must never run any chance of being kicked out of any important news center."[57]

However strongly they may have been felt or expressed, Cortesi's pro-Fascist sympathies were not enough to spare AP from the Fascist regime's anger. The Italian ambassador in Washington suggested to Mussolini at one point that Italy should distribute its own news internationally without involving AP, which was not cooperative or "fair minded."[58] In a report forwarded to Cooper early in 1927, Percy Winner acknowledged instructions from New York "to maintain a fair and impartial attitude towards Fascism." But in the current political climate, "a man who is neutral is considered anti-Fascist no matter how carefully he justifies his neutrality. We are considered representatives of an organization unfriendly to Fascist [*sic*] and to Italy. . . . All our efforts fall on fallow soil since we are treated with diffidence and suspicion."[59] This was especially evident in AP's deteriorating relations with Stefani—a situation that United Press was successfully exploiting. UP, Cortesi reported, was trying to separate the smaller European agencies from

AP and identified Stefani as the best place to start.[60] A campaign was launched to spread the idea that UP "is permeated through and through with the spirit of Fascism and that the UP of all newspaper organizations is the one best fitted to broadcast Fascist propaganda through the world." The campaign included inviting the Fascist official who controlled Stefani, Manlio Morgagni, to New York, where he visited UP headquarters in September 1927 and was guest of honor at a celebratory meal. Once back in Rome, Morgagni was "furious against the AP because of what he calls its Anti-fascist attitude" and threatened to give Stefani's news service to UP in defiance of the cartel contract.

Working relations between AP and Stefani journalists were deeply unsatisfactory. Winner described Stefani's news service as horribly inaccurate and worse than useless. Its employees were "clerks" who didn't understand the necessity of speed in news coverage, not professional journalists. When he visited the Stefani newsroom to urge that news should be relayed to AP more quickly, he was treated as an intruder and at times was "told politely but firmly to get out and stay out." Some Stefani employees were paid under the table to provide prompt news tips to UP and individual newspapers, with the result that "news frequently gets to our competitors before it gets to us." Meanwhile, UP news was widely published, with credit, in many Italian newspapers, including the Fascist organ *Popolo di Roma*, while AP was virtually unknown.[61]

In October 1928, Italian government protests about one story in particular brought Cooper into the debate about Italian censorship. Quoting a newspaper published in Brussels by Italian émigrés, AP reported that King Victor Emmanuel, who was believed to be unhappy with Fascist changes to the constitution, was going to abdicate.[62] The Italian ambassador to the United States complained in person to Charles Stephenson Smith, the editor in charge of AP's foreign news operation. Smith was sympathetic, telling the ambassador that the newspaper's connection with opposition politicians in exile should have been spelled out and the story written to make clear that it was "merely the talk of disgruntled Italians."[63] Smith assured the ambassador that AP was "flagging many unfavorable stories which do not seem reasonable" and would exercise greater vigilance about reports "of uncertain origin and doubtful character." But he also suggested that a relaxation of censorship in Italy "would protect the Mussolini government against unfavorable stories of this sort."

Cooper elaborated on this argument in a remarkable letter to Cortesi that was obviously intended to be read by the Fascist authorities.[64] Under different conditions, he wrote, the abdication story would never have been carried, but it was difficult to maintain AP's traditional approach of providing unbiased news under "the strict supervision" exercised over all news reports sent out of the country. No one dreamed of getting French news from outside France or German news outside Germany, because there were no restrictions on journalists' activities there. In Italy, however, censors suppressed or delayed reports they considered unfavorable, with the result that Italian news "is picked up wherever it can be obtained."

Cooper asked Cortesi to present his arguments directly to Mussolini, whom he had met in person—and from whom he had received an autographed portrait—during his extensive European tour a year earlier. This was a meeting, Cooper wrote, that he would never forget. In fact, since he returned from Europe, Mussolini's photograph "has hung in my office here. I have been looking at it as I have been writing." He recalled Mussolini telling him "that all he asks of The Associated Press is that it tell the truth about Italy," and that was exactly what AP wanted to do. If Mussolini arranged matters so that Cortesi's dispatches would not be held up or interfered with, it would be "a major step forward in protecting Italy's good name abroad by preventing wide publication of rumors." Mussolini was known for flattering foreign visitors,[65] especially influential journalists, and this had evidently succeeded with Cooper, who hoped that his personal appeal to the Duce would be accepted. Mussolini did not exempt Cortesi's dispatches from censorship, but AP had at least one bit of good news from Italy as 1928 came to an end: Morgagni had changed his views about AP and was now, in the words of Reuters' chief editor, "dead against the United Press, whose untrustworthiness and whose exaggerations in the handling of Italian news have aroused his political indignation."[66]

Stefani remained under Fascist control, however, like the Italian press generally, and it was under these conditions that AP sought to develop a closer relationship with the agency in the following years. For example, Cooper's office files include a detailed description by Giovanni Cappelletto, Stefani's general manager, of its "telephone service of propaganda from Italy to Austria and Hungary.[67] This was a substantial operation, sending around two thousand words a day; Cappelletto proudly noted that "every day every newspaper in Austria and Hungary contains some news favorable to Italy. . . . News which is purely Italian or Fascist propaganda is regularly published even in newspapers which are avowedly unfriendly to Italy." Within the complex internal politics of Stefani, Cooper considered Cappelletto to be "our friend," expressing gratitude "for his effort to expose the exaggerations of the United Press."[68] Cooper's public denunciations of European agencies' government connections and propaganda functions were, in some cases, muted to the point of silence in the context of the competitive struggle with UP.

* * *

At the end of 1925, *ABC*, a leading newspaper in Madrid,[69] contacted Cooper to inquire about the possibility of receiving AP news. Just as Italy was Havas territory under the cartel contract, so was Spain and its news agency, Fabra. (In fact, Havas was the majority owner of Fabra until 1926.[70]) The Spanish market had obvious appeal to AP; as Cooper told Noyes, *ABC* and its Madrid competitor *El Sol* were "outstanding examples of modern journalism of the North American type."[71] Both considered the service they received from Fabra—mostly French news from Havas and nothing from the United States—wholly inadequate. *El Sol* had already reached an agreement with United Press, giving UP access to its excellent local and provincial news coverage in return. Cooper asked Charles Houssaye of Havas whether AP might be allowed to have access to *ABC*'s news before publication in exchange for AP news, as a supplement to what the newspaper already received from Fabra.[72] AP had no intention of making any Spanish paper an AP member, and no fee would be charged for the use of AP news: "It would merely be an effort on our part to advantage ourselves with the cooperation of ABC to overcome the cooperation that the United Press receives from El Sol." Houssaye, however, was in no mood to offer concessions and told Cooper to abandon the idea.[73]

AP's frustration increased as time went on; by 1927 United Press was supplying almost all of *ABC*'s foreign news, while AP had to turn down additional requests for coverage from Spanish publications.[74] AP's Madrid correspondent, Robert Berry, considered Fabra "absolutely unsatisfactory in every way." He relied instead on personal contacts with Madrid journalists who were willing to supply news, with some payment usually expected.[75] As in Italy, censorship was a problem. Whenever Berry tried to call Paris to file a story, "they always tell me the line is not working, for all of them know I am on the Press and that I am using the phone for the purpose of sending news."[76]

* * *

AP journalists faced fewer obstacles in France than in Spain and Italy, although cables were occasionally held up or altered for political reasons.[77] But

Cooper was especially impatient with the performance of AP's Paris bureau and highly critical of the news coverage that Havas provided. As Elmer Roberts, AP's long-serving Paris bureau chief, explained, all of Havas's profits came from its extensive advertising business.[78] Relations between AP journalists and their Havas counterparts were mostly cordial, although Cooper's deputy Jackson Elliott observed during a visit to Paris that Roberts and his staff "are afraid of Havas—or at least fear to precipitate any clash by making requests for service."[79] Havas was also less than straightforward with AP, denying that it had any interest in the Radio Agency—which supplied news to AP's bitter competitor, United Press—when in fact it owned a majority of Radio shares.[80]

The Paris bureau supervised AP newsgathering operations in a large swath of Central Europe and North Africa, which gave Roberts a broad overview of the challenges and opportunities facing AP in the European market.[81] He saw a clear connection between AP's ambitions and the United States' growing position of power in the world: "Leadership is being thrown upon our government and upon our finances," and AP "can and ought to take an active part in the world press agency business."[82] AP's interests were not well served; in many European countries "no news service worth considering exists outside the semi-official agencies, AP's allies," all of which received government funds.[83] Beyond that, the smaller agencies dealt almost exclusively with Reuters and Havas. Having little contact with or knowledge of AP, they never considered its requirements, forcing AP to hire its own local correspondents.[84] The Paris staff regularly dealt with government officials who had never heard of AP and who "must first be convinced that we are not some obscure American newspaper interest in competition" with UP.[85] Cooper was also concerned about reports that the smaller agencies paid such heavy fees to Havas and Reuters that little was left for the development of their domestic news services and that they were considering leaving the cartel and signing up with United Press for this reason.[86]

After the embarrassment of the AP Paris bureau's inaccurate reports about transatlantic flights in 1926,[87] a further series of missteps came to a head in 1929 in what was—in the news agency world, where being a few minutes behind United Press on a major story was occasion for severe criticism and soul-searching—a debacle. The *Graf Zeppelin*, attempting its second transatlantic crossing with eighteen passengers and forty-one crew members, lost four of its five engines and was forced to make an emergency landing in Toulon, France.[88] Somehow United Press reported the landing at 3:20 a.m., while AP's story was not filed for another hour and twenty minutes—despite the fact that AP was allied with

Havas and UP was not. Cooper, who would soon be traveling to Europe, was furious. "The list of these failures throughout the last three or four years while not only discouraging is indicative of something that calls for radical action," he told Roberts.[89] "In no other place in the entire world have we had such misfortune in meeting our competition. . . . Havas may be partly to blame. If the time has come when we must settle the matter with Havas, we will meet that situation. . . . The matter has reached a crisis."

The radical action that Cooper threatened was taken soon after he arrived in Paris on June 2. Three days later, Roberts was receiving letters of appreciation on the occasion of his retirement from AP.[90] Cooper described his replacement, Joseph Sharkey, as "much more aggressive than Roberts. . . . He acts whenever necessary and goes to Havas and we get action."[91] Sharkey's appointment, and Cooper's frank expression of dissatisfaction to Houssaye while he was in Paris,[92] brought some initial improvements. But before long the Paris bureau was once again the target of angry criticism. When the former French premier Georges Clémenceau died, United Press beat AP by half an hour.[93] In a sensational story about the fatal shooting in Nice of Fred Nixon-Nirdlinger, a prominent theatrical producer from Philadelphia, by his third wife (they had met when she was a seventeen-year-old contestant in the 1923 Atlantic City beauty pageant), AP was eighteen minutes behind UP, even though the local newspaper had a Havas correspondent in its office.[94] As a result, the *Philadelphia Inquirer*—one of the model AP newspapers that took neither UP nor INS—was now giving "serious consideration to buying an additional news service for protection."[95] In 1932 a false flash from AP's Paris bureau that Amelia Earhart had crashed on her flight to Europe was killed before any AP paper printed it, but Cooper was furious once again.[96] With Havas focused on its own interests—its advertising business, its connection to the Radio Agency, which also supplied news to UP, or its service to Latin America—and lukewarm at best to its nominal ally AP, and with United Press taking advantage of a productive network of connections to French newspapers, the problems with AP's news supply from France were unlikely to disappear. And because Havas was one of the two chief beneficiaries and enforcers of the cartel system that Cooper found increasingly intolerable, he was disposed to be more critical of it than of the smaller agencies—in Italy and Japan, for example—with which he hoped to develop new, independent connections.

* * *

By 1929 AP's board of directors was moving beyond the idea of merely improving the supply of foreign news for AP's U.S. members and toward distributing AP news to newspapers in other countries for its own sake. Ochs and Robert McCormick of the *Chicago Tribune* were broadly critical of Reuters, making it clear they were prepared—eager, even—to end AP's relationship with the British agency and the cartel in which it played the leading role. United Press was "making a good deal of capital out of our relationship with Reuters by stating that Reuters being under governmental subvention everywhere, we incidentally are parties to it," Ochs observed at a board of directors meeting, and he urged Cooper "to go ahead and serve American news to foreign countries where it is desirable."[97] McCormick, whose truculent and suspicious attitude toward everything British had been forged when he was a student there thirty years earlier, denounced Reuters as "a national propaganda news service:"

> [He had] an idea or a conviction that it approaches a duty for us to put our news service all over the world. . . . I would like to see us accomplish for this country in the news what the movies have done for this country in the news reels. I would like to have them get a good American service abroad . . . anything that is American and represents the real country, instead of having it strained through this poison filter that it does go through now.[98]

Cooper took up the theme enthusiastically, widening the scope of the critique from Reuters' shortcomings in China and Japan to include the failures of the cartel agencies in France and Spain.

"Don't you think . . . it is time for us to get militant all down the line?" asked E. Lansing Ray, publisher of the *St. Louis (MO) Globe-Democrat.* Cooper agreed: "I have lost all patience." In an indication that other board members were considering radical action, Cooper was asked how much it would cost to replace the news that Reuters provided. Cooper replied that he did not know but suggested that AP's foreign news operation could be made self-supporting by charging fees to international newspapers that received it, thus contradicting the assurances he had given Jones that AP sought an exchange of news with newspapers in Britain and elsewhere only in order to improve international coverage for its U.S. members. While Cooper did not believe that it would ever come to the point of a clean break, "I do not think Reuters can get along without us as well as we can get along without them."

Some objections were raised to this assessment. Ochs raised the possibility of Reuters making an agreement with UP for U.S. news in the event of a split with

AP, but Cooper replied that Roy Howard had assured him "that if we break with Reuters he will not take them on." (This might have seemed over-optimistic, but in fact AP and UP did sign an agreement to this effect when the break with Reuters came five years later.[99]) Noyes warned that it would cost a great deal to replace Reuters and wondered how AP could do without Reuters–Press Association coverage of the British Parliament. More generally, the suggestion that AP would

> establish a world-wide news service and that we should collect the news and distribute it to the Japanese newspapers—to the French newspapers—to the Italian newspapers—and make a world service out of it, that is something different than we have ever contemplated doing. . . . I am in full accord with anything that will improve our incoming services . . . but I would be very loath to go in on the theory that it is the duty of The Associated Press to establish an American hegemony in all the countries of the world.[100]

Noyes's voice still carried a great deal of weight, but on this occasion, he was the only director to close the door so firmly on selling AP news in what was still the exclusive territory of Reuters, Havas, and their affiliated agencies. He and Cooper were duly instructed to devise a plan for "enlargement and development of the AP foreign service"—a formula vague enough to cover a wide range of possibilities.

More than a year later, Cooper delivered his plan. His main point was that United Press, through its connection with at least 150 European newspapers, was becoming so strong internationally that it was a serious and growing threat to AP. UP could never challenge AP's position in the U.S. market unless it offered better coverage of international news, which it now had and which was AP's "only vulnerable point." This vulnerability was the direct result of the many failings of AP's allies, made worse because the cartel contracts prevented AP from making the kinds of alliances with progressive newspapers that had put UP in such a strong position. In 1893 AP had no choice but to rely on the cartel agencies for international news, but "what was then a bulwark is today the bar to our greater efficiency abroad." All of AP's European allies, unlike AP, were proprietary and profit-making, and many had a focus, like advertising for Havas, that took their attention away from news. Fabra and most other small agencies—there were twenty-four allied agencies in all—"have no news of their countries except what they clip from newspapers." To make up for the agencies' deficiencies, AP had greatly expanded its own foreign newsgathering operation, which now included twenty-two foreign bureaus, costing almost half a million dollars a year. AP's coverage was so much better that the agencies often relied on it for news of their own countries. If this situation did not change, AP would be in the impossible position of having to "collect more and more money at home to spend abroad in order to save our reputation at home." Beyond that, many of the allied agencies were compromised by reliance on government subsidies, which meant that AP was supporting "methods that are abhorrent to the principles of our journalism"—methods that European newspapers were increasingly rejecting. With all these deficiencies, it was

> no wonder that the United Press can find and is finding a fertile field in most any country. The United Press is rapid. Few of the agencies are. It is progressive. The agencies are not. It is free from government influence. The agencies are not. It does not carry propaganda. The agencies do. It endeavors to mold its work upon the very standards of accuracy and impartiality upon with The Associated Press is founded.[101]

Far from being the purveyor of sensation and inaccuracy that Cooper had denounced a few years earlier, UP was now a formidable challenger in every way.

Cooper's analysis of the strategic challenge that AP faced was uncompromising, and the solution he proposed was radical. AP should set up one or more subsidiaries—preferably in England, and perhaps also in France, Germany, or Italy—to gather and sell news. As a cooperative providing news to members only, AP itself was prohibited from selling news, but this should not apply to its foreign activity. The cooperative idea—which Cooper frequently lauded in public as the only form of organization that guaranteed independence and impartiality—"is not adapted to an aggressive campaign," he explained. "Membership and that sort of thing. I want a corporation that can do things that this one cannot do."[102] If revenue from sales to foreign newspapers exceeded the cost of newsgathering and distribution, the profit would be remitted to AP. Selling news internationally, seeking to make a profit, and acting on its own rather than through the cartel agencies would be enormous changes in AP's basic and longstanding methods of operation.

Cooper's presentation was met with a round of applause but also many questions. Noyes had not "made up [his] mind at all" about Cooper's proposals and had grave doubts about how the subsidiaries would be organized and controlled.[103] Ochs, however, was in favor of drastic measures, as was McCormick: AP's contracts with the cartel agencies should not be renewed on the existing basis.[104] Clark Howell of the *Atlanta Constitution* asked how Roderick Jones would respond to the proposed changes, a highly relevant question at a time when AP was in the midst of negotiations with Reuters about getting a free hand in China and Japan in the context of a proposed alliance against UP. "It would be all right," Cooper replied, "if we did not disclose the full plan to him."[105] The issue was left in Noyes's and Cooper's hands, with authorization to take whatever action they agreed was necessary.

Despite Cooper's emphasis on the gains UP was making in Europe, Japan remained AP's top priority. Glenn Babb, AP's Tokyo bureau chief, considered Japan the one area of the world "that offers opportunities for big money operations, comparable to the field you [Cooper] opened up in South America."[106] The prospect of substantial revenue from Japan was the key to AP's entire Pacific strategy, as it would help defray the costs of the otherwise unprofitable service to Honolulu and Manila.[107]

In Cooper's eyes, at least, revenue was not the only consideration. He consistently emphasized Rengo's cooperative form of organization, both in public, where some hyperbole about the purity of AP's motives might be expected, as well as in private. In correspondence with Noyes, he compared AP's role in Japan to the decisive part it played in establishing Canadian Press as a nonprofit cooperative:

> In Canada it was releasing the newspapers from the Canadian Pacific Railroad [*sic*] domination. In Japan it is releasing the Japanese press from the domination of a proprietary agency. . . . The cooperative Associated Press must not compromise the cooperative principle in dealing with a struggling cooperative association after its own pattern.[108]

Noyes, however, was just as consistently skeptical of this line of argument. Rengo was owned by a group of wealthy publishers who were quite able to pay a fair fee, and it received subsidies from the Japanese government as well.[109]

Noyes and Cooper did agree on the ultimate goal of obtaining a free hand for AP in Japan (and China)—a goal formally adopted by the board of directors in January 1930[110]—but had different interpretations of what this would mean in practice. The 1927 Reuters contract specified that AP could provide news to Rengo, but Reuters was to be fully compensated for any reduction in revenue as a result, and all AP news sent to Rengo was also to be made available free of charge to Reuters for use throughout the Far East. Noyes and Cooper agreed that these two provisions should be eliminated but disagreed about the requirement that Reuters should be involved in any AP-Rengo discussions, with any agreement subject to its approval.

AP's subsequent discussions with Reuters left a great deal of room for misunderstanding on this and other points. After meeting with Jones in Rome in March 1930, Noyes reported that they were in agreement: Rengo would be entirely free to do as it wished when its current Reuters contract expired in 1933. They also agreed that Reuters should be consulted before AP and Rengo signed a contract so that Rengo would not be in a position to play off one against the other over financial terms.[111] (Cooper took exception to this: "A free hand to me would mean to do as we please without taking anything up with Reuter at all."[112]) In London, meanwhile, Jones told the Reuters directors that a joint approach—coordinating the financial terms of AP's and Reuters' contracts with Rengo and cooperating in their competition with UP in China—would work to the advantage of both Reuters and AP.[113] Cooper, however, had already told the AP board (but not Jones) that he had no interest in shoring up Reuters' position in China and Japan by joining forces.[114] His goal for AP was to achieve the greatest possible degree of independence. AP would never "come to a solution with the agencies with Reuter in an overlordship, as I call it, and making great profits; and anything that we do that brings it to modernity, that improves our situation, or hurts their situation, I do not believe that Reuter would ever let us do it."[115]

When Cooper met Jones in London that summer to translate the Rome agreement with Noyes into a detailed contract, he believed that the only outstanding issue was the amount of the fee that each would receive from Rengo. To his surprise, Jones presented an entirely new proposal for a formal AP-Reuters alliance against UP in China. This would require Reuters to withdraw its service from any English-language newspaper that published UP rather than AP news (with compensation for any revenue that Reuters lost as a result); limit AP's service to news of North and South America, the rest of the world being covered by Reuters; and forbid AP from charging less for its service than Reuters charged for its own, or serving any newspaper that did not also take the full Reuters service. In Japan, AP would be free to make any arrangement it wished with Rengo, but the requirement to reimburse Reuters for any lost revenue remained.[116]

Cooper told Jones that this appeared to be taking everything up anew, putting him in an awkward position because he had understood from Noyes that everything except Rengo's subscription fee had been settled. The possibility that

Cooper might have misunderstood Noyes left him sufficiently uncertain that he was unwilling to reject Jones's proposals categorically and agreed to bring them back to the AP board. His tense relationship with Jones—more strained than ever after Jones took offense at Cooper's complaint that Reuters was "sitting up late at night trying to find petty little charges" to be levied against AP[117]—added to his unease. Back in New York, however, Noyes was not handicapped by any such uneasiness. Their entire conversation in Rome, he told Jones, had been about "changes to the status quo, not its maintenance," including a free hand for AP in China and Japan.[118] There had been no suggestion that Reuters would be compensated for lost revenue in the event of a Rengo-AP contract. Cooper added that AP did not want to include any mention of the fee AP proposed to charge Rengo in its contract with Reuters but would merely "do everything it can, consistent with its own best interest, to take Reuters' interest into consideration also."[119]

Jones, while expressing regret that what he characterized as the "provisional agreement" with Cooper was not acceptable, offered to reconsider any aspects of it that "seemed . . . not to harmonise" with his and Noyes's discussions in Rome. But he continued to maintain that compensation for lost revenue in Japan would merely be "a fair business return" for Reuters, which had accepted inadequate returns for many years in the hope of eventually reaping "a legitimate reward . . . as the Japanese press became stronger and richer."[120]

The main result of this confusing series of interactions was that Noyes and Cooper sent a detailed and explicit statement of AP's requirements for a new contract to Jones at the end of December, rejecting virtually every element of the proposal Cooper had brought back from London.[121] AP wanted a free hand in China with no limitations on the scope or cost of its service. A section written by Cooper laid out rather abstract but far-reaching provisions about the freedom of major and minor agencies to deal directly with each other. If AP and Rengo (or Stefani, or Fabra, or any other of the allied agencies) wished to deal directly with each other, Reuters and Havas would have nothing to say about it, no claim for compensation, and no right to be consulted. Language about the inevitability of "natural" alliances among agencies—"geographical propinquity, international trade, travel and communication routes and the international political contacts determine after all the route of prime news exchange"—echoed Cooper's 1922 manifesto on the same subject.[122] If these principles were not followed, "only the competitors of the allied agencies"—that is, UP—"would benefit." AP acknowledged Reuters' wish to avoid price competition between the two agencies in their relations with Rengo, but the terms of either agency's agreement with Rengo had no place in a contract between the two of them.

In Europe, competition with UP was the key issue. Not only were AP's allies indifferent toward UP's expansion in their territories, but the existing arrangements prevented AP from competing effectively on its own. Noyes concluded by setting out several essential conditions to be included in the next contract: AP must be free to make direct arrangements to sell or exchange news with any newspaper anywhere, regardless of its connection to any other agency; any agency not covered by the AP-Reuters contract (such as Rengo) must be free to choose the agency with which it wished to have its primary connection; and the contract should cover only news from each agency's national territory, with any original news coverage from outside its national territory being the subject of a separate agreement. Under this provision, AP would send U.S. domestic news to Reuters in London but not any news that it collected elsewhere in the world, while Reuters would provide news from its much more extensive national territory—which was defined as including the United Kingdom and the whole British Empire—to AP in New York.

As in 1926 and 1927, AP's plan was first to reach agreement with Reuters and then to include Havas and Wolff—which, although still a member of the four-party cartel, had been confined to German territory after World War I and was by this point more like a strictly national agency. AP also expected Havas and Reuters to make their separate contracts with subsidiary agencies like Fabra and Stefani conform to the overall agreement, allowing AP to sell directly to newspapers in all of those countries. These demands raised immediate concerns in London. Reuters' news manager warned that the absence of any limitation on the terms of AP's eventual agreement with Rengo "means unrestricted competition." Allowing AP to make direct arrangements with any newspaper in any territory would mean "a complete breakup" of the *agences alliées* system—"all the continental agencies will be against this."[123]

Jones accepted AP's argument that it wanted more freedom in order to compete with UP, telling one member of the Reuters board that UP's success was "goading the A.P. into adventures and activities upon which, but for the U.P., they would never embark."[124] But he also wanted AP to agree that it had no ambition *except* to meet the challenge from UP, a more dubious proposition. In his understanding, AP's desire to have its name appear in European newspapers was mainly intended to give AP correspondents a higher profile and make it easier for them to do their work of serving U.S. newspapers, not because AP "wanted to play the part of news salesman in foreign lands in competition with other Agencies."[125] Much of the back-and-forth of the subsequent negotiations involved Reuters, Havas, and their allies trying to formulate ways of allowing AP to compete with UP but not with them, which ultimately proved impossible. "The whole truth is that all the correspondence is filled with the fact that our setting up these services would be competitive" with the cartel agencies, Noyes told the board. "It could not be anything else but competitive."[126] After hearing a report on the progress of negotiations, Ochs commented that "if they know just what we have in view it is possible that they would not be so favorable to it."[127] Foreign news was now the most expensive part of AP's news-gathering operations, Cooper observed, and "if there is a possibility of revenue abroad, we want it"—no matter at whose expense this was done.[128]

Reuters' and Havas's fears about the likelihood of AP competition were well-founded, so the question arises, Why did they agree to a contract that gave AP almost everything it asked for? There was one crucial difference between 1931–1932 and 1926–1927: AP was now genuinely prepared to end its relationship with the cartel if the changes it considered essential were denied. "If we are ever going to get any place with this thing, we will have to state our position to Jones very firmly and stand by," Cooper told the board in 1930. "And you won't expect me to come back with the best I can get as you did three years ago. . . . If I have to come back and report to the Board in October that it seems hopeless, I will have to do so."[129] On Cooper's instructions, his foreign news editor drew up a detailed estimate of what it would cost—about $150,000 a year—to replace the cartel's international news and the Press Association's coverage of British domestic news.[130] AP's establishment in 1931 of a British subsidiary, Associated Press of Great Britain, led to widespread speculation that a break with Reuters was imminent,[131] and Reuters was certainly aware of this. In April, UP's European manager visited Jones in person to ask whether Reuters would be willing to make an alliance with his agency in the event of a break with AP.[132] Jones insisted that there was absolutely no truth to the rumors, but "if by an effort of imagination I do suppose such a thing . . . then REUTERS naturally would consider alternative arrangements. Primarily we were merchants. Our merchandise was news. We should be willing to sell to the United Press or to any other respectable buyer who would pay our price."[133] Jones reported to his board of directors in June that the European subsidiary agencies were strongly opposed to AP's demand to deal directly with newspapers in their territories— which raised the question whether Reuters should stand with AP and break with the allied agencies, or vice versa, if AP "took up too strong a line."[134] The mere posing of this question showed how much things had changed since 1927. Underscoring the shift, Noyes asked Jones what Reuters would do if AP and Havas were unable to reach an agreement, saying it would be "a great misfortune . . . if there should be any interruption of the intimate relations" between AP and Reuters.[135] Noyes still wanted to maintain AP's connection with Reuters, but only if AP gained the freedom of action it demanded.

The final contract included almost everything AP wanted. "It is a tremendous advance in our present relationship and is a further and as far as I can see final step . . . in a relationship that stood in exactly one position for 34 years," Cooper told the board.[136] The only disappointment was that Reuters' and Havas's contracts with subsidiary agencies remained in force and could not be modified to allow the unrestricted sale of AP news to newspapers in their territory before they expired. Charles Houssaye of Havas expected difficulties in convincing Stefani to agree, but Cooper believed he had an ace up his sleeve: "I may be optimistic, but I think it would take only five minutes with Mussolini personally to get the Italian Agency looking at things our way."[137]

AP now had the ability to sell its news anywhere in the world—including Japan, once Rengo's existing contract with Reuters expired in 1933. The theoretical concerns that Reuters and its allies had about competition from AP were about to become much more immediate.

6

The Japanese Gambit

We cannot possibly be crusaders. No Press
Association can. . . . Our correspondents are
guests of the nation they are assigned to, living
under certain restrictions. They have to keep
faith with the country, and they have to cover
the news. It is sometimes a ticklish business.

—Kent Cooper, *Editor & Publisher*, May 18,
  1931

Between the spring of 1933 and February 1934, Cooper accomplished something
he had been single-mindedly pursuing for years: freeing AP completely from
the restrictive cartel contracts that hampered its ability to operate around the
world. It was a watershed moment in AP's history and in the overall organization of the international news system, setting the stage for AP to become one
of a few truly global agencies. The achievement of this central strategic goal
followed directly from another long-desired accomplishment: establishing an
alliance between AP and the Japanese agency Rengo. Roderick Jones's furious
response to the inroads that Cooper made in Japan finally achieved what fifteen years of patient effort on Cooper's part had not, convincing Frank Noyes
that after operating by the cartel's rules for forty years, AP no longer needed it.

* * *

Early in May 1933, Cooper—accompanied by his wife, Marian, and executive secretary, Sally Gibbs (whom he went on to marry nine years later, after
Marian divorced him)—set out on the first leg of his long-anticipated trip to

Tokyo to negotiate a contract with Rengo. En route to Vancouver he had an unpleasant surprise. "I was amazed . . . to confront Roy Howard on the same train," he reported to Noyes, and "consternated to learn he is going to Japan, and, as he put it, 'wherever you force me to go, besides.'"[1] Howard had phoned Cooper a week before his departure to say that he knew about the trip but did not mention that he intended to come too. His presence reminded Cooper all too clearly of what had happened in South America almost fifteen years earlier when Howard "followed me around South America. I say 'followed,' but he really accompanied me, because he was always on the same train." Now the same thing was about to happen in Japan, making an already complicated situation even trickier: "With his long experience of the Far East, and his superior attitude in respect to Oriental news, you can imagine that he will not make a congenial travelling companion." (Howard, for his part, reported gleefully to Karl Bickel that after Cooper took a day to sort out his reaction to Howard's presence, his demeanor was "frostier than a traffic judge's smile."[2]) Aboard the *Empress of Russia* bound for Yokohama, Howard told Cooper—"assuming I knew it," which he did not—that UP's Japanese ally Nippon Dempo and Rengo were going to be merged into a single government-subsidized agency.[3] Howard agreed with Cooper's suggestion that UP would not object to signing a contract with an agency directly controlled by the Japanese government, which was recently the subject of international condemnation for its 1931 invasion and occupation of Manchuria: "All this means that apparently [Howard] hopes to get a contract with a subsidized Japanese agency which he says is in the forming."[4]

Howard's unwelcome presence was not the only unexpected complication Cooper had to face in Tokyo. Roderick Jones had learned about the voyage too and dispatched his Far Eastern manager, Christopher Chancellor, to Tokyo with instructions to "remain with me constantly."[5] Chancellor was ordered to sit in on Cooper's meetings with Rengo and Japanese newspapers, but Yukichi Iwanaga, Rengo's general manager, refused to allow it.

As Cooper soon learned, Rengo was in desperate straits. The steep depreciation of the Japanese currency had effectively doubled the already heavy payments it made to Reuters, and Rengo would go out of business if this continued. This would be a catastrophe for AP: "If Rengo does not survive I see no hope for [AP] in the Orient."[6] Meanwhile, Iwanaga was furious at Reuters after learning that United Press, which had been charging Nippon Dempo a much lower fee for a better news service to begin with, had cut the amount further to alleviate the exchange-rate shock. Cooper hoped that Reuters could be persuaded to match UP's reduced fee and to divide this amount equally with AP. On the face of it, this seemed quite unrealistic, as Reuters had come to take for granted that the Japanese foreign ministry subsidy to Rengo would effectively cover whatever fee it charged. But the ministry had recently notified Rengo that it planned to stop the subsidy, and the newspapers that jointly owned Rengo were not prepared to make up the shortfall.

Cooper also learned a great deal about the strength of the UP–Nippon Dempo alliance in competition with Rengo, Reuters, and AP. UP treated Nippon Dempo as a real partner, charging reasonable fees and making sure it had the foreign news coverage it needed. Reuters' international operations, on which Rengo relied, were not nearly as extensive as UP's, and its news service was simply not as good. Nippon Dempo had never accepted government subsidies and, having to work harder "to succeed solely on its merits," was financially successful. Rengo's efforts, by contrast, were "dulled perceptibly" by its reliance on subsidies. But UP's strong connection with Nippon Dempo meant there was no chance of AP making a new alliance in that direction: Rengo was AP's only hope. Although Cooper had been working closely with Iwanaga since 1926 and believed him to be sincere, it was from his competitor Roy Howard, not his ally Iwanaga, that he learned of the Japanese government's plans to merge the two agencies. In fact, Iwanaga first expressed astonishment that Cooper knew about this but then told him everything.

It was a grim situation. While Japanese newspapers were suffering financially from the Depression, the government was becoming dictatorial and was determined to end both the subsidy paid to Rengo and the independence of Nippon Dempo. Iwanaga was prepared to accept the merger if the government turned the ownership and management of the new agency over to all Japanese newspapers collectively, but this left many questions unanswered. If the merger took place, would AP, alone or in partnership with Reuters, become the main international news partner of the combined agency? What would happen if Rengo sold out to Nippon Dempo, with its perpetual UP contract? Or if Reuters rejected Rengo's financial demands and allied with Nippon Dempo instead? In the face of so much uncertainty, the agreement that Cooper reached with Iwanaga was merely provisional and did not include the all-important item of the fee that AP would charge. It simply made AP news available to Rengo at least until the next scheduled meeting of the AP board of directors in October. This would protect Rengo from being left without any source of international news if Reuters made unacceptable demands when their current contract expired on July 1.

The interim contract did, however, establish a direct relationship to provide news to and receive news from Rengo, as AP had wanted to do since at least 1926 and as the 1932 agreement with Reuters specifically allowed. Worried that Reuters might preemptively cancel its current AP contract if Chancellor reported that Cooper's aim in coming to Japan was "to cut Reuters' rate," Cooper would not reach a definitive agreement with Rengo without first discussing the situation with Jones. AP, "as well as Reuters, has so much at stake in this situation here that it behooves me to try to have a conference with you at the earliest opportunity" he wrote to Jones at the end of May, proposing to meet in Paris on his way back to New York.[7] But at the same time Cooper agreed with Iwanaga that Rengo's fee should be sharply reduced to the amount that Nippon Dempo paid to UP, and he was not willing to accept less of this amount than Reuters received.[8] This meant that Reuters would be expected to settle for the equivalent of nine thousand dollars instead of the twenty-four thousand dollars it was currently receiving from Rengo for general news. Iwanaga was to begin a new round of contract negotiations with Reuters within a few weeks, knowing that AP would provide an affordable and complete supply of international news if Reuters proved unwilling to reduce its fee very substantially. The AP-Rengo contract also included standard language specifying that each party's contractual territory included its "Possessions, Dominions, Colonies, Protectorates, and Mandated Territories," which meant that Rengo would have exclusive rights to AP news in the Japanese puppet state of Manchukuo, the Manchurian territory that Japan had illegally invaded and occupied, drawing condemnation from the U.S. government among others. Cooper expressed concern about many aspects of AP's relationship with Rengo, but there is no indication that this was one of them.

Cooper was right to be concerned about Chancellor's reports to Jones. On the same day that Cooper was completing his wide-ranging report on the Japanese news situation, Jones informed the Reuters board of directors in London that Cooper had signed a separate agreement with Rengo. This was not objectionable in itself, but the suggestion that AP would receive the same amount of revenue from Rengo as Reuters did was disturbing: "This interference ... between Reuters and Rengo could not be tolerated."[9]

As Jones's angry comment showed, it was hard to see how Cooper's stated wish that both AP and Rengo would continue in alliance with Reuters could be reconciled with his promises to Rengo about the financial terms of its agreement with AP. On his way back to Europe, Cooper sought to justify his actions in a long missive to Jones. AP had been shoring up Reuters' position in Japan for twenty years, he asserted, with very little revenue to show for it and for much of the time no satisfactory coverage of Japanese news from Rengo, while UP "gets both news and money" from its ally. Rengo's problems were now acute and it desperately needed relief from the heavy charges that Reuters exacted. AP was prepared to provide Rengo with a complete news service on its own for eighteen thousand dollars a year, but Cooper urged Jones to accept a partnership in which Reuters and AP would have "equal responsibility and equal returns." Unfortunately, this would mean "a small financial loss for Reuters" of about fifteen thousand dollars—"a negligible amount . . . in the magnitude of Reuters' income around the world."[10] Detailed financial terms were not spelled out in the AP-Rengo agreement, but they were clearly laid out here.

Cooper's apologia made little difference. Even before receiving it, Jones told the Reuters directors that Cooper was "a dubious friend, superficially always most friendly," but acting in ways that were "inconsistent with our conception of loyalty to allies."[11] AP was trying to undermine Reuters in the Far East and would do the same elsewhere if possible. In part, this reflected the "strong pan-American feeling" that was dominant in AP circles—a desire "to get American news and American ideas across in foreign countries." British interests had played a dominant role in the Far East for the last sixty years, but now "America is becoming our rival in an increasing way." The British ambassador in Japan had recently told Jones that U.S. interests were entirely hostile to those of Britain, and it was under these circumstances that Cooper had been "secretly conspiring against us" for the past year. In Jones's account, he and Cooper had reached a gentleman's agreement in 1932 that once AP was permitted to enter the Japanese market, it would negotiate a new contract with Rengo "hand in hand" with Reuters. Instead, Cooper had left New York in secret—"not the act of an ally and a friend" but of a potential enemy. The AP contract would allow Rengo "to put a revolver at our head if we are weak enough or foolish enough not to call their bluff." Jones therefore took a drastic step, asking for authority to cancel Reuters' contract with AP, effective January 1, 1934, on the premise that "the best defensive is the offensive." AP had taken for granted that "good old Reuter is there and good old Reuter will do just what they want" for too long. The goal was to sign a new AP agreement that would be fairer to Reuters, but if this could not be achieved, Reuters would have to find other allies—and UP "would be only too glad to come to terms with us tomorrow."¹²

John Buchan, the novelist and long-serving Reuters director—who had been Jones's close colleague when Jones was in charge of British news propaganda during the First World War—joined in the vilification of Cooper. There would be no peace for Reuters as long as Cooper, "a low stamp of American, of a different class altogether from the old Associated Press men," remained in charge. Melville Stone, Jones added, would "turn in his grave" to see the methods that Cooper used. Noyes, while a personal friend, was "just as pan-American as any of them . . . extremely nice, but hard." After Jones answered a few mild questions, the board agreed unanimously and enthusiastically that he should have "full authority to do whatever he thinks best." At the beginning of July, Reuters notified AP that it was canceling their current contract and sought a new agreement "in line with the Company's requirements."¹³

Within a few months it became clear that Reuters had made a colossal strategic blunder, but there were no second thoughts when Jones and Cooper met on July 27. In Jones's accounts of this crucial encounter, he spoke hard truths to an ill-at-ease and penitent Cooper, telling him that expressions of friendship "were worthless when they masked activities which rightly or wrongly we could only regard as altogether hostile."¹⁴ Cooper responded not with indignation but with "a mourning protest that . . . the innocent and philanthropic motives of [AP] had been misrepresented and misunderstood." AP's agreement with Rengo was only provisional, and anything in it that interfered with Reuters' forthcoming negotiations with Rengo could be dropped. Cooper's main concern was Reuters' termination of its contract with AP, which came as a great shock and was "the last thing he or [AP] wanted." Cooper asked for the notice of termination to be withdrawn so that AP and Reuters could discuss amicably whatever changes to the contract were desired, but this, Jones replied, was impossible. There was no point in discussing the broader contract until the situation with Rengo was cleared up to Reuters' satisfaction.

In Cooper's version of events, he also emphasized that he was willing to set aside the Rengo contract if it was a barrier to continuing relations with Reuters.¹⁵ He told Jones that when Iwanaga started to discuss a reduction in the fees that Rengo paid to Reuters, he had immediately replied that there could be no definite agreement on this without consulting Reuters; Reuters and AP had agreed that AP "would not go into Japan cutting rates." This was true in a narrowly literal sense, but Cooper's June 11 letter to Jones made it clear that his strong preference was for Reuters to accept a financial loss. Cooper did not tell Jones about a telegram just received from Iwanaga: Rengo's directors had voted to make its main news agreement with AP if Reuters rejected its new contract proposals. The "pistol in Rengo's hands to use against Reuters," as Jones described it, was now loaded.

By Cooper's account, the uncompromising line that Jones was now taking was largely the result of personal irritation. Iwanaga's nephew, the Japanese ambassador to Holland, had spoken with Jones several times and told Cooper that "it was ninety percent a case of Sir Roderick's pride being hurt and that the wound could only be healed by [Cooper's] coming to his office to make amends, and above all, for Iwanaga to come." When Cooper told Jones that Iwanaga would indeed be coming to London, he "showed real fire by pounding the desk and declaring, with his teeth set: 'That's his only chance!'" Cooper said he was amazed that Jones had canceled the overall AP contract with no preliminary warning or discussion, to which Jones replied, "One challenges quickly when one's pride is hurt."

Iwanaga arrived in New York on August 21 en route to London. According to Cooper, he was angry to learn that Reuters was canceling the AP contract and proposed to return directly to Tokyo without going on to London at all and "stand upon his relationship" with AP.[16] Cooper, however, persuaded him to go "for the good of the common cause. . . . Frankly I did all this because I thought it is what you [Noyes] wanted done." In London, Iwanaga signed a new agreement with Reuters for general news that sharply reduced the annual cost to £2,400, very close to the US$9,000 that Cooper had previously suggested.[17] Jones acknowledged to the Reuters directors that the agreement involved a substantial reduction in revenue but considered it satisfactory because it "bound Rengo to Reuters more closely for five years minimum" and strengthened Reuters' position in relation to AP.[18] At Jones's suggestion, Iwanaga signed a contract with AP on his way back to Tokyo that was an exact copy of the new Reuters agreement.[19] The contract specifically allowed Rengo to forward AP news to China and occupied Manchuria (Manchukuo); sending news from Japan to those territories had been one of Rengo's major goals since it was founded, and this was the main reason for the large subsidies received from the foreign ministry.[20]

DeWitt Mackenzie, AP's London bureau chief, reported that Jones had suggested Reuters might sign a contract with United Press instead of AP,[21] and this
possibility was taken seriously. Early in August, Karl Bickel of UP met George
Turner, Reuters' overseas news manager, and Chancellor in London to discuss
the prospects of cooperation in the Far East (excluding Japan) and South America. While no definite agreement was reached, Turner reported that Bickel was
"keen as mustard on any sort of contact with Reuter, small or big, but preferably
big" and described him as "alive, quick-thinking, understanding, reasonable,
and we believe, quite a straight fellow. What a gulf of difference between him
and K.C.!"[22]

Resolution of the relationship with Rengo did not weaken Jones's resolve to
tear up the AP-Reuters contract. His new proposal called for dramatic changes.
News exchange between Reuters and AP would be limited to their own news
of the British Isles and the United States, respectively, and the domestic news
each received from allied agencies in North America and Europe. If AP wanted
access to Reuters' news from the British Empire or anywhere else in the world—
including Australia, New Zealand, South Africa, India, Egypt, Siam, Singapore
and other Straits settlements, China, the Dutch East Indies, and other countries
of the Far East, excluding Japan—it would have to pay an annual fee of fifty
thousand dollars. In exchange, Reuters offered to pay five thousand dollars for
AP's news of Central and South America.[23] These demands came as a shock
to AP. Elimination of the fee paid to Reuters and its allies since 1893 had been
one of the main achievements of the 1926–1927 contract, a clear sign that AP
was now Reuters' equal, and it was hard to imagine AP agreeing not only to
its restoration but to a substantial increase as well. The contract proposals and
Jones's explanation were "a major, if not the major disappointment of my life,"
Noyes wrote in reply, indicating "a very low estimate, on the part of the Directors of Reuters and yourself, of the value of [AP] in the close association that
has existed for so many years."[24]

Cooper, meanwhile, was actively making plans for news coverage of Britain
and Europe without Reuters and its allies, using a private cable address that
sent communications to his Park Avenue apartment instead of AP headquarters in order to maintain secrecy.[25] DeWitt Mackenzie, who had returned to
New York to take charge of AP's foreign service, assessed whether the Exchange Telegraph Company (Extel)—another London-based news service,
to which AP had subscribed until earlier that year—could make up for the

possible loss of Reuters news coverage in Britain, Europe, Africa, and the near and far east.[26] Extel's world news service, he estimated, could be obtained for around five thousand dollars a year, but since it also served UP and INS, AP would not have the news exclusively. The network of correspondents and stringers AP already maintained around the world could make up for gaps in Extel's service just as it had done with Reuters. Cooper acted quickly on this advice, ordering Frank King, the new London bureau chief, to propose a new five-year contract to Extel without delay.[27] King was also making discreet arrangements to hire string correspondents in areas of Europe where AP would need additional protection: "Heralding the fact that we are hunting for correspondents throughout the Empire would soon create much gossip throughout Fleet Street."[28]

On January 10, AP's board of directors voted unanimously to reject Jones's proposed contract and made no counteroffer. The board, Noyes told Jones, had concluded that "our point of view is so entirely divergent from that expressed and reiterated by you that the two cannot be reconciled."[29] The summary account of board decisions presented to AP members in that year's annual report was, if anything, even more laconic than usual: the board had simply considered Reuters' proposal to renew their news exchange contract on condition of AP's agreeing to make an annual payment "and decided not to accept the conditions suggested."[30] There was no further acknowledgment that an alliance that had been the foundation of AP's approach to international newsgathering and news distribution for forty years was at an end.

Cooper immediately made overtures to all the major agencies affiliated with Reuters—Havas, Wolff (which had recently been forcibly merged with another agency by the Nazis as Deutsches Nachrichtenbüro), and the Press Association—about establishing independent connections with AP.[31] He had already told Charles Houssaye of Havas that Reuters was demanding a forty-five-thousand-dollar differential and suggested a separate AP-Havas agreement with no fees involved for either.[32] Houssaye accepted in principle the idea of AP paying a differential for Reuters news of the British Empire and Far East but was "entirely ignorant" of the amount demanded and did not want to consider the possibility of a split between Reuters and AP or to decide between the two.[33] Even while making these approaches, Cooper instructed the Paris bureau chief to make arrangements for AP to cover French news on its own, "just as if there were to be no future relationship with Havas."[34]

Cooper also complained about Reuters' financial demands to Hans Mejer, the new head of Deutsches Nachrichtenbüro (DNB). It was preposterous that AP's relationship with DNB would have to end unless AP accepted Reuters' demand for an "exorbitant and unwarranted" payment. AP did not need Reuters' news, because it already had a better world news service than any other agency.[35] Would DNB, "revitalized by your own activities, and intensely interested in maintaining its rights internationally as befits the German nation of today," allow Reuters to dictate its future relationship with AP? If not, he forwarded as a model for a new two-way relationship the contract that AP had recently signed with Stefani. National news from each agency's territory would be exchanged with no payment, but a differential would be charged if DNB wanted AP's world news as well.[36] (It did not, however, include a clause from the Stefani contract specifying that the Italian agency could "suppress any news which it may consider unsuitable for publication in Italy, or to modify the form thereof in order that it may meet the requirements of the Italian press.") Cooper was well aware by this time that DNB had become a propaganda agency under strict Nazi control.[37] His Berlin bureau chief, Louis Lochner, reported that DNB's news coverage was faster than it previously had been—at least for whatever "non-political and official news" was permitted by the Ministry of Propaganda. But AP should not forget "that we are living in a dictatorship and therefore, no matter how we tie up, there will be news which a German bureau cannot give us."[38]

Cooper also approached H. C. Robbins of Britain's Press Association (PA). Although the PA became the majority owner of Reuters in 1926, it had largely left Jones to run the agency as he saw fit. Cooper praised the PA service as a crucial element in AP's connection with Reuters but expected that a direct relationship with AP would not be permitted. Robbins replied in very friendly terms, saying that in view of the mutual ideals of AP and the PA—both newspaper-owned cooperatives—the PA would be happy to continue the relationship, but this would be impossible if the split with Reuters was irrevocable.[39] However, he urged AP to keep negotiating and suggested that Reuters would be prepared to withdraw its proposals and return to the status quo. Mejer also said it was impossible for his agency to break with Reuters and urged mediation, as did Houssaye, who asked the AP board to withhold a final decision until he could discuss the situation with Reuters.[40] But even as Cooper tried to maintain relations with Reuters' European allies, he seemed untroubled by the prospect that none would be in a position to work directly with AP. He was, he told Noyes, "very happy and confident of the future of [AP] abroad, more happy than ever before and confident for the first time."[41]

AP's decision to let the Reuters contract lapse set off a feverish round of discussions with United Press by both parties. Jones told the Reuters directors that a contract with UP would give Reuters an alternative source of U.S. domestic and international news, and UP "would be only too glad to come to terms with us tomorrow." But when this possibility had been raised at an AP directors meeting several years earlier, Cooper assured the board that Roy Howard had told him "that if we break with Reuters he will not take them on." As events turned out, Cooper was right. In a series of phone calls between Jones and Bickel in January, Bickel expressed concern that a connection with Reuters would also mean a connection with Havas, UP's bitter competitor in South America.[42] Even though Jones held out the prospect of "epoch-making business" for UP, it soon became clear that any agreement including a connection between UP and Havas was impossible.[43] UP's contract with its subsidiary, British United Press (BUP), giving BUP exclusive rights to use UP material in the British empire, was another obstacle.[44] Jones then proposed to continue the discussions in New York, not only with UP but also with AP. On January 31, he cabled Noyes: "Granted your good will I am determined my dear friend to settle this trouble. I am sailing Berengia Saturday to see you."[45] Cooper was sure that this new approach "on a suddenly newly asserted friendship and good will basis" was the direct result of UP's reluctance to sign a contract with Reuters.[46] "Jones was also thrown into a panic by summary demands from Havas," he told Noyes; its substantial subsidy from the French Foreign Office for disseminating government-approved news internationally was predicated on a continuing connection with AP and its distribution network.[47]

On the same day that Jones sent news of his departure for New York, Cooper proposed a radical departure in AP's relations with UP, its chief competitor: an agreement that neither "would make any exclusive news availability contract with any European agency."[48] This would "take the wind out of Jones's sails forever," guaranteeing that neither AP nor UP could make a contract with Reuters unless identical terms were also offered to the other agency. With Jones set to arrive in New York within a week, AP's negotiating position would be "greatly strengthened" if the AP-UP agreement was already in place. Noyes raised some reasonable questions: Why would Bickel want equal access to the news of the Press Association, for example, when UP already had an agreement to exchange news exclusively with its own British subsidiary? In "the back of my mind is the thought that after all the United Press is our real competitor and that this fact should always be kept in mind."[49] Cooper replied that his main concern was to forestall the possibility of UP making an agreement with the Press Association that excluded AP. It would be better for AP to retain its exclusive access to PA news through Reuters rather sharing it with UP, but accepting Reuters "domination of our activities" around the world was too high a price.[50]

UP's motives were equally straightforward. As the New York bureau chief of the Soviet agency TASS reported to his head office in Moscow, Bickel had told him that he was "watching the collapse of the old Alliance under the domination of Reuter and acquiring what advantage might be possible for the United Press. . . . What he desired most of all was a relation with Tass," which had an exclusive contract with AP for the use of its news in North America.[51] After the new AP-UP contract was signed, Cooper and Bickel agreed to visit Moscow together to discuss joint arrangements with TASS.[52] UP was also to gain access to the news of Stefani, similarly tied to AP in an exclusive arrangement.[53]

The AP-UP agreement, reached after less than twenty-four hours of discussion, was signed two days before Jones's first meeting with Noyes.[54] It guaranteed that any arrangement AP had with any European agency (including Reuters and the Press Association) had to be available to UP on the same terms and vice versa.[55] If one of AP's European allies insisted on terms for a contract with UP that UP considered unfair, AP would be required to cancel its existing contract. Roy Howard sent "hearty congratulations" by telegram: "Think foreign news agreement most important achievement since Stones property right news decision stop. Hope marks beginning long overdue intelligent cooperation between two agencies."[56]

The UP agreement gave Cooper and Noyes the whip hand in their discussions with Jones. The altered balance of power was immediately evident in Jones's initial meeting with Cooper—there would be no return to the status quo. "I told [Jones] promptly that it seemed to me wholly futile to discuss anything unless he would agree to let us negotiate directly with the Press Association because all I wanted was the Press Association report of the British Isles," Cooper recounted to his close ally, Fred Livesay of Canadian Press.[57] After "a great deal of talk," Jones said that "he would favorably consider the utmost that I would ask, so anxious was he to retain the connection" with AP. But when Jones added that he wanted exclusive rights to distribute Reuters news in Canada—where Canadian Press received Reuters material at no additional charge through its relationship with AP and was gravely concerned about being required to pay heavily for Reuters news if the AP connection ended—Cooper flatly refused: "You will just have to consider that for the purposes of any negotiations The Canadian Press and The Associated Press are one and the same thing."[58] After some hesitation, Jones agreed to this as well. AP's other major demands were that Reuters would supply all of its news from the British Empire and other countries in Africa and Asia in exchange for AP's news of North America and U.S. possessions, with no differential to be paid either way, and that AP would be free to make separate contracts with any of Reuters' allied agencies. These provisions were all adopted without amendment in the final contract.[59] Livesay, for one, was jubilant: "You have certainly bottled up Sir Roderick tight as far as we are concerned. . . . The whole thing must have been to him a terrific blow, but he brought it on himself by his arrogance and vanity."[60] In presenting the new contract to his own board of directors, Jones played down to the point of deception the extent of Reuters' losses. (Or perhaps, as the historian of Reuters, Donald Read, has written, it was just an example of Jones's "talent for self-deception."[61]) Jones presented AP's right to make a separate contract with the Press Association—a major concession that Reuters would never have accepted except under duress—as nothing more than "a face-saving gesture" to assist Cooper in his relations with the AP board.[62] Abandonment of the claim for a forty-five-thousand-dollar differential, acceptance that AP's domestic news was worth as much as all of Reuters' international news, the end of any limits on AP's connections with Reuters' allied agencies and clients—none of these was apparently mentioned.

Since AP and Reuters were now entirely free to supply news to newspapers, radio stations, and any other journalistic organizations in each other's territory, they were competitors at least as much as allies. In light of this, AP was determined that Reuters staff in New York should not have access to any of its news from outside the United States and Canada. The result was that Reuters journalists, who previously had been welcome in AP's newsroom, were barred from entry as of March 31. Reuters' New York office, which (along with the New York bureaus of the close AP allies Canadian Press and Rengo) had been within and part of the larger AP headquarters, would have to be made physically separate. (In London, AP moved completely out of the Reuters–Press Association building on Fleet Street.) Jones entrusted the new arrangements to his chief editor, Bernard Rickatson-Hatt, who had recently spent a year in New York as Reuters' chief U.S. correspondent and made a thorough study of AP's methods while he was there.

The day after Jones left New York, Rickatson-Hatt was summoned to the office of Lloyd Stratton, Cooper's executive assistant and right-hand man. Stratton, "a K.C. yes-man through and through" and "slippery as an eel," informed Rickatson-Hatt that while AP journalists would be glad to see him personally, "I was not so welcome in my official capacity."[63] Relations between AP and Reuters were "now on an entirely different footing and can never be the same again." From now on, Stratton and another senior executive were to be his only journalistic contacts; other AP staff had been instructed "to have as little to do with Reuters as possible."[64] This was a significant loss—being cut off from AP's international news coverage "cramps our style a great deal."[65]

At the end of February, Cooper sailed for Europe to negotiate new contracts with TASS, Havas, DNB, the Press Association, and other Reuters allies. The negotiations with TASS went smoothly; Bickel of United Press visited Moscow at the same time as Cooper, and in accordance with the AP-UP agreement on non-exclusivity, both signed contracts with TASS.[66] (The fact that the United States and the Soviet regime had established diplomatic relations just six months earlier, and that the USSR was about to join the League of Nations, no doubt had something to do with its desire for more extensive connections with U.S. news agencies as well.[67]) The situation with Havas and DNB, whose relations with AP were no longer governed by the previous four-party contract, was more complicated. AP's proposal to both was based on inequality: their use of AP news would be restricted to their respective national territories, while AP would be entitled to use the news they provided anywhere in the western hemisphere.[68]

Jones was equally concerned about Reuters' relations with DNB and Havas, traveling to Paris for discussions with Mejer and Houssaye a few days after Cooper arrived in Europe. The Havas representatives were angry, suggesting that Jones had looked after Reuters' interests in the negotiations with AP "but had not manifested any particular concern for Havas." The new AP proposal was an insult, implying that Havas was less important than Reuters, "worthy only of the treatment due to underlings." Why had Reuters not done better for its ally of many years' standing? Jones responded with anger of his own. He had never pretended to negotiate on Havas's behalf. In fact, thanks to its "weakness amounting almost to desertion," he had arrived in New York in a compromised position after Havas told him that a break with AP was unthinkable because of its commitment to disseminating French propaganda news in North and South America—dissemination that relied in large measure on the AP connection.

Under the circumstances, Jones had done well by managing to reach an agreement that avoided the disastrous consequences of a permanent break between Reuters and AP while also guaranteeing Havas access to AP's U.S. news. He did eventually press AP to offer Havas and DNB the same terms as Reuters had negotiated, but Cooper refused, telling Jones that "he did not care whether he had a contract with them or not. Havas were moribund, and had been for twenty years, and D.N.B. were nothing but a Government Propaganda Department."[69] Meanwhile, AP bureau chiefs in London and Paris were instructed to keep developing their own sources of news and not to use any material from Reuters, PA, or Havas unless absolutely necessary.[70] Havas eventually signed the basic contract that Cooper proposed, paying a minimum of one thousand dollars a month extra for the right to use AP material in South America and the Far East.[71]

A similar contract was signed with the Italian agency Stefani.[72] But AP followed a different course in Spain, where the relationship with Fabra was "injuring our prestige. . . . The news was being garbled and badly handled; only a few of the papers were crediting The AP, etc."[73] Instead, AP provided a news service from London to the Madrid daily *El Debate*.[74] Rex Smith, the Madrid bureau chief, had reported favorably on the prospects of an agreement even before the new Reuters contract was signed, but warned Stratton that "we cannot get away from the fact that Debate is a Catholic-Monarchist organ."[75] Smith acknowledged that he was sympathetic to both Catholics and monarchists "personally and as a journalist," but an overt alliance with "any political or religious organ" would damage AP's reputation for impartiality. He nonetheless believed that a connection with *El Debate* was a good idea as long as AP's independence was not compromised.[76] Besides receiving considerable revenue, AP had exclusive rights to use the news collected by *El Debate* and its provincial associates, including *La Vanguardia* of Barcelona. Just as Cooper had long hoped, the arrangement also generated much favorable publicity for AP, since *El Debate* was "playing our news in a way new to Spain."[77] This approach of dealing directly with prominent individual newspapers rather than an unsatisfactory national agency "undoubtedly will become a general program," Stratton wrote.[78]

* * *

In Germany, conditions for journalists, including international correspondents, deteriorated sharply after the Nazi regime took power in January 1933. For the next eight years, Louis Lochner struggled to find a way to carry out what

he considered to be his journalistic responsibilities under these restrictions—
though he concluded after the war that he was able to report less than half of
what he knew.[79] Cooper, however, painted a much more favorable picture of
the journalistic environment in Germany than was really the case, for strategic,
tactical, and perhaps political or ideological reasons.

Two months after Adolf Hitler became German chancellor, Lochner sent
Cooper a remarkably candid assessment of the situation, speaking frankly about
the new pressures he was facing. One incident was particularly telling, raising
issues of journalistic integrity that Lochner, and AP, regularly confronted until
December 1941, when Germany declared war on the United States, the AP bureau in Berlin was closed, and he and all other American correspondents still
in the country were arrested and interned. The incident was this: a contact in
the German Foreign Office had warned Lochner that detectives were on their
way to raid the office of AP's news photo subsidiary, Associated Press GmbH,
because it had allegedly distributed photos of a Jewish businessman in Munich
who was forced to walk through the streets in short pants with an antisemitic
placard around his neck. Lochner reported that the picture had indeed been
available but that he and AP GmbH's photo editor (a German citizen) had
decided against using it, "having carefully studied the censorship decrees, and
knowing that the Nazi and Nationalist photo concerns were merely waiting
for us to slip a cog and give an excuse for shutting us up." The decision not to
distribute the photo led to a cabled complaint from AP's head office: "Nazi attacks on Jews played big. Licked here first pictures." For Lochner, however, it
was "more important for us to remain in the field here, even if occasionally we
are licked, than to risk having our whole organization destroyed by publishing
a picture to which the regime in power objects." He hated censorship and felt
"terrible that we cannot report everything we know." But if AP wanted to fulfill
the functions of a news agency in a country where freedom of speech and freedom of the press were curtailed, it must try "just as long as possible to remain
within that country." Correspondents for individual newspapers might well
risk ejection by taking a bolder approach, but the fourteen hundred members
of AP "want us to stick to our posts."[80]

Lochner's decision in this case, and the justification he offered, set out the
essence of the dilemma that AP faced in covering Nazi Germany. What limits
should a journalistic organization accept in order to keep operating inside an increasingly authoritarian state that relied heavily on propaganda? Recent research

by Harriet Scharnberg and Norman Domeier has shown that AP GmbH—AP's German-registered subsidiary that was subject to German laws—served Nazi propaganda purposes at times, both before and during the war.[81] Scharnberg's work led to a detailed review by AP of all its operations in Germany in the years leading up to and during the Second World War.[82] The review concluded that while AP made mistakes, particularly in its photo operations, "in the totality of its conduct [AP] fulfilled its mission to gather the news in Germany forthrightly and as independently as possible for the benefit of its audience and for the benefit of the truth."[83] Among other things, this review documented the constraints on regular news coverage and the often ingenious ways that Lochner tried to make the most of the limited opportunities for factual reporting. What was not discussed in this report, however, is how Cooper—in his public accounts of AP's operations in Germany at the time, and even in high-level internal discussions—depicted the journalistic environment there.

Lochner, an American citizen of German descent who had worked for Henry Ford during the First World War as an opponent of U.S. involvement, had been a journalist in Berlin since 1921, joining AP in 1924 and becoming bureau chief in 1928. His fluency in German and wide network of contacts, especially in conservative, monarchist, military and cultural circles (his second wife, Hilde, was a German citizen from a well-connected family) made Lochner a formidable gatherer of news.[84]

Once the Nazis took power, they moved quickly to exert control over all forms of media, especially journalism, creating a situation unlike anything Lochner had ever experienced. Journalists working for Wolff, AP's ally in the Reuters-led cartel, were "scared stiff, and don't dare publish unfavorable things," he reported to Cooper in March 1933. A Nazi official in Wolff's newsroom "goes over every item and decides whether it can be sent out or not." There was no official censorship of reports sent out of Germany by foreign journalists, but Lochner was "reliably informed that all our cables are being read." Under these circumstances, Lochner decided not to use any information from sources who, fearing for their lives if identified, wanted to remain anonymous. This included many credible reports of atrocities against opponents of the regime. Some correspondents for individual newspapers did use material of this kind, risking expulsion, "but they are people whose offices don't care whether or not they stay," because they were confident that AP would continue to provide coverage. In this unfamiliar landscape, where any AP report that displeased the regime was publicly denounced, Lochner concluded that the best course was to "accept the German nationalistic revolution as a fact and give the new regime a chance"; refuse to file "sensational or alarmist stories unless those who supply the facts are ready to stand for them in case I am questioned"—in other words, refuse to cite anonymous sources; "live up to the laws and the decrees of this country even though they seem irksome and contrary to journalistic ideals"; maintain AP's reputation among Nazi officials for "fairness, integrity and objectivity," even when it came to stories that the authorities might "frown upon, but that must be carried by a non-partisan organization like the A.P. if it does not want to lose its reputation"; and finally, "always remember that, no matter what may happen, the A.P. will want to have a bureau in Germany."[85]

While Lochner's position was, essentially, to accept the rules of the game established by the Nazis, he sometimes successfully resisted the regime's pressure. For example, the Nazis immediately took action to strip Jews of their civil rights. This included official discrimination against AP GmbH, which had Jewish employees.[86] AP had established this news photo subsidiary as a German company, and thus subject to German law, in 1931.[87] Lochner reported to Cooper in the spring of 1933 that he had protested to "various Nazi friends" about the anti-AP discrimination and believed that "by simply sticking to our guns we can hold our ground without even dismissing our Jewish staffers." Even after adoption of the Schriftleitergesetz, or Editor's Law, in October, specifying—among other measures amounting to the legal termination of press freedom[88]—that only Germans of non-Jewish descent could be licensed to work as journalists, Lochner tried to protect AP GmbH's six employees who did not qualify as Aryan.[89] By the end of 1935, however, AP complied with the law, discharging or (in one case) reassigning outside of Germany the employees classified as Jewish. Several subsequently emigrated to the United States with AP's assistance.[90] The *New York Times*, whose Wide World news photo service was similarly registered as a German company, shut down the operation in 1935. There is no indication that AP considered anything similar.

On one occasion, Cooper sharply criticized Lochner for trying to protect journalists' rights. In September 1933, three journalists from the USSR, representing TASS and the newspapers *Pravda* and *Izvestia*, were prevented from attending the trial of five men charged with setting fire to the Reichstag. The TASS and *Izvestia* correspondents were later arrested. Lochner, believing that Wolff had sent out a misleading report about the incident under Nazi direction, wrote a letter of complaint, urging Wolff to take up the criticism with its overseers.

Cooper replied sternly, "It is not for you, nor for us, to make representations" on TASS's behalf. He feared that "the fine cooperation" AP had been receiving from Wolff would end as a result of the letter. A complaint to the authorities could be justified only if AP was "directly hindered in our work in Germany as were the Tass representatives."[91]

Lochner replied that he was miserable to hear of Cooper's disapproval but also defended his actions. He was not interfering on TASS's behalf but wanted only to "secur[e] objective reporting" from Wolff and point out the dangers that all foreign correspondents in Germany were facing. His complaint had not caused any difficulty with the propaganda ministry—whose officials had recently described Lochner as producing "the most objective reports in the American press concerning the German revolution and the New Germany"—or with Wolff. But Lochner also promised never to do anything similar without consulting Cooper first. If not for the friendly tone of Cooper's admonishing letter, he would have resigned from AP; Cooper's expressions of confidence had "kept me buoyant despite the terrifically difficult situation" that foreign correspondents in Germany now faced.[92] The psychological pressure on Lochner, and his acute concern about approval or disapproval—whether expressed by Nazi officials, his ostensible allies in the Wolff agency, or his own head office—were plain to see. None of Cooper's fears about negative repercussions were borne out.[93] But now, even the limited room that Lochner had to maneuver had been further reduced—this time through the actions of his own superior. The message was clear: to minimize any risk of expulsion, Lochner should always err on the side of caution.

On January 1, 1934, Joseph Goebbels's propaganda ministry forced Wolff and its competitor, Telegraph Union, to merge into a single agency, Deutsches Nachrichtenbüro, which was directly (although not publicly) Nazi-controlled.[94] Wolff had been indirectly controlled or subsidized by the Prussian and later the German government and had privileged access to official news and public transmission facilities since the 1860s, and the German government acquired outright majority control in 1931.[95] While Cooper had long been a forceful public critic of government-subsidized or government-controlled news agencies, AP's immediate response to the formation of DNB reflected more practical concerns. United Press, AP's rival, was allied with Telegraph Union and after the merger would probably insist that it should receive DNB's news report, Lochner predicted. This meant that AP would lose the exclusive access to Wolff's German domestic news that it had previously enjoyed under the cartel contract.[96] (In the event, DNB continued Wolff's connection with the cartel agencies, not Telegraph Union's link with UP.[97]) Even though Wolff would not provide news "that is in any way harmful to the present regime," Lochner considered it an indispensable source of government news, and it would be the only source of such information after the merger. AP should therefore do everything it could to maintain its alliance with Wolff/DNB, "imperfect though it is." Cooper had already shown that he realized the importance of maintaining a strong connection with the newly formed DNB after the collapse of AP's relationship with Reuters.[98]

Lochner, who was sometimes accused of being pro-Nazi, or at least too inclined to accept Nazi interpretations of events at face value, also disclosed some of his personal views after the first months of the Hitler regime. While he abhorred Hitler's antisemitism and lamented the end of judicial independence, he also believed that "the Hitler movement has wonderful sides to it." There was "something great and noble in the idea of a 'Volksgemeinschaft'—a real community of interests between all classes of society."[99] In a letter to his daughter attending university in Chicago, he described the government's approach of criticizing the foreign press for everything that went wrong as short-sighted, making it "increasingly hard for those of us who try to be objective and to extol all the good things that the government does alongside our mentioning the bad."[100] In general, Lochner was more critical of France than of Germany. France, he told Cooper, should be blamed "more than any other single factor for the condition in which Germany now finds herself," through its insistence on full payment of heavy war reparations.[101]

Cooper was reluctant to say anything in public about the difficulties that international journalists faced in Germany. In November 1933, Lochner spelled out clearly to DeWitt Mackenzie, AP's London bureau chief and de facto head of its European news operation, the restrictions under which he and other correspondents operated.[102] Wolff ignored any news that would show the Nazi regime in a bad light, and German newspapers could not be relied on for information, because "no editor dares say anything that is not agreeable to the Propaganda Ministry." German contacts who could provide information on "problems like the Jews, the churches, the treatment of foreigners, even the diplomatic situation" were afraid to speak to foreigners on the phone, making it necessary to meet sources in person and clandestinely. By 1935, DNB was sending out propaganda ministry material—including falsehoods, distributed "with the utmost brazenness"—as its own stories without acknowledging the source.[103]

(DNB's sarcastic nickname was "Darf Nichts Bringen," or "not allowed to deliver anything.") Until 1939, about two-thirds of the news that it gathered was reserved for the exclusive use of Nazi officials, and this increased to four-fifths after the outbreak of war.[104] Nazi authorities, meanwhile, were directly attacking foreign news organizations. At one point in 1935, the propaganda ministry and Nazi Party put AP on a blacklist, but Lochner insisted that AP must continue to cover controversial subjects such as attacks against Jews or the problem of food shortages and rising prices; otherwise, it would be presenting a "mendacious picture" of life in Germany.[105] Even so, at times he (and other journalists) substantially minimized the extent of atrocities in order to avoid reprisals. After covering the explosion of antisemitic violence throughout Germany on Kristallnacht—November 9–10, 1938—Lochner told his daughter that he and other correspondents had effectively "lied in the sense that they understated many times rather than even approach the truth for fear that their authentic sources might be led to new torture if they were revealed."[106]

Despite clear evidence of how severely AP's newsgathering inside Germany was restricted, Cooper presented a much more favorable picture. "The rest of the world is getting a good picture of what is going on in Germany," he told a group of AP members in September 1934. While German newspapers "do not give all the world news to their readers," there was "no censorship on the news coming from Germany."[107] The German authorities "do not care for world opinion," and "what the rest of the world thinks does not bother them"—assertions that directly contradicted Lochner's frequent reports of official retaliation for unfavorable stories and outright suppression of news. After 1939 the gulf between Cooper's depiction of the situation facing journalists in Germany and the reality became even wider.[108]

*   *   *

Beyond Europe, AP was quick to explore the possibilities presented by its newfound freedom of action in 1934. Gideon Seymour, a former bureau chief in Buenos Aires, was sent to assess prospects in South Africa, Australia, and New Zealand.[109] Despite the obvious competitive purpose of his mission, Seymour had the assistance of Reuters staff in South Africa and expected to receive similar cooperation in Australia.[110] Somewhat surprisingly, the fact that AP had everything its own way in the 1934 contract led not to bitterness but instead to a period of apparent good feeling between the two agencies. Jones told Cooper that they were "building up a new relationship . . . on a new basis, a basis of greater freedom vis-a-vis the other than either hitherto has enjoyed."[111] To Chancellor, he described the new contract as giving Reuters valuable new opportunities to sell its service in the United States and elsewhere, which should be exploited "without disturbing the much better relationship" with AP.[112] But Jones's suggestion that the change in AP's attitude was the result of "Reuters' bearing throughout the crisis in our mutual relationship" and AP's growing appreciation of "the solid worth of Reuters as a world news organization" was, if not outright dissimulation, at least very wishful thinking. Friction between Reuters and AP had indeed abated, but this was mainly because Reuters, as a direct result of Jones's overplaying of his hand, had given AP practically everything it wanted.

With all the new developments in AP's international activities—greatly expanded coverage of foreign news, staff increases, and the systematic investigation and exploitation of new markets—its relationship with Rengo, which had been the immediate cause of the break with Reuters, no longer occupied center stage. In fact, the actual as opposed to the imagined relationship with Rengo brought with it some new concerns. When it seemed in early February 1934 that the Reuters-AP relationship might not continue on any terms, Iwanaga told Cooper that Rengo would do everything it could to strengthen AP's position in the Far East, especially in China, Korea, and occupied Manchuria (Manchukuo).[113] Glenn Babb, AP's bureau chief in Tokyo, welcomed the expression of support but warned Cooper that it was dangerous to rely too heavily on Rengo "in controversial Japanese-Chinese situations." AP would probably need its own correspondent in Japanese-occupied Manchuria before too long: "Rengo will not be good enough when unbiased judgment of a controversial situation or colorful writing on the spot are required."[114] According to Roy Howard, AP did not succeed in neutralizing Rengo's imperialist bias as Babb recommended. After a visit to Manila in 1935, he told Cooper that Rengo's bias was also affecting AP's original coverage of China. The AP news appearing in Manila newspapers "is so palpably tinged with Japanese propaganda and has presented such a ridiculously untrue picture of what is going on in North China, that I am certain you would personally raise hell about it if you were on the scene."[115]

Meanwhile, the Japanese government went ahead with its plan to merge Rengo and Nippon Dempo into a new agency, Domei, under closer government control; this was accomplished in 1935 and 1936.[116] Domei was even more heavily subsidized than Rengo had been, but the policy of denying the existence of any such subsidies continued.[117]

By the mid-1930s, the autonomy that AP gained in its long struggle with Reuters went along with close relations with news agencies in Japan, Germany, and Italy that were clearly controlled by Fascist or militarist/authoritarian governments. AP's policy of maintaining a presence in any country where that was possible without publicly criticizing restrictions on press freedom, and accepting limits on coverage of systematic violations of citizens' rights and military aggression, did not apply only to dictatorships of the right, as its continuing relationship with TASS indicated. But as the tensions between fascism and democracy grew sharper in the late 1930s, the complications that arose from this position also became more acute. And at the same time in the United States, AP as an institution was becoming increasingly aligned with big-business opposition to major elements of Roosevelt's New Deal.

7

New Media

This broadcasting business is the bane of my
existence. . . . I can do nothing.

—Kent Cooper, November 8, 1932

Throughout its long history, journalism has been shaped and reshaped by the
emergence of new technologies in a process that was always complicated and,
in many ways, unpredictable. The nature of journalism as a business, the institutional imperatives of its organizations, the social and political context in
which it operated, the perceived demands of its audiences and ideas about how
journalism should (and should not) be practiced all played a part in winnowing
down the many possibilities that any new technology presented to those that
appeared to be, in retrospect, natural.

During the 1920s and 1930s, two new technologies severely disrupted the
journalistic landscape: radio and the same-day transmission of news photographs, known as Wirephoto. Cooper, whose understanding of the journalistic
uses of different technologies was the foundation of his ascent at AP, understood the potential of these new arrivals very well and worked hard to have
them adopted. But his efforts to get AP to embrace radio and Wirephoto were
hindered and at times derailed entirely by internal tensions—reflecting in part
the broader competitive environment in which AP and its rivals operated—and
by disagreements about the journalistic legitimacy and necessity of new approaches. In the case of radio, debates about how AP should respond dragged
on inconclusively for almost twenty years. With Wirephoto, Cooper was able
to overcome determined opposition much more quickly and definitively. The
question was never about technology in general but specific technologies in

specific contexts. This left a great deal of room for different outcomes, even in the same organization and with the same person in charge.

*   *   *

U.S. newspapers struggled to come to terms with radio for most of the 1920s and 1930s.[1] Publishers were divided into bitterly opposed camps: some wanted to obstruct or try to control the new medium, emphasizing the threats it posed to established ways of doing journalism, while others embraced it, hoping to take advantage of the new opportunities it presented. The struggle was particularly intense and prolonged within Associated Press, whose cooperative structure gave supporters of each approach frequent opportunities to insist to their fellow members, to the board of directors, and especially to Cooper, on the correctness of their views and the disastrous folly of their opponents. For Cooper, whose instinct with radio, as in most things, was to modernize rather than preserve the status quo, the years between 1925 and 1939 were deeply frustrating—not only because a great deal of AP members' anger was directed at him personally but also because AP's competitors, United Press and International News Service, took lucrative and strategically important advantage of AP's near-paralysis whenever radio was involved.

AP news was first used on the air in 1920. Radio was still mostly considered a harmless novelty when the local newspaper member in Pittsburgh provided AP's presidential election returns to station KDKA in November.[2] Little more than a year later, AP informed its members that the news report was intended only for publication in newspapers, and no other use—including broadcasting—was permitted. On receiving this notice, *Editor & Publisher* reported, radio stations immediately stopped using AP news.[3]

Publishers soon began to wonder how the free distribution of news over the air would affect them when radio receivers appeared in thousands of homes. The effect on extra editions of afternoon papers that printed late sports scores was one particular concern. Would readers still be interested, one executive wondered, in a "flowery, slangy play-by-play two-column account of the game" once they already knew who won? Publishers of morning newspapers were less worried, believing that readers who heard a brief radio report the night before would be eager for a more detailed account the next morning. This difference of opinion between publishers who thought radio news would displace newspapers and those who thought it would stimulate interest in a more complete, printed account of any particular story proved to be long-lasting. An executive of the Westinghouse Electric and Manufacturing Company—which either owned or had an interest in most of the fifteen to twenty broadcasting stations in operation at the time—played down the threat, saying:

> [Radio] is not and never will be a competitor of the newspaper. . . . It is true that an item of news can be radioed to listening millions almost instantaneously. But such messages are necessarily ephemeral; they reach only those actually listening in at the time, and they must be stripped of practically all detail. The only result, from a newspaper standpoint, of radio-phoning an important piece of news is the selling of more newspapers the next morning.[4]

For the time being, Westinghouse stations stopped broadcasting news flashes. But as radio's popularity grew, the questions raised were likely to become more urgent. By April 1922, AP was aware of seventy-five newspapers that were involved in the broadcasting of news.[5]

AP's effective ban on broadcasting news faced its first serious challenge in 1924, from one of its most influential members: Robert McCormick, publisher of the *Chicago Tribune* and a member of the AP board. As the U.S. presidential election approached, he announced that the *Tribune* would challenge the rule that prevented AP members from broadcasting election returns. This included the local results they compiled themselves, which, under AP's bylaws, were the exclusive property of the cooperative for any use other than in the printed newspaper.[6] It was not surprising that the *Tribune* should be the one to launch this challenge—newspapers that became involved with broadcasting in a serious way were typically larger and wealthier, and the *Tribune*'s station, WGN (for "World's Greatest Newspaper"), eventually became one of the founders of the Mutual Broadcasting System network.[7] With a preponderance of larger newspapers on the pro-broadcasting side and smaller newspapers on the anti-broadcasting side, the question of radio put additional pressure on fault lines that already existed within AP. The successful Hearst-led campaign against AP's oligopolistic bondholding system in 1927 relied heavily on the rhetoric of small versus large newspapers, and this was to be repeated in public battles over the rapid (and costly) transmission of news photos in 1934 and 1935.[8] In an editorial, the *Tribune* described the conflict over radio as "a clash between the Old and the New" and said the AP rule smacked of "monopolistic control."[9] Harry Chandler, publisher of the *Los Angeles Times* and *Mirror*, also protested.[10] Radio, he wrote, "is here to stay as a great and dependable medium for the dissemination of news," and AP's refusal to recognize this was like refusing to use the telegraph or the telephone when they were new.

The *Tribune's* protest was just the beginning of AP's problems. Within days, Karl Bickel of United Press announced that client newspapers with radio station affiliations in New York, Boston, and seven other cities would broadcast UP's election returns.[11] "No one can eliminate radio from this field," Bickel declared, and UP intended to use radio "where we properly can. . . . Whether we like it or not . . . has nothing to do with the fact that it is here."[12]

On Election Day, twenty-eight newspapers broadcast the results using UP and Hearst returns, reaching an estimated 10 million listeners.[13] The *Chicago Tribune* was among those that relied on UP, backing away from its threat to use AP results without authorization. Others did use AP returns, however, and eventually thirteen members, all from larger cities, faced charges of violating AP's bylaws.[14]

While the most senior levels of AP management were taking a hard line against radio, Cooper—still assistant general manager at this point, though soon to replace Martin in the top position—adopted a much more conciliatory tone. In January 1925 he urged AP's regional superintendents to use radio "to enlighten the public" about AP and how it carried out its work.[15] Each superintendent was to prepare a short talk explaining what AP was, including "interesting anecdotes of how news stories . . . were covered in an unusual or dramatic manner." The talk should be broadcast over as many nearby stations as possible, whether affiliated with AP newspapers or not. Cooper made a similar argument about radio's promotional benefits in recommending to Noyes that the speech of U.S. vice president Charles Dawes at AP's annual luncheon should be broadcast: "I am not so much concerned about what the Vice President may say . . . as I am of the opportunity of enlightening the public upon the work of The Associated Press."[16]

Debates over AP's approach to radio dominated the 1925 annual meeting. Chandler, McCormick, and five other publishers wanted AP to allow the broadcast of news of "transcendent national importance . . . which by its very nature cannot be exclusive," such as the results of presidential elections.[17] They were not proposing, as Edgar Piper of the *Portland Oregonian* explained, that all of AP's news be made available to radio: "There is no possible method by which the radio news—general news—may be broadcast through radio stations and be interesting to the public at large. Nobody is going to a receiving set to hear the news of the day." It was simply a question of providing to broadcasters the major news bulletins that AP publishers already made available to the public on bulletin boards outside their offices. As Noyes pointed out, however, the geographical reach of radio signals made them quite unlike bulletin boards. When a local publisher posted a news report on a bulletin board, only that member's interests were affected. But a broadcast bulletin was thrown "into the air so that [a newspaper] a thousand miles off" was affected; the broadcasting member had no right "to invade their territory in that way" and possibly cut into print circulation. The whole AP system was based on exclusive local territories, and radio threatened to destroy that exclusivity for newspapers that stayed aloof from radio. Fewer than fifty of AP's members embraced broadcasting. Should they be allowed to broadcast the news "gathered by the joint effort of twelve hundred members . . . to the manifest disadvantage of all the rest"?[18]

Most of the arguments for and against broadcasting of AP news that were advanced over the next fifteen years were presented for the first time at the 1925 meeting. Chandler observed that non-AP newspapers interested in radio had a tremendous advantage over AP members "because they are free to do anything they want to do." They could and did buy other news services for their broadcasts, and used AP bulletins without permission:[19] "You cannot bottle the news in this day and generation, with millions of radio listeners and hundreds of broadcasting stations; and if we do not keep up . . . I think we will make a very great mistake." Irwin Kirkwood of the *Kansas City (MO) Star* argued that a ban would hurt AP's prestige because news of major events like presidential elections would be broadcast without AP getting any credit. To which James Stahlman of the *Nashville (TN) Banner* replied that if millions of people heard broadcasts of AP news, "wouldn't that simple act very seriously detract from the function and opportunity of a newspaper?"[20] Anything AP did to help radio would multiply the number of stations in competition with newspapers that wanted to stick to their traditional business, ultimately forcing many to adopt radio unwillingly, for self-preservation.

Competitive forces of several different kinds were at work simultaneously. Big-city AP newspapers that favored broadcasting were at odds with AP members in nearby smaller towns that did not want to get involved with radio and feared encroachment on their markets. Jay Hayes of the *San Jose (CA) Mercury Herald*, with no radio affiliation, wondered what would happen if a disaster considered of transcendent importance occurred in his city. Chandler in Los Angeles would be able to broadcast the AP report (which might well include the *Mercury Herald*'s own reporting of the event) "to my subscribers before I am able to publish it." AP members that were involved with radio vied with non-AP competitors that did not face the same restrictions, and AP as an institution competed with UP and INS for prestige and eventually for revenue. For Joseph Knowland of the *Oakland (CA) Tribune*, it was obvious that if AP did not broadcast news, its rivals would, and radio stations would be compelled "to take on other competitive services."[21] Despite the objections of Noyes, Ochs, and others, an overwhelming majority (130 to 10) voted to allow broadcasting of major news bulletins. Many supporters of the resolution acted on assumptions that turned out to be quite unrealistic—that radio would never be a serious competitor for advertising, for example—and the frankest assessment may have come from McCormick: "I do not know where we are drifting. We are drifting somewhere, and we are controlled by a current that is very much stronger than we are individually or collectively."[22] In any case, radio's popularity as a news medium was increasing; a survey by the American Newspaper Publishers Association found that 132 newspapers were now providing news in one way or another—either through ownership or by supplying programs or bulletins—to 113 stations, accounting for almost 20 percent of all stations operating in the United States and almost half of the most powerful stations.[23]

The approval of bulletin broadcasting emboldened advocates of radio, with Cooper's enthusiastic support. George Miller of the *Detroit (MI) News* suggested that summer that broadcasting AP's play-by-play telegraphic account of the World Series would be a master stroke.[24] From the beginning, Cooper's approach to radio was based on his awareness that UP and INS would exploit its possibilities if AP did not; as he told Noyes, the World Series "will be broadcast anyway, and [AP] might as well have the radio audience."[25] Eventually eighty stations broadcast AP's play-by-play report.[26] The reaction from members was mostly favorable—although some non-broadcasting smaller papers complained that this hurt their circulation and destroyed local interest in the play-by-play bulletin boards outside their offices.[27] Cooper followed up immediately by allowing AP's play-by-play reports of prominent football games to be broadcast.[28]

In this atmosphere of rapid change, many AP members were confused about exactly where the line was to be drawn. "Just what is the radio broadcasting rule now of The Associated Press?" E. Lansing Ray, a member of the board of directors and publisher of the *St. Louis (MO) Globe-Democrat*, asked Cooper at the end of December. It might stimulate sales of his newspaper if some of the main stories to appear the next day were mentioned on the air at around 9 p.m., but he was not sure if this would be allowed.[29] Cooper replied that broadcasting was in a stage of experimentation; Ray should try what he had in mind and report the results to the board.[30] On New Year's Day 1926, Cooper himself was host of a nationally distributed broadcast intended to show "the extent to which radio has become the art of instantaneous communication," including AP bulletins from European capitals.[31] The loosening of restrictions had some immediate results: in June, the editor of the *Boston Evening Traveller* gratefully advised Cooper that the paper was canceling its contract with United Press now that AP general news could be used on the air.[32] In 1927 the board approved Cooper's proposal that members be allowed to broadcast any AP reports that were eligible to be posted on bulletin boards as long as AP and the local newspaper were given explicit credit.[33] Broadcasting was no longer limited to news of "transcendent national importance," a significant easing of restrictions.

Cooper's embrace of a suggestion by the head of RCA's broadcasting division that AP itself should provide bulletins directly to major New York stations faced more resistance.[34] The publisher of the *New York Telegram* was astonished to learn that AP was proposing to allow broadcasting of sports results throughout the afternoon without having consulted members. Late-afternoon editions with that day's sports scores were popular, and this step "might mean considerable inroads on their sales."[35] Cooper's rejoinder—that UP news was already being broadcast by at least one New York station, and that AP should not give up "whatever good will is accumulated from this public service"—evidently did not carry much weight; the executive committee rejected the idea.[36] An agreement with the New York members that they would put pressure on UP to drop its own service to local stations had virtually no effect.[37] As 1927 came to an end, Cooper's deputy Jackson Elliott complained bitterly about a recent incident in which two New York stations broke into their regular broadcasts for a two-minute UP report on the hopeless position of six men trapped in a U.S. Navy submarine that sank off Cape Cod. Radio listeners "all across the country learned of the enterprise of this opposition agency," while AP was "constantly being placed in the rear seat in spite of the fact that we belong out in front."[38]

As in 1924, the 1928 presidential election put additional strain on the fault lines underlying AP's radio policy. In October, Cooper accepted a proposal from his longtime friend M. H. "Deac" Aylesworth, the president of NBC, to provide AP's complete election returns to the network, which had also arranged to receive UP and INS returns.[39] The broadcast would not be sponsored but presented "solely as a public service." Cooper accepted on the condition that AP would be given specific credit for every one of its bulletins read over the air.[40] An AP story on October 16 reported that "the American people . . . can sit at home and have the election returns brought to them by radio" in November. Immediately after this story was transmitted, Cooper received a flurry of complaints. C. B. Blethen of the *Seattle (WA) Times* described the arrangement as "perfectly rotten." Radio was "one of the worst competitors the newspapers have" and was rapidly taking away advertising revenue. Why should "our own Associated Press proceed to knock out our bulletin boards and our general news service?"[41] As J. Earl Langdon of the *Sacramento (CA) Bee* observed, the NBC agreement would allow AP results to be broadcast by stations with no AP connection that were "trying everything humanly possible to take business away from newspapers."[42]

In response, Cooper emphasized that this was not just a decision that he or the directors had made by themselves: "The Board has been trying to follow the expression of the [1925] annual meeting"—when members voted overwhelmingly to provide bulletins, specifically national election returns for broadcasting—"and that's all."[43] But Cooper's own radio appearances (he was the featured guest on the nationally broadcast *Collier's Radio Hour* shortly before the election) and widespread knowledge of his friendship with Aylesworth made it difficult to put entirely to rest suspicions that his actions reflected personal partiality to radio. In fact, Cooper's connection to NBC was close and long-lasting (as illustrated by network chairman David Sarnoff's attempt to hire him away from AP in 1930[44]). Cooper was not among those in the 1920s and 1930s who expressed concern about private ownership of the public airwaves, the dominance of a commercialized as opposed to a public-interest approach to broadcasting, or the possible dangers of consolidation when newspapers and radio stations came under the same ownership.[45] He never spelled out his views on these questions explicitly, but it probably struck him as quite natural that the profit-oriented, advertising-based model that had served newspapers so well would also apply to the new medium.

A plan by the *New York World* to broadcast AP's 1928 election results nationally over the CBS network in cooperation with local stations and individual AP newspapers raised other concerns. Several radio stations asked local AP members to pay for the privilege of being associated with the broadcast. The

Philadelphia Bulletin complained that the *World* was going to broadcast "over stations located in the territory of other members, material which those members
have helped to collect."[46] Once again, the geographical reach of high-powered
radio stations threw the zones of local exclusivity that were a basic element of
AP's structure into disarray. Cooper, however, warned against interfering with
the *World*'s plan, which aimed to enlist more than 150 stations across the United
States. It would not harm AP or any of its members "to have the air saturated
that night with mention of The Associated Press." UP was "in somewhat of a
panic about the fact that they are getting no radio presentation this year. Four
years ago it was all their own way. I'd like to see it all our way this time."[47]

A few days after the election, Cooper declared that he was pleased with the
prominence of AP news on the NBC broadcast. During one hour of the program, AP was mentioned more than twice as often as UP and four times as often
as INS.[48] Aylesworth was also pleased but not surprised to learn that "the great
newspapers of this country had the largest circulation for the day after elections
in the entire history of journalism."[49] Many AP members saw things differently,
however. AP members' groups and newspaper associations in California, Texas,
Utah, Idaho, Oregon, and Washington called for a variety of restrictions on the
broadcasting of AP news, including a complete ban, prohibition against using
AP news in sponsored programs, or limiting its use to radio stations affiliated
with local AP members, with no availability to networks.[50] Broadcasting of
news was "getting out of hand," Elliott warned Cooper.[51] A growing number of
advertisers were sponsoring news broadcasts so that they, rather than AP or the
local AP member, got the credit.

AP's opposition to sponsorship of news broadcasts was a long-lasting—
though, as it turned out, not permanent—aspect of its overall approach to radio
for several reasons. AP's character as a cooperative that did not sell news (unlike
UP and INS) but made it available to members on a nonprofit basis was central
to its identity. The fact that AP had no commercial motives, Cooper and others
regularly asserted, guaranteed the quality and reliability of AP news. (The fact
that, as a matter of course, AP news was printed in profit-oriented newspapers
that did rely on advertising was rarely mentioned.) For the many individual
members that objected to radio, the potential loss of advertising revenue to
sponsored broadcasts was an immediate threat, and it was inconceivable that
AP itself should allow its news to be used in this way. The institutional and
individual-member imperatives against sponsored radio news powerfully reinforced each other for many years.

AP's board of directors was quick to respond to the growing tide of complaint, imposing the first restrictions on Cooper's freewheeling experimentation. Two months after the election it was decided that no member could establish a network of stations that broadcast AP news in another member's city without the local member's approval and sharing of on-air credit and that AP news could not be used in sponsored broadcasts.[52] This marked the beginning of a period of uneasy stasis. AP's approach to radio was on the agenda for both the 1929 and 1930 annual meetings, but the subject was simply referred back to the board of directors both times.[53]

A damning report about the impact of radio released on the eve of AP's 1931 meeting by a committee of the American Newspaper Publishers Association (ANPA)—which represented newspapers generally, not just AP members—finally seemed to set the stage for some decisive action. Publishers, the committee concluded, had "lulled themselves to sleep while the greatest competitor they ever faced" grew "from infancy to full-fledged manhood."[54] Major advertisers had reduced their newspaper spending by 12.5 percent between 1929 and 1930, while their radio spending increased by 63 percent. Radio advertising revenue as a proportion of newspaper advertising revenue had more than tripled since 1928. Arguing that the ANPA was in a better position than AP to convince all three news agencies to work together in limiting the use of their news on the air, members passed a resolution urging the directors to respond favorably to whatever recommendations emerged from the ANPA's annual meeting the following week.[55]

UP, meanwhile, continued to take advantage of AP's restrictions, allowing its news to be used on sponsored programs such as Lowell Thomas's high-profile *Literary Digest* broadcast and charging a fee to stations that used its news, generating a substantial amount of new revenue.[56] "We have tightened the use of radio as demanded by many of our members," Elliott observed glumly in a memo to Cooper, "and the result is just what you predicted."[57] One glimmer of hope was that in the face of growing concern about radio, INS decided that its news could be used on the air only to promote the circulation of INS client newspapers. These had "a right to protest vigorously against the news being sold or used by such competing agent[s] as the radio."[58]

The journalistic frenzy over the kidnapping of Charles Lindbergh's infant son on March 1, 1932, further sharpened the tensions between newspapers and radio. United Press had been providing news bulletins regularly to NBC and CBS but stopped the practice after a chaotic night when representatives of both networks were expelled from the UP newsroom, where they had been phoning late bulletins about the kidnapping back to their news studios.[59] Karl Bickel of UP told *Editor & Publisher* that he had been waiting for more than two years for the ANPA to announce its position; once that was done, "it will not be so difficult for a press association to work out a policy." Meanwhile, UP client newspapers that owned radio stations were allowed to use its news on the air "because it is our business to aid our clients to the best of our ability in whatever way we can."[60] At AP's 1932 annual meeting, however, Roy Howard was applauded for saying that no agency should allow its news to be freely used on radio and that bulletins should be broadcast only if newspaper circulation was not adversely affected.[61] Once again, though, no action was taken; a proposal to stop providing AP news to radio under any circumstances was postponed indefinitely on a fairly close vote of 64 to 53.

As a result of the annual meeting's inaction, the 1925 resolution authorizing the broadcast of bulletins about major news events such as presidential elections remained in effect. However, Cooper's plans to broadcast the 1932 presidential election results in a way he believed was consistent with this policy ended up subjecting him, and AP, to a flood of furious anti-radio sentiment. The final decision to provide AP returns to both NBC and CBS was not made until the last minute, and AP members were only informed on Election Day, November 8.[62] This was a result of eleventh-hour jockeying with UP. It had initially offered to provide results to the two networks for one thousand dollars each, while Cooper's position was that AP would not sell its results. After NBC refused to pay the fee, UP canceled its contract with CBS as well and announced, ostensibly high-mindedly, that it was acting "in response to what it interprets as the wishes of a great majority of its newspaper clients."[63] Cooper then agreed to provide AP returns to both networks. To an AP publisher who urged Cooper to follow UP's example and withhold results from the networks, he replied that UP always had two goals in mind: "First, to make money, and, second, to put The Associated Press in a hole.... I hope you or no other member will move to hamstring AP and thus let the United Press win on both of their coveted points."[64] On Election Day Cooper issued a message to all members that underscored how much he already felt on the defensive: "That you may not be led to misunderstand the entire situation respecting broadcasting of the Associated Press election results." Clearly rattled, he apologized the next day to Clark Howell, a member of the board of directors and publisher of the *Atlanta Constitution*, for writing him heatedly on the mistaken assumption that

Howell wanted AP to follow UP's example: "This broadcasting business is the bane of my existence. Even though the members themselves decided the thing, those who are opposed to broadcasting vent their spleen in messages to me. I can do nothing."[65]

In the days following the election, marked by prominent use of AP news on the air, Cooper was inundated with angry complaints over what many AP members considered "treason within the ranks."[66] In a detailed and widely distributed defense of his actions, Cooper argued that broadcasting election results was allowed and in fact required under the 1925 members' resolution. He concluded by asking reasonably, if somewhat plaintively, that if the members wanted a change in direction, they should take "some action . . . which would make it possible for the management to answer satisfactorily the communications of a conflicting nature, which constantly are being received."[67] But members were in no frame of mind for explanations of why Cooper's course of action had been correct.[68] "Someone down there should have been sufficiently close to the newspapers and their problems to know that 1932 is not 1925 as relates to the radio problem," one wrote. Had AP management, another asked rhetorically, shown "straight thinking in delivering the private property of AP newspapers collectively to the National and Columbia broadcasting newspaper destroyers?" Will Campbell of the *Helena (MT) Independent* wanted Cooper to have "one letter in your files which tells you the exact truth: You should resign at once and admit your unfaithfulness to the members of The Associated Press."[69] Many suggested that Cooper's close friendship with Aylesworth was behind his decision.[70] But Cooper mournfully denied any suggestion of personal bias; if his critics really knew him, "they would . . . know I love [AP] more than they do and that I would be the last person in the world to be guilty of letting a friendship outside [AP] sway me in a matter of this kind even if I had an authority."[71] UP salesmen were stirring up resentment against him, but he had faith "in the justice of men who know that I have given my life to The Associated Press."

The furor over the election broadcast was the catalyst for a decisive change in AP's approach to radio and the approach of the newspaper industry generally. The ANPA quickly set up a national committee of publishers to develop a common policy on radio competition.[72] A month after the election, AP's executive committee sent out a questionnaire, the results to be used to frame a recommendation for the 1933 annual meeting.[73] These actions, *Editor & Publisher* predicted, "are expected to force a showdown between newspaper publishers and radio."[74]

Some of the questions submitted to AP members were straightforward ("Do you favor permitting broadcasting by members?") and others more directive ("Do you favor denying members permission to broadcast any news belonging to [AP] . . . disregarding the advantages both financial and of prestige that would accrue to competing news agencies who permit such broadcasting?"). Of the more than 90 percent of members who responded, a majority (57 percent) wanted to forbid members from broadcasting over stations they owned, with almost 70 percent against network broadcasting.[75] In an analysis of the results, Elliott noted that 60 percent of 233 members involved in broadcasting subscribed either to UP or INS in addition to AP. There was a significant difference between wealthier newspapers that took AP's full leased-wire service and those that took a more limited pony service; the 43 percent who favored allowing members to broadcast on stations they owned accounted for 57 percent of AP's revenue. In a separate survey, Elliott found that of the one hundred members paying the largest assessments, two-thirds favored broadcasting.[76] In reporting the questionnaire's results to AP members, Noyes took pains to keep alive the possibility of broadcasting by those who owned or had other affiliations with stations. If this was prohibited outright, the ninety broadcasting members that relied solely on AP would be forced to patronize one of its competitors.[77]

The right of members to broadcast over local radio stations that they owned or were affiliated with was preserved at the 1933 annual meeting—but just barely. After a tumultuous debate, members banned the provision of AP news to networks under any circumstances, limited broadcasting on individual stations to brief bulletins with credit to AP and the local newspaper, and required payment for bulletin broadcasting.[78] Bulletins could be no longer than thirty words; only one bulletin could be broadcast on a single topic; no connection with advertising would be allowed; and, except for the most momentous news events, bulletins could be broadcast only during the member paper's hours of publication, typically 9 a.m. to 7 p.m. for afternoon papers and 8 p.m. to 6 a.m. for morning papers.

One argument in favor of allowing bulletin broadcasting was that it would deter radio networks from establishing their own news divisions, but this hope proved to be illusory. By September, Cooper was trying to discourage Frank Gannett, whose Rochester, New York, radio station was affiliated with CBS, from providing its local news to the nascent Columbia news service.[79] In preparation for the October board meeting, Elliott devised a plan to drive a wedge between CBS, with its aggressive approach, and NBC, which still hoped to avoid open competition with newspapers and established news agencies.[80] He suggested that AP should provide NBC with a sharply edited summary of news events, "designed to stimulate the sale of newspapers by whetting listener appetites for more details." The report could not be sold to advertisers, and prominent on-air credit was to be given to AP and the local newspaper. The current Columbia service was terrible but was nonetheless making inroads. Radio networks could not compete with newspapers in covering spontaneous news locally, nationally, and around the world except at tremendous expense, but if they joined forces and made their reports available to newspapers as well, AP and its members would face real danger. Elliott suggested the alliance with NBC tentatively, "because to many it will look like giving up the fight, but I see in it a victory for the newspapers which likewise could benefit radio."

Elliott's recommendations foreshadowed a significant rapprochement between news agencies and broadcast networks. The Biltmore Agreement of December 1933, signed jointly by CBS, NBC, AP, INS, UP, and the ANPA, went even further than Elliott's proposal. In exchange for a heavily restricted supply of radio bulletins from the three news agencies—limited to one five-minute broadcasting period after 9:30 a.m. and another after 9 p.m., in order not to beat morning and afternoon newspapers, respectively, with each news item limited to thirty words or less—CBS agreed to scrap its own news service.[81] The bulletins would be written and provided to CBS and NBC by a new joint organization, the Press-Radio Bureau (PRB).

Problems with the new arrangement arose almost immediately. Radio stations were not interested in broadcasting bulletins hours after the news had been published in newspapers, and AP members who owned radio stations wanted to broadcast their local news with no restrictions.[82] Herbert Moore, a former UP reporter and senior editor of the now-defunct CBS news division, quickly established a competing service, Transradio, that offered news to radio stations with none of the PRB's restrictions.[83] As of mid-May, while the PRB had 160 stations as clients, Transradio had already signed up 28. A year later, with Transradio serving 190 subscribers, a central pillar of the Biltmore Agreement collapsed.[84] UP and INS, deeply concerned about Transradio's success, decided to sell up to four fifteen-minute news broadcasts a day that could be sponsored.[85] The explicit intent was to produce as much revenue as possible—revenue that then allowed UP to offer its main news service to AP members at sharply reduced rates.[86] This was a tremendously worrisome situation for Cooper, who strongly believed, in the words of Howard's deputy William Hawkins, that "he cannot afford to let the UP get any revenue which he can possibly prevent the UP from getting."[87] In response, AP allowed members to use AP general news on the air for up to an hour a day for a small additional fee and their own local news without charge. Sponsorship remained forbidden, however, which meant that AP-affiliated stations and AP itself could not match the revenue gains of their competitors.[88]

AP's board of directors did not consider a more far-reaching response until 1938. In a circular to members, Noyes said the board had received many recommendations that sponsored broadcasts of AP news should be allowed, particularly since UP and INS were receiving substantial revenue on this account.[89] Members who used AP news in broadcasts supported by advertisers would pay higher fees, and some of this additional revenue would be applied to AP's general expenses. This would postpone, or perhaps make entirely unnecessary, across-the-board assessment increases to meet AP's growing expenses so that all members—not just those involved in broadcasting—would benefit. With the establishment of the PRB, Noyes observed, the debate over whether to broadcast AP news or not was over; the question now was "whether we can in a self-respecting way get any revenue for our members and for ourselves from a service that is inevitably going on."[90] But with 80 percent of members not involved in broadcasting, the proposal was, yet again, postponed indefinitely.[91] Meanwhile, of the 249 AP papers involved in broadcasting, many more used UP, INS, or Transradio news than AP's non-commercial service.[92]

There was no choice but to try once more in 1939. By this time the PRB had finally ended its tortured existence, with NBC taking AP news on a non-commercial basis and CBS opting for UP, INS, and sponsorship.[93] Early in the new year—belying his public assertions that he had no role in matters of policy that should be decided by members alone—Cooper outlined a new strategy to present to the annual meeting.[94] Individual directors, he complained, were giving mixed signals about what AP's policy should be. All, Cooper urged, should advocate one and only one proposal: the use of AP news in sponsored broadcasts would be allowed but without AP being identified as the source. This was a gradualist approach intended to weaken objections to the commercialization of AP news. Cooper realized, one director wrote, that "we could not expect the members to go the whole distance now. . . . He would be quite content if we attained a half way station on the next jump."[95]

After the 1938 defeat, little was left to chance this time. AP's president, Robert McLean, attended several state meetings, reporting that "the only thing really that does the trick" was to present a stark choice: higher assessments for everyone or new revenues from radio advertising.[96] An even more gradual approach than Cooper proposed was adopted at the annual meeting. Noting that a growing number of members "have been compelled to purchase the news of competing agencies for . . . sponsored programs, and that an impairment of state circuits and loss of membership and territorial representation in the news report is threatened," the resolution merely urged the board to consider these problems and give interested members an opportunity to make representations in person a month later.[97] In response to a further questionnaire, several members stated that they would drop UP, INS, or Transradio if AP news was available for sponsored broadcasts.[98]

After three days of deliberation at AP's new Rockefeller Center headquarters in May, the executive committee approved the sale of AP news for sponsorship, charging a premium of 25 percent on top of the current assessment for those who took advantage. Sponsored network broadcasting was not allowed, although non-commercial use of networks was permitted. On local stations, sponsored newscasts were to be credited to the local newspaper, not AP itself, and the use of news from any other sources was forbidden.[99] Members could also continue to use AP news in unsponsored broadcasts for a 5 percent surcharge. For *Editor & Publisher*, this was a precedent-shattering and history-making decision; it had taken AP seventeen years to come to this point.[100] The ban on identifying AP as the source of sponsored newscasts was quietly dropped a few months later, and by the end of the year 25 members were broadcasting sponsored news, while 115 others were broadcasting without sponsorship.[101] Cooper continued his efforts to mollify the remaining opponents, but by now the balance had shifted decisively. Even James Stahlman of the *Nashville (TN) Banner*, a leader of the anti-radio forces for many years, changed his mind: "Since the other press associations are doing it, I can't see why The Associated Press shouldn't go ahead and get what it can out of the situation," he wrote in response to yet another questionnaire. "It can't hurt me more than the UP and the INS have already done, so change my vote from 'no' to 'aye.'"[102]

Most remaining restrictions were successively dropped, and in 1940 AP earned almost $250,000 in extra assessments from members who used its news on radio—more than twice what it cost to provide the service.[103] The final major change came in January 1941 when—following Cooper's recommendation—AP's radio activities were handed over to a frankly profit-seeking subsidiary, Press Association (not to be confused with the British domestic news agency of the same name).[104] By the mid-1940s, the subsidiary was remitting a net profit of $600,000 a year to its parent organization, and more than half of the 950 U.S. radio stations were broadcasting Press Association news.[105] In 1946 radio stations were admitted as associate members, and by 1951 radio "provided a substantial portion of total income."[106]

*　*　*

AP's long struggle over radio was an agonized process that left it almost constantly on the defensive, trying (and usually failing) to find consensus among its members and respond effectively to decisions by United Press, INS, and Transradio. But when it came to the adoption of another technological innovation—the rapid transmission of news photos, known as Wirephoto—Cooper was able to seize the initiative, keep control of the process firmly in his hands, and thoroughly outmaneuver AP's competitors. It was a welcome reversal that he and the AP board pursued enthusiastically and at times ruthlessly.

Cooper wanted to establish a photographic service for AP soon after becoming general manager, but it took two years to convince the board of directors. Slow distribution was a major obstacle. While printed news sent by telegraph was more or less instantaneous, pictures were sent by mail, which meant they were mostly suitable only to illustrate non-news features. As early as 1925, Cooper urged AT&T to develop equipment for the rapid transmission of photos and provide it exclusively to AP.[107] When AT&T refused on the grounds that this would violate its public utility status, Cooper asked that all agencies simply be notified when the equipment was available. (Scripps-Howard, the Hearst organization, and the *New York Times* all operated their own photo services.) According to John Hightower, a long-serving AP journalist whose in-house history remains unpublished, Cooper was operating on the assumption that AP's competitors would find the cost prohibitive, allowing AP to make an exclusive agreement.

A year after Cooper's promotion, his successor as traffic chief proposed a renewed appeal to the board to establish a photo service.[108] By now, AT&T's telephoto service—a way to transmit photographs from point to point over telephone lines—had become "very efficient." It took just seven minutes to send a photo from New York to San Francisco, and as the service was extended to more cities, publishers would increasingly consider photos a form of spot news. Competition, as always, was an important consideration. If AP acted quickly, it could take the lead, but if it delayed, another organization would act first "and forestall us." Cooper, however, was not interested in an arrangement in which AT&T would occasionally and on request transmit individual AP photos. Instead, he wanted a leased-wire system for photos as AP had been using for news since the 1870s—a network of permanent circuits that AP would operate itself, making the transmission of news photos a regular, rather than exceptional, occurrence.[109] Larger newspapers across the country, he told the board in January 1927, "are urging us to do something of that kind."

AP's photo service went into operation on August 1, 1927, long before the rapid-transmission network that Cooper envisioned was in place.[110] As with the news service, the photo service was based on exchange among members. Even with this modest beginning, it was not unanimously popular: Julian Mason of the *New York Evening Post* told Cooper that he opposed the idea because the photos were not available exclusively and would "merely increase our expense."[111] Cooper offered his standard response to objections about the cost of additional services: AP photos would be better and cheaper than those provided by its private competitors.[112] Overall, like the feature service introduced at the same time, AP's photo service was a success. By 1930, Cooper reported, it was supplying more newspapers than any of its competitors. "Pictures," he declared, "have come to be news."[113] By 1932 all four major picture agencies—AP's photo service, Acme-NEA (owned by the Scripps-Howard chain), INS, and the *New York Times'* Wide World service—were relying extensively on telephoto transmission for coverage of major stories such as the kidnapping of Charles Lindbergh's baby.[114] Still, the approximately one hundred newspapers willing to assume the extra cost of receiving photographic prints remained a distinct minority among AP's thirteen hundred or so members. Most opted for the less expensive and less timely "mat" service, directed at newspapers that did not have the capacity to make their own photo engravings.

As with AP's basic leased-wire news operation, there was an inverse relationship between the number of subscribers to the photo service and the cost. If two members in the same city received photos, each paid half as much for transmission as a single member would pay. Lower costs encouraged more members to subscribe, reducing costs further and setting a virtuous circle in motion. Cooper understood this clearly; he always wanted to make optional services compulsory if possible, or at least to create extra incentives for subscribing and disincentives for not doing so. The board decided accordingly in 1932 to penalize latecomers to the photo service in any city where another member already subscribed, imposing an automatic one-year delay before the service could begin and an equalization fee to compensate the first subscriber for bearing the whole cost alone until that point.[115]

In June 1933, AT&T announced that it was canceling its telephoto service, writing off almost $3 million in accumulated costs.[116] It was, Cooper wrote later, an "imperfect, impractical effort" that reached too few cities, offered poor-quality reproduction, and failed to attract enough business.[117] Meanwhile, AT&T's engineering division advised Cooper that it had developed a new and much improved method of transmitting photos. Cooper once again wanted exclusive use of the new technology but understood that AT&T could not grant this directly. He suggested that the new equipment be offered to all four U.S. photo services but only on the condition that at least twenty-five machines were ordered, establishing a network that would cost around $1 million annually to operate.[118] As expected, none of the other photo services was prepared to assume the heavy expense involved, and through the autumn of 1933, Cooper and Norris Huse, manager of the AP photo service, worked to enlist as many of the larger and wealthier AP members as possible. The *New York Daily News*, a photo-based tabloid, was among the first to sign up, joined soon after by the *Los Angeles Times*, *San Francisco Chronicle*, and the *Oakland (CA) Tribune*.[119] It was an unprecedentedly expensive service, which Cooper estimated would cost each subscriber between three and fifty times more than the regular photo service. For example, the *Daily News* agreed to pay $18,000 a year, but even this was based on the assumption that nine New York dailies in all would divide the cost among themselves.

Wirephoto, as the new service came to be called, soon became the subject of bitter internal controversy, largely because the competing photo services that it would immediately outdistance were operated by organizations that also owned many AP newspapers.[120] But while AP under Cooper's leadership was accustomed to conflict with the Scripps and Hearst interests, this had never been so in its dealings with the *New York Times*, the owner of Wide World. On the contrary, the *Times* was one of the founders and strongest supporters of the post-1893 AP. Adolph Ochs, now approaching the end of his life, had served on the AP board since 1900 and was one of its most influential members. He was revered by his fellow directors, by AP members generally, and especially by Cooper, whose ascent to the top position was a direct result of Ochs's enthusiastic personal support. In this case, however, Cooper and the AP board treated the *Times* as roughly as it treated it other rivals. While Huse and Cooper were canvassing prospective subscribers, they made sure not to approach or otherwise tip their hand to newspapers affiliated with any of the competing photo agencies, including the *Times*. The AP board discussed the plan only at meetings that Ochs did not attend due to illness, and Ochs was never told what had happened in his absence.[121] Robert McLean, a board member at the time, recalled years later that Ochs was "bitterly upset" when he learned what had happened.[122] Early notice was similarly withheld from Hearst- and Scripps-owned AP members until others, including their direct competitors, were given an opportunity to subscribe.[123]

Any remaining secrecy was dramatically brought to an end at AP's 1934 annual meeting when John Francis Neylan, the chief counsel of the Hearst organization, demanded to know whether AP had signed a contract with AT&T to establish the rapid-transmission photo service. Noyes replied that Cooper had planned to brief the members on these developments later that day but would report then and there. A regular flow of same-day news photos was "the newest and biggest departure in newspaper work since words were telegraphed," Cooper told the members.[124] To date, thirty-five members had signed five-year contracts. Neylan, however, charged that AP and Cooper had been duped into buying leftover telephoto equipment that AT&T no longer wanted. Clark Howell, publisher of the *Atlanta Constitution* and a board member, rose to Cooper's defense, rejecting suggestions that the board should have sought members' approval before proceeding. Wirephoto was strictly optional; members could subscribe or not, as they wished, and non-subscribers bore none of the cost. By sending photos to major distribution points across the country more quickly, the new network would also mean better, faster service for the many smaller papers that relied on mats. While the 1927 agreement to extend protest rights and reduce the dominance of long-established, wealthy members in board elections had led to a more cooperative relationship between Hearst and AP,[125] the return to confrontation brought renewed attacks on Hearst as fundamentally anti-AP. Noyes observed that only two or three Hearst papers contributed photos to AP's existing photo service "because Mr. Hearst has a picture service of his own, and it isn't essential to him to cooperate with us." Similarly, only two Scripps-Howard papers contributed their photos to AP. Surely Neylan did not expect AP or Cooper "to base his activities on what was especially pleasing to Mr. Hearst's picture interests, or Mr. Howard's picture interests."[126]

Roy Howard and Frank Knox—a former Hearst publisher—tried a different tack, arguing that there were simply not enough compelling spot-news photos available to justify the cost of a full-time network. Cooper replied that in the depths of the Depression, same-day news photography "would revitalize the newspapers. . . . It is going to do more than anything else that can be done to get the newspaper back so that the people will look at it." Howard then raised the really crucial point that underlay Cooper's strategy: "Is there any question in your mind that if [AP] launches this service, its competitors will not be forced to resort to the same service?" They would have to introduce and maintain an expensive new distribution network of their own just to keep up, something they desperately wanted to avoid. (Hearst in particular was having serious financial problems at the time.[127]) These concerns about cost were decisive, Cooper observed later:

> They would like to see the art of newspaper making improved if this will do it, but with labor organizations making their extravagant demands, with the [Newspaper] Guild marshaling its strength, with the question of the price of print paper, with the question of restoring cuts in salaries to their white collar class . . . it would be impossible for any further things to be undertaken.[128]

In any case, the objections on behalf of Scripps and Hearst did not seem to trouble the members, who voted unanimously to express confidence in Cooper and in the board.[129]

This, however, was only the first skirmish in what became a yearlong battle. After the annual meeting, Arthur Sulzberger of the *Times* expressed anger about the "great lack of frankness" in the discussion:[130] "It's an unpleasant situation when a Board of Directors meets and either discusses or does not discuss an important matter depending upon whether this or that director is present." Noyes denied that Ochs had been deliberately kept in the dark. But if that was true, why had Cooper apologized, telling Sulzberger "how badly he felt about having had to do what he did in keeping the matter from [Ochs]"?[131]

Searching for an ally, Neylan told Sulzberger that the AP board acted illegally in withholding information from Ochs.[132] He wanted to make sure that if it came to a lawsuit, Ochs would "not be persuaded to issue any statement which would let the A.P. off," something he might be inclined to do in view of his long tenure on the board. But despite the way he had been treated, Ochs would not cooperate with Hearst or Scripps. Sulzberger himself sympathized with some of Neylan's arguments, but a suggestion that the ailing Ochs might be called to testify against AP settled the matter: "I left Mr. Neylan in no doubt that we would do everything to block and avoid this."

By June 1934, Scripps and Hearst had decided definitively that none of their papers would subscribe to Wirephoto.[133] Together with the *Times*, they proposed that the photo distribution network should be left in AT&T's hands, with all four photo services (including AP) jointly guaranteeing it against any loss. This would essentially be a return to the former telephoto system using improved equipment. It would not provide a regular supply of photos to subscribers across a network—an individual newspaper would order an individual photograph if it was considered sufficiently newsworthy. Scripps-Howard's William Hawkins estimated that no more than three or four photos a week justified the cost of transmission, making the full-time network a "wholly unnecessary extravagance."

As he had done with great success in 1926–1927,[134] Neylan presented Wirephoto as being particularly harmful to the smaller newspapers that made up the great majority of AP members. He argued that no small or medium-sized newspaper could possibly afford Wirephoto and that those competing with nearby big-city newspapers that did adopt the new service would suffer from having nothing but comparatively outdated photos to offer their readers.[135] Less publicly, the *New York Times* remained deeply dissatisfied about the situation that AP's actions had created. If the *Times* and *Herald Tribune* each subscribed at fifty thousand dollars a year, "competitively we are not one cent's worth better off . . . than we were before," the editor of the *Times'* photo-heavy rotogravure supplement told Sulzberger. "And think how grateful we should be to the Associated Press crowd which handed this to us!"[136]

None of the criticism delayed the introduction of Wirephoto on January 1, 1935. The initial response from subscribers was highly favorable, with several stating that the availability of a steady supply of up-to-date photos revolutionized journalism, stimulating readers' interest and, in some cases, increasing sales.[137] The trial of Bruno Hauptmann, charged with kidnapping and murdering Charles Lindbergh's infant son, began on January 2, the service's second day, and subscribers were especially gratified to have same-day photos of what H. L. Mencken described as "the biggest story since the Resurrection." For Roy Roberts of the *Kansas City Star*, the service "demonstrated beyond argument that even on ordinary events, movement of pictures by mail is as obsolete as movement of news by mail." Frank Knox was less impressed, estimating that the service was only really useful for six stories a week.[138] Frederik Murphy of the *Minneapolis Tribune* acknowledged that Wirephoto was expensive, costing forty-five thousand dollars a year, but it largely replaced the paper's even more expensive rotogravure supplement.[139] The service sent out around forty-five items each day, including maps, charts, and diagrams as well as photos.[140] A photo from an afternoon baseball game in Boston could now be developed, transmitted to Kansas City or Dallas, and printed in a late edition in as little as ninety minutes.[141]

Faced with this apparent success—which increased the pressure on competing photo services to offer something similar—the Hearst organization redoubled its efforts to stop Wirephoto. Neylan returned to his 1927 playbook and set up a committee to solicit proxies, hoping to amass enough votes to pass a series of spoiling resolutions at the 1935 annual meeting. One would require a plebiscite of all members to approve "any radical innovation or pledging of the credit" of AP; members would also vote on whether to continue Wirephoto or scrap it.[142] Another resolution, unconnected to the photo service but reflecting Neylan's strategy of appealing to smaller newspapers, specified that the board of directors should have three members representing cities whose population was less than fifteen thousand.

In a lengthy response to the twenty-five AP publishers and editors who joined Neylan's proxy committee, and circulated to all other AP members as well, Noyes described Neylan's proposals as "a thrust at the very vitals of our organization."[143] AP simply could not operate if any initiative that might be considered a radical innovation had to be submitted to a plebiscite and was thereby made known to its competitors. The board of directors' challenge was to strike a balance between the interests of larger and wealthier newspapers that collectively paid about two-thirds of AP's bills—but accounted for less than one-sixth of the overall membership—and those of smaller newspapers that were more numerous but provided much less revenue. Neylan's attempt to drive a wedge between these two groups would destroy AP, Noyes argued. In fact, the AP board had consistently protected the interests of smaller newspapers and would give them more representatives on the board once the current proxy battle was over. Meanwhile, a competing members' committee began soliciting proxies in opposition to the Neylan group.

The battle for proxies raged all through March and most of April. Hearst representatives fanned out across the country, visiting as many AP members as possible and concentrating on the small-town publishers most susceptible to Neylan's appeal. Even more than usual, Cooper insisted publicly that as a mere employee of AP he had no role whatsoever to play in this conflict, which was to be decided by members alone.[144] In fact, he was deeply involved in the proxy campaign, receiving frequent updates and planning strategy with AP publishers across the country.[145] William Pape, publisher of the *Waterbury (CT) Republican* and head of the anti-Hearst proxy committee, put Cooper as an individual squarely at the center of the debate in his appeal to smaller newspapers to support Wirephoto. Cooper was AP's "star half-back," the author of many improvements to AP's services in recent years: "He is the man who carries the ball and if the opposition kills or cripples him, who will ever want to take his place and do his job as he has done it?"[146]

At the 1935 annual meeting, the board reported on the first three months of Wirephoto operations and responded to every criticism. Wirephoto was simply the latest manifestation of AP's commitment to provide an adequate photo service to its members, protecting them from "the arbitrary tactics of commercial syndicates."[147] It was vastly superior to the withdrawn AT&T telephoto system. Its greatest strengths were integration with the overall AP news photo service and "its network operation, firmly joined by proved channels of transmission" connecting all subscribing points simultaneously. The AT&T system, by contrast, was "not a news photo organization, it had no photos, it was not in the newspaper business, it knew nothing of the needs of newspapers or the use which could be made of its facilities." Wirephoto was also good for smaller newspapers that received their photos in mat form. For the "ridiculously low" amount of $2.50 a week, the papers were promised an expedited service that would bring them a constant supply of more up-to-date images, and the time advantage in publishing photos enjoyed by their big-city competitors would be no greater than under the previous system.[148] All the costs of Wirephoto equipment and staff were borne by subscribers, and receipts for the first three months of operation had exceeded expenses by almost $60,000.

Not surprisingly, this did little to mollify the well-organized opposition. The ensuing debate was, in the words of *Editor & Publisher*, "one of the most bitter internal battles ever waged" at an AP meeting.[149] Eventually all of Neylan's Wirephoto-related resolutions were heavily defeated. A separate resolution favoring more representation on the board for small newspapers was passed, but in a non-confrontational form that left subsequent action in the hands of the current directors. All in all, it was a rout for the anti-Wirephoto forces. Looking back years later, Roy Howard concluded, "We never had a chance to win."[150] AP's actions had "made it absolutely necessary that the UP shall furnish a picture service, regardless of whether it wishes to do so, and regardless of whether it can do so at a profit." Cooper would have been delighted to hear the strategic bind he created for his competitors described so clearly.

Now that Cooper's aggressiveness in establishing Wirephoto had been vindicated, he indulged in some self-congratulation. To Roy Hollis of the *New York Daily News*, the photo-oriented tabloid that remained the only New York subscriber, he boasted that Wirephoto was the only "perfect method of transmitting photographs to more than one point at a time." As AP's chief executive, he "naturally ha[d] to think of serving more than one paper. That's why I conceived the idea of a circuit upon which all members could receive the same photos at the same time. . . . That is press association operation."[151] Hearst's system of sending individual photos to individual customers on a per-occasion basis was deeply flawed because every photo could be transmitted to only one recipient at a time. If all thirty Hearst newspapers wanted the same picture without unnecessary delay, it would require thirty sending machines operating simultaneously.

In one of an occasional series of musings on various topics sent to the whole editorial staff, Cooper argued that 1935 would one day be seen as a landmark year in the history of American journalism, with Wirephoto responsible for "the changed pictorial aspect of newspapers."[152] For major stories like the recent death of Will Rogers in an Alaska plane crash, newspapers were using more photos and larger photos. As local editors became more aware of the possibilities presented by up-to-date news photos, they demanded more and faster coverage. A revolution was under way, Cooper concluded, that would "turn things entirely upside down before it ends."

Cooper's argument that photographs deserved a more prominent role in newspapers generally was likely to gain favor with at least one powerful board member. Robert McCormick of the *Chicago Tribune* criticized AP for being insufficiently picture-minded and urged Cooper to hire some outsiders to make up the deficiency.[153] Echoing McCormick's critique, Cooper said AP was

> skimping on the cost of getting pictures and we are away over staffed in getting the news, because all our newspaper men in America were brought up to write and not to snap a picture. So they all think they must have

words, words, words. Throw them in the waste basket! They must have more words! Throw them in the waste basket![154]

AP had to decide whether it was "just a news service with a few side lines" or whether its picture service was equally important.

Cooper's underlying preference had always been that any service AP provided—not just its core news operation but features and photos as well—should be, in essence, compulsory. This would lower the cost to each individual member and reduce the likelihood of anyone buying a similar service from one of AP's competitors. In that spirit he proposed to the board in October 1937 that non-subscribers in larger cities should be required to pay half of Wirephoto's leased-wire costs.[155] This suggestion alarmed some board members, who feared it would lead to resignations, but Cooper was unconcerned. This was the only way to dissuade members from signing up with competitive services, and even if some did resign, "we would ultimately get them back on their knees." Displaying some of the arrogance that increasingly characterized his relationship with the board after McLean succeeded Noyes as president, he loftily brushed objections aside. "Well, I am willing to leave this now," he replied when one director continued to ask about the prospect of losing members. "I don't think any purpose would be served by going on with this thing until you are ready to discuss what is the future of [AP]."[156] Six months later, the board unanimously agreed that all members in cities where Wirephoto was available would share the cost, whether they participated or not.[157] This had the desired result: by September 1939, Wirephoto had one hundred subscribers. James Stahlman of the *Nashville Banner*, one of the staunchest opponents in 1935, was among those who signed up, describing Wirephoto as "one of the finest things that [AP] has done now that it is available to the smaller newspapers at a price which practically everybody can afford."[158] By the end of the decade, photos did not occupy half of all newspaper editorial space, as Cooper recommended, but the number of photos used in newspapers had increased by almost 40 percent.[159] Deploying his considerable institutional resources to push for the development and then the widespread adoption of Wirephoto, Cooper set the stage for news photography to become a central element of daily journalism.[160]

One question that remained unresolved was the relation between AP and Wide World. Since Wide World concentrated on feature photos, emphasizing creativity and artistic quality as compared to AP's focus on daily news photos, one might have expected relatively little direct competition between the two.

For Cooper, however, any competition had to be forcefully opposed. After Ochs's death in 1935, the *Times* was not represented on the board of directors for seven years, so it was no longer necessary even to try to conceal AP's anti–Wide World actions.

By the end of 1939, Wide World was struggling to cover its costs. Cooper, meanwhile, wanted the AP board to take action against Wide World's "plain competitive actions," which he described as "amateurish but disturbing."[161] Immediately after the April 1940 board meeting, Cooper made an offer to buy Wide World for $250,000. When this was rejected, AP made a concerted effort to detach subscribers from Wide World, ratcheting up the financial pressure. Sulzberger, who had taken over as *Times* publisher, was warned in June that Wide World's deficit was growing amid clear signs that AP was out to get its business.[162] On August 1, 1941, AP purchased Wide World for $250,000, assuming some $125,000 in severance costs as part of the agreement.[163] Cooper recommended to the board that Wide World should become the fourth pillar of AP's operations, complementing the daily news service, news features, and news photos.

The cost of Wide World service to members, however, would be about twice as much as it was under *Times* management. This reflected in part a concern to make sure that broader availability of Wide World material did not weaken the competitive position of existing subscribers, mostly relatively wealthy newspapers in larger cities, by giving smaller newspapers in nearby communities better photos. Paul Patterson of the *Baltimore Sun* warned against leaving the impression that Wide World "is only for the metropolitan papers," but McLean denied that the effect on smaller papers was intentional. The price of Wide World "had to be high to be successful. . . . It wasn't a deliberate effort to exclude the smaller paper; it was merely that the very operation would not commend it on account of price to the small paper."[164] The concerns that smaller AP members expressed in 1935 and at other times about unequal access to AP's supplementary services were not misplaced.

AP's record of adapting to new media during the 1920s and 1930s was profoundly mixed. Radio affected every member directly, one way or another. Under AP's one member, one vote governance structure, the numerically larger group of smaller newspapers that feared radio prevented any significant easing of restrictions for many years, even while UP and INS made large gains from sponsored broadcasts. For years Cooper was unable to steer AP toward the embrace of radio that he favored from the beginning. The balance shifted only when radio revenue came to be seen as a way of preventing assessment increases that every member would have to pay. In the case of Wirephoto, Cooper was able to operate on more favorable ground. Unlike radio, Wirephoto did not have any immediate dollars-and-cents effect on most AP members. Cooper was able to direct and manage the process of introducing Wirephoto almost entirely in accordance with his own wishes. The Hearst interests ultimately failed to turn the debate into another big-paper-versus-small-paper conflict, leaving him free to fight the kind of battle with UP and INS that he was quite familiar with. The addition of the *Times* to the anti-Wirephoto forces did not significantly alter the balance, even though Cooper's (and the board's) rough treatment of one of AP's staunchest members was unprecedented. In both cases, though, he demonstrated a far-sighted understanding of how new technologies could affect the business and practice of journalism and contribute to AP's institutional strength.

8

Politics, External and Otherwise

Along with factual accuracy, Cooper and other AP executives and journalists consistently described political impartiality as a defining characteristic of its journalism. Yet critics—notably, critics on the left, such as Upton Sinclair, George Seldes, Morris Ernst, and Harold Ickes—frequently denounced AP as politically biased, dominated by wealthy business-oriented morning newspapers and by Republican and Republican-leaning publishers and directors.[1] In the voluminous documentation of Cooper's AP career, there are no overtly partisan statements in his own voice to be found. Cooper made many declarations, publicly and privately, about the need to maintain political impartiality at all costs and took action accordingly on many occasions. Yet he had clear Republican leanings in his youth, his early years in journalism, and after retirement, and according to Alan Gould, who worked closely with Cooper for decades, by the 1930s he was "a strong Republican, a qualified card-carrying Roosevelt-hater."[2]

During the 1928 and 1932 presidential elections, Cooper and AP faced criticism from member newspapers—Republican supporters in the first case, Democratic newspapers in the second—of failing to reflect their candidates' positions fairly. Neither was an open-and-shut case of bias, but the way each was handled sheds light on the prevailing political climate within AP. After 1932 AP as an organization became directly involved in politics when it took a leading role in opposing New Deal labor legislation, eventually asking the Supreme Court to declare the National Labor Relations Act unconstitutional. Byron Price, the Washington bureau chief who became Cooper's second in command and heir apparent, wrote later that it was "humiliating . . . to see the high apostle of impartiality embroiled in litigation in the role of front runner for all the labor baiters who had aligned themselves against the Wagner Act," the law requiring corporations to recognize and bargain in good faith with unions.[3] If Cooper had any similar qualms, no record of them has survived.

*   *   *

Herbert Hoover and Al Smith, the Republican and Democratic candidates for president in 1928, had very different approaches to dealing with the press. Hoover, as J. L. Williams of AP's Washington staff told Cooper, had "a horror of being misquoted" and rarely allowed himself to be quoted at all, and then only on the most inconsequential matters.[4] He did speak to journalists but insisted that he not be identified as the source for any stories that emerged from these conversations—putting reporters, who considered attribution of statements to named sources a basic element of objectivity, in a difficult situation. It was a sharp contrast to the approach adopted by Smith, who "allows himself to be quoted almost every day."

As Election Day approached, Republican newspapers began to complain that AP reporters covering Smith were doing a better job than those with Hoover. Cooper rushed to respond, asking Williams and Hoover himself whether they agreed with the criticism. (He told Hoover that he did not believe AP journalists were to blame for any dissatisfaction with campaign coverage but was prepared to reassign staff if Hoover felt otherwise.[5]) Cooper agreed that AP's coverage of Smith was more interesting than its stories about Hoover, but this was so because "Hoover is a poorer news subject," not as a result of any failing by James West, the main AP reporter with the Hoover campaign. "Unless and until Mr. Hoover removes the ban against being quoted in the personal talks he has with our man, you and various heads of Republican organizations will not be happy," Cooper told one dissatisfied publisher.[6] In fact, Williams reported, West was personally sympathetic to Hoover—so much so that one senior Republican official commented half-jokingly that campaign staff considered West "almost a Hoover adviser and . . . did not want to see him get into trouble."[7] W. H. Cowles of the *Spokane Spokesman-Review*—whose views, as a member of the board of directors, carried particular weight—wanted AP to devote more coverage to Idaho senator William Borah, whose powerful oratory compensated to some extent for Hoover's low-key approach to campaigning, but Cooper disagreed:

> To artificially stimulate amount of Republican news by carrying Borah for instance beyond news merits would be departure from practice of twenty-five years. Borah is largely repeating same speech wherever he goes. Surely you don't want us to keep repeating that speech. . . . I am personally disinterested in both sides but will say privately to you that just at this time Republicans are not making news that they could but Associated Press must not make it for them.[8]

In these exchanges, Cooper actively resisted the idea of going beyond "news merits" to remedy what Hoover supporters considered inadequate coverage, asserting the twin virtues of journalistic independence and impartiality.

This, however, was only the first in what soon became a barrage of Republican complaints centering on AP's coverage of Borah. The catalyst was a fighting speech Borah delivered in Minneapolis, firing back at Smith for trying to link Hoover to corruption charges against former cabinet colleagues and—at least according to the *Minneapolis Morning Tribune*—"electrifying" a crowd of twenty-five thousand people into "a spontaneous frenzy of enthusiasm."[9] AP sent only a distinctly mild five-hundred-word report of the speech, provoking immediate complaint from, among others, former Kansas governor Henry Allen, who was also owner of the *Wichita (KS) Beacon* and publicity director for the Republican National Committee. On Cooper's orders, the Washington bureau chief met Hoover and Allen with instructions to ask for specific instances of inadequate coverage and assure them that Cooper was "most anxious to correct any shortcomings."[10] Hoover had no personal complaint but conceded that the Republican National Committee might feel that "lesser lights of the party"— Borah, obviously—were not adequately covered. Allen was more explicit, saying the most serious complaint concerned Borah's Minneapolis speech, "the outstanding political speech" of the campaign so far. AP's reporter "mishandled it . . . and we have had a good many kicks about it."[11]

Within days of the Minneapolis speech, Cooper changed course, promising Republican critics that from now on Borah would be covered more extensively—"all [news] we have must be relayed."[12] After Frank Noyes joined the chorus of complaint, Cooper went further, assigning a staff reporter to cover Borah on a full-time basis.[13] Williams reported that this "would probably remove all complaint from [AP] as far as the [Republican] National Committee was concerned"—and so it did.[14] Cooper wanted Borah's speeches to be "fully covered on their news merits," a somewhat ambiguous formulation making clear to anyone involved that it would be wiser to err on the side of more rather than less coverage. The new arrangement was approved by the board of directors' executive committee.[15] In the face of explicit political pressure from Republican AP members, Cooper retreated from his initial assessment that Borah's speeches were tangential to the main contest between Smith and Hoover. That assessment may have been wrong—he and Williams eventually agreed that Borah's Minneapolis speech had not been adequately covered after all[16]—but in the absence of concerted pressure from Republican AP members, Borah would not have been assigned full-time staff coverage.

As the campaign drew to a close, Cooper instructed reporters with both campaigns to solicit statements testifying to AP's impartiality, which were cited in a news story on Election Day.[17] AP was commended on all sides "for its success in adhering . . . to impartial but thorough news coverage." Verbatim statements to this effect from both parties' presidential and vice presidential candidates followed. A few weeks later, a compilation of members' favorable comments was printed up in booklet form, demonstrating, as Cooper wrote, that AP's election coverage "brought no complaint or criticism, for the first time in memory." As the events of the previous weeks showed, this was hardly true. It was clearly of great importance to proclaim AP's impartiality, but in this case pressure from some Republicans among AP publishers did change the nature of its coverage.

Charges that AP's election coverage was biased arose again in 1932, this time from the Democratic side. While the two cases are not directly comparable, Republican-affiliated publishers were more successful in changing the balance of AP's election coverage in 1928 than their Democratic counterparts four years later. According to John Hightower, a senior AP journalist whose history of the agency remains unpublished, concern about the direction of AP's political reporting first arose when Cooper—with the Depression devastating the American and world economies—instructed the Washington bureau to provide more "good news" stories. Some AP journalists were suspicious of Cooper's motives, emphasizing that "trivial 'good news' items could be construed as political manipulation" while a presidential election was going on, Hightower wrote.[18] News of the edict reached an AP member in Kentucky—most likely Judge Robert Bingham, publisher of the staunchly Democratic *Louisville Courier-Journal* and *Louisville Times* and later U.S. ambassador to the United Kingdom. After the publisher complained to Cooper, the instruction was rescinded.

Bingham also complained about AP reports that he said included "editorial comments displaying bias" against the Democratic candidate, Franklin Delano Roosevelt.[19] One story stated that in a radio address on July 30, Roosevelt "delayed outlining how he could bring about a redistribution of wealth, which he called for in a speech at Atlanta last Spring." An earlier story on Roosevelt's speech accepting the Democratic nomination noted that he "did not mention modification of the Volstead Act to allow beer and wine as provided in the platform." These may not appear at first glance to be egregious examples of bias, and the waters were further muddied when Bingham added a similar complaint about how a Hoover speech had been covered. But in Bingham's view, when AP reporters noted how Roosevelt's (or Hoover's) current statements accorded with, contradicted, or apparently ignored his past statements, they were injecting opinion into what was supposed to be a rigorously factual account. The question of political bias in these instances was therefore mixed up with the movement, championed by Cooper since 1925, to allow AP writers more leeway—not only to include more color and human interest in their stories but also to state conclusions and draw inferences that they believed were justified by their knowledge of the facts. When Bingham circulated his complaint to AP members generally, asking them to send their responses to Cooper, many made this very point. The editor of the *Fort Myers (FL) News-Press*, "an unwavering Democratic newspaper," would rather print the Republican-leaning coverage provided by the *New York Herald Tribune* "than the moribund service Judge Bingham would have you give us."[20] F. A. Miller of the *South Bend (IN) Tribune* wrote that one of AP's failings in the past had been "leaning backwards in the endeavors to avoid anything that could invite a charge of partisanship." Since Cooper had become general manager, however, "AP reports have been enlivened by the elimination of wholly colorless writing."[21] The managing editor of the *Portland (OR) Journal* had no complaints, but if he did, "it would be that there is not enough bias, or, perhaps, color in Associated Press political dispatches. . . . When it comes to political coverage, there is more red meat in the United Press stuff."[22] While Cooper himself tried to respond to the substance of Bingham's complaint—he noted that an incomplete version of the original AP story appeared in the *Louisville Courier-Journal* and made the hair-splitting concession that "deferred" might have been a more appropriate word than "delayed"—he also defended what he described as "informative statements" rather than "editorial expressions." If the board of directors ordered these to be eliminated, it would be a revolutionary change in AP's journalistic practices, turning the clock back by more than twenty years.[23]

For some members, Bingham's charge of pro-Republican bias hit home. Lessis S. Read of the *Fayetteville (AR) Daily Democrat* (owned by the Fulbright family) told Cooper that he frequently cut out material from AP copy that showed a Republican bias.[24] Alfred Harrell of the *Bakersfield (CA) Californian* said that he had been concerned earlier about AP sending "what was patently propaganda for Mr. Hoover" and that "the partisan coloring and editorializing is becoming more obvious as the campaign develops." That was why his telegraph editor preferred UP's coverage.[25] This was a minority opinion, however. Of 141 letters received in response to Bingham's complaint, more than 70 percent expressed belief that the stories in question did not include problematic "editorial expressions," while almost 15 percent thought they did.[26] Still, it was noteworthy that a significant minority of AP members had concerns about pro-Republican bias in its political coverage.

Bingham presented his complaint in person to the board of directors in October. Anyone who expected fireworks would have been disappointed. In the typically bland prose of directors' minutes, the board concluded that there was no evidence of partisanship, and Bingham was "satisfied there was no such intent."[27] Adolph Ochs's private comment that Bingham had made "a mountain out of a mole-hill" was probably a more accurate reading of the board's feelings.[28] In any case, Cooper identified unspecified faults in the stories that Bingham cited, cautioned correspondents "to avoid all possible grounds for complaint," and was commended for taking steps to avoid any appearance of partisanship.[29]

Whether Cooper considered it justified or not, any public complaint about possible bias in news coverage went to the heart of AP's reputation for impartiality, one of the pillars of its dominance of the U.S. domestic news market. As the controversy spread, he moved away from his initial defense of the practices that Bingham criticized, advising AP staff that he wanted to get through the election campaign without "a single just criticism" for bias. All AP journalists should be especially careful and "go searchingly at copy on political matters to prevent cause for criticism."[30] Soon afterward, he complained to Byron Price about a Washington bureau story describing a dispute between the Democratic-controlled House of Representatives and the Hoover administration about the operations of the Reconstruction Finance Corporation. The story stated that the administration "maintained a watchful attitude, fully ready to blame the Democratic control of the House for the [proposed] legislation if bad results would follow."[31] Cooper told Price that the sentence should have ended after "attitude," eliminating the observation about possible political repercussions. There was "far more looseness in writing political matter this year than ever before," and curbing this tendency was to be one of Price's "intensive duties until further notice." Price responded with some frustration, saying Bingham's objection to mentioning significant omissions in political speeches—a practice that went back at least to 1914—was "untenable."[32] The phrases criticized as expressions of opinion, Price said, were nothing more than "plain, undisputed statements of fact." AP members demanded "more understandable and less superficial writing," and Price worried about taking "a step backward by making Associated Press dispatches even more superficial than they have been in some past campaigns." Some members of the board of directors agreed, with Houston Harte of the *San Antonio (TX) Standard Times* telling Cooper that he had been regularly complaining to Price precisely "because of the lack of interpretation" in AP's Washington coverage.[33] Cooper was adamant, however. Bingham's complaint had "put the Democratic members of [AP] in a state of alarm," and they were now scrutinizing the news report for any evidence of pro-Republican bias.[34] Cooper's clampdown seems to have had the desired result. No further complaints of bias were received during the rest of the campaign.

While Cooper took action in response to politically motivated complaints in both election years, there were some significant differences. In 1928 the nature of campaign coverage was positively changed to accommodate Republican wishes that a more colorful campaigner than Hoover be highlighted, regardless of Cooper's initial assessment of Borah's news value. This decision was not publicized and was made in response to behind-the-scenes pressure by Republican publishers and board members. The move in 1932 to eliminate anything that could be seen as interpretation originated with a Democratic publisher, but the change toward unassailably neutral coverage affected everyone equally. The controversy was played out in public, ending with a formal minute of the board of directors that reaffirmed the importance of preserving AP's reputation for impartiality. Public knowledge of the 1928 decision would not have had the same effect.

*   *   *

Franklin Delano Roosevelt's freewheeling, bantering press conferences as president made a spectacular and, at first, favorable contrast to the strict limits that Hoover and Coolidge before him imposed on interactions with journalists.[35]

Within a few years of his election, however, Roosevelt's relationship with the press became increasingly antagonistic as publishers lined up in opposition to many New Deal reforms.[36] AP was in the forefront of this movement, taking its opposition to New Deal labor laws all the way to the Supreme Court.[37] By September 1934, Roosevelt was (off the record) describing some AP reporting as "a lie."[38] Campaigning for his second term in 1936, he asserted that 85 percent of the U.S. press was engaged in a "very definite campaign of misinformation" against him.[39] A poll by *Editor & Publisher* showed that 60 percent of publishers opposed Roosevelt's reelection, a stance that—as the crushing Democratic victory in 1936 showed—put them increasingly at odds with public opinion.[40]

One of Roosevelt's bitterest critics was his former Groton schoolmate Robert McCormick of the *Chicago Tribune*.[41] In the final weeks of the 1936 presidential campaign, McCormick sent an urgent inquiry: a *Tribune* correspondent was reporting that a Communist publication from Moscow had endorsed Roosevelt's reelection. Could Cooper confirm or contradict the report?[42] Cooper instructed AP's Moscow correspondent to make inquiries, and later that day he responded with extensive excerpts from the August edition of *Communist Internationale* magazine. Roosevelt was described as being insufficiently reliable to suit the purposes of Wall Street, which had decided that "the puppet [Alf] Landon" should be sent to the White House instead.[43] AP would not file a story on the magazine's comments, Cooper told McCormick, because it was "not an organ of the Soviet government" but of the association of Communist parties in different countries. Ten days later McCormick asked Cooper to check the veracity of a report that portraits of Roosevelt, Rex Tugwell (the former Columbia University economist who was then a prominent member of Roosevelt's brain trust), and William Bullitt (who had just completed three years as U.S. ambassador in Moscow) were hanging in the Lenin Museum in Moscow. Cooper again referred the query to his Moscow correspondent, who reported that there were no such portraits and that, in any case, the museum did not contain any material from after Lenin's death in 1924.[44] McCormick also relayed complaints from a Republican operative that (once again) speeches by Senator William Borah were not being properly covered, because the AP correspondent in Idaho "is a New Dealer and won't put them on the wire."[45] Cooper investigated and reported that AP had in fact filed twelve thousand words about Borah between October 10 and October 14, adding that the senator himself declared that his activities had been covered "fairly and adequately."[46] As these incidents show, Cooper was not stampeded by McCormick's ultraconservative suggestions and was prepared to stand up for AP's journalism against unfounded suggestions of bias. But the successive inquiries provide a telling indication of the atmosphere in which he operated.

In general, there were few complaints about AP's coverage of the bitter 1936 campaign. Addressing a group of AP managing editors in November, Byron Price acknowledged that AP's reporting had been "less spicy and less spectacular" than that of opposition news services, but the result was "an impartial report, and a safe report."[47] Relatively soon after the election, however, Roosevelt's press secretary Stephen Early—a respected former AP journalist—publicly denounced an AP story asserting that Roosevelt's Senate allies were urging him to withdraw or severely scale back his plan to change the balance of the Supreme Court by appointing six additional justices.[48] A few months later, Early collected (at Roosevelt's direction) several AP stories that ostensibly demonstrated "distinct bias against the President and the Administration."[49] This eventually led to a meeting between Robert McLean, now AP's president, and Roosevelt, at which Roosevelt invited McLean to follow up with Early about "one or two items."[50] But when McLean went over the apparently problematic AP stories with Early, he left with the impression that Early "was apologetic and he felt the President was overstressing trivial instances."[51] Ultimately little came of this. McLean defended the overall quality of AP journalism while acknowledging a few, relatively minor, errors in judgment. There was probably little doubt before this that AP's political coverage was carefully scrutinized for any anti-Roosevelt bias; if they accomplished nothing else, the complaints by Roosevelt and Early made it clear that close scrutiny would continue. In that spirit, Cooper queried the new Washington bureau chief, Brian Bell, early in 1939 about an AP story reporting Roosevelt's charge that newspaper owners and politicians were spreading lies about his foreign policy.[52] "A bitter smile curled [Roosevelt's] lips" as he made these charges, the report added. "I have been sitting here trying to contort my face into a bitter smile and at the same time curling my lips," Cooper wrote, "and I will be damned if I know how it can be done without making it a sneer instead of a smile."[53] If AP's general manager was making detailed inquiries about such minor matters, the message could not have been lost on anyone involved in political reporting. Whatever the broader currents of news coverage may have been—to say nothing of AP's institutional involvement in political controversy—at the level of individual stories and individual phrases, AP's reporting was to remain impartial and safe.

* * *

Despite some evidence that AP was more attentive to Republican than to Democratic concerns about its political coverage, impartiality remained both a central public stance and, most of the time, a feature of its day-to-day journalism. But in its vigorous opposition to unionization of editorial employees and the New Deal labor legislation that mandated collective bargaining, AP as an employer was far from neutral.[54] Of all large U.S. employers, it was AP—supported by the fervently anti-union American Newspaper Publishers Association—that challenged the Wagner Act all the way to the Supreme Court. After AP lost its court challenge, Cooper's attempt to demonstrate openness to employees' wishes, as AP was then legally bound to do—while simultaneously endeavoring to slow down the process and limit the scope of unionization—exposed him to some of the most vehement personal attacks by AP members that he ever faced.

The National Industrial Recovery Act was one of several major items of legislation introduced by Roosevelt in the first one hundred days of his presidency, all intended to alleviate the economic crisis of the Great Depression. It required employers in different industries to develop codes that would limit competition, prevent reductions in prices and wages, and encourage hiring. It also recognized the right to collective bargaining, which was further enshrined and protected two years later in the National Labor Relations Act (commonly known as the Wagner Act).[55] As the legal climate for unionization became more favorable, the American Newspaper Guild (ANG) began trying to organize AP's editorial employees.[56] No headway had been made by October 18, 1935, when Morris Watson, the ANG's vice president for wire services and a member of AP's New York staff, was fired.[57] AP told *Editor & Publisher* that Watson was fired because of dissatisfaction with his work and said it was ridiculous to claim that his organizing activities were the reason. Watson, however, noted that the firing came a few hours after AP was notified that the ANG wanted to begin collective bargaining on behalf of the New York staff. The guild appealed to the National Labor Relations Board (NLRB), the tribunal charged under the Wagner Act with enforcing collective bargaining rights, to order Watson reinstated; AP replied that the law was unconstitutional and refused to recognize the labor board's authority.[58]

In January 1936, AP went to federal court in an attempt to forestall a scheduled labor board hearing, arguing that the Labor Relations Act did not apply to AP because it was not engaged in interstate commerce, which was the condition that justified federal regulation of relations between employees and employers.[59] This argument was rejected, and the labor board subsequently ordered Watson's reinstatement and the holding of a vote among AP's New York employees about whether they wished to be represented by the guild in collective bargaining.[60] Charles Clark, dean of the Yale University Law School and trial examiner in the Watson case, rejected AP's assertion that an order to reinstate Watson would infringe upon freedom of the press—nor did the First Amendment justify "opposing unionization of editorial employees and paying them less than the unionized mechanical employees."[61] Recognizing the guild would not give the union control over editorial decision making, specifically about stories involving labor or the labor movement's political aims as AP claimed. "The supervising editors of course are left complete freedom as to the material which should be sent out and its form," Clark observed. AP refused to abide by the labor board's order, leading to a further hearing in the U.S. Circuit Court of Appeals and another rejection of its claim that legislation establishing the labor board was unconstitutional. AP, the court ruled, was engaged in interstate commerce just as broadcasters and telegraph companies were and therefore fell under the labor board's jurisdiction.[62] The reinstatement of Watson was upheld, and AP was ordered to stop trying to discourage membership in the guild or discriminate against those who joined. Meanwhile, AP's editorial employees in New York voted 81–30 to have the Newspaper Guild represent them. AP refused to negotiate, however, saying it would appeal the circuit court decision to the Supreme Court.[63]

Editor & Publisher predicted that the circuit court's decision would "open the door wide to the organization of individual newspaper editorial rooms." If it was upheld by the Supreme Court, publishers would have to exercise "sound economic statesmanship . . . to keep the A.F.L.-Farmer-Labor Guild from dominance in their news departments."[64] (The ANG passed a resolution supporting the reformist Farmer-Labor Party at its 1936 national convention.[65]) In its appeal, AP contended that if Watson's reinstatement and the whole regime of collective bargaining were upheld, freedom of the press would be "severely jeopardized." AP must have the right to fire any employee whose "viewpoint has become so colored that he is unable to write the unbiased type of news article" that was AP's stock in trade.[66] Cooper, who had not taken a prominent role in this high-profile public dispute to date, supported this position. AP, he asserted in a staff newsletter, was uniquely unbiased—a remarkable achievement, considering that its member newspapers were dominated by "varying degrees of partisanship"—and its employees must remain "completely aloof from personal participation in the advocacy of any economic, social or political cause." If the Wagner Act was upheld and the Newspaper Guild represented AP reporters and editors, they would face "the more or less humanly impossible task" of writing about labor—a subject on which they had taken "an active, biased stand"—in an unbiased way.[67]

In a 5–4 decision, the Supreme Court affirmed the constitutionality of the National Labor Relations Act in April 1937.[68] The majority opinion agreed with the lower courts that AP was involved in interstate commerce and that reinstating Watson did not violate the First Amendment. AP had the right to dismiss any employee who actually demonstrated bias in handling the news, but not on the hypothetical possibility that this might happen, and was "not immune from regulation because it is an agency of the press."[69] The dissenting justices, however, insisted that any restriction on the ability of a journalistic employer to fire an employee was an unconstitutional violation of press freedom.[70]

The day after the court ruling, Watson returned to work at AP and the attempt to negotiate a collective agreement resumed. The board of directors, however, refused to accept the ANG demand that all editorial employees should be guild members. This was described as a "closed shop" and was a key point of opposition for employers who resisted unionization. The alternative, the so-called open shop, made union membership and payment of dues voluntary, weakening the union's ability to maintain the support of a majority of workers. Since the New York chapter of the guild insisted on this point, the directors concluded unanimously that "these negotiations were futile and therefore declared them ended."[71] Before negotiations could begin with employees in any other location, the question of whether unionization should take place on a national or local basis had to be resolved. The board wanted a single, nationwide bargaining unit rather than separate local bargaining units, which it claimed would lead to the adoption of different rules in in as many as sixty different offices. The directors did not add that it would also take much longer and be more difficult to attract the support of a majority of AP editorial employees nationally rather than organizing bureaus one at a time.

On January 5 and 6, 1938, Cooper spoke for AP at an NLRB hearing to consider the applications of editorial employees in Washington, Philadelphia, and Boston to be represented by the guild. By *Editor & Publisher*'s account, it was a low-key affair, a somewhat tedious exercise in what seemed likely to become a drawn-out bureaucratic process.[72] Others in attendance, however, were struck if not astonished by some of Cooper's comments. Elinore Herrick, who presided over the hearing, wrote to the White House with the surprising news that Cooper had given his blessing to the Wagner Act, saying among other things that he had been "educated" in the previous year and now realized that labor relations were part of his job.[73] Public controversy erupted when the next edition of the ANG newsletter appeared with an explosive front-page headline: "About-Face by AP Hinted by Cooper; Open to Guild Shop."[74] Cooper had expressed a "frank desire" to negotiate a national contract with the guild, the article stated. This and other remarks by Cooper—"Thank God for the Wagner Act, because it relieves the employer" and "Watson and those who feel as he does are doing a swell job"—suggested "a possibly complete about-face" in AP's attitude. Then the newsletter quoted this somewhat cryptic remark, an apparent repudiation of the board of directors' flat refusal to consider a closed-shop contract:

> I have no feeling about the closed shop, whether it should be or not. I would assume, if there is a closed shop, it would be a Guild shop to begin with, which I think is a far better closed shop for newsmen. . . . If it is a Guild shop and the employees by a majority vote said they wanted it, we could then go from there and build our future on a national basis.[75]

Cooper's comments quickly came to the attention of Elisha Hanson, counsel for the American Newspapers Publishers Association.[76] Hanson informed several others, including the staunchly anti-union James Stahlman of the *Nashville Banner*, who complained to several directors that if Cooper had been quoted correctly, his remarks were "contrary to the welfare" of AP.[77] At a board meeting of the Southern Newspaper Publishers Association, Cooper's remarks caused a "great commotion," with some members proposing a resolution of condemnation. "We were all left wondering," Adolph Shelby Ochs of the *Chattanooga (TN) Times* confessed to Arthur Sulzberger, "whether Mr. Cooper had gone 'haywire' or whether he was speaking with authority from his own Board of Directors."[78] Cooper's allies on the board rose to his defense, suggesting that the ANG newsletter account of his testimony and the NLRB's stenographic record were seriously inaccurate.[79] Clark Howell of the *Atlanta Constitution* told Stahlman that Cooper's main point had been the impossibility of having separate contracts for different locations as opposed to a single national agreement, but he also suggested that Cooper had been misquoted and reaffirmed the board's opposition to a closed shop.

Some of the criticism was sharply personal. Eugene McKinnon, chairman of the ANPA, complained to McLean that even if the accounts of what Cooper said were only half true, "it is still a very damaging statement for a man in his position to make," giving guild negotiators "a lever and a weapon . . . through which they intimidate and terrorize smaller publishers." Cooper "was besieged with dangerous delusions, and I had hoped that with a change in the Presidency taking place, a stronger control over autocratic tendencies of this individual would be exercised."[80] Some sympathetic board members expressed bewilderment. While reading the NLRB transcript, Paul Bellamy of the *Cleveland (OH) Plain Dealer* "had to pinch myself repeatedly and ask myself whether or not Kent [Cooper] had lost his mind, because so much of the testimony is filled with the most glaring non sequiturs."[81]

> Then I realized how hard it is for me sometimes, sitting in the board room, to get what Kent is driving at. He has a way of talking in a very low voice as if he were communing with himself. The result is that I have often thought he lacked the capacity to explain his own position. Evidently in this hearing they let him have his head and he rambled.[82]

Robert McCormick's judgment was harsher, if grudgingly supportive. Cooper, "with his weakness for unlimited talking, [was] an easy mark for any cross-examiner," he told the *Chicago Tribune*'s business manager. "He has the big head and has been excessively flattered by some of the directors. At that, he is probably as good a man as we can get for that job."[83] Questions were also raised about Cooper's health. One board member told Stahlman that Cooper had recently been "extremely nervous, excitable and irritable"—so much so that the board ordered him to take some time off in Florida. "Maybe this accounts for his incoherence," Stahlman suggested.[84] Cooper was apparently suffering from "some form of gastritis . . . intensified by nervous strain."[85]

While Cooper recuperated in Florida, McLean and Noyes tried to restore calm. In a letter to all directors and Cooper's chief critics, Noyes noted that Cooper was responsible for negotiating with the guild under the terms of the Wagner Act and "properly felt that he must act with an open mind on any and all proposals made by our employees."[86] The excerpts published in the guild newsletter were not a fair summary of Cooper's remarks. In fact, his testimony brought out the essential fact that AP's directors had unanimously agreed that AP "cannot consider a closed shop" for editorial employees. Thanks to Noyes's letter, Paul Bellamy concluded, the furor might finally begin to blow over.[87]

Cooper eventually sent a detailed defense of his conduct to Noyes and other supporters.[88] Some of the fiercest criticism was based on inaccurate quotation: "Somebody, somewhere, purposely perverted this record." Cooper did not say that a guild shop would be "a far better closed shop for newsmen" but that it would be better *than* a closed shop. (These terms were often used loosely, but in general a closed shop meant that anyone hired had to be a member of the union already, significantly limiting management's discretion in hiring, whereas in a union or guild shop, anyone hired would have to become a member subsequently.[89]) Mainly, Cooper argued that his approach was intended to disarm the guild (and the labor board) and succeeded in this: his opening statement, which stressed that he had "no opposition whatever to labor unions, . . . completely took the Guild off its feet." In response, the guild's attorney tried to establish that Cooper's ostensible openness to unionization was disingenuous because the board had already stated clearly that it would not accept one of the ANG's central demands: the closed shop. Trying to avoid being backed into a corner, Cooper doggedly insisted that he "would honestly approach that issue as all others with an open mind."[90] The true villains of the piece were some publishers' associations and their lawyers (the ANPA and Hanson, clearly) who "play[ed] on the prejudices of Associated Press members and start[ed] another movement against me personally." Now that his approach had been violently derailed, the only way forward was for Cooper to withdraw entirely from bargaining.[91] To the New York unit chairman of the guild, Charles McGrady, Cooper said he had no bitterness about the NLRB's rejection of his plea for a single national bargaining unit. But if McGrady should ever again begin negotiations with an employer who

> has thought things over day and night for two or three years and finally says to himself: "Maybe I haven't done enough to learn this new game which must have something or a lot of sane men wouldn't think it had and after all I have no personal prejudices in the matter." . . . Don't, for God's sake, blame anybody but yourself for your ultimate failure if you slam the door in his face and make him return braving a storm so furious by now as to prove to him that he was a damned fool to make the advance.[92]

It was not entirely clear whether Cooper's stated willingness to consider the idea of a closed shop was simply tactical, as he suggested to Noyes and others, or whether he genuinely thought it might have some merit. In a draft letter to Stuart Perry, a close ally on the board, Cooper mused that as general manager he should consider "how an application of it would actually affect the reportorial task, but first . . . hear what can be said in its favor."

> If the union is recognized as the sole bargaining agent and as such it presents only one issue for bargaining, namely the closed shop, a refusal to bargain on that issue would be held by the courts (in their present frame of mind) as refusal to bargain and therefore a violation of the law.[93]

For public consumption, Cooper stressed that he had never heard arguments in favor of the closed shop and would want to consider these thoroughly before presenting—or not presenting—the issue to the board. "My mind is not foreclosed against consideration of anything that the employees feel concerns their happiness and terms of employment," he said in a statement to *Editor & Publisher*, adding one crucial caveat: "The final decision . . . rests with the board, which is the supreme authority."[94]

On the question of pay scales, Cooper was less open-minded. As Washington bureau chief, Price was sharply critical of the relatively low pay for AP journalists, which he believed was one of the main reasons for the lackluster quality of much of its journalism. (This was also one of Walter Lippmann's criticisms of U.S. journalism in general.[95]) Appointed executive editor in 1937, Price was directly in charge of AP's news service and became management's representative in negotiations with the ANG's New York unit. While Price resisted some of the guild's demands, he supported the push for higher salaries—leading Cooper to reproach him for "betraying the memory of Melville E. Stone."[96] In 1938, with negotiations at an impasse, guild representatives asked to present their case directly to the board. It was a low-key and respectful session, with the guild emphasizing that it did not seek any improvements in working conditions beyond the status quo.[97] AP was "outstanding in the treatment of its employees in so far as security is concerned," Watson said, "but we want to have it in a contract." AP's position that any partisan political activity by the union should be banned remained a stumbling block, however. A contract was eventually reached with the New York unit in March 1940, based on an earlier United Press–ANG agreement. It did not include a closed shop, Cooper reported to McLean, and "does not call for us to do anything that we are not already doing."[98]

*   *   *

At times during the early 1930s, the pace and scope of change that Cooper faced (and often set in motion) seemed relentless. But much as he and AP were embroiled in struggles over radio and Wirephoto, an existential confrontation with Reuters, radical reorganization of international alliances and operations, and the years-long conflict over New Deal labor legislation and union recognition, AP's basic raison d'être remained what it had always been: providing a steady supply of daily news to its members. In this respect, an upbeat gathering of AP members' managing editors in November 1933 marked—in the words of Malcolm Bingay of the *Detroit Free Press*—"the ascendancy of Kent Cooper."[99] In a front-page paean to AP after the gathering, Bingay praised Cooper's "flawless poise and disciplined imperturbability" and cited "the 100 per cent endorsement" that AP's news report had received.[100] After this auspicious beginning, the AP managing editors meeting became an annual event. Alan Gould later described it as "one of the most positive things done to improve the news report."[101]

It was not surprising that Cooper got credit when things went well or blame when they did not. By 1934 the centralization of authority he established soon after becoming general manager was complete.[102] At one point he dictated ninety-two letters of instruction in a single day, which McLean saw as an example of Cooper's "tendency to do everything himself."[103] An assistant general manager, two executive news editors (reduced to one in 1937), six executive assistants (in charge of foreign news, features, photos, personnel, membership, and traffic), and dozens of "strategic bureau" chiefs reported directly to him.[104] AP was a large and complex organization; by the early 1930s it had around sixteen hundred employees, and by 1941 more than nineteen hundred, of whom about three-fifths were reporters and editors, with an annual payroll of more than $6 million.[105] In 1930 AP compiled and delivered an average of three hundred thousand words of news and features a day from 1,850 locations in the United States and around the world, distributed over 220,000 miles of telegraphic circuits. One unusual organizational wrinkle was the broad range of sensitive duties assigned to Cooper's secretary, Sarah (Sally) Gibbs, who in 1942 became Cooper's third wife. She was responsible for coordinating all matters presented to Cooper from all sources and for keeping track of all records and correspondence. She was also in charge of making sure that any direction to Cooper's subordinates was carried out. As well, she kept "minute details of everything, including successes and failures" of everyone who reported to Cooper.

One perennial critic cited Gibbs's role as one of many weaknesses in Cooper's relations with his staff. Bernard Rickatson-Hatt, Reuters's editor in chief, sent a series of detailed (and sometimes maliciously gossipy) reports to Roderick

Jones from New York about the prospects for Reuters' continuing relationship with AP after the disastrous contract renegotiation in 1934.[106] Beyond the small group of executives who "do his every bidding," Cooper was "much disliked for his brutal and inconsiderate methods" by the great majority of AP staff, though many admired him as a newspaper executive. According to Cooper and his immediate staff, he "has the Board in the hollow of his hand," but some younger directors reportedly distrusted him. In terms of politics, Cooper "was on the inside during the Hoover regime and is now on the outside during the Roosevelt era." The fact that Sally Gibbs drew a salary of more than one hundred dollars a week (two and a half times the AP average) was widely known, which "has not done Cooper any good. . . . It certainly infuriates the feminine staff."[107]

Rickatson-Hatt's comments may have been unfair; he knew that Jones relished any observations that showed Cooper in a bad light. But others within AP made similar judgments. Ben Bassett, whose forty-three years as an AP journalist and senior editor began soon after Cooper became general manager, wrote later that Cooper's "whims and vanity were notorious."[108] He provoked "strong views within the staff, from those warmed by the Cooper glow or chilled by a curt thumbs down," and was "cold-blooded toward some who fell from favor." Alan Gould, who worked closely with Cooper for more than twenty years, recalled that he made decisions "abruptly . . . too capriciously" and "often permitted his personal prejudices or offhand judgments [to] prompt decisions that he learned to regret."[109] Arbitrary decision-making about personnel was common among U.S. newsroom managers in the pre-guild era,[110] but Cooper appears to have been a particularly striking example of this approach.

A gathering of all U.S. bureau chiefs in New York in 1939 underscored the importance of Cooper's personal judgments about those who worked for him.[111] Everyone who attended had to submit a written assessment of the event, and the ensuing correspondence showed that just as Cooper relied on flattery in dealing with influential directors, he was not averse to flattery himself.[112] "There were magic in your presence and wisdom in your words," one bureau chief wrote, praising Cooper's "matchless leadership and inspiration to all of us."[113] Cooper evidently did not find these words excessive, declaring in reply that he was "profoundly impressed at the generosity of your greetings and good wishes" and referring encouragingly to "the horizon that is yours."[114] Cooper was more critical of the Albany bureau chief, who asked no questions during the gathering, "so apparently already knew it all." But Cooper was impressed by a detailed memo the bureau chief prepared for his own staff after the meeting, "so I will omit and forget comments that I could make and derive satisfaction from the fact that broadly you see your views not out of harmony with my own."[115] One of the gathering's main themes had been a challenge to "weed out mediocre men,"[116] and no one who was there could have been left in doubt that Cooper's sometimes offhand, very personal assessments of each of them would weigh heavily when judgments were made about who was mediocre and who was not.

In dealing with one influential board member, however, Cooper was consistently deferential. "Please never fear you are troublesome," he wrote in response to one suggestion from Robert McCormick. "I respect your ability and your news judgment and I want to hear from you any time you have time to write me."[117] No query from McCormick was too implausible to merit a detailed response, including one about a photo of a circus employee in Paris who had ostensibly escaped from a charging lion. "No man can out-run a lion and this man [in the photo] doesn't seem to be running very hard at that," he complained to Cooper. "I believe it is a trained lion."[118] Cooper referred the inquiry to his Paris bureau chief, who dutifully tracked down the photographer. It was an unrehearsed incident, McCormick was assured; the keeper had dropped his whip "and was moving as fast as he could out of harm's way."[119] But as Cooper also did during the 1936 election campaign,[120] he sometimes diplomatically resisted invitations for AP to join the *Chicago Tribune*'s anti–New Deal crusades. In the summer of 1936, McCormick told Cooper that one of his associates was "quite worked up over the way the New Dealers are using Yale profs as cat's paws. . . . It seems to me that if Yale has a lunatic on its faculty, that it is news." Cooper replied mildly that this was a topic of legitimate news interest, but he did not think AP should produce a story "pointing to the lunatic fringe on the faculty at Yale" or other colleges.[121] This was better left to individual newspapers—like, presumably, the *Tribune*. In 1938 McCormick asked whether AP had "gone Red," citing a story that described the labor policies of Michigan's pro–New Deal governor, Frank Murphy, as conciliatory.[122] McCormick was concerned that one of AP's member newspapers might be controlled by the Congress of Industrial Organizations (CIO)—presumably because of a Newspaper Guild contract—and that its coverage, now politically biased, was being forwarded to other AP newspapers. Cooper denied the charge. If there was a genuine cause for concern, AP should do "what it has done in all instances where a local member or his staff holds prejudices—Republican, Democratic, CIO, A.F. of L. or Communist—namely, be certain that any Associated Press dispatches from that source are true and unbiased." (Cooper did, however, repeat McCormick's description of Harold

Ickes, Roosevelt's secretary of the interior and a vigorous critic of newspaper publishers—including McCormick in particular—as "the polecat."[123])

To mark the tenth anniversary of his appointment as general manager, Cooper presented a forceful review of his accomplishments to the board of directors in October 1935.[124] Most current members had joined the board after 1925, and with the gradual changing of the guard, Cooper was much more willing to criticize Melville Stone's legacy than in the past. AP, he said, was moribund before his appointment because management paid little attention to members' needs and wishes. Basic standards of administration had been neglected. When Cooper took over, he found "numerous cases of bureau chiefs who were crooks," collecting the salaries of bogus employees or claiming thirty dollars a week for an employee who was actually paid twenty dollars a week and pocketing the difference. One of Cooper's main goals had been to expand beyond the basic news service and provide, on a cost-recovery basis, any service that would be better and less expensive than the members could get elsewhere. There were now forty-four such special services, including Wirephoto and features. Other major accomplishments were increasing membership by reducing the geographical scope of protest rights (though he did not mention the wholesale extension of protest rights to all members in 1927); broadening the scope of AP news coverage and paying more attention to human interest, in subject matter and in style; and making it possible for AP to "take its rightful position among the world's news agencies," escaping from a degrading subordination to Reuters.

The key challenge that remained was competition with UP. As a result of UP's making its news available to radio stations for sponsored broadcasts, it was receiving substantial additional revenue to support its news service. AP needed to improve its own service in response, but assessment reductions since 1932 had left it with less revenue. AP was operating in "a highly commercialized field and may have to act in conformity with the situation in which it finds itself." Although Cooper was careful not to be too explicit, he was preparing the ground for a new approach that would allow AP to sell its news to newspapers and other organizations that were not eligible for regular membership. Creating a new category of associate members with limited rights would accommodate not only the current Scripps-Howard and Hearst members that did not comply with AP's bylaws but also radio stations. This would provide new revenue from broadcasting if the board ever decided (as it eventually did in 1939[125]) that this was necessary. If members were unwilling to pay more, AP would be transformed "into something it had never been . . . in order to survive."[126]

Cooper's presentation to the board focused on the broad changes he had made since 1925 and those yet to be introduced rather than the long-standing fundamentals of AP's approach to news: impartiality and, above all, accuracy. This was probably just as well; the annual meeting a few months earlier had "rocked with laughter" when a heckler deflated an assertion of AP's sure-footedness by reminding members of a recent devastating failure in its news coverage.[127] The conclusion in February 1935 of Bruno Hauptmann's trial for kidnapping and murdering Charles Lindbergh's baby was the high point of newsworthiness in what was already one of the biggest stories of the decade.[128] In an effort to report the verdict before any competitor, AP's New Jersey bureau chief had secretly installed a telegraph operator in the attic of the Flemington, New Jersey, courthouse.[129] The telegrapher was connected to another AP employee in the courtroom by short-wave radio. As soon as the verdict was announced, the courtroom observer was to send a prearranged signal to the telegrapher, who would then send a flash over the wires before any of the other reporters could get word to their telegraph operators. Unfortunately for AP, the system did not work as planned. The telegrapher, believing he had received a signal from the courtroom—though not the signal that had been agreed on—mistakenly flashed that Hauptmann had been found guilty with a recommendation for a sentence of life in jail. The actual verdict, pronounced fifteen minutes later, was guilty with a sentence of death.[130] By then, many AP newspapers had started printing extras trumpeting the erroneous report—"because of the reputed accuracy of the Associated Press, many newspapers were ready to roll on the AP's say-so," *Editor & Publisher* noted with perhaps a hint of schadenfreude—and hundreds of thousands of radio listeners heard it over the air, credited to AP, through the Press-Radio Bureau. AP sent a "kill" notice eleven minutes after the flash, but a great deal of damage had been done. William Hawkins and Roy Howard exchanged incredulous and jubilant telegrams; the false verdict was "one of the worst black eyes AP has received in many years," Hawkins wrote from Los Angeles. But from Hawkins's location on the West Coast, Howard replied, it was "impossible you get any sense Rocks' [AP's] agony today." His telegram continued:

> Apparently believing had inside tip from jury or officials they flashed wrong verdict fifteen minutes before announced in court then gave to PRB which put out with full credit to Rocks stop. Later PRB corrected placing blame on Rocks and latter in fumbling disingenuous apology balled situation hopelessly stop. . . . Situation so terrible I actually feel sorry for Kent.[131]

Newspapers that relied solely on UP made sure their readers knew how AP, and their local competitors who used it, had failed.[132] In a statement to the staff, Cooper acknowledged "the serious damage that this incident has caused."[133] The bureau chief, wholly in the wrong for having set up the secret relay system in the first place, was suspended indefinitely without pay, and the telegrapher who sent the flash was fired.

Four days later, AP made another high-profile error. The Supreme Court was scheduled to release a ruling in the so-called Gold Clause cases, involving a challenge to legislation that detached the U.S. dollar from the price of gold. In a complicated decision, the Court criticized the legislation but ruled, none-theless, that obligations to redeem U.S. government bonds in gold could not be enforced—effectively sustaining the administration's position. AP's initial version of the story, splashed over newspaper front pages across the country, stated wrongly that the obligation to redeem bonds in gold had been upheld.[134] Speaking to a group of AP managing editors a few months later, Byron Price acknowledged that AP had committed "a straight-out fumble in reporting . . . and our [editing] desk made matters worse trying to clear up this confusion."[135] AP's error affected the stock market, while "hundreds of AP newspapers had to eat their words."[136]

A few weeks later, Edwin "Jimmy" James, managing editor of the *New York Times* and a persistent critic of AP's journalism, sent one of his last memos to the gravely ill Adolph Ochs. James charged that—as the Hauptmann and Su-preme Court errors illustrated—AP put too much emphasis on speed rather than waiting for solid confirmation.[137] This approach, he wrote, "will inevitably produce other such errors." All in all, a growing feeling among *Times* editors that AP "is not to be depended upon in every case causes wider psychological doubts." The *Times* was far from being a typical AP newspaper, but a lack of confidence in its accuracy on the part of one of the agency's most important members was a serious matter.

Among the many changes that Cooper set in motion at AP, one important development was entirely out of his hands: Robert McLean's replacement of Frank Noyes as president in April 1938.[138] McLean had been an AP director since 1924, filling the board seat that his father had occupied since 1900, and took over as publisher of the family-owned *Philadelphia Bulletin* in 1931. He was "a Prince-ton man"—a patrician by comparison to the self-made Cooper—which may have contributed to the stilted relationship between the two.[139] While Cooper had sometimes been frustrated by Noyes's reluctance to break with Reuters,

Noyes had always treated him with warmth and deference. Their relationship, beginning when the thirty-year-old Cooper was a relatively junior AP employee and Noyes, seventeen years older, was already well established as president, had something of a father-son character. The situation was more or less reversed when McLean, twelve years younger than Cooper, came into office. Cooper was then in his late fifties, strongly established as AP's dominant executive, and in no need of a mentor even if McLean had been inclined to act as one. (He was not.) Looking back years later, McLean recalled that Cooper did "a magnificent job as General Manager," but as a result of Noyes's indulgence, he was "definitely somewhat spoiled when I came into office. There is no other word to describe his attitude at certain times than discourteous, even verging on the insubordinate."[140]

After several weeks of rest in Florida in the winter of 1938—where Cooper spent at least a month every year—he had apparently recovered from the illness that coincided with the furor over his musings about a guild closed shop. But in the spring of 1939, his health deteriorated drastically. McLean recalled later that Cooper had trouble adjusting to his new boss: "He'd only worked for one man, and that was Frank Noyes. . . . It was our relationship which was causing him distress."[141] By the beginning of May, Cooper was in Rochester, Minnesota, for an extended process of diagnosis and treatment at the Mayo Clinic. Very few people knew about this, and Cooper took determined steps to maintain secrecy. "After three weeks of being turned inside out and upside down," Cooper was diagnosed with chronic gastritis.[142] "I am being taught how to eat and what to eat," he told McLean, one of the few who knew about his illness, "and I am being warned that if I ever crook an elbow with you, . . . I shall have to set out at once and buy a ticket for Rochester and do this all over again. Am I going to drink? I am not!" He was also told that he must "put no pressure whatever on my existence if I want to get well," making him "the damnedest, laziest amoeba that you ever saw." This meant three months of complete rest after finishing his treatment in Minnesota, an absence sufficiently long that an acting general manager had to be appointed. In the first acknowledgment that Cooper, who had now been at AP for almost thirty years, would retire at some point, McLean observed that whoever was chosen would be seen as Cooper's probable successor but hastened to add that he had no immediate plans for a change in leadership: "I have hoped that your restoration to full health would find you eager to carry on."[143] Cooper's temporary replacement, they agreed, would be Price, who had left Washington to come to New York as executive editor, responsible for all aspects of the news service, two years earlier. This move was part of a larger reorganization that reduced the number of those reporting directly to Cooper from more than one hundred to four.

As his stay in Minnesota dragged on, Cooper was evidently unaccustomed to having a lot of time on his hands, leading to some unusually candid reflections on his own behavior. No executive in any organization, he told McLean, had ever enjoyed the "marvelous and comforting, well-wishing support" that AP's board of directors had given him since 1925: "These associations have been the greatest thing in my life, and I have been ashamed at times of my petulance and impatience, which I can only put down to the state of my health."[144] McLean was intrigued to learn about a possible psychological dimension to Cooper's illness.[145] He had noticed that several things, particularly the tense negotiations with the guild, "tend to upset [Cooper] nervously and emotionally."[146] Later he was told that the Mayo Clinic physicians had identified an emotional background for Cooper's recurring health problems but could not determine exactly what it was: "They had actually devoted some days to psychoanalysis when Kent called a halt."[147]

At the end of May, Cooper returned from Minnesota to continue recuperating at home in Irvington, an affluent suburb of New York.[148] A week later he began coming in to AP's new headquarters at Rockefeller Center for a few hours each day but left most things to Price and his other assistants.[149] He promised Noyes that if he and McLean "will let me take it easy this summer, . . . my health will continue to improve and [AP] will go further. All I need to do is to learn to let others carry on the detail, and I have actually learned that that can be done."[150]

By the time Cooper returned to work full time in September, the international tensions that had been steadily mounting through the last half of the 1930s had come to a head, with Germany and Russia's invasion of Poland leading to a declaration of war by Britain (and several of its former colonies, including Canada, Australia, and New Zealand) and France. War and the events leading up to it presented new challenges to the integrity of AP's journalism and, eventually, unprecedented opportunities for worldwide expansion.

Kent Cooper in 1926, a year after he was appointed general manager of Associated Press. He began his journalism career in Indianapolis more than twenty-five years earlier, and the inscription reads: "To the boys at 'IN' from whence I came." (Courtesy Lilly Library, Indiana University, Bloomington, Indiana)

Melville Stone, a towering figure in AP's history, was general manager from 1893 to 1920. Cooper accepted Stone's offer of a job in 1910 despite his belief that AP was "moribund." (Source: Associated Press)

Cooper's trip to Tokyo in 1933 to negotiate a contract with the Japanese news agency Rengo marked a turning point in the evolution of the international news system. Cooper (seated, right) worked closely with Yukichi Iwanaga (center), Rengo's managing director, and AP's Tokyo bureau chief, Glenn Babb (left). The man standing at rear is unidentified. (Courtesy Lilly Library, Indiana University, Bloomington, Indiana)

Adolph Ochs, publisher of the *New York Times*, was one of AP's longest-serving and most influential directors. He was also one of Cooper's strongest supporters, though he considered some of the breezier AP coverage that Cooper introduced "the vilest rubbish." (Source: Associated Press)

In 1928 Roy Howard (second from left) was no longer president of United Press, AP's great competitor, but remained its *éminence grise* for decades. He and Cooper, seen here at Sea Island, Georgia, in 1928, first met when beginning their journalistic careers around 1900. Their rivalry—leavened by a somewhat wary friendship—lasted for almost sixty years. (Courtesy Lilly Library, Indiana University, Bloomington, Indiana)

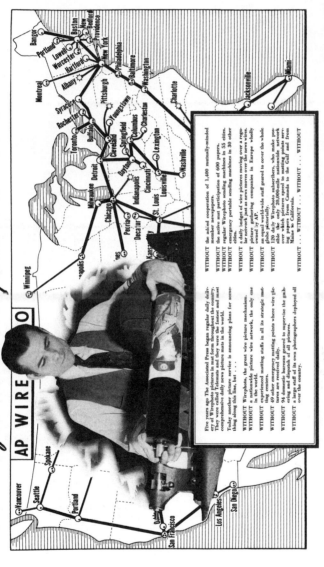

Cooper's introduction of Wirephoto—the same-day transmission of news photos—in 1935 was a milestone in the evolution of news photography. It was also, as this advertisement shows, a huge advantage for AP over competing photo services (Source: Associated Press)

Competition with AP's rival United Press was always one of Cooper's main preoccupations. Here he speaks with UP's president, Hugh Baillie, at a New York club luncheon in 1938. Of all UP's chief executives, Baillie was the most combative and the most skeptical of Cooper. In one widely distributed memo to UP staff, Baillie mocked Cooper, who "seemed to feel that we were being rather unclubby" by drawing unwelcome attention to an AP factual error. "I am sorry we hurt Kent's feelings." (Courtesy Lilly Library, Indiana University, Bloomington, Indiana)

By the 1940s, Robert McCormick—the arch-conservative publisher of the *Chicago Tribune*, and a long-serving AP director—was Cooper's closest ally on the board. In December 1943 he sent Cooper "a line to say that I consider you one of my Christmas presents of this year." (Source: Associated Press)

Cooper developed an increasingly close friendship in the 1940s with Robert McCormick, publisher of the *Chicago Tribune* and an AP director. One result was the broadcast in September 1943 of an operetta composed and written by Cooper, *About the Girl*, on the *Tribune*-owned radio station, WGN. With Henry Weber (left), conductor of the WGN Symphony Orchestra, and Marion Claire, who sang the lead role. (Courtesy Lilly Library, Indiana University, Bloomington, Indiana)

Cooper in 1942 with three men who powerfully influenced his career. From left: Robert McLean, AP's president from 1938, with whom Cooper had an awkward relationship; William Haley, a member of the Reuters board of directors, who convinced Cooper to set aside his deep-seated distrust of the British agency; and Frank Noyes, AP's president before McLean and the person most responsible for Cooper's ascent. (Source: Associated Press)

During World War II, DeWitt Mackenzie was best known as the author of AP's popular daily war summaries. He had another, unpublicized role as ghostwriter of *Barriers Down*, the book about AP's international expansion that turned Cooper into a high-profile advocate of press freedom. (Source: Associated Press)

Edward Kennedy, AP's Paris bureau chief, scooped the world in May 1945 with his exclusive story about Germany's surrender. Accusations that he had violated a promise to hold the news until it was officially released led to a high-profile public controversy and his eventual dismissal. (Source: Associated Press)

In 1944, Cooper was at the height of his authority and influence, underscored by the board of directors' enthusiastic acceptance of his recommendation to spend up to $1 million a year for the expansion of AP's international operations. (Source: Associated Press)

From left: Christopher Chancellor, Reuters' general manager; Cooper; Reuters director and British publisher Esmond Harmsworth (Viscount Rothermere); and McLean at AP's 1948 annual meeting. Chancellor praised Cooper publicly for his press freedom campaign while complaining privately to colleagues about "the appalling difficulty of dealing with this man." (Source: Associated Press)

Cooper with his four assistant general managers in 1943. From left: Frank Starzel (who became general manager himself five years later), Alan Gould, Cooper, Paul Miller (the Washington bureau chief and future AP president), and Claude Jagger. (Courtesy Lilly Library, Indiana University, Bloomington, Indiana)

In 1946 Cooper published a highly speculative fictionalized biography of Anna Zenger, the wife of Peter Zenger, the colonial printer whose acquittal on libel charges is a milestone in the history of American press freedom. Cooper's third wife, the former Sally Gibbs (who was also his former executive secretary), is credited with research for the book, but the story line—depicting a beautiful and intelligent but unheralded woman who was the real power behind a dull, stolid, and more famous spouse—suggests she may have had a hand in writing it as well. (Courtesy Lilly Library, Indiana University, Bloomington, Indiana)

Cooper reviews AP's communication network in Germany with bureau chief Wes Gallagher in 1948. AP "moved in with the troops" beginning in 1944 and quickly made major inroads into the German newspaper market. (Source: Associated Press)

Cooper unwillingly handed over all AP operating authority to Frank Starzel in 1951 but was still considered "the grand old man of the news agency world." Here he delivers the toast to the British news agency Reuters at its centennial gala in July, attended by the British prime minister, the archbishop of Canterbury, and scores of other dignitaries. (Courtesy Lilly Library, Indiana University, Bloomington, Indiana)

Cooper and Sally in the summer of 1964. Cooper, now eighty-four, was in declining health after major surgery the previous year. He was admitted to a hospital on January 22, 1965, after suffering a heart seizure and died nine days later. (Courtesy Lilly Library, Indiana University, Bloomington, Indiana)

Roderick Jones, the general manager/managing director of Reuters from 1915 until 1941, seen in an undated photo. He was Cooper's bête noire for twenty years, enforcing the cartel restrictions that kept AP confined to North and South America. Their disdain was mutual. (Source: Reuters Archive)

9

The Shadow of War

In his annual report to AP's members in December 1943, Cooper heaped praise on AP's war correspondents and photographers for doing "one of the most brilliant jobs of reporting in history" in "an epic story of journalistic heroism and enterprise,"[1] echoing sentiments that he expressed throughout the Second World War. The story of AP during the war usually, and understandably, focuses on its correspondents and photographers—five of whom died in the course of their work—and their extensive coverage of the conflict.[2] But while Cooper led the public praise of AP's journalists, he had very little involvement in day-to-day news coverage after Byron Price became executive editor in 1937.[3] Instead, he focused during the war on AP's long-term strategic goal of international expansion, its response to the U.S. government's antitrust prosecution, and a handful of more immediate news-related controversies.[4] Two of these involved high-profile AP correspondents: Louis Lochner, the Berlin bureau chief until his arrest in 1941 and subsequent expulsion from Germany, who faced accusations from some AP members and others that he was too easy on the Nazis, and Edward Kennedy, whose hotly debated scoop about the end of the European war in 1945 eventually led to his dismissal from AP. In both cases, Cooper's determination to protect AP's public image—and perhaps his own position—led to ethically questionable decisions. Meanwhile, he became increasingly dyspeptic, expressing dissatisfaction with his own institutional role and responding furiously to criticism of AP by its members. For a time Cooper virtually stopped dealing with his immediate superior, Robert McLean—with whom his relationship had never been easy—even while forging a close friendship with another AP director, the ultraconservative and deeply controversial publisher of the *Chicago Tribune*, Robert McCormick.

*　*　*

Censorship was one of the issues that consistently occupied Cooper's attention. Within days of the British-French declaration of war in 1939, he protested vigorously about the British censorship regime, in which every form of communication from Britain to the outside world had to be approved by censors, regularly leading to substantial delays. In London, the crucial transit point for most of AP's European coverage, the British military exercised a "vise-like grip" on war news, consistently favoring secrecy. This situation, Cooper complained to the British authorities, was "most oppressive and hampering to [the] best interests not only of England and [the] Empire but to the reasonable requirements of the work of the Associated Press in America and throughout the world including British Empire."[5] In its place he recommended what he described as the "most workable and reasonable" system of "responsibility censorship" adopted in Germany and other European countries. Under that system, international correspondents were free to transmit stories without prior censorship. This was an important advantage for routine news, but correspondents in Germany could be, and often were, subjected to harassment and other sanctions, including expulsion, if what they published displeased the Nazi authorities.

Cooper was well aware of Germany's draconian press controls, official retaliation for unfavorable stories, and outright suppression of news through the reports he received from AP's Berlin bureau chief, Louis Lochner.[6] Why, then, did he gloss over the drawbacks of the German approach? It was not just a matter of trying to put pressure on the British authorities by praising the approach of their authoritarian enemy; Cooper made the same arguments in private to his own colleagues. He told AP's Paris bureau chief in 1940 that "the Germans all along have been liberal in that they have passed our matter without censorship. . . . However, we would not want to take the responsibility of sending something we think they might question[,] so in such cases we ask them to look at the copy."[7] In effect, Cooper equated the absence of formal censorship in Germany with the absence of *any* meaningful restrictions on international correspondents' reporting. It would be more accurate to describe this as a system of self-censorship, requiring journalists constantly to make judgments about what to report and what to omit, with severe consequences for whatever might be considered an incorrect decision. For Lochner, the constant effort to guess whether stories would bring official retaliation was exhausting.[8] "The fact that there is allegedly no censorship here imposes all the greater responsibility" on every foreign news organization, he told Cooper:

> In a way straight censorship is much easier than this "personal honor" system, for it means that one must watch the moods and peculiarities of the top men all the time and know when one can risk treading on otherwise forbidden ground and when it is time to shut up and not spill what one knows.

Lochner told Alan Gould that it would be hard for anyone in New York to appreciate "what weighing of the possible effects on our continuation as a Berlin bureau goes into every story." Frequently the whole staff debated "whether this or that item may be sent at all or whether it falls under the ban; if to be sent, in what form it may be presented; whether putting this or that idea into the lead will cause us trouble with the authorities, etc."[9] Yet in a 1940 review of censorship in Europe, Cooper lamented that AP no longer had the "unlimited facilities for collecting news" that it had enjoyed in both Germany and Britain before war broke out. In fact, only Britain had provided anything like "unlimited facilities."[10]

Cooper vigorously defended his policy of cooperating with the authorities in any country where AP correspondents worked, and he rejected the idea of trying to evade censorship. "I have always gone on the theory that our men are guests of the countries to which they are accredited and that they should not abuse their hospitality," he told the concerned editor of one AP newspaper in September 1939.[11] This was the only way to avoid having AP correspondents expelled. AP must "do the best it can in sending the true news from any country in the world" and could not do this "if it has a policy of combating censorship or if it tries to circumvent censorship." This might mean not sending some stories, "but it leaves us in good standing constantly to educate the censorships (as we continually do) that any policy of suppression is short-sighted." (While Lochner often defended his reporting against the German authorities' objections, there is no indication that this resulted in any education of the kind Cooper suggested.) Cooper told another AP member that Lochner was writing "with freedom" under responsibility censorship—a contrast to the situation in Britain and France, where censorship was "rigid indeed."[12] In the spring of 1940 he urged the German government through its chargé d'affaires in Washington to lift recently imposed censorship so that AP could continue to make "its frequent assertions that Germany does not censor its news from Berlin."[13] A year later he told the editor of the *Chicago Daily News* that while the German government was "reacting unfavorably toward all Americans, including correspondents, because of the attitude of the United States government toward the German government," he was "personally astonished and appreciative . . . at the cooperation the German authorities have given the Associated Press staff."[14]

As his comment about the U.S. government's attitude toward Germany suggested, Cooper was a forceful proponent of American neutrality between 1939 and 1941 (as were many other Americans).[15] Many AP editors disagreed, however. In June 1940, after German forces rolled through Belgium, the Netherlands, and northern France to corner more than three hundred thousand British and French troops in Dunkirk, Cooper sent a circular to all news editors and bureau chiefs, rejecting "unjustified criticisms . . . of our factual reports from abroad which at present are unfavorable" to the Allies.[16] The United States was "longing for pro-Allied and anti-Nazi propaganda," but AP should resist the pressure. The United States was not at war, and AP should not "get off-side ourselves by whooping it up for either belligerent on any idea it is our duty to whoop it up for either."[17] He maintained this approach until the eve of U.S. involvement in the war, sharply criticizing in October 1941 editors of AP newspapers who "would have our men leave the Axis countries while our country is officially at peace, come home and write like rocking-chair radio commentators talk—hell-bent for getting us in the war."[18]

Cooper took pains to defend Lochner—one of three American correspondents invited personally by Hitler to accompany the rapidly advancing German forces in the spring of 1940—against charges that his coverage was pro-Nazi, or at least not sufficiently critical. His firsthand accounts, presenting a vivid and accurate picture of German military successes, got front-page display in many AP newspapers. But often he used language that—at least to some observers—suggested, if not outright sympathy, an equable or even admiring attitude toward the invaders. In one story, he described the warm welcome he received from a senior German commander and the "twinkle in his eye" as he pondered rapid victory. In others, he commented on the "death-disdaining courage" of German soldiers or—even while noting "the hatred in people's eyes" in one Belgian town destroyed by the German advance—expressed surprise at "how quickly the local population and occupation army made friends."[19] One AP newspaper, the *Oklahoma City Times*, denounced Lochner as a Hitler propagandist, and a group of Maryland and Delaware members unanimously condemned his reporting as biased and pro-Nazi.[20] Some of Lochner's fellow correspondents also criticized his work, with Joseph Harsch of the *Christian Science Monitor* describing him as unduly pro-German and William Shirer of CBS placing him among those who "played the Nazi game, a little . . . if only to get a beat, a scoop."[21] Cooper, however, told the Oklahoma City editor that Lochner's accounts of German gains were not much different from those in Winston Churchill's speeches and that neither was "good reading to anyone who longs to see the allies win." He told one dissatisfied reader of AP coverage that Lochner's job was to report "what he sees and . . . what he is told by the highest authorities" and that he was carrying out these duties honestly and accurately. Lochner was "fully reliable . . . a natural born and loyal American and a thoroughly experienced Associated Press man."[22] The complaints against Lochner were considered by the board of directors, which voted unanimously to express its confidence in the work of AP's foreign staff.[23]

Lochner was personally as anti-interventionist as Cooper. After September 1939, he strongly urged—as he had done in 1917—that the United States should not go to war with Germany. "I don't see why we should fight for the decrepit English sham democracy, however much I may be averse to authoritarianism as a principle of state," he wrote to his son in May 1940.[24] In the summer of 1941 he told his daughter that his overriding aim had always been to promote better relations between Germany and the United States, even at the cost of hard-hitting coverage: "For twenty years I gave all there was in me to bring our two nations together, and now it looks as though all my labor had been in vain. I can claim that I was more than a reporter: in every possible way . . . I tried to foster German-American understanding."[25] Morrell Heald, who edited a collection of Lochner's letters to his family, has suggested that the depth and duration of Lochner's connection to Germany, including family ties and many close personal friendships, made it hard for him to understand how the Nazi regime's actions appeared to outside, and especially American, critics.[26]

Lochner's distaste for Germany's opponents was matched and possibly exceeded by Cooper's. Gould recalled later that Cooper had "strong opinionated attitudes toward the participants in the war. . . . He detested the British and French." On one occasion, Cooper's vigorously expressed opinions shocked both Gould and Price:

> I wouldn't say [Cooper] was pro-German, though in effect some of his privately expressed opinions would indicate he was happy to see France collapse early on and thought the Germans would finish the job with England if they

invaded across the channel. . . . There was one day after a session including much strong talk about the war that Price and I left his office and turned to each other and simultaneously said, "For crissakes let's hope that what we've just been listening to is confined to the corner [office]. Not only pretty hot stuff but it could be very upsetting if it got involved in any AP [coverage]."[27]

Walton Cole of Reuters, who also knew Cooper well, commented in 1944 that AP in general and Cooper in particular were "violently anti-French"[28]—a legacy, no doubt, of many years of tension between AP and Havas.

Cooper continued to cooperate actively with the official German news agency DNB in the early years of the war, instructing his Washington bureau chief in 1940 to intercede with the State Department on behalf of a DNB correspondent who needed a visa for the United States.[29] There were sound practical reasons for doing this: if AP did not offer assistance, "our facilities in Germany would have been cut off and probably our men would have been deported."[30] AP intended to continue its "loyal cooperation" with DNB as it had done with Wolff for fifty years and expected the same from DNB in return. Lochner, however, suspected that DNB's correspondent in New York sent back to Berlin "all the things he can lay his hands upon that in any way are unfavorable to us."[31] Praise for DNB's loyalty was hardly consistent with Lochner's suspicions and his detailed accounts of the agency's record of suppressing news and deliberately spreading falsehoods, including accusations against AP.

While Lochner and AP's news staff struggled under difficult conditions, AP's German-registered photographic subsidiary, whose employees were all licensed by the propaganda ministry, was directly implicated in Nazi propaganda activities both before and after 1939, as both Harriet Scharnberg and Norman Domeier have shown.[32] In the spring of 1941, Harold Ickes—Roosevelt's secretary of the interior and a prominent critic of the press[33]—expressed concern to Noyes about AP's photo operations and its news coverage. Ickes said he understood the difficulties that American correspondents working in Germany confronted: "But I sometimes wonder whether we would not be better off without dispatches from that country if the alternative is to be fed daily doses of arsenical propaganda."[34]

Ickes enclosed sections of a recent report he had seen about AP's activities in Germany; he did not identify the authors but assured Noyes they were "able and sincere men" whose only aim was "counteracting Nazi propaganda." During the First World War, he and others considered Lochner to be distinctly pro-German. The report cited Lochner's coverage of the rapid German advances a year earlier and concluded that he was "an easy victim for many a Nazi trap"—for example, by reporting that Belgians were "glad when the Germans arrived to liberate them from the British and French 'invaders' who looted their communities."[35] The report went on to outline the legal limitations under which AP's German subsidiary operated—including the requirement that all of its employees must be Aryan Germans—and identified one of its senior employees as "an ardent Nazi." One staff photographer was simultaneously a member of the German army's Propaganda Kompanie; another photographer employed by AP GmbH, Franz Roth, had to flee Austria in 1935 because of his activities on behalf of the illegal Austrian Nazi Party. (Roth was also a member of the SS Propaganda Kompanie.[36]) Other German citizens, similarly licensed by the propaganda ministry, worked in the news department. The report praised Lochner for "honestly striv[ing] at impeccable neutrality and . . . loyally serving American interests." He was "known to be opposed to Nazism" but had very close relations with high-ranking German military officers, and his efforts to gain the Nazis' favor had sometimes gone too far. More broadly, the authors questioned whether "American interests can be well served by maintaining an allegedly American news agency in Berlin which employs a predominantly German staff in both its news and news picture departments, and thus exposing itself to the direct influence of the Propaganda Ministry."

Noyes dismissed the report, declaring that whoever wrote it fundamentally misunderstood AP's mission.[37] Lochner (who had won a Pulitzer Prize in 1939) was doing a magnificent job. His reporting during the invasions of Holland, Belgium, and France was "tragically and prophetically true and the criticisms examples of wishful thinking." Lochner had not been deceived into sending propaganda "save as is done in transmitting official claims." Cooper was deeply grateful for this vote of confidence, repeating his strictly neutralist analysis: "Because of the majority pro-English feeling in this country it is only natural that our boys in Germany who are telling the truth are going to receive the brunt of criticism against [AP]."[38]

The report and Ickes's complaints were referred to the board of directors, which considered them for several hours.[39] Cooper identified many of the individual stories that were criticized and concluded that the information provided about them was "inaccurate, misleading, or not substantiated by the facts." Concerned that the report might be made public, McLean drew up the board's response, a broad denial.[40] He and the board fully agreed with Cooper's view that "controversial discussions arising at this time will only exacerbate the problem." No specific response was made to the allegations about the Nazi or

SS affiliations of employees of AP GmbH, and there is no indication that any discussion took place about the significant restrictions that journalists working in Germany faced.

Four days after the Japanese attack on Pearl Harbor brought the United States into the war, Lochner, four other American correspondents working for AP, and the remaining correspondents for other U.S. news organizations in Germany were arrested. They were detained for five months before returning to the United States in an exchange for German journalists similarly detained there.[41] John Evans, AP's foreign editor, noted that the stories AP correspondents filed after leaving Germany contained no new revelations, demonstrating that they had reported effectively while there: "Censorships and the over-emphasized fear of reprisals had never prevented the essential truth of things from getting out."[42] This observation failed, however, to acknowledge the importance of forceful contemporaneous reports of events, the chief stock in trade of any news agency. What might have been the effect on U.S. public opinion and political attitudes toward Germany if Lochner and his colleagues had reported everything they knew about Kristallnacht and other antisemitic atrocities as those events occurred? Would this have affected U.S. attitudes toward threatened democracies like Czechoslovakia and the embattled British-French alliance after 1939? These questions are impossible to answer. What is certain, however, is that part of the story of what went on inside Germany was conveyed to the readers of AP newspapers but by no means all of it, which was surely the purpose of the tight German control exercised over the activities of international journalists.

Limited though the coverage was, resourceful journalists like Lochner and his colleagues provided more information to the readers of AP newspapers than would have been available if they left Germany or were expelled, leaving Goebbels's propaganda ministry and the highly compromised DNB as the main sources of information. In that sense, the decision to continue operating under the Nazi regime's restrictions, exercising careful and continuous self-censorship to avoid expulsion, was defensible, even if critics like Ickes might legitimately raise questions about how much journalistic freedom was lost, and how many ethical compromises made, in the exchange. But the strength of this defense depended on knowing how extensive and substantial the compromises were. Cooper's repeated public assurances that Lochner and other AP journalists were operating "with freedom" and without (formal) censorship meant that the editors of some fourteen hundred AP newspapers, their millions of readers—and perhaps the directors as well, who relied on Cooper to describe the conditions that AP journalists inside Germany faced—knew very little about exactly which compromises were made, leaving them in no position to make accurate judgments about the adequacy of coverage. The editors of AP newspapers who charged that Lochner's reporting was too easy on the Nazi regime would have been more vociferous and probably more numerous if they knew more about the systematic regime of intimidation, pressure, and self-censorship that shaped it.

Why did Cooper consistently give a misleading public account of the restrictions on foreign journalists inside Germany? Clearly, he wanted the AP bureau in Berlin to remain in operation for as long as possible and may have believed that accurate public statements about press restrictions would bring retaliation of the kind he urged Lochner to avoid at all costs. But if that was Cooper's chief concern, remaining silent would have sufficed. Why make statements that were positively misleading? One explanation is that, in the face of criticism, Cooper wanted to assure the editors of AP newspapers and their readers of the quality and truthfulness of AP coverage. Cooper's anti-French views and insistence on U.S. neutrality after 1939 suggest another explanation: that he considered it possible—as many others did at the time[43]—that Germany would win the war. In that event, AP would want to be on at least neutral terms with the victorious Nazi regime in order to continue reporting from Germany and to have a continuing relationship with DNB, whose scope of operations outside Germany would expand significantly.

Taken together with AP's documented failings in the operation of its German photo subsidiary, Cooper's misleading statements about the restrictions on AP's main news operation suggest a further explanation: that AP in the 1930s was an immature organization in its international operations. AP had maintained its own correspondents in European capitals since the early 1900s, but its repudiation of the Reuters-led cartel in 1934 opened up a broad canvas of international possibilities, leading to major expansion after 1944. The international strategy was almost entirely Cooper's work. He had enormous discretion over how it was handled—specifically, over the balance among opening up foreign markets for AP news and photos; making, maintaining, or changing alliances with foreign news agencies; and defending AP's journalistic practices and reputation. Cooper did not have a sophisticated understanding of international affairs, and the judgments he made reflected his own somewhat isolationist views and immediate practical concerns rather than a thoughtful analysis of how a news agency that valued truthfulness, accuracy, and impartiality could or should operate in an increasingly authoritarian international environment. The board endorsed those Cooper-inspired trade-offs of which it was aware but—meeting only twice a year—was not in a position to exercise effective oversight. In any case, the journalistic accomplishments of AP's news staff in Germany were compromised by Cooper's systematically misleading account of the significant ways in which they were limited. Readers of AP news from Germany for most of the 1930s did not know they were receiving an account that was substantially constrained by the Nazis' elaborate formal and informal methods of press control. After the publication of Scharnberg's revelations about the extent of Nazi influence in AP's German photo subsidiary, AP commissioned an in-depth report on the operations of its Berlin bureau between 1933 and 1941. One of its recommendations was that AP should be "transparent with staff and the outside world about what compromises if any have been made for access to a leader, or a government, and be willing to justify them."[44] This was emphatically not done at the time, mostly because of Cooper, and the board did not exercise any meaningful independent supervision.

*   *   *

Along with censorship restrictions, the beginning of war in Europe presented new problems with costs and competition. Finding alternative channels for news from Europe in the wake of Britain's clampdown on all outgoing cable traffic was an immediate challenge.[45] Throughout the fall of 1939, AP scrambled to establish direct channels from Berlin, Paris, Rome, and other European capitals as the volume of transatlantic copy soared to five times its normal rate. Losing ground to United Press was a major concern. "London exasperatingly slow," Cooper complained in mid-September in an urgent telegram to AP's chief European news executive. "Being beaten Berlin [and] Paris frequently."[46]

The unprecedented volume of coverage, combined with the need to cobble together alternative channels for the prompt transmission of news, led to a sharp increase in costs for AP and for its rivals.[47] UP and INS responded by raising their fees substantially, while AP did not—prompting anger among the private agencies' subscribers and expressions of gratitude to AP. After several months of phony war, the spectacularly successful German blitzkrieg attacks on Denmark, Belgium, the Netherlands, and France in May 1940 brought to a head the tension between keeping costs under control and not being beaten on news coverage. Early in May, the publisher of the *Daily Oklahoman* demanded an explanation for the "terrible beating" that AP suffered at UP's hands when

Belgium and the Netherlands were invaded.[48] Cooper acknowledged that AP had been behind on the landing of German paratroopers in both countries but was ahead by two days in reporting that the German army was marching to occupy the Netherlands and by lesser amounts on other major stories. Overall, he estimated, AP was ahead of its rivals about 75 percent of the time, and this could not be raised to 100 percent even if AP increased its spending tenfold.[49]

For more than a year, Cooper and AP took pride in telling members that AP's economies made it unnecessary to increase assessments to meet the high costs of war coverage. By the beginning of 1941, however, Cooper argued that it was time to recoup some of the $1.2 million cut from members' assessments during the depths of the Depression. AP's basic service had improved in many ways since then, he told the board of directors, all at no additional cost to members: better (and better-paid) writers; an improved feature service and basic photo service; a greatly expanded Washington bureau, providing more coverage of developments affecting individual states and increased state-level coverage generally; a larger sports staff; the establishment of departments to cover finance, science, the arts, and other specialized subjects; adoption of a five-day week for employees; and doubling of the foreign staff. The extra costs of war coverage were on top of all this. AP's recent decision to allow the sale of its news to radio stations brought in some extra revenue, but this would not reach an appreciable amount for four or five years. Meanwhile, UP had not cut its basic fees in the 1930s as AP did, was currently receiving around $1.5 million a year in radio revenue, and had recently raised its rates by 15 percent. "I shudder to think what could have happened . . . if the enormous additional collections of our competitor had been applied to improve its news services," Cooper told the board of directors.[50] Early in 1941 the board approved the recommended increase, recouping about half of the 1932 reduction.[51]

*   *   *

Despite his vow while undergoing treatment at the Mayo Clinic to rein in his "petulance and impatience," Cooper's expressions of dissatisfaction became louder in the early 1940s. Eight years after his rapturous reception at the first AP managing editors meeting, his remarks to the group in 1941, ostensibly humorous, were strikingly bitter. Cooper expressed astonishment at the volume of criticism directed toward AP; newcomers to the gathering were "shocked to hear you say the service is so rotten, with hardly a favorable comment."[52] In fact, AP was "the finest flower in the journalistic garden of the world." The only thing preventing it from coming to "full and radiant bloom" was that AP members "and you, their managing editors, are 90% to blame, because of their lack and your lack of interest and their and your lethargy." He ended by musing aloud that "when I am fired or when I quit, whichever comes first," he might adopt a suggestion by his friend Deac Aylesworth, the president of NBC, who, on the day of his retirement, wanted to make a live statement over the whole network that "all you bastards out there who think you know it all can go to hell." Additional remarks that Cooper prepared but did not deliver showed that he still regretted the decision not to accept Roy Howard's offer to return to United Press in 1916 with a promise of advancement to the top position. If he had accepted the offer, UP and not AP would now have Wirephoto; AP would never have "throw[n] off the shackles by which Reuters and the allied agencies" kept it confined to North America; and Frederick Roy Martin would still be AP's general manager.

Cooper's relationship with McLean was occasionally warm but at other times close to being dysfunctional. At one point in the early 1940s, Alan Gould recalled, Cooper "abruptly decided that he would delegate to Lloyd Stratton all contact" with McLean:[53] "It was incredible. McLean would telephone Cooper's office and ask for KC and the answer was that he was not available and they wished he would talk with Mr. Stratton." In April 1943, while Cooper was on his annual winter retreat in Palm Beach, McLean expressed great concern that for several months "there appears to have developed a feeling of restraint in your and my relationship which I have been unable to pierce."[54]

> For the sake of the whole organization it is important that we should operate in an atmosphere of mutual confidence and, I hope, cordiality. If that is difficult for any reason it is important to know what obstacles stand in the way and I trust we can sit down frankly and talk it out.

When McLean complained in 1945 about the poor organization and choppiness of an AP story based on a U.S. military briefing in Guam, Cooper's reply had a testy, patronizing edge. Without checking the story in question, he informed McLean (as if McLean did not know) that an AP reporter faced "thousands of edition times"—not just a single deadline that the reporter for an individual newspaper had to meet—and had to write the story as it developed. If AP's reporter waited until he could "compose himself a nice little piece in a workmanlike manner, it would get in late compared with the competition. Perhaps you think this should be done; or do you?"[55] This hardly reflected the instruction Cooper recently issued to bureau chiefs to welcome suggestions or criticism from AP member newspapers enthusiastically, making clear "that it is just what you wanted."[56]

Cooper was unhappy about his title as general manager as well. He had avoided using the term for the past few years, he told Noyes in 1941.[57] The general manager's only function was to direct the news report—something Cooper had been less and less involved with since 1937—while he had been occupied with "a great many other things, either corporate or blazing new trails." He was given the additional title of executive director in 1943, which he considered a more accurate description of his role.[58] This also allowed Cooper to remain AP's top executive even after he gave up the general manager's job five years later. His 1941 salary, almost $64,000 (roughly equivalent to $1.1 million in 2020), was more than three times higher than that of any other AP executive.[59]

At one point in the late 1930s, Cooper considered retirement, but those plans were abandoned in the wake of personal and institutional developments.[60] Immediately after the Japanese attack on Pearl Harbor brought the United States into the war in December 1941, Price—widely seen as Cooper's likeliest successor—was appointed U.S. director of censorship, responsible directly to Roosevelt.[61] Alan Gould, Price's replacement as executive editor, was well-regarded as a newsman but never a candidate for the top job, leaving AP with no obvious general-manager-in-waiting.[62] After Cooper's divorce from his second wife, Marian, in 1940, he complained that he was wiped out by the financial settlement, telling Gould that now "he couldn't afford to retire."[63]

Cooper's marriage in February 1942 to Sally Gibbs, formerly his executive secretary for almost twenty years, gave him another reason for wanting to maintain his income. Cooper kept news of the marriage, which took place while he was in Florida for his usual winter sojourn, largely to himself, informing the small group of executives who met with him every morning in AP's Rockefeller Center boardroom only on the day the ceremony took place.[64] In an unusually emotional and self-revelatory note, Cooper described Sally as the only person who had kept him from leaving AP while Martin was general manager. One day in the early 1920s, Cooper recalled, she told him not to lose patience and informed him of "an obvious conclusion"—that he would soon become general manager—demonstrating an "enduring philosophy of patience and detached reassurance the likes of which I have never seen." Over the next twenty years, she "never once faltered in trying to make my plans succeed." During this time, Cooper asked her several times to marry him—some of these proposals must have been offered while he was still married to Marian—but she refused. When he thanked Sally for her loyalty to him, she replied that she was primarily loyal to AP and that Cooper was simply an "incident." Now, he told his colleagues, "I am going to be an 'incident' no longer. . . . I am going to transfer her loyalty from the A.P. to me and with such devotion and affection as I am capable of I am going to make her like it." For her part, Sally confided to Lloyd Stratton that she intended to make the mercurial Cooper "the happiest man in the world. . . . I know that is a task, but I think I know his moods, his weaknesses and his strength."[65]

For Cooper, now sixty-two, his new marriage brought a degree of personal contentment that he had not known for many years. "I can't remember ever being as happy in my life as I am now," he told McLean.[66] One manifestation was a prolonged burst of musical creativity. As a young man, Cooper had dabbled in composing popular music. Now, after years of inactivity, he churned out song after song: in 1942 alone, "I'll Not Forget," "Love Is," "The Magic of the Violin," "They'll Make Love Our Way!," and "Yankee Doodle Dixie Dandy."[67] Cooper's rapidly growing catalog of songs also played a part in his increasingly close friendship with McCormick, who arranged for Cooper's music to be broadcast on the *Tribune*'s radio station WGN and other stations on the Mutual network. This culminated in WGN and Mutual's 1943 broadcast of *About the Girl*, an operetta written and composed by Cooper.[68] The plot involved "vigorous outdoor action of the Alaska Highway builders and machination of saboteurs . . . set against a backdrop of romance."[69] Cooper was deeply grateful to McCormick, declaring somewhat rhetorically that the broadcast brought him "the only fame I shall ever have. . . . I shall never forget your sincere friendship."[70]

Cooper increasingly expressed sympathy with McCormick's political views. "I can't stand the Williams broadcasts any better than you can," he wrote in October 1940 in response to McCormick's criticism of Wythe Williams, a Mutual network commentator who strongly supported Roosevelt's lend-lease policy of providing armaments to Britain.[71] On one WGN broadcast in August 1941, McCormick charged that poorly trained American soldiers could not "defend themselves for a day" against German forces.[72] Cooper, forewarned by McCormick's office, assigned an AP reporter to write a story on his remarks, adding that he listened to McCormick's Saturday broadcasts whenever he could because "I think what you are doing is a great undertaking admirably accomplished. Saturday night you were at your best and of course what you said was entirely true."[73] But Cooper also continued to defend aspects of AP's news coverage that irritated McCormick, such as referring to Britain and France as "allies": "As they are allies and they frequently refer to themselves as allies, we have to use that term occasionally," he observed with mild reasonableness. He also held McCormick to account for violations of AP policy, as when he forwarded a complaint that an AP story's reference to "President Roosevelt's 'Lend-Lease' Bill" had been changed in the *Tribune* to "President Roosevelt's dictator bill."[74] On another occasion, a board member complained that the phrase "target of a New Deal purge campaign" had been added to an AP story in the *Tribune* referring to Republican senator Gerald Nye, a prominent isolationist.[75] The unnamed director, Cooper wrote, considered this a "violation of the assurances that you gave a couple of years ago that such paragraphs would be bracketed if inserted or else left out entirely." None of this, however, seems to have affected their developing friendship. When McCormick congratulated Cooper on his marriage in 1942, he replied that matrimony was one of the two most important things that had happened to him in the past year—the other being "really getting acquainted with you. . . . I am always yours to command."[76] As 1943 came to an end, McCormick sent Cooper "a line to say that I consider you one of my Christmas presents of this year."[77] Nonetheless, in McCormick's eyes there remained a substantial difference in status between himself and AP's most senior employee, who was "after all . . . always inferior to the board members."[78]

* * *

In the spring of 1945, AP and Cooper became embroiled in a major journalistic controversy, one that left its members bitterly divided and its reputation for integrity in doubt. It began with what appeared to be the biggest scoop imaginable: an exclusive report on May 7 that the Second World War in Europe was over. "Germany surrendered unconditionally to the Western allies and Russia at 2:41 a.m. French time today," AP's Paris bureau chief Edward Kennedy reported.[79] His story was an eyewitness account of the surrender being signed at Eisenhower's headquarters (known as SHAEF, for Supreme Headquarters Allied Expeditionary Force) in Reims, France. Soon after the report began appearing on the front pages of American, British, and French newspapers, however, Allied headquarters announced that no official statement about the surrender had been issued, and AP was peremptorily cut off from all communication facilities in the European theater.[80] Cooper immediately sent a cable of protest to Eisenhower, saying that AP had not received any notice of the suspension or the reasons for it.[81] The blanket suspension was lifted after seven hours, but Kennedy and two AP colleagues were forbidden from using any military communication channels, which meant that in the crucial early hours of the controversy, AP was unable to get any explanation from Kennedy of what had happened. In the meantime, other, highly critical accounts of Kennedy's actions came flooding out of Paris. In a letter to Eisenhower, fifty-four war correspondents denounced Kennedy for breaking a pledge not to send news of the surrender until it was officially released and demanded that the ban on all AP communications be reinstated.[82] Brig. Gen. Frank Allen, the officer in charge of public relations for Allied headquarters, accused Kennedy of breaking a promise to maintain secrecy until the surrender was officially announced, using "unauthorized methods of communication in order to commit his deliberate violation," and endangering the lives of U.S. troops.[83]

The charge that Kennedy had broken his word was a product of the unusual circumstances around the surrender ceremony. On May 6 Allen summoned seventeen journalists to an airfield in Paris, where they boarded a military plane. Once in the air, Allen informed them that they were going to Allied headquarters to witness the German surrender and had them pledge not to release the news until it was officially announced.[84] All, including Kennedy, agreed. As Kennedy noted in his memoir, this provision was not unusual—it was one among hundreds of cases during the war when news was given to correspondents with the stipulation that it could not be disseminated until officially released. On arrival in Reims, the correspondents witnessed two senior German officers signing the surrender documents in the presence of U.S., British, and Russian officers. They were then told that the news would not be released until 3 p.m. local time on May 8—some thirty-six hours later.[85] In Kennedy's account of events, Allen told the correspondents that Eisenhower wanted the news released earlier, but his hands were tied at "high political levels" and nothing could be done about it.[86] When Kennedy returned to Paris, army public relations officers told him that the Russians wanted the surrender to be announced later in Berlin, where they would then be the occupying power.[87]

Just after 2 p.m. on May 7—still more than twenty-four hours before the official release time—Germany's provisional government announced the unconditional surrender in a radio broadcast addressed "to the men and women of Germany."[88] The provisional government was based in Flensburg, a city under Allied occupation on the German-Danish border, and Kennedy knew that the broadcast would not have been permitted without approval from Eisenhower's headquarters. He concluded that SHAEF had authorized the Germans to release the news in order to end German military resistance and save lives. Kennedy told the chief U.S. military censor in Paris that he was no longer obliged to maintain secrecy; once a release agreement was broken by anyone, it was "the universal practice . . . to regard the news as released generally and to proceed with its publication."[89] (Alan Gould, who held AP's top news position at the time, endorsed this view: "In and out of war, at home and abroad, once a major story has been broken by a major organization, then all bets are off and all restrictions." So did Wes Gallagher, who replaced Kennedy as Paris bureau chief in 1945 and became AP's general manager in 1962.[90]) Furthermore, Kennedy concluded that the news was being withheld for political reasons, not on the basis of military security. In view of Eisenhower's assurance that there would be no political censorship of news, its release was justified on these grounds as well.[91] The censor told Kennedy to do as he pleased, believing that the AP correspondent was simply letting off steam and that it would be impossible for him to get around military censorship of all outgoing communication channels.

This assumption was incorrect. Correspondents had regularly been allowed, on an informal basis, to use the military telephone system, which was not subject to censorship. Kennedy knew that he could place an unmonitored call to the AP bureau in London through the Paris military switchboard and did so.[92] He dictated about three hundred words before the line failed. The London bureau then forwarded the story to New York using a stamp that exempted it from British military censorship because it was "in transit" from another military theater and had—presumably, but in this case not actually—been cleared there.[93] Kennedy was later criticized for not consulting his superiors at AP before filing the story, but it is difficult to see how he could have done so. The back-channel military phone connection to London had gone dead after a few minutes; if Kennedy had used this channel to seek advice instead, it would have been at the expense of reporting the momentous news of the surrender. Communicating with AP headquarters through regular channels would have allowed U.S. military censors to stop the story from being sent. In his unpublished history of AP, John Hightower concluded that Cooper "ignored the realities of censorship" when he eventually insisted that Kennedy should have told New York about his plans.[94]

Cooper's initial reaction—before he knew anything about how the story had been sent or why AP had been suspended—was to congratulate Kennedy. "Wish you were here to help read the staggering pile of messages commending you," he telegraphed on May 7.[95] But in the wake of fierce criticism from the U.S. military authorities and Kennedy's fellow correspondents—many of whom worked for influential AP members—Cooper's position became more complicated. In a confidential report to the board of directors on May 8, Cooper argued that the hold-for-release agreement that Kennedy and others had accepted was far from being sacrosanct. The time may have come, he wrote, "when government, or even military authority, may so far project autocratic actions as to render ridiculous the zealous application by the press of its self-imposed rule respecting observing a confidence." An AP reporter was the casualty this time, but "the entire press may ultimately be the casualty if the press does not apply its self-imposed rules with reasoned judgment, as well as with conscience."[96] Cooper also telegraphed the War Department in Washington, drawing attention to the "avalanche of comment[s] favorable to Kennedy and Associated Press and entirely unfavorable to military authorities" from AP members.[97] To an AP publisher who suggested that members contribute to a fund to reward Kennedy, Cooper replied, "You know me well enough to feel certain that Kennedy will be rewarded to his complete satisfaction."[98] The next day, however, responding to charges that Kennedy had violated a confidence, he issued a public statement saying that "observance of all obligations voluntarily assumed has been, and will continue to be a cardinal principle of The Associated Press and its employees."[99] But he had not had an opportunity to speak to Kennedy in person or to the military authorities and would not prejudge the case.

Cooper's attempt to withhold judgment was torpedoed on May 10 when McLean issued an unqualified apology, repudiating Kennedy's actions. AP, he wrote, "profoundly regrets" the distribution of the surrender story, "which investigation now clearly discloses was distributed in advance of authorization." AP's "whole, long, honorable record" was based on "the observance of obligations voluntarily assumed"—quoting part of Cooper's statement but omitting his insistence on not rushing to judgment.[100] AP members were profoundly divided: some denounced Kennedy; some complained about McLean's statement; and others praised Kennedy for, as one Texas editor wrote, acting "in full keeping with the traditions of a free press in the United States. . . . The news of the people's victory was not the property of either the politicians or Army brass hats to barter."[101] AP carried a running roundup of editorial comments from member newspapers, about evenly divided between pro- and anti-Kennedy opinions.

SHAEF announced on May 14 that Kennedy was disaccredited as a war correspondent and had been ordered to return to the United States. By now, Cooper was coming around to the position that he would maintain for the rest of this controversial period: Kennedy should have told his superiors about his plan before filing the story.[102] But as McLean adopted an increasingly critical position, encouraged by Sulzberger and Noyes, he and Cooper were increasingly at odds.[103] McLean was concerned that some AP members "place their judgment of what the public is entitled to know—and when the public is entitled to know it—above that of even the highest constituted authority," and he asked whether Cooper's advocacy of press freedom had led AP staff to think "that they are carrying a torch for the newspapers and the public."[104] Noyes wanted Kennedy fired and McLean was leaning strongly in this direction, although other AP directors disagreed.[105] In response, Cooper noted that McLean's repudiation of Kennedy was generally seen as a disavowal of his position that the case should not be prejudged but acknowledged that it was perfectly proper for McLean to use his own judgment in speaking on behalf of the members.[106] McLean, meanwhile, told an AP member who supported Kennedy that in issuing the condemnation, he had to act quickly, "doing promptly that which it was obvious it was going to be necessary to do sooner or later."[107]

Cooper also asked McLean to forward any comments that were critical of him specifically.[108] McLean obliged, relating his conversations with Arthur Page, a vice president of AT&T who was working for the Truman administration in a public relations capacity. Page had told McLean that the tone of Cooper's initial telegrams to Eisenhower and the secretary of war, "and the general vigor of your offensive before it was possible to judge completely what had happened," had made the situation worse.[109] "Perhaps it was my duty just to take it," Cooper replied, "not ask for an answer, not to make any protest and wait. That would have been satisfactory to the military and to Mr. Page. However, I did not do it."[110] An editorial in the *Philadelphia Inquirer* denounced Cooper for bombarding Eisenhower with "petulant, peremptory messages" at a time when the allied commander was "up to his ears" winning the war.[111] Cooper was feeling the weight of disapproval. "I am in the position of having been dissected by adverse comment and affectionately and feelingly sewed up by favorable comment," he wrote to Sulzberger. "Though the body is still in one piece it is curious to know: Who is to administer the coup de grace?"[112]

Hoping to keep the controversy under control, AP refused to make any public statement about Kennedy's status—a stance that was to be maintained for the next year—but this only raised more questions. AP's Philadelphia bureau chief reported that he had been plagued by questions about Kennedy at a recent gathering of Pennsylvania members but was told that AP had no further comments on the case.[113] After Kennedy returned to the United States, AP said only that his status was "inactive."[114]

On arrival back in New York, Kennedy damaged his already shaky position further. Asked by reporters whether he thought he had been in the right, he replied, "I'd do it again if I had the chance."[115] In a subsequent interview with *Editor & Publisher*, he insisted that he was not "bellowing defiance" and added an important qualification: he would have sent the story, "but with the flat statement that it was not passed by SHAEF censors, so that [AP] would have known exactly what it was." This was close to an acknowledgment that he accepted Cooper's criticism of his failure to inform AP about the unusual circumstances surrounding the story, but the concession seemed to have come too late.

By this point Cooper was saying that he had agreed with McLean all along, and his aim was to bring about "the termination of [Kennedy's] services as inconspicuously as I could."[116] At a board of directors meeting in October 1945, Cooper reported that Kennedy's employment with AP would end as of October 31; the board unanimously approved.[117] Cooper also realized that at least as many AP members believed that Kennedy had acted properly as did not. Any publicity about his firing "would have stirred up both sides . . . and would not have been a good thing for AP." Cooper had not had any contact with Kennedy since July, but his executive assistant, Claude Jagger, did speak to Kennedy in September, who reportedly said that he wanted "just one more month."[118] On this basis, a check marked as severance pay was deposited into his bank account on September 30. Kennedy, however, insisted that he had never been told he was being fired and refused to cash the check. Again, no public statement was made.

With McLean's peremptory and essentially premature judgment that Kennedy was in the wrong (valuing deference to authority well above journalistic initiative), Cooper's shifting account of what Kennedy should have done, and AP's evasiveness about his status, its handling of the Kennedy affair was questionable enough at the time. It appeared worse in retrospect. In July 1946, Senator Sheridan Downey, a Democrat from California, told the Senate that Eisenhower had reviewed the suspension of Kennedy's credentials and would not prevent him from being reaccredited as a correspondent covering the U.S. military in future.[119] The War Department continued to believe that the original decision was justified and did not rescind it, but Eisenhower clearly held no grudge, wishing Kennedy every success. Downey also tabled a memorandum from Eisenhower's chief of staff stating explicitly that SHAEF had ordered the German provisional government to broadcast news of the surrender, confirming Kennedy's contention that SHAEF itself had broken the embargo.[120] Kennedy, who had made no public statements since the original *Editor & Publisher* interview a year earlier, now said only that Eisenhower's action "speaks for itself."

Kennedy's firing did not become public knowledge until his military credentials were reinstated. The AP story on Senator Downey's statement added somewhat cryptically in the second-to-last paragraph that Kennedy "has been doing free lance work and writing a book."[121] This indirect acknowledgment that Kennedy was no longer with AP prompted angry inquiries from some AP members. Jack Harris of the *Hutchinson (KS) News-Herald* told Cooper that additional details about where Kennedy was and what he was doing should have been included in the story as a matter of routine. But a fellow editor who asked for such details was told there would be no further comment. "Isn't this deliberate news suppression at the source of the very sort against which the AP has been leading a worldwide fight, and hasn't the AP been hoist by its own petard?" Harris asked.[122] *Editor & Publisher* provided some additional details, notably that Kennedy had offered to resign several times but was refused—presumably because this would have led to unwelcome publicity—and that he had never been officially told that he was fired.[123]

AP remained sensitive for years about criticism of the way it had treated Kennedy. In the summer of 1947, *Editor & Publisher* declared in an editorial that Kennedy's story "will go down in the books as one of the greatest journalistic beats in history."[124] McLean immediately proposed that the publication's editor be told why he was wrong.[125] Cooper agreed, and a lunch was duly organized where McLean, Cooper, Stratton, and other senior news executives told Bob Brown, the editor, that "he was wrong and why."[126] The next year, Kennedy wrote a detailed account of the incident for *The Atlantic*, provocatively titled "I'd Do It Again."[127] Here he argued that while around four-fifths of newspaper editorials and personal letters supported his actions, the *New York Times*, which "was powerful in the Associated Press directorate . . . applied strong pressure on McLean." Cooper, Kennedy wrote, refused either to accept his resignation or to fire him outright, suggesting instead that Kennedy admit he was wrong and ask for forgiveness, which Kennedy rejected as a "false and cowardly way out."

Eight years later, the now-retired Cooper published his own account of the Kennedy affair in his book *The Right to Know*. He sought to appear evenhanded, saying the incident involved both "history's most flagrant misuse of military censorship" as well as the most flagrant instance of its violation, and neither could be justified. He acknowledged that Kennedy did not file his story until after news of the surrender had been broadcast, with Allied approval, by the German provisional government—a crucial element in Kennedy's own defense of his actions. But Cooper did not mention the journalistic practice of treating an agreement to hold news until officially released as nullified once the embargo had been broken by anyone (much less by its own authors, as in this case). He asserted that McLean's explicit denunciation of Kennedy's actions did not undermine his own position that Kennedy should have an opportunity to explain his actions before any judgment was made, contradicting his statement to McLean at the time.[128] Kennedy's fatal errors were that he violated a pledge of confidence that the military authorities considered to be still in force (although Kennedy had told the chief military censor in Paris what he was going to do) and that on returning to New York said he would do the same thing again. Cooper also stressed that Kennedy had left his supervisors "in the dark" by filing the story without any notice about its irregular nature.[129]

Kennedy responded in an article for the North American Newspaper Alliance, a feature syndicate serving many AP newspapers.[130] In the many years of Cooper's pronouncements about freedom of the press, Kennedy wrote, this was the only occasion when his convictions were put to a serious test, and Cooper "equivocated for a long time and then furtively lined up with elements which had taken a stand against the right of the people to know." Cooper's account was greatly distorted, with facts misstated and essential information omitted. The insistence that Kennedy should have informed Cooper about what he was doing was not only impractical given the poor telephone connection to London; as an AP bureau chief in other places, Kennedy had frequently sent sensitive stories with no explanation and on those occasions had been congratulated. Only when "one came along that required stamina on the home front" did Cooper—after the fact—decide that a preliminary note was essential. (Kennedy's UP counterpart from 1945 had a less flattering version of those earlier instances, saying Kennedy had previously violated censorship in Egypt, Italy, and southern France, "and got away with it. Why should he shrink at Reims when the stakes were greater in every way?"[131]) A few months later, Cooper's successor, Frank Starzel, sharply reprimanded an AP bureau chief for giving a speech that dealt with the Kennedy affair, noting that publication of *The Right to Know* had "revived the story and then it was the subject of some bitter exchanges."[132] At the time, the Kennedy incident "created a serious schism in the membership and your statements likely will cause another uproar." Eleven years after V-E Day, AP was still trying to tamp down the controversy, aptly described by AP's former CEO Tom Curley and historian John Maxwell Hamilton as "one of the worst moments in AP history."[133]

10

"The Government Suit"

For AP's critics, the bylaw that gave existing members the right to exclude new competitors made it responsible for journalistic monopolies in cities across the United States.[1] The rule had been declared illegal in 1900 when the Illinois Supreme Court ruled that AP, then based in Chicago, improperly monopolized the supply of news. In response, AP moved its headquarters to New York and reincorporated under the much more forgiving terms of New York State's membership corporation law, often used—as critics regularly pointed out—to incorporate hunting and fishing clubs.[2] In 1915 the U.S. attorney general concluded that it was not a violation of new federal antitrust laws for AP to withhold membership from some newspapers.[3] After this, while there were major battles within AP over the application of the right of protest,[4] the basic structure went unchallenged for more than twenty years.

The Roosevelt administration's shift away from the early New Deal emphasis on economic coordination and toward vigorous enforcement of antitrust laws in the later 1930s set the stage for renewed scrutiny.[5] In the spring of 1939, Robert McLean reported to the board of directors that the Department of Justice had started, but subsequently called off, an investigation to determine whether AP exercised a monopoly.[6] A year later, the board heard that Robert McCormick's cousin Eleanor (Cissy) Patterson, who had recently bought two Hearst newspapers in Washington, D.C., and merged them as the *Washington Times-Herald*, threatened to take legal action after she was unable to obtain AP news. Thurman Arnold, the trust-busting assistant attorney general, urged Patterson to file a formal antitrust complaint, she told AP's annual meeting in 1942, but as a fourth-generation newspaper publisher, she "didn't like the smell of it, and . . . refused to act."[7] The real conflict came in Chicago, where McCormick's *Tribune* was the only morning newspaper in the city after Hearst's *Herald and Examiner* ceased weekday morning publication in 1939.[8]

In April 1941, McCormick brought a resolution to the board of directors that launched Cooper into an important new role as a public champion of international press freedom (at least as defined by AP). This "crusade," as Cooper later described it, was inextricably tied up with three major issues that AP faced during the rest of the decade: the antitrust litigation, which eventually began in 1942; AP's ambitious plans for global expansion after 1945, bringing to fruition the quest for international freedom of action that Cooper had pursued since 1918; and Cooper's ultimately successful struggle to prevent AP news from being used in what he considered government propaganda services, notably the Voice of America, as the Cold War took shape in the later 1940s.[9]

McCormick's resolution called for a narrative to be written outlining AP's role "in opening up the world to the circulation of free and unbiased news"—something McCormick had strongly supported for years.[10] This book, he said, would be

> of tremendous value at this time for the public to know the part taken by [AP] in changing the history of news coverage by agencies in foreign countries; the successive steps that transformed a rigidly controlled individual or agency news service, to the free exchange of news between all countries, and especially to the international distribution of Associated Press news.

The suggestion that the book would influence public opinion in AP's favor was significant. McCormick had heard rumors beginning in 1939 that Marshall Field III, heir to the Marshall Field department store chain and a strong supporter of Roosevelt, was planning to purchase the struggling *Chicago Herald and Examiner* in order to compete directly with the *Tribune*. Nothing came of this, but in the spring of 1941, Field was discussing the possible purchase of two other newspapers in Chicago.[11] As the chief financial backer of *PM*, a New York daily with a strong liberal bent, Field was already a controversial figure in the newspaper world, and it did not take much imagination to see him bankrolling a strong competitor—both in commercial and political terms—to the ultraconservative *Tribune*. But unless Field could purchase a Chicago morning paper that already had an AP membership, the *Tribune* could prevent him from getting AP news and photos. McCormick, it seems likely, anticipated that the Justice Department could bring an antitrust action against AP if that occurred. Certainly when *Barriers Down*, the book that was the result of McCormick's resolution, was published, both he and Cooper saw it as an important part of AP's public relations response to the antitrust case that eventually arose from Field's launch of the *Chicago Sun* in December 1941. "I was charged with raising the issue of international press freedom to defeat the government's aim against [AP]," Cooper declared in a public speech in 1945.[12] When the manuscript was completed at the end of 1942, McCormick urged Cooper to delay its release until "two or three days before the [antitrust] trial opens," thus guaranteeing "a barrage of literary reviews all thru the trial."[13]

*   *   *

The first edition of Field's *Chicago Sun* appeared on December 6, 1941, the day before the Japanese attack on Pearl Harbor brought the United States into World War II. AP news and photos were conspicuously absent. The new paper, the advertising trade magazine *TIDE* reported, "will support the New Deal top to bottom, especially on foreign affairs."[14] Chicago had a substantial audience that was "vociferously demanding a new morning paper"—around one hundred thousand people had recently signed a petition calling for an alternative to the isolationist *Tribune*. After a first-day press run of almost nine hundred thousand copies, daily circulation stabilized at around three hundred thousand—by no means as much as the behemoth *Tribune* but a solid basis for continuing publication.[15]

Field applied for AP membership in September, soon after publicly announcing his plans to publish in Chicago.[16] He also discussed the project with Roosevelt—with whom he had a strong connection as chairman of the FDR-supporting Business Men's League and president of the United States Committee for the Care of European Children, whose honorary chair was Eleanor Roosevelt.[17] The president welcomed the news; at his instruction, press secretary Stephen Early replied to a citizen complaining about isolationist news coverage that the new publication would give Chicago readers "a newspaper in which they can find the news truthfully printed."[18]

The response to Field's inquiry about AP membership was predictable. Since waivers of the protest right had not been obtained from the *Tribune*, the *Herald*

American (which still held the rights to a morning franchise in Chicago after the *Herald and Examiner* ceased weekday morning publication), and the *Daily News*, the board of directors could not act on the application.[19] It could not even be considered until AP's next annual meeting in April 1942, and even then the application would be accepted only if four-fifths of AP members present voted to override the protests. Complaining to Cooper about the delay, Field forwarded a legal opinion that AP's membership rules amounted to "a contract or combination in restraint of trade."[20] At the invitation of McLean—who wanted the record to show AP's willingness to deal with the application "in a fully considerate manner"—Field and the *Sun*'s publisher met the board's executive committee, reporting that they were negotiating to buy the weekday morning AP franchise of the *Herald American*.[21] The attempt was unsuccessful, however, with Field offering $250,000 for the membership and Hearst demanding $1 million.[22] The day before the *Sun*'s first edition appeared, Field complained to McLean that the inability to obtain AP news and photos was a severe handicap and proposed that until the *Sun*'s membership application could be considered, AP should make available the news and photo services that it was selling to nonmember radio groups and nonmember newspapers. (AP had decided earlier that year to sell its news to radio stations whether they were connected to AP newspapers or not.[23]) Each additional day's delay "causes damage to me and to The Chicago Sun," Field wrote.[24] Adding to the pressure, Thurman Arnold told Field that the appearance of a new paper in Chicago, "is an exceedingly welcome bit of news to the Antitrust Division," especially in view of Field's "disinterestedness and objective attitude toward public affairs, your sincere patriotism and your devotion to public welfare."[25] McLean—who was AP's chief interlocutor with the government in the case—noted after a meeting with the attorney general, Francis Biddle, that "very great pressure was being brought on everybody connected with AP in Field's behalf."[26]

AP's response to the prospect of an antitrust suit was chaotic, reflecting deep internal divisions and much wishful thinking. Most members had protest rights that allowed them to exclude new competitors and did not want to give up this advantage. An exclusive local franchise was an asset that had monetary value, as Field's $250,000 offer for a Chicago membership had recently shown.[27] On the other hand, AP's lawyers advised that an antitrust prosecution would probably be successful, which, members were warned at the 1942 annual meeting, could lead to "the dissolution of the corporation, thus jeopardizing the existing rights of all members and impairing the value of their newspaper properties."[28]

The crucial question was whether AP members were willing to make revisions to the bylaws that would either forestall an antitrust prosecution entirely or strengthen AP's position enough that it could be defended in court.

The board of directors was sharply divided, with McLean supporting a broad liberalization that would allow the *Chicago Sun* (and any other newcomer in a large city) into membership and McCormick bitterly opposing the *Sun's* admission.[29] Complicating matters further, a committee of members appointed in 1940 to consider changes to the membership rules insisted on making its own recommendations regardless of what the board of directors decided. This group wanted to accept new competitors on payment of a substantial sum to the established newspaper as compensation for a reduction in the value of its exclusive franchise.[30] Cooper, meanwhile, had his own agenda. He wanted change, describing the existing rules as "a monstrosity . . . inconsistent, contradictory."[31] But he was not particularly concerned, at least in late 1941 and early 1942, about the possibility of an antitrust suit. Instead, he mainly wanted to make it easier for the fifteen afternoon papers that now relied on United Press or other services for their Sunday editions to get access to AP despite the opposition of morning members in those cities.

Although Cooper insisted in public that he was not involved in AP's deliberations about membership matters, he had a major role behind the scenes. As the board struggled to develop a resolution for the 1942 annual meeting that would not bring it into open conflict with the members' committee, Cooper proposed his own solution. The right of protest would be abolished and a new member could be elected by a simple majority of those attending the annual meeting. The newcomer would be required to pay the established newspaper(s) 10 percent of the total assessments levied in that city since 1900, which, in a place like New York or Chicago, would amount to a substantial sum (around five hundred thousand dollars for a paper in Chicago, by Cooper's estimate).[32] The justification was that a new member would benefit from previous payments that built up AP's resources and organizational strength and should be required to make its own contribution. Arthur Moynihan, AP's attorney, pointed out clearly (and correctly) that the Department of Justice would see this simply as an attempt to assign cash value to the right to exclude a competitor, an obvious violation of antitrust law. The payment would not be required in cities where no competing AP newspaper was already in operation—a fatal flaw, showing that the value of AP membership "is due to nothing except the protest rights." But this potent objection was ignored.

Cooper also proposed an additional requirement that he expected no would-be competitor would accept. Any service to which the new entrant had exclusive rights—including comic strips and other popular features—would have to be made available to every established AP member in that field. "Nobody is eligible who has got exclusive contracts for services that are competitive with [AP] unless he says that he will throw his open in exchange for getting into the Associated Press, and that he won't do," Cooper told the board. "None of them will do it."[33] The new member would even be required to ensure that the provider of the exclusive service also offered it to the existing AP members. This, it was generally recognized, was beyond the power of any applicant to do. To appreciative laughter, one speaker at the annual meeting declared it to be the only good aspect of the proposal, because if the new entrant "can't deliver, he doesn't get the A.P. membership."[34] What one director described as "Kent's proposed white rabbit" was unanimously approved on the assumption that the members' committee could adopt the proposal as its own.[35]

McLean, who had met Arnold and other Justice Department officials several times to discuss their expectations, had a better understanding of the legal situation than anyone else on the board. He realized clearly—and said so repeatedly—that only one thing would put the threat of prosecution entirely to rest: admitting the *Chicago Sun* (and any other applicant in a similar situation, such as Cissy Patterson's *Washington (DC) Times Herald*) as an AP member: "Where there is a bona fide applicant, a legitimate newspaper corporation . . . he should be admitted."[36] Even if AP changed its bylaws to elect new members by a simple majority vote, an unfavorable result would probably still lead to prosecution. McLean wanted a unanimous vote of the board to recommend approval of Field's application but could not persuade a majority to agree. "Your views," McCormick complained, "are at variance with all of the other members of the Board and with three quarters of the membership."[37]

According to *Editor & Publisher*, the annual meeting that was to revise the membership rules and vote on the *Sun*'s application featured "some of the stormiest debate in AP annals."[38] What was described at the board meeting as "the Cooper proposal"—abolishing the right of protest, providing for election by a simple majority, and requiring the applicant to pay a substantial fee to existing AP members and to guarantee their access to any exclusive services to which the applicant subscribed—was adopted. But the applications of the *Sun* and *Times-Herald* were then decisively rejected. "Despite the relaxing of the rules, the club members were still being mighty exclusive," *Newsweek* commented.[39]

More than 40 percent of the votes cast for and against the *Sun* were prox-ies. McCormick personally brought in 190 anti-*Sun* proxies, accounting for more than one-fourth of all the anti votes.[40] In the weeks leading up to the an-nual meeting, McCormick's proxy-gathering campaign came to the attention of the Justice Department, resulting in a counterproductive decision to have FBI agents interview him and other AP publishers, apparently to determine whether improper pressure had been exerted to secure their support. McCor-mick denounced this intervention as Gestapo tactics.[41] In all, twenty-six agents questioned sixty-six publishers, most of them in Illinois.[42] In McLean's view, this led many AP members to "rally behind the man who was being investigated," McCormick.[43] Noyes's assessment was that if "there wasn't the question of the Government messing in the thing"—presumably by the threat of prosecution and the resort to FBI interviews—the board, at least, would have endorsed membership for the *Sun* "practically as a whole."[44]

Shortly after the *Sun* was rejected, Thurman Arnold told McLean that a decision had been made to prosecute AP.[45] The requirement that a new member pay compensation to existing members was simply "capitalization on an exclusive right," just as Moynihan had warned. The department's recent practice was to pursue antitrust cases criminally, but if AP provided its news service to the *Sun* pending a court ruling, the case could be pursued through a civil action.

AP directors and senior executives generally—and correctly—believed that Roosevelt was personally involved in the decision to prosecute. He famously described McCormick, along with his cousins Joe Patterson of the *New York Daily News* and Cissy Patterson, as "the McCormick-Patterson Axis," later telling librarian of Congress and playwright Archibald McLeish that they "deserve nei-ther hate nor praise—only pity for their unbalanced mentalities."[46] The president took a keen interest in the Chicago situation all along, and in mid-March 1942 he again discussed it personally with Field and his attorney, Louis Weiss.[47] In a memorandum for Roosevelt summing up the case for prosecution, Weiss wrote that the unfairness of AP's restrictive rules for admission was "more flagrant" in view of the *Tribune's* "violent form of isolationism":

> A newspaper which is seeking in every way to support the government is kept at a grave competitive disadvantage by the arbitrary action of a com-petitor whose editorial position runs counter to the government's entire policy.... The government's effort to obtain the full support of the people in the war effort must be sustained by all possible means.[48]

When Roosevelt met McLean to discuss the case, his parting words were "Will the *Sun* be elected?" McLean replied that he did not know.[49]

Biddle, the attorney general, made sure that Roosevelt approved the decision to prosecute before telling Arnold to proceed.[50] He warned that all the newspapers in the United States would be up in arms, to which Roosevelt replied that this would be "nothing new, eighty percent of the newspapers were always against him." When Biddle predicted that the prosecution would be seen as biased, a way of favoring a newspaper that supported him, Roosevelt asked "whether I thought he should not help his friends but only those who were against him." In midsummer, AP's reporter assigned to the Justice Department related Arnold's comment "that I knew as well as he did that the decision on the kind of action to be taken against the AP would be made at the White House."[51]

Confusion continued to reign as AP struggled to respond to the now-definite threat of legal action. On the one hand, the AP board decided early in July to resist prosecution "as without merit in either law or fact."[52] But a week later, in the hope that some way might still be found to admit the *Sun* under the existing rules, a resolution was passed allowing the *Herald American* to sever the weekday morning franchise in Chicago that it controlled but no longer used from the valuable Sunday membership that went with it, which it did use. Field could then purchase the weekday morning membership that he wanted. Whether by accident or design, the resolution was introduced and passed after McCormick, who would have opposed it strongly, had left the directors' meeting.[53] When he heard about the decision, McCormick was furious, threatening to sue if it was not immediately rescinded.[54] It was passed "for one purpose only, namely, to enable the Chicago Sun to acquire a six-day morning membership."[55] Cooper told McCormick that he was personally distressed about the dispute but argued that separating the weekday and Sunday components of an AP membership had always been permitted.[56] After his initial burst of outrage, McCormick struck a tone more of sadness than anger, telling Cooper he was "much more hurt by the conduct of my friends in voting away my property rights in my absence and without hearing me, than I am at the act itself. . . . This was not a deliberate action of the board, but was a sudden grasping of an out by tired, harassed men."[57]

Cooper himself was strikingly inconsistent in his actions. He frequently declared that he could have nothing to do with the lawsuit, telling McLean at one point that he did not want to receive any more information so that he could tell inquiring directors that he knew nothing about it.[58] Weeks later, however, he assumed a very active role, urging the board to call a special meeting of all members to vote on his new suggestion that any newspaper regularly publishing for two years should be admitted to membership.[59] The directors unanimously rejected this idea, but Cooper continued to insist that the board had to do a better job of keeping members informed about the rapidly changing developments.

In mid-August, Cooper learned that the antitrust suit was going to be filed within the next few days. It would be a civil suit rather than a criminal prosecution, but that was no relief: the Justice Department had "drawn up the complaint so adroitly and has so confined itself to issues that have clearly been decided in favor of the government in other litigations that I have a conviction that the government will be successful."[60] If so, AP would confront the greatest crisis in its history and would be forced to reorganize. Members would lose the right to elect (or reject) new members and the right to be compensated for loss of local exclusivity. The reservation of their local news for AP's exclusive use, one of the organization's greatest strengths, could be threatened as well. These losses would come as a great shock to unsuspecting members, in part because the board had ordered Cooper to avoid covering the antitrust issue in AP's news report for fear that public speculation might precipitate immediate action by the Justice Department.[61] He urged the board to hold a referendum asking members to decide between facing the lawsuit and making further amendments to AP's membership rules that would forestall it. Until these questions were settled, Cooper himself would try to persuade the Justice Department to postpone the prosecution.

While awaiting the board's response, Cooper went to Washington "entirely on my own responsibility, to try to get an audience with whatever individual I can find" who had the authority to order a delay. If the Justice Department agreed to postpone the suit until the result of the members' referendum was known, he would then attempt to "negotiate the minimum of by-law changes that will be acceptable." Cooper also wrote directly to Biddle—whom he hoped to meet in Washington the following day—while acknowledging that "you do not know who I am or what are my responsibilities."[62] Repeating phrases that were about to appear in *Barriers Down*, he argued that a successful prosecution would threaten "the highest moral principle ever originated in America . . . true and unbiased news" by driving AP members into the arms of privately owned and profit-oriented news agencies. Any step that damaged AP would hurt the U.S. war effort, raising public fears of an assault on freedom of the press even if that was not the government's intention. Not surprisingly, this effort did not succeed.[63] Cooper also met Roosevelt in person in an effort to reach a settlement, only to be dismissed with the comment that "all we're trying to do is get you a new member."[64] The board accepted Cooper's proposal for a referendum, but by now it was too late.[65] On August 28 the Justice Department announced that AP was being prosecuted in federal court for "illegally restrain[ing] and monopoliz[ing] interstate commerce in news."[66] This began a three-year legal odyssey—regularly described by Cooper and others at AP as "the Government suit"[67]—that would not end until the case reached the U.S. Supreme Court.

The suit was to be heard by a special expediting court of three appellate judges of the Southern District of New York—Learned Hand, Augustus Hand, and Thomas Swan—whose ruling could be appealed directly to the Supreme Court.[68] In the spring of 1943, after AP provided thousands of pages of information in response to more than three hundred specific queries from prosecutors and received extensive information about the government's case in return, the Justice Department argued that there was no significant disagreement about the facts and proposed that the court should issue a summary judgment based on the written evidence that had been amassed rather than hearing directly from witnesses.[69] As Biddle explained to Roosevelt, this approach—never previously adopted in a major antitrust case—would avoid a long trial "at which the Associated Press would have an opportunity to make speeches about freedom of the press."[70] AP strongly opposed the move, and both sides presented their arguments at a six-hour hearing in July, which turned out to be the only occasion when lawyers addressed the court in person.[71]

As Biddle predicted, the prosecution, naming AP, its directors, and all of its members as defendants, brought forth vociferous charges of government interference with press freedom. Comments from scores of AP members were solicited and printed in *Editor & Publisher*; their headlines—"U.S. Control of News Means End of Free Press," "Mortal Blow to Press Freedom, "Patently a Revenge Suit, "Government Action Must Please Hitler"—provide a quick summary of the views expressed.[72] AP's lawyers relied heavily on First Amendment arguments, as they did six years earlier in the unsuccessful challenge to the Wagner Act.[73] If the government had "the right to determine who may be associates in collecting and distributing news," it could also claim "the right to determine what news could be collected under what conditions."[74] Requiring AP to provide its news service to anyone who wanted it would make it a public utility, like the railroads and, like the railroads, subject to government regulation.[75] (The government's response was that AP would remain free to discriminate

among applicants for membership but not on competitive grounds.) A successful prosecution would destroy the cooperative principle "the cornerstone of the
AP" and would in fact make a monopoly in news more likely by removing the
main reason—inability to obtain an AP franchise—that led many newspapers
to sign contracts with United Press or INS. In Cooper's affidavit, submitted as
part of AP's defense, he argued that if AP news was available to everyone, there
would no longer be any incentive for members to contribute to its development,
making it "merely another commercial news agency."[76]

Cooper had little direct involvement with AP's legal strategy, which was
controlled by a subcommittee of the board of directors. To Frank Gannett, an
AP publisher (and then-chairman of the Republican National Committee), he
acknowledged that as the head of AP's news service, he should "not become
entangled in the political fight of the government against [AP]."[77] But he also
complained that even in private the board had little interest in his views. Cooper
wanted AP to mount a vigorous public campaign rejecting the government's
charges: "The Board ought to see that this law suit is tried all over the lot. . . . The
members should be inspired to take an active interest by way of discussions not
only in their newspapers but to the political minions in Washington." However,
these ideas were too militant for AP's lawyers "and therefore too militant for
the board." One aspect of AP's defense strategy particularly bothered Cooper.
The charge that AP's membership rules unlawfully restrained competition was
answered by saying that AP membership was not essential to the successful
operation of a newspaper. This led to the somewhat surprising assertion by
AP's attorneys that either UP or INS was quite adequate on its own. A series of
supporting affidavits from executives of United Press and competitors of AP's
Wirephoto network underscored the point that, in the words of one, there was
"no instance where access to the service of a particular news agency has been
determinative of a newspaper's success or failure."[78] Cooper, who had spent most
of the previous twenty years insisting that AP was the preeminent American
news agency, could not contain his anger when McLean proposed sending
thank-you notes to all those who had provided affidavits for the defense:

> If by this you mean to thank the United Press officials for the terrific destruc-
> tion their affidavits wrought upon the poor old Associated Press, I hope
> you won't do it. You have no idea of what use the United Press is making
> and will continue to make of the voluntary resignation of [AP] from its
> leading place in world journalism.[79]

Cooper's situation was complicated by the fact that McLean, his immediate superior, and McCormick, his closest ally, were bitterly divided over the correct approach. McCormick was not only opposed to the *Sun*'s application but was also virulently critical of Field personally, raising unfounded doubts about his record of service in World War I and making much of his treatment by a New York psychoanalyst who, in the *Tribune*'s words, "refashioned Field from an international playboy into a rootin' tootin' New Deal whooper upper."[80] According to McCormick, Field was "not a legitimate newspaper man" but "part of an alien and radical conspiracy against our republican form of government."[81] Yet McLean had "tried to get the Sun in by every kind of subterfuge that his ingenuity could devise. . . . I do not think he ought to be [re]elected president."[82] McLean, on the other hand, thought it was "a little ignominious that we as publishers so lack confidence in our abilities that we are not prepared to meet all comers under a fair set of rules. . . . Bert McCormick would grow in stature and influence if he were to take the opposite position. However, I fear he will not."[83]

The district court issued its decision in October. There was no need for a prolonged trial with witnesses and cross-examination; the relevant facts, provided by both parties in their extensive written submissions, were not in dispute. By a two-to-one majority, the court ruled that while AP was not a monopoly, its bylaws did violate antitrust law. It was not necessary to prove that withholding AP membership made it impossible for a newspaper to operate successfully. The crucial point was that AP "is a vast, intricately reticulated organization, the largest of its kind, gathering news from all over the world, the chief single source of news for the American press, universally agreed to be of prime consequence."[84] Depriving any newspaper of such a service "is to deprive the reading public of means of information which it should have; it is only by cross-lights from varying directions that full illumination can be secured."

The majority opinion firmly rejected AP's First Amendment defense. The judgment did not restrict in any way the right of an AP newspaper to print whatever news it chose: "All that we do is to prevent him from keeping that advantage for himself." The fact that the case involved news, and not ordinary goods like steel, machinery, or clothing, made the restrictions on competition more harmful, for the newspaper industry "serves one of the most vital of all general interests: the dissemination of news from as many different sources, and with as many different facets and colors as is possible." As long as no restrictions were imposed on what anyone could print, it was the reading public rather than publishers who needed First Amendment–like protection. AP's existing membership bylaws, therefore, were unlawful and could no longer be enforced, and any replacement must state explicitly that an applicant's ability to compete with an established member must not be taken into consideration when membership decisions were made. Dissenting from the majority opinion, Justice Thomas Swan concluded that the restrictions on competition were not sufficient to constitute an antitrust violation. Furthermore, in ruling that newspapers were subject to public-interest considerations not applied to other industries, the court was exercising authority that should properly be left to legislators.

The district court ruling anticipated an appeal to the Supreme Court, and AP's board of directors unanimously agreed to do so. Asked to comment on the court's decision, Roosevelt demurred but asked instead, "Does the country club still exist?"—a mocking reference to the patrician character of the board and AP's exclusivity.[85] AP's coverage of the ruling featured prominently a sharply critical statement from Frank Noyes, now its honorary president. Noyes said the court's reasoning made him feel like "an octogenarian Alice in Wonderland," given its conclusion that despite not being a monopoly and not seeking to impede competition AP had nonetheless violated the antitrust statutes.[86] Cooper, who chafed under the limitations on AP's coverage dictated by its lawyers, defended the decision to present a more critical view now: "Since this was the first time that anybody has ventured to speak up for [AP], there was news in your statement."[87] He was also concerned that members did not fully understand what was at stake, seeing this as only a "Chicago matter in which they have no interest," and that they would be shocked to learn of the heavy legal expenses involved.[88] Everyone at AP objected strongly to the aspect of the ruling that gave the government continuing oversight of AP's membership practices. At the same time, McLean mused privately that the changes demanded to AP's bylaws "are not greatly different from those which [AP] will of necessity impose upon itself in the near future or yield primacy to the United Press."[89]

The Supreme Court heard oral arguments on December 5 and 6, 1944. Robert Jackson, who was attorney general when the antitrust investigation began, withdrew, leaving eight justices to consider the case. The chief justice, Harlan Stone, was sympathetic to AP's argument that the anti-competitive impact of its bylaws was not sufficient to warrant a Sherman Act conviction, but Felix Frankfurter took the opposite view: "Competition doesn't mean that you can't get on without it. Competition means that you have not something that your rival has."[90] At one point, Wendell Berge, presenting the Justice Department's case, cited a recent magazine article by Cooper—one of many published as part of his increasingly high-profile press freedom "crusade"—in which he urged that journalists everywhere should be free "to seek out news with equal access to all," that newspapers should be able to publish news freely, and that news agencies should be free to compete with each other.[91] "We agree with what Mr. Cooper says," Berge commented. "Maybe Mr. Cooper hasn't instructed his counsel," Frankfurter observed drily.

Six months later, the court delivered its verdict. Five justices upheld the lower court's ruling and three called for it to be overturned; five separate written opinions were delivered in all.[92] Without saying so explicitly, the majority opinion rejected the district court's reasoning that the Sherman Act should be applied more stringently to newspapers than to other businesses because of their crucial role in a democracy. The restraints on competition created by AP's bylaws were no different from those previously declared illegal in the trade in tiles, enameled ironware, lumber, women's clothing, or motion pictures, and AP should be treated just as these other businesses were. (In his concurring judgment, Frankfurter differed on this point: journalism "has a relation to the public interest unlike that of any other enterprise pursued for profit.... Truth and understanding are not wares like peanuts or potatoes.") AP was not being declared a public utility, obliged to serve all comers on equal terms. The court strongly reaffirmed the lower court's conclusion that the First Amendment offered no protection: "Freedom to publish is guaranteed by the Constitution, but freedom to combine to keep others from publishing is not." In dissent, Justice Owen Roberts largely adopted Swan's district court position: the evidence did not prove that AP's practices "must inevitably result, or that its activities have in fact resulted, in any undue and unreasonable restraint of free competition." The district court ruling did make AP into a public utility, usurping a regulatory role that should be left to legislators. Furthermore, making AP subject to continuing supervision by the courts "may well be, and I think threatens to be, but a first step in the shackling of the press, which will subvert the constitutional freedom to print or to withhold, to print as and how one's reason or one's interest dictates."[93]

Now that the legal process had run its course, AP had to decide how to respond. McLean initially favored the narrowest possible reworking of the membership bylaw to conform to the letter of the ruling, but Cooper saw an opportunity to make broader changes.[94] In particular, he wanted AP to accept organizations other than newspapers—including radio stations—as associate members, one of his long-standing goals.[95] Although it was expressly forbidden to take local competitive factors into account when making membership decisions, AP did not have to accept all applicants: every member must publish "a *bona fide* newspaper, continuously issued to a list of genuine paid subscribers." This was meant to assuage the concerns of smaller members in particular, some of whom feared the emergence of predatory competitors who could essentially extort concessions by the mere threat of beginning publication.[96] Cooper also wanted to eliminate any reference to hours of publication.[97] This would finally solve the problem of newspapers with afternoon memberships that were prevented by local morning newspaper competitors from using AP news in their Sunday editions. "I wish I could get you and every member of [AP] to look upon [AP] as a news service, which is all it is, and not as a means of trying to keep publishers publishing within the hours where their competitors feel they do them the least harm," he told McLean. "It won't work. It hasn't worked for thirty years."[98] For once, AP had an opportunity "to throw off the shackles that have never bound our competition."

After more than three years of struggle, the final decision to admit the *Sun*, the *Times Herald*, and two Hearst newspapers came as something of an anticlimax, reflecting the fact that AP had been "licked all along the line from the first chapter until the last period in the last chapter of the book," in the words of director George Booth.[99] Rejecting these applications now would expose AP and its members to contempt of court citations, and the rejected applicants could sue for triple damages.[100] The *Sun*'s application for associate status (the contract it had signed with United Press when AP service was denied in 1941 made it impossible to provide its local news exclusively to AP, as regular members were required to do) was approved by a vote of 949 to 34, with even more lopsided results in favor of the other applicants.[101] The new bylaws, following Cooper's blueprint in virtually every respect, were adopted unanimously.

Immediately after the Supreme Court turned down AP's appeal, McCormick launched a parallel effort to nullify the court's ruling through legislation, sending Cooper a draft bill that would effectively exempt AP and other news agencies from antitrust prosecution.[102] McLean was skeptical. AP's lawyers believed that such legislation could only be drafted "with great difficulty, if at all," and there was considerable doubt about whether Congress would approve it.[103] Cooper, however, was encouraged by the "earnestness and eagerness of the smaller members to go at this thing," concluding that "with leadership and an organized effort, something can be done."[104] Several AP publishers were members of Congress, and mobilizing their support would be an obvious first step.[105] By the time

AP accepted the *Sun*'s application, three members of Congress had introduced legislation exempting news agencies from the antitrust laws, with Rep. Noah Mason, an Illinois Republican, taking the lead.[106] At AP's 1946 annual meeting, members strongly supported a request to Congress to amend the Sherman Act so that it would not "prohibit any press service company from exercising its own discretion in the selection of its members."[107] However, Mason's bill was eventually rejected by a House of Representatives subcommittee.[108] With AP's board of directors divided about the wisdom of the idea, there was little chance of its being resuscitated.[109] McCormick did not seek reelection to the board in 1948, bringing his decades-long tenure—but not his relationship with Cooper—to an end.

As many observers noted at the time and subsequently, AP's loss in the antitrust suit did not have the dire consequences that were predicted. "The sky did not fall," Cooper wrote in his autobiography ten years later.[110] McLean considered the freedom of action that the ruling gave AP "a valuable thing."[111] The outcome solved one of AP's most stubborn problems by making the news service available to Sunday newspapers that had previously been prevented from receiving it; it also set the stage for radio stations to become associate members, bringing in substantial additional revenue.[112] Roy Roberts, publisher of the *Kansas City Star* and a long-serving director, told a group of AP managing editors in 1958 that he often wondered whether Cooper, "really, secretly, down in his heart, didn't want the AP to lose the fight":

> Because the outcome didn't hurt the AP. It made the AP, opening the doors where it had to sell the membership. It provided the bankroll that let the AP go to town. . . . Those it really hurt were the owners of the papers . . . who had franchise rights worth millions.[113]

The ruling also meant that fewer newspapers had a reason to sign contracts with United Press or INS because AP was not available to them; it was "no accident," John Hightower concluded, that AP's two main rivals merged in 1956.[114] The eventual cost of the suit to AP was $474,314, about one-fifth of what AP had spent on all of its foreign newsgathering in 1944.[115]

AP had now gone head-to-head with the federal government in two high-profile legal proceedings and had lost both times. To the extent that the two things can be clearly separated, both involved AP's corporate interests rather than the news service per se. In 1946 AP once again took an uncompromising stand against a new federal government proposal, one that would have a direct effect on its news operation.

11

The Crusade

Barriers Down, the book that did more than anything else to bring Cooper's name to public attention, was published in December 1942—three months after the antitrust suit was launched but more than six months before the case was actually heard. It was mainly a narrative account of how AP overcame the cartel restrictions that prevented it from selling its news outside North America—first in South America during the First World War, then in Europe (very slowly) after the establishment of its British subsidiary in 1931, and in Japan after 1933. AP's, and Cooper's, struggles with Roderick Jones of Reuters were covered extensively. AP's emancipation from the cartel broke down "the barriers that hindered the exchange of news between the press of all nations—the kind of news exchange that brings peoples of all nations to understand each other and thus reduces to a minimum the causes of wars."[1] As a nonprofit cooperative committed to impartiality, AP stood for "true and unbiased news—the highest original moral concept ever developed in America and given to the world."[2]

The book concluded with recommendations for reform of the international news system, which Cooper repeated frequently in published writing, speeches, and efforts to gain political support over the next several years. All postwar peace treaties should include binding rules to "guarantee freedom of the press around the world as we know it."[3] All news organizations should be guaranteed equal access to official news and transmission channels, with no preferential treatment of its own national agency by any government. In addition, every agency should be free to make news exchange agreements with any other agency, with no limitations of exclusivity; at least one agency in every country should be jointly owned by the newspapers it served (like AP and unlike its chief U.S. competitors); and "the intentional covert inclusion . . . of biased international propaganda" should be prohibited.

"Press freedom" was the shorthand term for Cooper's program adopted in *Barriers Down* and repeated in the public discussions it inspired, but the version of this potent idea that he proposed was limited in some significant ways. Cooper considered American journalism a model that *should*, ideally, be adopted around the world, but he always realized that it would be impossible to establish U.S.-style press freedom in every country. This was little more than a hope, with no mechanism to enforce it. The rules that Cooper wanted to see established in international agreements focused on the freedom of news agencies to operate in foreign countries, not the universal adoption of something like the First Amendment. Cooper did believe, though, that AP's news was an antidote to government-backed propaganda, and in that way its availability in other countries—at least in those where it could be printed—was in itself an important contribution to press freedom.

With its focus on removing obstacles, *Barriers Down* reflected ideas that had been central to American thinking about international trade for decades. Woodrow Wilson's Fourteen Points, for example, called for removal of all barriers to global commerce, and in 1935 the assistant U.S. secretary of state described "the breaking of barriers"—political, economic, and cultural—as "the major problem [of U.S.] foreign relations."[4] The book's argument that American journalistic practices were a model for the rest of the world was a media-specific variant of the long-standing idea that the United States had a duty to spread its uniquely democratic values everywhere.[5] By 1942, elite and public opinion was converging around the notion that, beyond setting an example, the United States had a responsibility to actively lead the emergence of a new world order after the war.[6] Cooper's call for internationally binding rules to prevent national governments from putting limits on the worldwide commerce in news was consistent with all these currents of thought.[7] The practical question was how the international news system should be structured and governed, whether by the cartel's quasi-imperial regime of extraterritorial exclusivity and preferential (often compromising) treatment by national governments, or by a new set of rules allowing AP—or any other agency with equally rich resources—to operate anywhere in the world with few if any limitations.

Cooper's authorship of *Barriers Down* was central to the reputation he developed after 1942 for "carr[ying] the banner for a world-wide free press and free interchange of news everywhere."[8] In fact, most of the book was ghostwritten by DeWitt Mackenzie, a senior AP journalist who had been chief of AP's crucial London bureau and subsequently the New York–based executive in charge of all foreign coverage. Mackenzie began working on the manuscript during the summer of 1941, submitting the first draft chapters of what he tentatively called "The Great Barrier" to Cooper with an explanatory note stressing that they were not "the finished product."

> I propose to do considerable rewriting. . . . The book is being dictated to the stenographer and then is edited roughly for mistakes. There will have to be changes, additions and deletions and the language of the whole book will be toned up. . . . The title "The Great Barrier" is tentative. It popped into my head and I put it down to give me something to shoot at.[9]

Cooper revised Mackenzie's draft substantially, adding details about many events in which he had been personally involved (such as his numerous conversations with Roderick Jones), rewriting (Mackenzie's references to "Kent Cooper" were changed to "I" and "me" throughout), and deleting material (including most references to his predecessor, Frederick Roy Martin, as general manager). Mackenzie kept up a steady stream of notes accompanying draft and revised chapters, with Cooper always having the final word. On one occasion, Mackenzie gently suggested deleting Cooper's warning that Americans might lose their own free press if journalists became "too deeply involved" in providing news to U.S. government information agencies, pointing out that to some extent this was already happening under wartime conditions. Cooper's reply was brusque: "Leave it in. I said 'if.'"[10] (Mackenzie accepted the decision cheerfully: "If you wish to keep the clause in, why then I'm your Boswell.") Other notes were brisk accounts of Mackenzie's progress, showing how he managed the process in accordance with Cooper's wishes. "I haven't done wholesale rewriting in these chapters," he wrote in January 1942, "because they didn't seem to call for it. . . . You begin reading today at Chapter IX, page 60."[11] A conservative estimate, based on a comparison of Mackenzie's draft and the final manuscript, is that about three-quarters of *Barriers Down* was Mackenzie's unaltered, or minimally edited, work. With one exception, however (a message from New York to AP's London bureau in 1941, stating that Mackenzie was "completing under associateds [*sic*] sponsorship a history of associateds relationships with foreign agencies and its fight for international freedom of press"[12]), there was no indication at the time or subsequently that anyone besides Cooper was involved in writing it. When the book was about to appear in print, Cooper took full credit in a message to AP directors, staff, and others who were sent autographed copies:

> I suppose sooner or later I had to do it. So I have written a book, entitled "Barriers Down." This book is not about the [antitrust] suit· It is about an activity of mine on behalf of [AP] for twenty years that I consider the most important thing I have ever done for [AP]. Moreover, in all modesty I think it's the most important thing that ever was accomplished on behalf of world journalism.[13]

Barriers Down contains no acknowledgments and Mackenzie's name does not appear anywhere in it. Cooper's lack of frankness about the authorship of a book that celebrates the importance of truth in journalism is a glaring example of his inconsistency.

Cooper described the book at the time as a personal project undertaken "on my own responsibility," presumably to avoid associating AP too closely with his own strongly expressed opinions.[14] But AP as an institution was deeply involved, given the board resolution calling for the project to be undertaken in the first place, the employment of a staff member, Mackenzie, to write the draft and revise it, and AP's spending more than fifteen thousand dollars to advertise the book and purchase copies for distribution to AP members, schools of journalism, and libraries.[15] It did not include any specific reference to the antitrust suit, but there were many vague allusions to the importance of the U.S. government never placing a "hand of authority" on AP or interfering with its "high mission."[16] (In keeping with the freedom-from-government theme, the account of AP's expansion into South America omitted almost all details of the State Department's strong direction.) Years later, after Cooper retired, he said the book was "written and published at the time the U.S. government was preparing to sue [AP]" and was "therefore, institutional in the extreme."[17]

Barriers Down was favorably reviewed by AP members and others but was hardly a best seller. It was variously hailed as "one of the most important achievements of our time, . . . a story of one of the finest examples of American idealism and initiative," and "breathtaking in its candor, inspiring in its idealism, fascinating as the story of a noble crusade."[18] Cooper himself was warmly praised.

Josephus Daniels (an AP publisher, secretary of the navy during the First World War, and former U.S. ambassador to Mexico) told Cooper that he had "earned the gratitude of your own country and the world by your persistent fight." Responses from some AP journalists—who could be expected to have a keen appreciation of the journalistic issues involved and might also have seen an opportunity to rise in Cooper's favor—verged on the rhapsodic. For the Oklahoma City bureau chief, Cooper's ideals "raise a standard and beacon for all of us who look to him for inspiration"; his counterpart in Pittsburgh considered *Barriers Down* the most important story in the history of journalism, "a work that qualifies KC for the next Nobel peace prize or some similar recognition."[19]

Cooper was worried about the possibility of more negative reactions from some quarters, however, congratulating the head of AP's British subsidiary for diplomatically misplacing his copy rather than lending it to Roderick Jones, for fear that this might be the prelude to legal action.[20] In *The Nation*, a critical observer poked fun at the book for presenting AP "as a pure and forlorn maiden in the clutches of a sinister international dragon and [Cooper] as the valiant knight who for twenty years fought to effect a rescue."[21] The author agreed wholeheartedly with Cooper's critique of the news agency cartel but described his account of AP's struggle against it as extremely disingenuous since a careful reading demonstrated that "his real opponents were not the foreign agencies, but Melville Stone." Privately, Roy Howard criticized "Kent's phony and at times melodramatic picturization of Cooper slaying the dragon, Reuters," seeing the book as an attempt to convince journalists that no news agency could be "clean or worthy" unless it followed AP's "so-called cooperative" model.[22] A month after the book appeared, thirty-five hundred copies had been sold in addition to those purchased directly by AP, barely covering the publisher's costs.[23]

Cooper was the featured speaker at AP's annual meeting in 1943—a high-profile platform usually occupied by members of the U.S. cabinet, senior government officials, or Supreme Court judges. He urged all AP members to join a "crusade that the people of all countries may be granted what is a constitutional right here—namely, a free press."[24] In practice, this would be done by including guarantees in peace treaties "that news at its source shall be freely available to all news men everywhere" and that "no country shall give preferential transmission facilities access to its own press." With minor modifications, Cooper advanced these recommendations to an ever-growing group of audiences over the next several years, reaching a peak between 1944 and 1946. He was to spend much of his remaining time at AP seeking support for this campaign.

* * *

Cooper made enormous strides after 1944 toward the goal he had been pursuing for more than two decades: making AP as dominant in providing news to countries around the world as it was in the United States. Besides delivering many public speeches about the need for unfettered access to international news markets, writing numerous articles, and being written about, he became directly involved in politics, pressing U.S. officials and Democratic and Republican legislators to make his quest a matter of U.S. national policy. As suggested by Arthur Sulzberger—whose election as an AP director in 1942 marked the *New York Times'* return to AP's governing councils after the Wirephoto-inspired absence—Cooper first wrote to Cordell Hull, the U.S. secretary of state, asking him to remember the importance of including "some stipulation in peace terms" about press freedom around the world and listing the recommendations set out in *Barriers Down*.[25] Hull promised to "keep this specially in mind."[26] The Washington bureau chief, Paul Miller, followed up with State Department officials, who raised some prescient questions about how Cooper's proposals might work in practice: Would TASS be considered a news agency with the same rights to operate anywhere in the world as AP or Reuters? Could Russia claim to have a free press?[27] Cooper also approached individual politicians directly, including William J. Fulbright, then a Democratic member of the House of Representatives and a member of the family that owned the *Northwest Arkansas Times*, a longtime AP newspaper.[28] Fulbright agreed enthusiastically that a requirement for worldwide press freedom should be included in postwar settlements and promised to work toward that end. He also took the opportunity to complain that news agencies paid too much attention "to the crackpots in Congress. . . . When one considers the Axis papers dominated by McCormick usually falsify all reports on foreign affairs, it seems too bad that the legitimate news services likewise give most of their space to these same peculiar individuals." Cooper instructed Miller to follow up on Fulbright's complaint, illustrating that the quest for political support could bring requests for favors in return.

Cooper's next step was to push for statements in favor of international press freedom to be included in the 1944 election platforms of both the Republicans and the Democrats.[29] He attended the Republican National Convention in Chicago, where, with support from the American Newspaper Publishers Association, the American Society of Newspaper Editors (ASNE), Sulzberger, and fellow AP director George Booth (a member of the Republican Platform Committee), the party adopted a version of the ASNE's free press proposal.[30]

The plank was aimed not only at totalitarian states but also at Roosevelt: it took up the cause of "peoples [who] have found themselves shackled by governments which denied the truth, or, worse, dealt in half-truths or withheld the facts from the public" and condemned any use of the press "as instruments of the administration and the use of government publicity agencies for partisan ends."[31] But it went on to say that "all channels of information must be kept open with equality of access to information at the source" and considered that it would be "a valuable contribution to future peace" if agreement about this could be reached with other nations. Ralph McGill, chairman of the relevant ASNE committee and publisher of the *Atlanta Constitution*, acknowledged that the plank was merely a gesture but considered it an important one. Reporters covering the convention mostly ignored it, however.[32]

Cooper played a bigger role at the Democratic convention, meeting in person with the platform committee at the invitation of senators Carl Hatch and Harry Truman.[33] The plank adopted by the Democrats endorsed "the right of all men to write, send and publish news at uniform communication rates, and without interference by government or private monopoly, and that right should be protected by treaty." This was less overtly partisan than the Republican version and closer to Cooper's original ideas, although the reference to "private monopoly" was, intentionally or not, a reminder that the government's antitrust suit against AP was still before the courts. Truman was less cooperative after he became president, vigorously rejecting Cooper's suggestion that the defeated nations should be required to guarantee press freedom in peace treaties: the United States was not prepared to "[cram] anything down the throat of an independent nation that will interfere with the peace settlement."[34]

The crusade, nonetheless, was gaining momentum. Cooper asked Fulbright to sponsor a congressional resolution—helpfully providing a draft—and enlisted the support of two influential senators, Democrat Thomas Connally and Republican Robert Taft.[35] Paul Miller, meanwhile, was making some headway with the State Department. After meeting with Cooper in June, Assistant Secretary of State Adolph Berle delivered a speech to the Foreign Press Association describing freedom of information as "a major necessity" of the new international organization that the United States, Britain, the Soviet Union, and China had agreed to establish.[36] A proposal for Roosevelt to issue an order instituting freedom of information in all areas under U.S. military control was now being considered, although Berle warned that the Russians "are going to be difficult on any such agreement."[37]

Fulbright introduced his resolution in the House of Representatives on September 7, setting off two weeks of frantic activity by AP's Washington staff and Cooper to have some version of it adopted by both houses of Congress before they adjourned for the presidential and congressional elections in November.[38] AP's coverage of developments was positive to the point of being promotional; according to one story, the proposal "that America lead a crusade for worldwide freedom of news, based on the thesis that lies promote war and truth is a mighty worker for peace, tightened on the imagination of Congress today."[39] Several roadblocks had to be removed or navigated around. Rep. Sol Bloom, the chairman of the House of Representatives Foreign Affairs Committee, which would have to approve the resolution, was not inclined to consider it until after the election.[40] "I am sure you can get Bloom to call a meeting of the Committee," Cooper told Miller, "or if necessary, get the State Department to get Bloom to call the Committee and report the resolution unanimously."[41] Miller's persuasion was evidently effective; the next day, in a friendly letter to Bloom, Cooper noted with satisfaction that Bloom was going to push the press freedom resolution, enclosed a warmly inscribed copy of *Barriers Down*, and invited him to meet for lunch the next time he was in New York.[42]

On the day before the Senate adjourned, Miller and other members of the AP staff brokered an agreement among Taft, Connally, and Sen. Arthur Vandenburg (former publisher of the *Grand Rapids [MI] Herald*) to resolve differences among their competing drafts. This version of the resolution—calling for free international news exchange "without discrimination as to sources, distribution, rates or charges," to be "protected by international compact"—was accepted by the House committee without amendment.[43] Then came a last-minute rush to have the resolution adopted by the whole House in the final hours before it adjourned. For procedural reasons, this would succeed only if the Speaker immediately recognized a member of the Foreign Relations Committee and allowed him to introduce the resolution. The plan almost failed when another representative—who, in Miller's words, "didn't know what was going on"—challenged the request for unanimous consent on the grounds that a quorum was lacking. Another AP staffer then "ran to the hallway outside the House, sent a messenger for the Congressman—and persuaded the Congressman to withdraw his motion."[44] As had happened in the Senate earlier that day, the House then approved the resolution unanimously. Throughout the years-long free-access campaign, Cooper repeatedly insisted that he was acting as an individual, not on behalf of AP, but in this case he relied heavily on AP's staff and reputation.

When politicians including Fulbright, Bloom, Taft, Connally, Vandenburg, and numerous others responded favorably to suggestions and direction from AP staff, or when they received effusive letters of thanks from Cooper, it is hard to believe that they thought they had gained credit with an individual but not an institution.[45]

Cooper next tried to enlist Roosevelt's support but less successfully.[46] When they met at the White House, Roosevelt told Cooper that he planned to make a statement on international press freedom, and Cooper related to reporters afterward that the president had described the cause as "so right."[47] This, however, seems to have been an example of Roosevelt's often-noted propensity to leave visitors thinking he agreed with them whether he actually did or not. Roosevelt eventually decided that he would not, after all, issue the statement that press secretary Stephen Early had prepared; it would have ordered the commanders of U.S. occupation forces in Europe and elsewhere to provide equal access to information and transmission facilities to all accredited correspondents and urged all members of the United Nations to do the same. "Quite frankly," he told Early, "I regard Freedom of the Press as one of the world's most microscopic problems."[48] Cooper continued to cite the president's "so right" comment, however, and was never publicly contradicted. And even without Roosevelt's support, the State Department continued to push for the United Nations to adopt some version of free press principles—though this effort eventually reached a dead end in the face of growing Cold War tensions and skepticism on the part of nonaligned nations about the power of U.S. news agencies.[49] Gen. Douglas MacArthur, however, earned Cooper's enthusiastic gratitude for imposing equal access to news and transmission facilities in U.S.-occupied Japan.[50]

One question that preoccupied Cooper was how United Press would respond to his campaign. A major reason for repeatedly stating that he undertook the campaign strictly as an individual was that if it was too closely associated with AP, this "would make our friends of the opposition jealous, which could hurt the cause."[51] Cooper was not trying to erase UP from the story (he acknowledged that UP "first blazed the trail of American news abroad," while AP became involved only belatedly[52]) but wanted to portray the two as equal partners. The situation was complicated because UP's president at the time, Hugh Baillie, had long held a wholly skeptical view of Cooper.[53] In the May 1944 newsletter of Sigma Delta Chi, the fraternal organization of U.S. journalists, Baillie presented a case that in many respects seemed virtually identical to Cooper's, asserting that "free and untrammeled interchange of news around the world" would make another world war less likely.[54] But the implicit message was that UP—which had never been part of the Reuters-led cartel, "participated in by the world's government news agencies"—was a more plausible standard-bearer for world press freedom than AP, a cartel member for more than thirty years before finally withdrawing just ten years earlier. Despite Cooper's assertions to the contrary, it was also clear that AP's growing reputation as a champion of press freedom had commercial value—as Cooper's executive assistant evidently realized when he sent copies of a recent speech by Cooper and a related article in *Life* magazine to bureau chiefs in London, Lisbon, Rome, Madrid, Cairo, New Delhi, and Johannesburg, suggesting these should be mailed to "prospects and others as you see fit."[55]

Throughout the autumn of 1944, buoyed by the campaign's recent political successes, Cooper delivered a series of high-profile public speeches; several articles by or about him were published at the same time. The titles of his speeches and writings give a good idea of the campaign's main themes: "Free News: First Step in Peace," "World Freedom of Press and Radio," "Freedom of Information: Head of Associated Press Calls for Unhampered Flow of World News," "So They Need Not March Again," "A Free Press in a Free World."[56] He now sharply criticized Nazi methods of controlling the work of foreign correspondents—as he refrained from doing before 1941—the effect of which was that "complete news coverage was impossible, and the world suffered for it."[57] One peculiar manifestation of the campaign was a nationally broadcast radio dramatization of *Barriers Down* on NBC, in which stereotypical citizens of England, France, Germany, Italy, and other countries repeated the twisted views of the United States and each other promulgated by "propaganda agencies for cut-throat international politicians."[58] An anonymous Frenchman blurted out, "M'sieu—M'sieu—the paper this morning reports that that criminals in your country shoot up Chicago! Mon Dieu, *vous etes sauvage*." An English voice, representing a Reuters journalist of the Roderick Jones era, asked, "Shall I send out this story, sir?" His superior, told that it might harm British interests, replied, "Then kill it." The script ended with a stirring call-and-response as four voices representing the citizens of the world together shouted, "We shall demand it!" or "That too!" as one element after another of Cooper's program was read out to them. It concluded with an appeal to listeners by Cooper himself to "help us to strike down forever the barriers that stand in the way of world-wide Freedom of the Press—to strike down forever one of the greatest barriers to world-wide peace."

Although most U.S. coverage of Cooper's crusade was highly positive, it attracted critical commentary elsewhere. *The Economist* charged that Cooper, "like most big business executives, experiences a peculiar moral glow in finding that his idea of freedom coincides with his commercial advantage."[59] He failed to acknowledge that "when all barriers are down[,] the huge financial resources of the American agencies might enable them to dominate the world. . . . Democracy does not necessarily mean making the whole world safe for the AP." Cooper promptly fired back, saying that *The Economist* could not want news agencies confined to their own countries—"as was largely the case before Reuters withdrew its cartel domination" of much of the world—and that any opportunities open to AP under his plan would be equally available to any British agency.[60]

In the United States, *Fortune* magazine was unusual in acknowledging that AP's opportunities for postwar expansion would be greater "if the way is cleared by an international free-press doctrine."[61] Cooper's reputation as a free press champion might also weigh in AP's favor in its antitrust case, soon to come before the Supreme Court.[62] But motives were almost always mixed in this way— "the ageless battle for liberty is also always a battle for private interests"—and if Cooper's campaign did succeed, he "will be entitled to a full twenty-one gun salute or whatever salute is given to great campaigners in a great cause." Some readers of Cooper's article in the November 1944 issue of *Life* magazine questioned his and AP's commitment to freedom of the press in view of the refusal to provide news service to the *Chicago Sun*. "If the AP wishes to run on the basis of a restricted country club membership, they are out of order in bringing up 'freedom of the press,'" one reader asserted.[63]

Another critique, published in the Soviet magazine *War and the Working Class*, applauded the principle of international press freedom but took issue with Cooper's claim that the USSR would never agree about its importance. In fact, the Soviet Union strongly supported freedom of the press, but "the Soviet people will never consent to replace its freedom of the press with the American one." In the United States and most European countries, press freedom was more theoretical than real because many newspapers were controlled by businessmen "who follow first of all their narrow interest." Cooper dismissed concerns about the heavy capital requirements of newspaper publishing and concentration of ownership, however; the crucial point was whether the newspaper owed its existence to the patronage of its readers, "who thus make it free and independent."[64] He also acknowledged that his crusade might be seen as "part of some sort of imperialistic scheme to expand American news activities around the globe." But real press freedom meant having a choice among news providers so that no country would have to receive most of its world news from New York—or from London, Moscow, or Berlin. Yet Cooper also believed that American journalism in general and AP journalism in particular "set the standard of objective news for the whole world."[65]

Objections to the business domination of U.S. journalism by the USSR and the European states that were now firmly in its sphere of influence soon became a fixture of debates about whether and how postwar international institutions should protect press freedom.[66] The tone of Soviet criticism grew harsher as East-West relations moved toward outright hostility: one *Pravda* commentator charged in 1947 that there was essentially no difference between U.S. news agencies and oil companies, warning that "the dying influence of capitalistic monopolies in the newspaper world . . . is going to come up inevitably at international world congresses."[67] Some American publishers took the anti-imperialism critique seriously: Sevellon Brown of the *Providence (RI) Journal-Bulletin*, a U.S. representative at the United Nations Conference on Freedom of Information in 1948, concluded that American journalists must make common cause with their colleagues from smaller and poorer countries "which have a real fear of American cultural imperialism and which sincerely feel that we have too much power in the possession of our global news organizations. . . . The feeling that all their [international] news is handled with an American slant is too strong to be disregarded."[68]

* * *

The first stage in Cooper's campaign was setting out the overall program in *Barriers Down*, and the second was mobilizing political and public support. Now came the third, really crucial, stage: taking advantage of the favorable climate he had worked hard to create by actually signing up new clients. AP had been providing news service directly to British newspapers since 1939 through Associated Press of Great Britain (APGB).[69] By operating through APGB and making London the editorial and distribution center for its worldwide expansion, AP could avoid implicating the U.S.-based nonprofit parent organization in a frankly commercial operation.[70] AP was then twenty years behind UP internationally, Cooper told the head of AP's European operations; even after the break with Reuters in 1934 gave AP a free hand in principle, substantial cuts in assessment revenue during the Depression meant little was done.[71] The outbreak of war put a halt to AP's European and Asian expansion efforts, but by the end of 1942 APGB was providing news to sixty-seven British subscribers.[72] In terms of quality and reputation, however, APGB was "never more than a token service," clearly inferior to UP's subsidiary British United Press and Reuters in the eyes of British editors.[73]

In the autumn of 1943, with growing prospects of an Allied victory, Lloyd Stratton was put in charge of "the news and newsphoto 'invasion' of the continent."[74] He was dispatched on an ambitious reconnaissance mission that took him to thirty-four countries, including Egypt, the Soviet Union, South Africa, India,and China, covering some sixty thousand miles over six months.[75] Based on the information he gathered, Stratton made a forceful proposal to the board of directors in October 1944 for an expensive and aggressive campaign to sell AP news internationally.[76] United Press, Stratton wrote, was currently the leading U.S. news agency in the world, and it could only be prevented from converting this advantage into dominance of the U.S. market "by first subduing it outside the United States." AP could no longer afford to see itself as primarily in the business of collecting international news for U.S. newspapers but must, as UP had already done, establish strong and lasting connections with publishers of major newspapers everywhere in the world. The revitalized Reuters, with its extensive international system of newsgathering and distribution, was also determined to succeed as a global agency at a time of "political, economical and commercial consolidation of the world."[77]

Stratton saw a clear connection between the United States' growing role in the world and AP's ambitions. In his travels, he was struck by "the tremendous magnitude of American installations"—many of them military bases, but also representing "lasting economic, commercial, political, governmental, or policing activities." Other countries had a growing appetite for news of the United States, "the most powerful nation in the world for a long time to come." In practical terms, AP had to strengthen its news staff in London, New York, and Washington and begin producing substantial daily news services for subscribers in Europe, northern and southern Africa, and the Middle East. These services would have to be carried at a loss for several years. The board's decision several months earlier to allocate ten thousand dollars on a onetime basis (later raised to one hundred thousand dollars) was clearly inadequate to carry out this program. AP faced a stark choice: "either meeting the opportunity, and the pace the opposition already has set, or becoming reconciled to the ultimate consequences."

Cooper strongly endorsed Stratton's conclusions, stressing that while AP had sharply reduced its assessments during the 1930s, UP kept its rates steady and imposed a substantial wartime increase. This gave UP more than $10 million in additional revenue since 1932 that it could use to strengthen its international news operation.[78] Now if AP wanted to compete aggressively around the world, "we are going to have to have money with which to do it and not expect to be on a paying basis for years to come."[79] Instead of a onetime appropriation of $100,000, international expansion would require an annual expenditure of $1 million, with any funds not spent in a given year carried over. The board, evidently convinced, responded with sustained applause. "Well, gentlemen," McCormick asked, "what are we waiting for?"[80] The open-ended annual commitment of $1 million was approved unanimously.[81]

* * *

Roderick Jones's forced resignation as chairman and managing director of Reuters in 1941 set the stage for a much improved relationship with AP.[82] Reuters had been owned by the Press Association, the cooperative organization of British provincial newspapers, since 1926. Jones, however, remained the dominant figure until the mid-1930s, when a new and more critical group of directors—including William Haley, then managing editor of the UK's *Manchester Evening News*—determined that he had to be replaced. The one-sided 1934 contract with AP, the direct result of Jones's miscalculation, was one of the key indictments against him, along with a compromising willingness to accept government influence in exchange for subsidies.[83] After Jones was gone, Haley led successful negotiations to bring the powerful London publishers into joint ownership of Reuters, with an agreement that their and the PA's shares would be exercised "as in the nature of a trust rather than as an investment."[84] Underscoring the rejection of Jones's willingness to work closely with the British government, the trust agreement specified that Reuters' "integrity independence and freedom from bias shall at all times be fully preserved." These commitments were to play an important role in the next major order of business: renegotiating the "intolerable" 1934 contract whose terms Cooper had literally dictated to Jones.[85]

Haley traveled to New York in April 1942, with instructions that Reuters should be prepared for a complete break with AP if the 1934 agreement could not be substantially changed. The most offensive provision was the clause giving AP access to all of Reuters' international news and all domestic British news provided by the PA in exchange merely for AP's North American news and none of its own international coverage. He waited three weeks before Cooper found time to see him.[86] Once Cooper and Haley did meet face-to-face, they began a marathon round of talks that took up dozens of hours on at least ten occasions over six weeks.

In a detailed account for the Reuters board, Haley described Cooper as "in many ways an extraordinary man." He was considered a genius by some AP directors, with a deep understanding of the news agency business. At first he seemed temperamental and volatile; repeatedly Haley would reach what he thought was an understanding on one difficult point or another, only to find at their next meeting that Cooper had "receded from the point to which I had brought him last." Eventually Haley realized that this simply reflected Cooper's deep distrust of Reuters; he was obsessed with Roderick Jones and what he saw as Reuters' failings under Jones's leadership. On five separate occasions Cooper recounted the story of how, more than twenty years earlier, Jones had coldly turned him down at their first meeting when Cooper offered AP's cooperation and help—dismissing as presumptuous the idea that AP, in the person of its relatively junior traffic chief, would have anything to offer the managing director of Reuters.[87]

Through patient effort, Haley convinced Cooper that Reuters had definitely changed for the better, and "once the ground had been won he was the staunchest friend." Reuters and AP—both now owned collectively by the newspapers of their respective nations, which Cooper had long considered the ideal form of organization for all news agencies— could be, in Cooper's words, "blood brothers" and "allies with a sense of common responsibility to the world." Cooper spoke more than once of his failure to have language about the free international exchange of news included in the Versailles peace treaties in 1919 because "Reuters and Havas had already plotted everything" in order to maintain the cartel system. Now he was enthusiastic about the prospects of AP and Reuters working together to promote international press freedom. In Haley's words, Cooper saw himself as "the Elder Statesman of the news agency world," the role he increasingly pursued after the publication of *Barriers Down*. At one point Cooper read long extracts of the manuscript-in-progress to Haley and eventually asked him to read all of it—now altered in light of their increasingly harmonious conversations to have a happy ending, at least as far as Reuters and AP were concerned.[88]

The motto of the new Reuters-AP relationship was "compete and co-operate." The 1942 contract did away with the inequality that had been integral to the 1934 agreement. Reuters and the Press Association would now provide only their news of Britain and the British Empire in exchange for AP's U.S. domestic coverage. The news that both agencies collected elsewhere in the world, amounting to most of their international coverage, would be mutually available only on a "bulletin protection" basis—that is, for use in a very short news item in case one agency had an important story that the other did not. "All the old anomalies are abolished," Haley told the Reuters board. "The news exchange is as exactly balanced as possible, and each clause is reciprocal."[89] For Cooper, the preamble urging "world-wide acceptance of the principle of a free press and international exchange of truthful unbiased news" was as significant as any of the practical clauses. Cooper told the head of APGB in London that the new relationship "should turn out to be one of the finest things that has ever happened" to AP.[90]

As AP began to pursue expansion more aggressively, however, competition came to the fore, jeopardizing 1942's hard-won emphasis on cooperation. With the end of the war in sight, AP rushed to take advantage of the collapse of news distribution networks in the Axis countries and the nations they occupied and to seek new opportunities in neutral countries like Switzerland and U.S. allies like Great Britain. Tensions came to a head in London, where the major national dailies represented by the Newspaper Proprietors Association (NPA) notified AP on May 4, 1945—three days before Kennedy's report of the German surrender—that they would discontinue their AP news service the following day. No explanation was given.[91] This development was of keen interest to Reuters, where an observer concluded that resentment of AP's "high-handed sales methods" was the main reason for the dramatic decision.[92] A week earlier, AP staff covering the founding conference of the United Nations in San Francisco reported prematurely that Germany had surrendered,[93] causing the London Sunday papers—many of which had to recall thousands of copies when the story proved to be inaccurate—"enormous embarrassment and considerable expense." Many British journalists believed that Cooper, supported by his $1 million annual budget, "was planning a grand campaign to make the world safe for American news."

Christopher Chancellor, Reuters' new chief executive, saw a direct connection between AP's London setback and its broader international thrust, "which in the eyes of many British newspapers is directed against Reuters."[94] The NPA-AP dispute gave Chancellor an excellent opportunity to counter AP's expansion plans and to weaken Cooper in the eyes of the AP board of directors. He pursued this opportunity adroitly and often duplicitously—praising Cooper to his face for his press freedom campaign while complaining at the same time to colleagues about "the appalling difficulty of dealing with this man, who never seems to remember what he has once said and who lives from brainstorm to brainstorm" and arguing that AP generally was "suffering from megalomania."[95] Chancellor was quite proud of his ability to present one face to Cooper (or others) and another to his colleagues, comparing himself at one point to a Spanish plenipotentiary during the long struggle for Dutch independence in the sixteenth century. "I am quite realistic about the AP," he told one Reuters director early in 1945. "But we must be cunning and bide our time. It was Philip the Second's representative in the Netherlands (Cardinal Granvelle) who operated always 'with the hand concealed.' Perhaps I am rather like the Cardinal."[96]

Chancellor's campaign to wring the greatest possible advantage from AP's difficulties received an unexpected boost when Arthur Sulzberger, now AP's vice president and a close ally of McLean, visited London on *New York Times* business. On a courtesy visit to Chancellor, Sulzberger heard for the first time about the problem with the NPA.[97] As Chancellor explained the situation— and as Sulzberger promptly told McLean—AP was experiencing a backlash against its overly aggressive sales tactics, "trying to accomplish in six months that which we should try to do in ten years." To make matters worse, the false German surrender report coincided with an AP advertising campaign stressing its journalistic virtues, with the result that "AP's name [is] mud."[98]

Sulzberger then began a round of meetings with the London newspaper proprietors and Reuters directors, hearing sharp criticism on all sides.[99] This crash course in the deficiencies of AP's approach to expansion was leading Sulzberger, in Chancellor's view, to question Cooper's leadership: "He realizes there is something seriously wrong with the AP management, and it is possible that we may hear of some interesting developments after he returns to NY."[100] Chancellor was particularly pleased to establish a direct channel to the AP board rather than relying on Cooper as the sole intermediary, especially since "there is a group in the AP Management favoring a break with Reuters."[101]

By the end of July, the immediate crisis came to an end: after Cooper apologized (using language proposed by Sulzberger), the NPA newspapers resumed their AP service.[102] AP was "still out to dominate the world," Chancellor reported to a Reuters director, "but after their recent setbacks they seem to be in a somewhat chastened mood." Nonetheless, the purported threats to cancel the AP-Reuters contract had shaken the board's confidence about the future of its relationship with AP.[103]

The atmosphere eventually became less fraught after Cooper unequivocally rejected any suggestion that the Reuters contract was in jeopardy.[104] In January 1946 he and Chancellor signed a new agreement that further expanded the scope of competition between AP and Reuters, with less reliance on each other's news and further erosion of the remaining traces of territorial exclusivity. AP could now include British domestic news supplied by the PA in its own service to Europe and Asia—areas that had been previously excluded—and Reuters could do the same with AP news of the United States in Canada, the West Indies, and South America.[105] The arrangement for bulletin protection on news from elsewhere in the world was scrapped, further heightening the competitive stakes. Now each agency had to rely exclusively on its own resources for international news. The new agreement, in Cooper's words, provided "the largest individual freedom of action that it was possible to work out."[106]

One significant remaining vestige of the post–World War I cartel system was dropped as well. As Stratton told Cooper, the greatest obstacle to AP's international expansion was the news exchange agreements that Reuters had with more than a dozen national news agencies in Europe, Africa, and Asia. Under the 1942 and earlier contracts, Reuters could provide the news it received from AP to these agencies as well. When asked about subscribing to AP, many accordingly responded by asking why they needed AP "when we receive the cream of AP's news through our agency's service from Reuters?"[107] These arrangements also compromised AP's efforts to sell its service directly to newspapers in those countries, which was the basis of its international strategy. The new contract effectively prohibited redistribution of AP news through the national agencies allied with Reuters.

For decades the international news system had been characterized by limits on competition[108]—both through the exclusive territorial arrangements of the cartel and the practices of national governments that traded preferential treatment and subsidies to nationally based agencies for influence over their news operations. Now AP and Reuters were committed to open competition everywhere in the world, with each operating increasingly on a truly global basis rather than focusing on historic spheres of influence. AP's emphasis was progressively more on establishing relations with individual newspapers, bypassing national agencies wherever possible. Nationality remained relevant, however, because journalistic conventions in many countries were different from those in the United States or Britain, meaning that potential clients had to be convinced of the desirability of AP or Reuters/PA news. This was one of many challenges that AP's ambitious post-1945 expansion plans had to confront.

* * *

In his annual report for 1944, Cooper noted that AP news was now being published in countries that "had not received objective news reports for nearly five years. . . . AP moved in with the troops as enemy territory was freed," in many cases with the assistance of American journalists who were now in military roles.[109] DNB ceased to exist with Germany's defeat, and in France, the successor to Havas, Agence France-Presse, was in the very earliest phases of organization, leaving an open field for AP and other international agencies to exploit.[110] AP had more than five hundred subscribers in Sweden, Italy, France, India, Switzerland, Denmark, Finland, Belgium, Holland, Norway, the Philippines, China, Japan, Korea, Turkey, Egypt, Greece, and Czechoslovakia by the end of 1945, with plans to include Austria, Yugoslavia, and Hungary the following year.[111] In Central and South America, AP served 210 newspapers and radio stations, an increase of more than 40 percent in two years. Stratton, who had day-to-day responsibility for AP's international operations, reported in the spring of 1946 that revenue covered only a little more than half the service's cost, estimating that an annual deficit of five hundred thousand dollars would be incurred for several years to come.[112] But the program was succeeding in its main purpose: while UP was still dominant internationally, it had been "stopped dead" in several countries and could no longer claim "unchallenged supremacy."[113]

Already, however, concern about the prospect of continuing heavy losses prompted Cooper, with McLean's approval, to rein in spending, both domestically and abroad. In February 1946, the American Newspaper Guild's newsletter reported that the growth of AP's worldwide operations had come to an abrupt halt. The increase in foreign staff was stopped and many were called back to the United States without being replaced.[114] McLean acknowledged that the report was accurate; he and Cooper agreed that in some parts of the world the rapid expansion outpaced not only current revenue but also any potential revenue.[115] Increased spending by itself, Cooper concluded, would not allow AP to "overcome the disadvantage of a late start."

The expansion program was thus severely curtailed about eighteen months after it began but by no means eliminated. Results varied widely from one country to another. Despite initial suspicions on the part of some German editors that AP was "the voice of the State Department," by 1947 its stories appeared more than twice as often in German newspapers as those of Reuters, its closest rival. A year later, the Berlin bureau chief reported that UP was so desperate about its deteriorating position in Germany that it was drastically cutting rates, to no effect.[116] At the same time, AP abandoned its efforts to sell news in India.[117] Two wide-ranging internal State Department reports in 1947 about the worldwide operations of U.S. news agencies showed that Reuters, thanks to its continuing connection to the national news agencies in many countries—a useful relic of the *agences alliées* system—was considerably stronger internationally than either AP or UP.[118] While AP was slightly ahead of or on an approximately equal footing with UP in several countries (Norway, Belgium, Sweden, Denmark, England, France, Turkey, Finland, and the Netherlands), it was behind almost everywhere in Latin America—generally the best international market for U.S. news—and seriously behind or shut out entirely in many other places (Portugal, Spain, Switzerland, South Africa, Czechoslovakia, Thailand, and Lebanon).

AP's efforts to make headway in in the Eastern European countries that were now firmly aligned with the USSR presented particular difficulties. As of November 1945, U.S. correspondents were at work in the capitals of all the Balkan countries and in Poland, Czechoslovakia, Hungary, and Austria.[119] Cooper reported that they were allowed to send dispatches covering many news developments, but their movements were restricted and they faced "varying degrees [of] political censorship." His views about dealing with what were, in effect, state news agencies—whether in the USSR, Soviet-bloc allies, or elsewhere—were complex if not downright contradictory. In the spring of 1947, he complained to the chief of AP's Paris bureau that French government news could only be obtained through Agence France-Presse, which would never be "anything other than a subsidized government news agency."[120] This meant that AP was helping to finance "a government news agency which sells government news, an outrageous thing that ought to be exposed if we can't break it down."[121] A few months later, however, Cooper took a more benign view of involvement with government-controlled agencies in his instructions to AP staffer Dan De-Luce about how to introduce the AP service into Romania, Bulgaria, Yugoslavia, and Poland. Cooper wanted to explore the possibilities not only of sending news from those countries to the outside world but also of importing news "so that we can tell those back of the iron curtain—. . . if there is one—what is going on in the rest of the world."[122] In Romania, for example, AP news could be made available to Romanian news agencies for a nominal amount with the understanding that AP material would not be manipulated "to say something we didn't say."[123] (A similar clause was already part of AP's contract with TASS.) As matters stood, AP news was being distributed in Romania anyway, without credit or any control over its use, and it was not practical to deal directly with individual newspapers. AP should therefore "work with what there is in any

country which does not have exactly the formula that we have in this country.
. . . Let's be cosmopolitan and adapt ourselves to the realistics on a friendly basis
in places where we must deal with governments."

This, of course, was very different from the position that for years Cooper
had advanced in public about the importance of American-style press freedom
being adopted in other countries. As had happened with Japan and Germany
in the 1930s, Cooper's focus on expansion and competition sometimes led to
practical arrangements with government-controlled or government-influenced
news agencies of the kind he regularly denounced elsewhere. At one point he
firmly corrected an AP bureau chief abroad for warning local newspapers that
their AP news service would be withdrawn if the government did not stop trying
to control correspondents' outgoing dispatches. AP, Cooper told his colleague,
should not try to "impose our standards on the will of a group of newspapers
or an agency that differs from us."[124] When operating in foreign countries, AP
should "adjust or apply the essentials of AP standards to the fullest extent possible to the practices of the substantial and responsible newspapers of the country." This was "merely tuning" AP's cardinal principles, not compromising them.

This may have been a realistic position for the head of a news agency that
wanted to operate in as many countries around the world as possible, but it was
also an acceptance of the limits on AP's freedom that accompanied international
expansion. As time went on, the situation for Western journalists in Eastern
bloc countries became steadily more difficult. AP correspondent Jack Guinn,
for one, was expelled from Hungary in November 1947, ostensibly because of
involvement in espionage.[125] Cooper did not protest the expulsion but succeeded in having a visa issued to DeLuce to replace him, telling the Hungarian
vice president that he was "certain that only Guinn is persona non grata and
that you wish Associated Press [to] have representative [in] Budapest."[126]

Despite these challenges, AP's postwar expansion program was strikingly
successful overall. By early 1948, AP had around eleven hundred newspaper
subscribers in fifty-six countries outside the United States, and its international
operations were breaking even by 1950.[127] When Cooper retired in 1951, AP news
was published in seventy countries outside the United States. The major markets were Latin America and the Caribbean (twenty-three countries), Europe
(nineteen), and Asia and Oceania (fourteen), with significant inroads being
made in Africa and the Middle East. Even without the adoption of free press
principles in postwar peace treaties or other international agreements, AP had
become a powerful force in most parts of the world.

12

The Voice of America

In Kent Cooper's public and private statements, AP's long campaign to withhold its news from the Voice of America (VOA)—which he forcefully led, with strong support from Robert McLean—was a simple matter of refusing to compromise AP's unbiased, impartial news report by association with a government propaganda agency of the kind he had seen in many other countries (and somewhat selectively denounced) for decades. The refusal to provide news to the VOA was in many ways a straightforward extension of Cooper's free press campaign, but it was also deeply entangled with two other challenges AP faced in the 1940s: the antitrust suit, which sharpened an antigovernment animus that had been building throughout the 1930s and left a bitter legacy, and the rush to take rapid advantage of opportunities to expand news sales internationally after the war ended. Despite sharply divided views among AP members and within the board of directors about U.S. government efforts to disseminate a positive image of the United States around the world, and despite strong and persistent pressure from the State Department and its supporters, Cooper and McLean were able to maintain a firm position against allowing the VOA to broadcast AP news. Eventually, as anti-Communist sentiment grew among publishers and politicians, a limited concession was made that eased the pressure on AP while avoiding any public acknowledgment of its cooperation and minimizing the likelihood of lost sales. In this increasingly fraught political atmosphere, it was remarkable that AP was able to resist as successfully as it did. In recent high-profile legal battles with the U.S. government over the Wagner Act and the antitrust prosecution, AP had consistently lost. This time, amid growing Cold War tensions, Cooper's full-throated defense of the idea that any direct government connection must be rejected—and that private ownership was the only proper form of organization for journalism—prevailed.[1]

*   *   *

Two months before the United States went to war with Germany and Japan in December 1941, AP's board of directors approved a request to deliver the same type of news service to the War Department as it had provided in World War I. The government paid for a leased-wire connection to AP's Washington bureau, and AP forwarded whatever news the bureau chief thought the department would find useful via a special sending operator.[2] This was done at no charge, Cooper wrote, because he was "opposed to taking Government money." This stricture, which Cooper often repeated, was actually observed in a hair-splitting way. AP itself, it was true, took no government money—but Press Association, its wholly owned and wholly controlled subsidiary that sold a condensed, broadcast-style news report to radio stations and other nonmembers, did, charging Army Intelligence and the Army Radio Bureau each one thousand dollars a month for its service.[3] There might be nonmonetary forms of compensation as well: the Washington bureau chief was instructed that in making the arrangements, he should "put the [War] Department under obligation to you so that [AP] will get some good out of it, perhaps in a news way." When it was proposed that the arrangement should be extended to the newly established Office of the Coordinator of Information—the immediate forerunner of the Office of Strategic Services and the CIA—Cooper identified another abiding concern. AP must get written assurances that its news would not be sent onward to South America "in competition with us," which would discredit AP "and might even put us out of business there."[4] Cooper realized from the start that a government agency's use of AP news in other countries would interfere with actual or potential sales.

In the summer of 1942, all U.S. government information programs—foreign and domestic—were consolidated in the newly created Office of War Information (OWI). It initially received (and paid for) the condensed Press Association report but wanted to install its own filing editor in AP's Washington bureau, with access to AP's entire news report.[5] By this point, AP had been charged with antitrust violations, and Byron Price (then the chief U.S. press censor) told Cooper that the prosecution would not be stayed on grounds that AP was an essential war service. Cooper saw a clear connection between the two issues. "There is considerable inconsistency in the world, isn't there?" he asked the Washington bureau chief, Paul Miller.[6] "One department of the government says we are not essential to winning the war and another says they can't get along without us!" AP initially refused the request, but this position did not last; by the spring of 1943, the OWI's office in Washington was connected to AP's main news wire, and the OWI was proposing similar connections to its offices in New York and San Francisco.[7] In a pointed letter to Henry Stimson, the secretary of war, Cooper demanded a guarantee that AP material would not be accessible to competitors or non-subscribers in areas where AP service was otherwise available.[8] This condition was carefully observed. For example, when AP began offering a news service to Swedish newspapers and radio stations in 1944, the OWI agreed to curtail its own service to Sweden.[9] Immediately after the war ended, the OWI's withdrawal from news distribution in Germany gave Cooper "fond hopes that we could get a good start" there.[10]

By the end of 1944, the State Department was making plans to continue some version of the OWI's international news operations in peacetime. When Cooper heard about this from Col. Noel Macy—a wartime State Department employee who, as publisher of a group of Westchester County newspapers in New York, had been an AP member for many years—he replied that U.S. news agencies, including AP, were already taking steps to provide "adequate, independent world news outside of the United States."[11] It would be difficult to develop these services, however, if the government continued to distribute news itself. Meanwhile he complained to Miller that the OWI was "compet[ing] with us on our own stuff all over the world."[12] Cooper also began to campaign publicly against continuation of the government's news operation overseas. In a late 1944 speech commemorating the adoption of the Bill of Rights—which included the First Amendment guarantee of press freedom—he denounced suggestions that the United States should engage in "foreign propaganda in the guise of news," which could be a first step toward "what brought on Germany's moral degradation as a nation."[13]

Soon after the war against Japan ended, President Harry Truman ordered the establishment of a permanent information program to present "a full and fair picture of American life and of the aims and policies of the United States government" to the world, stressing that this would not compete with private

American media organizations and would focus only on areas of the world where they did not operate.[14] AP's news story about the announcement described it as establishing "America's first peacetime foreign propaganda program," adding that Truman was taking "revolutionary steps in the conduct of American foreign policy."[15] William Benton was hired as assistant secretary for information and cultural programs with a mandate to put the new program in place.[16] Benton retired from the New York advertising agency that bore his name, Benton and Bowles, in 1936 and then went on to positions as assistant to Robert Hutchins, president of the University of Chicago (and head of the Commission on Freedom of the Press), and as publisher of the *Encyclopedia Britannica*. The new program would require congressional authorization and a budgetary appropriation (unlike the wartime-emergency OWI), and the cooperation of AP, UP, and INS was considered crucial to avoid accusations that the government was usurping the role of privately owned news organizations. The OWI's shortwave broadcasts to Europe during the war were known as the Voice of America, and Benton adopted this name for the whole program of international broadcasts.[17] For the next two years, he waged a high-profile, high-pressure, and almost constant campaign to persuade AP to provide its news to VOA but never succeeded. Benton's vigorous public criticism essentially backfired, causing some AP publishers who might otherwise have sympathized with his cause to dig in their heels—although it's far from certain that a more diplomatic approach would have been any more successful.

When Macy and Benton first approached McLean to discuss the availability of AP news for the new program, he referred them to Cooper, who spent no more than ten minutes in discussion with Macy before recommending that he make his case to the board of directors.[18] During a half-hour meeting in November, the directors' only questions to Macy were about how the government program would affect AP's international news distribution. The board was very concerned, Lloyd Stratton told Macy afterward, that AP's expansion plans would be compromised by "competition with itself on its own news product."[19] AP's counteroffer was strictly limited in duration and geographical scope. The VOA would be allowed to use AP news only in the few areas—such as Germany and the Balkans—where it was not already available to newspapers directly. News would not be delivered to any VOA offices in the United States but only at the nearest point to the area in question and only in the local language. So, for example, AP news for broadcast to Germany would be made available in German in London or Paris. Macy replied that while he understood AP's concerns about competition, the proposal was unworkable. All VOA broadcasts were produced either in New York or San Francisco; it had no staff anywhere else in the world, "so a news report delivered elsewhere would be of no use to us."[20] Nor would it be possible to limit the use of AP news to broadcasts in individual languages, because in an effort to keep costs down a single newscast was prepared and only then translated. Removing AP stories "in some languages and not in others would present very real operational difficulties." In short, if the AP report was not made available in the United States, the VOA could not use it anywhere. Macy then repeated the initial request—that AP continue to provide its news to the VOA in New York and San Francisco as it had done during the war.

The board definitively rejected this request in January 1946. A resolution drafted by Arthur Sulzberger—who generally was in favor of the government's international information program, except for AP news—declared that "news disseminated by non-governmental news agencies is essential to the highest development of mankind and to the perpetuation of peace between nations."[21] The borrowing of Cooper's language from *Barriers Down* and many recent speeches was clear. While it might be useful for governments to maintain official libraries of information around the world, the resolution concluded that "government cannot engage in newscasting without creating the fear of propaganda which necessarily would reflect upon the objectivity of the news services" that supplied it. AP immediately stopped providing news to the VOA as successor to the OWI.

This flat refusal—announced to the world a few days later on the front page of the *New York Times*—left no room for negotiation and set off a furious campaign by Benton to force AP to relent.[22] His immediate response, sent to McLean, all other AP directors, and the press, was that the decision "jeopardizes American interests, American security and the cause of peace itself."[23] It also impugned the integrity of UP and INS, which were continuing to provide their news to VOA. The VOA did not engage in propaganda but was under constant pressure to keep its broadcasts objective and impartial. Worst of all, AP was continuing to make its news available to the Soviet news agency TASS (and to the government-supported British Broadcasting Corporation [BBC]), giving "the Russians the benefit of the doubt which they refuse to give to the government of their own country."

The argument that AP should not withhold its news from the U.S. government while providing it to TASS was difficult to answer. The day after Benton's letter was published, Sulzberger reported to McLean that he was receiving letters and telegrams "asking why [AP] takes action against its own State Department and does not restrict its news from other governments who might also abuse it."[24] McLean agreed, telling Cooper that this was "the most serious charge" that AP had to meet.[25] Sulzberger wanted the board to pass a second resolution stating that AP would withhold its news from foreign governments that received it either directly or indirectly, but this was postponed so that Cooper would have time to discuss the necessary contractual changes with TASS and other AP partners. Stratton had already started working on this. The BBC was to be told that the service would not be available for international broadcasting after the current contract ended; AP's close ally Canadian Press would also have to stop making AP news available for the international broadcasts of the Canadian Broadcasting Corporation (CBC).[26] Benton, meanwhile, continued to hammer at AP's weak point. It was inconceivable, he said in another statement for the press, that a citizen of a European country should "be able to listen to the Russian radio and the British Broadcasting Corporation about developments throughout the world, prepared from material furnished by an American news agency, and yet listen to an American shortwave broadcast from which the same source of news is withheld."[27] James Byrnes, the secretary of state, said AP (and UP, which by now had followed AP's lead in withdrawing service) were exercising "discrimination against our government. . . . You should be willing to agree that as long as you continue to furnish news service to any foreign government you will either give or sell the same service to the United State government."[28]

Cooper's blanket rejection of any form of journalistic organization other than private ownership underlay his position on the use of AP news by its international allies. It was no more acceptable for public broadcasters like BBC or CBC to use AP news in international broadcasts than it was for TASS to do so; all were subsidized by governments and therefore equally tainted. McLean and others at AP, however, recognized that the BBC's international shortwave broadcasts were successful precisely because of the company's reputation for impartiality.[29] BBC governors insisted that all of its foreign-language broadcasts must be "objective and non-propagandist."[30] In the U.S. context, Cooper saw government-sponsored international news broadcasting as a kind of Trojan horse; if it was accepted, the next step would be establishment of a government-controlled news service, to be "utilized domestically by the party in power."[31] Cooper was like many supporters of profit-oriented commercial broadcasting in the United States—the so-called American system—who, in David Goodman's words, refused to admit "any distinction between public

funding [of broadcasting] and government 'control.'"³² Cooper never admitted
the possibility that public-service journalism might serve readers and listeners
as well as privately owned news organizations. In his defense, it could be said
that he had seen many examples during his career of news agencies whose independence was compromised by government support or outright control; he
rarely acknowledged, however, the ways that private owners (and a system of
private ownership) could shape news coverage to suit their own interests. Nor
did he acknowledge in public the ways in which AP did accept government assistance, such as in China, where AP, UP, and other American correspondents
relied heavily on U.S. government transmission facilities.³³

The State Department's international information program had three distinct
elements involving news, and its impact on AP depended on which of these
was being considered. One was the direct cable and wireless news service that
OWI provided to newspapers and radio stations abroad during the war. It was
now supplied only to news organizations in Germany, Austria, Japan, and a few
other countries, and Benton pledged that even in these places it would be dis-
continued as soon as private news agencies were able to operate there. In this
connection, the government's policy was to do "everything within its power to
break down the artificial barriers to the expansion abroad of private American
news agencies . . . and not to compete with it."³⁴ A second element was the daily
wireless bulletin sent to U.S. embassies and missions abroad, which included
four or five paragraphs of "miscellaneous press," using material from newspapers
and news agencies. It was for the personal information of U.S. diplomats who
received it, not to be published locally, and therefore "not competitive to the
wire services." AP disputed this, however; Stratton said local distribution of
news from the embassy bulletins "has caused more competitive difficulty than
anything or from anybody else."³⁵ (The conflicting accounts of how the bulletins
were used eventually led to a serious misunderstanding between Cooper and
McLean.) But Benton insisted that shortwave broadcasts, the third element of
VOA's news distribution plan and accessible to anyone with a suitable radio,
were different: they must include news agency material in order to "present a
well-rounded picture of the American scene." McLean was prepared to allow
AP news to be used in embassy bulletins with strict protection against local
distribution, especially since it would "take some of the 'heat'" off AP.³⁶ But
AP could not agree to widespread shortwave broadcasting, he told Byrnes. Its
reputation around the world was "a national asset of inestimable value," which
could be endangered if it supplied news to the VOA in this form.³⁷

Competition with United Press also played a part in AP's stand. In Cooper's triumphant recounting of events, AP's unequivocal rejection of cooperation with the VOA put its rival into "a paroxism [*sic*] of anguish" that it had not already taken this step.[38] A few days after AP's decision, UP also notified the State Department that its news would no longer be available, on essentially the same grounds. In Roy Howard's words, "Any news dissemination by the State Department . . . will inevitably be regarded as propaganda" and "wreck one of our great national assets . . . the world-wide acceptance of the objectivity and freedom from propaganda of the news report of the American press associations."[39] Cooper feared that any backtracking on AP's part now would allow UP to portray itself "as the sole standard bearer of the principle that our government keep out of news collection and dissemination at home and abroad." Competition with UP—a matter of self-interest rather than principle—may not have been the main reason for AP's position, as Benton asserted, but it was certainly one reason.[40] The third major U.S. news agency, INS, continued to provide its news to VOA for use in areas where private news agencies didn't currently operate on a temporary basis, but it had considerably less original international coverage than either AP or UP.[41]

In the wake of several discussions in person and much correspondence between Benton and McLean, a proposal that the State Department could use AP material in the news section of its wireless bulletins—for the personal information of State Department staff and not to be distributed otherwise—was presented to the board of directors in February.[42] This was along the lines of McLean's discussions with Benton, but Cooper objected vociferously to the suggestion that the directors should approve this step by a mail-in vote before their next scheduled meeting. He felt justified in putting forward his personal opinions so emphatically because the board's VOA decisions to date had been made at his "insistent recommendation," although he continued to insist for public consumption that he kept his personal views strictly to himself.[43]

Cooper's argument placed much emphasis on the current U.S. political context. Benton was struggling to gain congressional approval for the significant new spending involved in the State Department's plans, with Republicans and conservative Democrats opposed to what they considered another New Deal program.[44] AP's decision to stop supplying news to the VOA seriously damaged this effort, undercutting Benton's assurances that the program would not compete with private news organizations.[45] Any change in AP's position now, Cooper warned, would amount to "a confession by us that we went too far (which we did not) and that the government scared us out of the moral stand we took."[46] When the State Department was informed privately after the directors meeting in January that AP would not provide its news to the VOA, no objection was heard; Benton "went into a violent public fit" only when the resolution was published, which he saw as "an attack on his efforts to get forty million dollars of government money. . . . If we had quit serving the State Department and never had published the Board's resolution we never would have heard a word from Mr. Benton." AP "set the moral standard for the world" by refusing to accept a tainted government connection, and any change in its position now would nullify that stand. In fact, publication of the board's decision restored AP's good name, "which had been clouded for fifty years" by its relations with many government-backed agencies. Supplying news to the State Department, to be redistributed free of charge, would also undermine AP's painstaking efforts to show international clients that its news was worth paying for. Benton's public attacks on the board's motives and his heavy-handed campaign to force AP to change its stance made it "inexpedient" even to consider any modification.

Cooper's recommendation to stand pat was accepted unanimously, leaving the April board meeting as Benton's next opportunity to present his case.[47] Benton continued to operate on two fronts at once, on one hand asking McLean in an ingratiating tone for advice about how best to approach the board—even while members of his staff considered launching a surprise pro-VOA resolution at AP's general meeting.[48] At the same time, he was advised to soften attacks on AP in a forthcoming speech. A proposed reference to the directors as "reformed alcoholics and Bourbons is not in good taste and will both offend our supporters and cause a permanent rupture with the Board," a colleague warned.[49]

This speech, focusing entirely on AP, was delivered to the New York Newspaper Women's Club at a public forum on press freedom in March. Sulzberger and Eleanor Roosevelt were among the other speakers. As he had done all along, Benton dismissed AP's stated concern about association with government propaganda.[50] The real, unstated reasons for AP's stand were "plain dislike of government," fear of competition for international subscribers, and the desire to "score a smart sales advantage . . . by beating the UP to the draw in proclaiming its purity." All of these did in fact have much to do with AP's position, but the propaganda argument was not so easily dismissed. Sulzberger rejected the "facile" charge of hidden motives; he was present when the AP board made its decision, and Benton was not.[51] Sulzberger's anger came through more clearly in his complaint to managing editor Edwin James about the *Times*' own coverage of the speech: Benton "made a vitriolic, ill-tempered, thoroughly wrong attack on the AP and, to my mind, that is not sufficiently conveyed to our readers."[52] This episode was a good example of how Benton's aggressive approach could alienate a potential ally. The *Times* made its own news available to the VOA, and Sulzberger generally supported the State Department's international information program. He also criticized Cooper's handling of the withdrawal of service: AP should have given at least a month's notice, as UP did. (Macy was told on a Friday that the service would end the following Monday.) "It seems to me that we were trigger happy and, after my experience with the London publishers this past year, I blame myself for not having raised the question of how we were going to cancel."[53] For McLean, Benton's speech provided further evidence that he "has small regard for facts" and showed that it was impossible to discuss anything with him without the risk that AP's position would be misrepresented.[54]

As the board meeting where Benton was to present his case in person approached, the legislative climate for the State Department's information program was becoming chillier. A bill to put it on a permanent footing was stopped in the House Foreign Affairs Committee, partly out of concern about AP's and UP's objections, while the House Appropriations Committee slashed the program's proposed $20 million budget in half.[55] (The money was restored a few months later, allowing the VOA to remain on the air.[56]) Meanwhile, if any doubt remained about the reception awaiting Benton, Cooper's speech to AP's assembled members at the annual meeting—a day before Benton's visit to the board—removed it.

In a long address that took most members by surprise and was apparently decided on only at the last minute, Cooper presented AP's ambitious international expansion program as the solution to all the problems enumerated in *Barriers Down*.[57] It would "make available to the people of all countries the blessed right to know—not, God forbid, through government propaganda but by the method that has given that right to the people of this country."[58] That method, of course, was AP's approach to news, with its adherence to principles of "objectivity, truthfulness, impartiality and accuracy," setting a standard for the whole world and "spreading the doctrine of a free press to all people hungry for unbiased information." But if AP went along with the State Department's demands, this program would be gravely threatened; newspapers in other countries wanted nothing to do with agencies that cooperated with governments spreading propaganda.

Responding to the charge that AP provided news to government-connected news organizations in other countries while withholding it from the U.S. government, Cooper pointed out that AP's agreement with TASS prohibited redistribution of AP news outside the Soviet Union: "AP news is therefore not involved in Russian international propaganda." The agreement that allowed Canadian Press to provide AP news to the "government owned" Canadian Broadcasting Corporation for use in international shortwave broadcasts was about to end and would not be renewed; a similar agreement with the BBC would end as soon as possible. Everywhere else in the world where AP provided news to government-connected agencies it did so only for domestic use "and not for international propaganda purposes." The AP news service carried a substantial story about the speech, emphasizing Cooper's plea for recognition of the altruistic motives behind AP's expansion plans and the "utter lack of any thought that the undertaking would be selfishly remunerative."[59]

In its session that day, the board of directors complained about unfounded allegations of hidden motives (by Benton, obviously) but also responded to "certain sober criticism" of AP's position. The claim that VOA broadcasts would not be propaganda but simply a fair representation of the news that AP reported reflected "a misunderstanding of what propaganda is. . . . Any broadcast designed to promote our way of life will of necessity be propaganda—good propaganda possibly, from an American viewpoint, but certainly not objective news presentation."[60] AP's acceptance around the world as objective was "an asset of inestimable value and makes its contribution to universal understanding since the reporting of events as they are is a basis of confidence between peoples." With AP's position set out so explicitly beforehand, the meeting with Benton was an anticlimax. The board listened to him politely for an hour, asked questions for forty-five minutes, and promptly reaffirmed the decision to withhold AP news from the VOA.[61]

With his efforts to engage directly with AP approaching a dead end, Benton sought to mobilize other publishers, most of them AP members, to support the VOA. There was certainly room for progress in this direction. A survey in *Editor & Publisher* showed as many publishers and editors in favor of the government program as were opposed to it, and an editorial called on AP and UP to reverse their stand.[62] A few days before AP's annual meeting, Benton addressed the American Society of Newspaper Editors, which took the welcome step of appointing a committee to study the State Department's information program—something Benton had unsuccessfully urged AP to do for months.

The ASNE also refused to endorse the stand taken by AP and UP.[63] Over the summer, the ASNE committee conducted interviews with State Department officials and representatives of AP, UP, and INS.[64] Edwin James of the *New York Times*, appointed to the committee at Sulzberger's behest, told his boss that the group had "a rather fiery time" in its session with Cooper, Stratton, and Alan Gould, with Cooper taking three hours to outline his views.[65] It was a "splendid speech," James reported, but both he and Sulzberger remained unconvinced by Cooper's uncompromising stand.[66]

After its New York meetings, the ASNE group had "a long and howling executive session" in which it became clear that there was no chance of a substantive agreement. The result was a "lame compromise . . . that the government ought to be doing something of the kind at this time, that what it is doing is dangerous, and that therefore it ought to be watched closely by competent news authorities."[67] A flat endorsement of the State Department program and criticism of AP and UP for refusing to participate—a possibility that Cooper had initially worried about—was averted, but he regretted that the day should come "when a group of American newsmen can accept the principle that humanity can be benefitted by the government going into the news business."[68] If the government "can get their oar in abroad . . . they will turn their experience into the domestic field," he warned the chairman of the ASNE committee. "Watch this, fellow. 'You ain't seen nothin' yet.'" Cooper's apocalyptic fears about VOA setting the stage for a large-scale domestic propaganda program may have been exaggerated, but he repeated the warning often.

The final ASNE report was a study in equivocation. It concluded that everyone involved—Benton and the State Department; AP and UP, with their staunch refusal to make their news available; and INS, which had continued to provide its news temporarily—had equally honorable motives. Most (but not all) members of the committee went along with Benton's request to avoid use of the word "propaganda." In fact, though, the report's affirmation that all VOA content was subject to "control of policy" editing—intended to "maintain America in its most favorable light"—made it quite clear that the broadcasts were not independent or impartial. The final conclusion was that "the present uncertainties in global relations" justified the U.S. government's desire to explain its actions and policies to people around the world, but the ASNE should continue to monitor the State Department program in view of "the dangers inherent in government dissemination of news."

Cooper's vigorous rejection of any government involvement in news also colored his response to the work of the Commission on Freedom of the Press, a private body established by Henry Luce and headed by Robert Hutchins, president of the University of Chicago. The commission was sharply critical of U.S. journalism—for reasons including growing concentration of ownership, its tendency to provide readers with a steady diet of sensation and gossip in pursuit of profits, and especially a lack of accountability—and concluded that the press must systematically improve itself or risk external regulation.[69] Cooper denounced the commission's volume on international communication because it appeared to "justify the government making up for the deficiencies of the American press associations" just as he, and AP, were marshaling in opposition to the VOA.[70] This report actually endorsed most of Cooper's proposals for postwar freedom-of-information agreements and stated specifically that private organizations rather than governments should have full responsibility for improving international understanding to the extent that they could accomplish this. But it also concluded that they were not fulfilling this responsibility as of February 1946 and recommended that the State Department should continue to provide as much of the international news service that had been operated by the OWI as private agencies "cannot or will not undertake."[71] Many American journalists and journalism organizations criticized the commission's work, with Cooper among the most uncompromising. Its final report, the work of "college presidents and professors," suggested that the American press "lacks responsibility which a political party in control of the government could supply."[72] This meant that "a form of the Russian Soviet conception of press control would be imposed." Wilbur Forrest of the ASNE had a more focused complaint: the commission's criticism of American journalism made it harder to convince journalists and government officials in other countries that the U.S. press was a model to be emulated.[73]

*   *   *

The enunciation of the Truman Doctrine in March 1947—which called for substantial U.S. aid to Greece's royalist government, fighting a Communist-led insurrection—was a milestone in the evolution of the Cold War, reflecting and heightening tensions between the United States and the Soviet Union. In his first press conference, the newly appointed secretary of state, Gen. George Marshall, described Benton's broadcasting program as "a very important matter. ... It seems to me absolutely essential that from somewhere—in this case, the

United States—we endeavor to cover the world with the truth."[74] The political atmosphere in Washington was changing; one indication was that Rep. Karl Mundt, the South Dakota Republican who had strongly opposed the State Department's information program a year earlier, now sponsored a bill authorizing the VOA operation.[75] Cooper was considering testifying before the House Foreign Affairs Committee—the program was something that "I, as an individual, if not as an executive of [AP], feel I should oppose on moral grounds"[76]—but McLean warned him to proceed carefully. The AP board had not taken a stand for or against the government's information program in general but only on the narrower question of AP's participation, reflecting a sharp internal division.[77] Cooper replied that he was astonished to be told that the board had not rejected the government's "broadcasting propaganda program" in its entirety.[78] If McLean felt so strongly that Cooper should "remain mum on this issue," perhaps the board should consider a speech that he was planning to deliver in Chicago later that month.

Cooper sought out comments from others as well on a speech that he obviously considered a crucial public intervention in the VOA debate. He forwarded a draft to Arthur Krock, the *New York Times* Washington columnist, saying he was "trying to get up the nerve" to ask Sulzberger to have it printed in the *Times*, which had "leaned over so far in its news columns in the direction of the Benton program" without presenting the other side of the question.[79] McLean sharply criticized the draft. Far from being a dispassionate appraisal, it was simply a plea "that the distribution of world news be left to private American enterprise and particularly to [AP]."[80] Cooper's opinions would inevitably be seen as an expression of AP's views, and he should not seek extensive publication of the speech, distribute copies except on request—and certainly not to members of Congress—or go beyond AP's normal practice in reporting it. Sulzberger, with mounting frustration, told McLean that Cooper was getting involved in an inappropriate way and should not make the speech at all.[81] The public battle lines were clearly drawn, with Marshall insisting before a House Foreign Affairs subcommittee that "so long as propaganda is engaged in, we are faced with the necessity of taking action ourselves," while a committee of the journalism fraternity Sigma Delta Chi (with Cooper and UP's Baillie among its members) registered its opposition to the program.[82]

Cooper was at his manipulative worst in responding to McLean's concerns about the speech. He raised—only to immediately discard as "pseudo-dramatic"—the possibility that he might resign so that he could deliver the speech without implicating AP. He also rejected the idea of submitting the text to the directors in advance. If they refused to approve it, he would also have to resign, producing "a rift in the membership that would be far more destructive" than anything he might say in public. It would be better if he went ahead and made the speech on his own responsibility, leaving the board free to take any action it wished afterward, "up to and including my resignation."[83] The threat, though couched in subjunctives, could not have been much more explicit. Cooper did make several revisions to the draft, however, and McLean eventually pronounced himself satisfied.[84]

The speech—delivered to a newspaper group, the Inland Press Association, in Chicago on May 26—was polemical, bitterly sarcastic, and full of dire predictions. Insisting, implausibly as ever, that he spoke only as an individual, Cooper presented the issue in stark terms, as a conflict "between government propaganda disguised as news, and news written without bias as sponsored by our free press."[85] It would have been more honest for the U.S. government frankly to admit that, since it could not control the international activities of American news agencies, it wanted one of its own, much as the Soviet government had TASS. In fact, the relevant branch of the State Department should be named TAUS—Telegraph Agency of the United States—on the Soviet model. The VOA broadcasts were more likely to backfire than succeed in their aims: propaganda distributed by shortwave would only inflame tensions without inciting listeners in the Soviet Union and its satellites to rise up against their authoritarian governments. Meanwhile, the simultaneous bursts of international news distribution activity by American news agencies and the U.S. government were creating "wonder and fear abroad whether this dual activity is the result of a secret pact between the government and the news agencies which forebodes American world imperialism."[86]

Cooper's free-enterprise views were forcefully stated. Not only did the VOA invade a field that should be left to private business; more broadly, providing "truthful news to mankind by private instead of government enterprise is more important than any other private economic function; also it is beneficially performed only by private enterprise."[87] Historian Quinn Slobodian has trenchantly criticized the notion of "market fundamentalism," noting that the rules of the market are set by regulations imposed by governments and international organizations.[88] Cooper's call for press freedom to be mandated around the world in postwar settlements, limiting the ability of national governments to regulate the operations of foreign-based news agencies, is a good example of this deliberate market-shaping activity. But when it came to the U.S. domestic market, Cooper was unequivocal in asserting that journalism must be wholly unregulated and left entirely in the hands of private business. These free-enterprise views were complicated, though, by his critique of the profit motive—at least as far as news agencies were concerned, although not their newspaper clients. He constantly cited AP's nonprofit status, in contrast to the commercial approach of UP and INS, as the guarantor of its independence and objectivity.

AP's story about the speech led with Cooper's spectacular charge that government propaganda is "a maelstrom of international self-seeking where wars are brewed," and the full text was published in *Editor & Publisher*.[89] For Sulzberger, Cooper had not observed either the letter or spirit of his exchanges with McLean: "Kent decries propaganda with such vigor that he becomes guilty of it.... I'm very much upset by it."[90] Cooper, however, was pleased with the public response, including congratulations from Roy Howard, who described the speech as "a honey."[91] Benton did not respond publicly for three weeks. Besides reengaging in the interminable debate about whether the VOA was engaged in propaganda, his most substantial point was that contrary to Cooper's assertions, there were still many areas of the world where U.S. agencies did not operate, at least for the time being and possibly for the foreseeable future.[92]

This was one of Benton's last skirmishes with AP. He left the State Department in September 1947, after VOA legislation had been passed in the House of Representatives. The Senate followed suit in January 1948, after a congressional delegation returned from a European fact-finding tour convinced that the VOA was absolutely necessary as a way of combating Soviet propaganda.[93] Benton's replacement was George Allen, a foreign service officer who had been U.S. ambassador to Iran.[94] Now that the program had solid bipartisan support in Congress and strong backing from Marshall, the State Department launched a new effort to gain access to AP and UP news.

A report prepared for Allen stated that about a quarter of VOA content was straight news, mainly material taken from New York metropolitan newspapers and supplemented by Reuters, INS, the Dutch news agency Aneta, and the radio news service Transradio.[95] The problem was that any items in the New York newspapers that came from AP or UP could not be used—and Reuters' coverage could not always be relied on, since it did "not always present the U.S. point of view accurately." Allen forwarded the memorandum to Sulzberger, saying the department was "severely handicapped, by lack of your service, in doing an effective job assigned to us by overwhelming vote of Congress."[96] The

U.S. government's involvement in international news broadcasting was "temporary, dictated by the world situation"; eventually news coverage would once again be left entirely to private enterprise, a system to which Allen was fiercely devoted. He also presented his case at the annual meeting of the ASNE, which urged AP and UP to provide "adequate summaries"—but not their full news services—to the VOA, citing "special circumstances arising out of the present crisis in Europe."[97]

Allen formally asked AP at the end of May 1948 to reverse its earlier refusal and begin supplying its news to VOA.[98] It was understandable that AP made the decision it did in 1946, when it was not clear that Congress would ever approve a permanent information program. But now that the Smith-Mundt legislation had been approved by an overwhelming bipartisan majority in both houses of Congress, that uncertainty no longer existed. Meanwhile, the reasons that led Congress to act had become even more pressing. After a Communist-backed coup, Czechoslovakia had fallen under totalitarian domination, and other European countries faced similar threats. In their propaganda programs, the Soviet Union and its allies had "declared war, so to speak, against the people and the way of life of the United States."

By now Cooper was ready to compromise—a little. He proposed giving VOA tacit permission to pick up and use any AP news after it was published or broadcast but only in order to confirm the accuracy of reports received from other sources: "In other words, if there is something that they receive from Reuters, or INS, or Trans-Radio and they are in doubt about its accuracy, they can use the newspapers to check what [AP] says."[99] VOA staff could also phone the AP news desk for up-to-date information on any particular story of urgent or vital interest.[100] The arrangement was not to be announced or otherwise made public, eliminating the possibility of harm to AP's reputation.[101]

The State Department was disposed to accept this proposal, although Allen bridled at Cooper's insistence that that it should not be acknowledged publicly.[102] It was ridiculous, he wrote, for AP to fear that it would be tainted if it were known that its news was provided to VOA. No other American corporation was condemned for selling its products to the government, and news was "a commodity just like cars or washing machines." A few months later, McLean complained that the new head of VOA, Charles Thayer, was only concerned about winning the Cold War and did not consider whether AP "gains or loses, whether the principle of unbiased and accurate news is lost in the shuffle."[103]

Cooper's fears that high-ranking U.S. government officials did not understand journalism were evidently well founded, at least in this instance.

AP's directors were not satisfied with Cooper's minimal concession, however. As tensions between the United States and the USSR mounted, many members of the board were reconsidering the blanket refusal to let the VOA use AP news. Fearing a complete reversal, Cooper asked his European bureau chiefs whether cooperation with the VOA would play into European journalists' fears that AP was the voice of U.S. foreign policy.[104] The Berlin bureau chief, Wes Gallagher—eventually one of Cooper's successors as general manager—replied that "propaganda-shy German editors, remembering the Goebbels days" and now inundated with Soviet propaganda, could easily lose confidence in AP if that happened.[105] Yet Cooper recognized that directors' opinions were changing and that they were becoming impatient with his protests. "I have become convinced that it is futile for me any further to point up the realities to the board," he told McLean in December.[106]

McLean shared most of Cooper's concerns about the damage to AP's reputation that would arise from working directly with the VOA but also wanted to offer some further concession that would mollify his wavering colleagues.[107] Eventually he and Cooper agreed that the State Department should be allowed to use AP items from its Washington city news ticker in the wireless bulletin sent to embassies around the world.[108] In addition, as Cooper had proposed earlier, the VOA could use the facts in AP news reports after they were published or broadcast, but AP news would not be delivered directly to the VOA newsroom.[109] This would "take a good deal of the heat off" AP, Cooper noted; the fact that news in the embassy bulletins was usually twenty-four hours behind AP's regular transmissions was another point in its favor. McLean then convinced Sulzberger and other pro-VOA directors to accept the new plan. If AP became directly involved with VOA, "the principle of international comity and honesty in news"—the moral concept that it, and the United States, had brought to the world—could be lost.[110] McLean's virtually wholesale adoption of Cooper's views and language was striking. On a more practical level, if the VOA used reports by AP correspondents inside the Soviet Union or its allied countries in efforts to foment discontent among their citizens, AP journalists—already often suspected of engaging in espionage—would be subject to expulsion or official harassment.[111] The board ratified the arrangement, reaffirming that AP's news report "should not be made available to any government, or agency of any government, for use in propaganda broadcasts," which would be a "denial of the basic objectivity to which [AP] is unalterably dedicated."[112]

McLean and Cooper worked together more closely than they had in years to achieve this result, but one significant misunderstanding arose between them. Cooper had been operating under the assumption—confirmed by his own State Department contact, a former AP war correspondent whom he respected—that the embassy bulletins were made available only to U.S. diplomatic staff and not to local journalists.[113] McLean, however, specified to the new secretary of state, Dean Acheson, that that the bulletins *would* be distributed to local press agencies and newspapers, and it was on this basis that the agreement proceeded. Cooper learned about the mix-up only when he received a complaint from AP's Singapore bureau in June. The general manager of the *Straits Times* newspaper had told the bureau chief that since he was receiving the wireless bulletin every day, the AP service was less valuable.[114] Under the circumstances, he wanted to reduce the amount paid to AP, and the bureau chief feared this was just the first of many such requests. Two weeks later, Cooper received a complaint from the Cairo bureau chief, whose story about an anti-Muslim purge in the Soviet republic of Turkestan was distributed via the embassy bulletin almost as soon as he filed it, "blunting [a] good exclusive."[115] McLean rejected Cooper's demand that local distribution be prohibited immediately, but it was eventually agreed that AP news in the wireless bulletin would be released locally in countries only where AP did not distribute its own news and without attribution.[116]

One more attempt was made to obtain AP and UP news for VOA broadcasts in 1950, when Allen was replaced by Edward Barrett, a former editor of *Newsweek*, with the support of Edward R. Murrow, who eventually became head of the United States Information Agency, which controlled the VOA. The request was summarily turned down.[117] A proposal from the newly established National Committee for Free Europe, organized by John Foster Dulles (with backing from the Central Intelligence Agency), to use AP news in its broadcasts was also rejected.[118] AP's policy was clear, McLean wrote; it refused "all use of the service in connection with any propaganda of foreign broadcasts by any person, government, or organization."

The struggle over AP's refusal to provide its news to the VOA had now gone on for five years. This was a pivotal period in both U.S. politics and international relations, when the world became firmly divided into antagonistic camps of West and East and anti-Communism became the dominant American ideology. Under these circumstances, it was striking that AP not only succeeded in refusing to participate but also wanted to refuse to participate in what Benton described as an essential tool to combat widespread misunderstanding of the United States around the world—even as other journalistic groups like ASNE, and many AP directors and members, strongly disagreed.

Cooper's uncompromising refusal to have anything to do with government propaganda—a characterization that could not convincingly be disputed in view of the VOA's systematic practice of "control of policy" editing and its overall intention to show the United States in the best possible light—was the product of mixed motives, as his actions often were. The fact that free, government-backed international news broadcasts using AP material would severely hamper AP's postwar expansion plans was a central and consistent element of Cooper's opposition to VOA (as was the realization that UP would benefit if AP supplied the VOA and UP did not). There were many inconsistencies in Cooper's own record of dealing with news agencies linked to government propaganda efforts. While his experience in the Reuters-and-Havas-led news cartel gave him genuine reasons to criticize agencies that were essentially government press bureaus, he took great pains to establish new connections with Rengo and Wolff/DNB in the 1930s and with government news services in Soviet-bloc countries in the late 1940s, agencies that were egregiously propagandistic. Finally, his free-enterprise fundamentalism rejected the possibility that public broadcasters like the BBC and CBC—which, while imperfect, largely operated independently of the governments that provided direct or indirect financial support—could serve a useful journalistic purpose. At the same time, Cooper mostly avoided critical scrutiny of privately owned, advertising-based news organizations. The result was that he put much too narrow limits on journalism's possibilities, especially in countries where the state was viewed more positively than in the United States.

But even with all of this in mind, was Cooper wrong or unfair to act as he did in the immediate postwar years? Editors in other countries were already suspicious of undue U.S. influence over their news supply.[119] The regular use of AP-credited news in VOA broadcasts—which, as time went on, became more overtly propagandistic—would have undoubtedly blurred the boundary between AP's news coverage and U.S. geopolitical aims and possibly have compromised the status of its correspondents abroad. It was ultimately good for AP to maintain its independence from perceived government influence, in a business where perception was directly linked to credibility.

Was it also good for the world? AP's expansion was a strategic business decision, not an exercise in altruism as Cooper so often described it, and he was not inclined to question AP's reflection of U.S. values and perspectives. But the international availability of AP as a separate and distinct news service meant that journalists and news consumers had at least one additional option available to them for world news coverage—an alternative or supplement to Reuters, UP, INS, AFP, TASS, the VOA, or Soviet propaganda, one whose value could be judged on its merits. There is evidence that editors in other countries did make such judgments; for instance, Richard O'Regan, a long-serving AP correspondent in Germany, told Cooper in 1959 that German journalists' initial concern about AP being the voice of the State Department was eventually overcome when they saw "as the years went by that the AP *really* delivers them an unbiased report."[120] In any event, in the face of a strong and sustained public campaign to make AP change its position, Cooper almost completely prevailed, with McLean's staunch support on the essentials. This was his last major campaign as general manager, and the outcome was about as favorable as he could have wished.

13

"Mr. Associated Press"

AP's annual meeting in April was one of the fixtures of the American journalistic calendar, and every year *Editor & Publisher* provided extensive, if generally uncritical, coverage. The edition of April 24, 1948, was no exception, but in three full pages of AP-related news there was no mention of the most significant board of directors' resolution in decades: Cooper's twenty-three-year-long reign as general manager (GM) was about to end.[1] On April 21 the board unanimously decided that Frank Starzel, AP's traffic chief, would take over as GM in October.[2]

McLean insisted on the change, Cooper wrote later. He was now sixty-eight, three years past AP's normal retirement age. Starzel was immediately given the title of senior assistant GM and put in charge while Cooper was absent on an extended tour of AP's European bureaus in June and July.[3] AP staff were told that Starzel was the acting general manager, but no public statement was made.[4] This began a three-year transition during which Cooper kept his position as executive director and was—at least nominally—Starzel's immediate superior, staying involved with a few issues that he felt strongly about while steadily handing over more and more responsibility.

For any close observer of the comings and goings at AP's Rockefeller Center headquarters, the change would have been evident soon after Cooper returned to the United States in August. Starzel had no idea when Cooper would reappear in the office, and a month later Walton Cole of Reuters reported that Cooper had been there only once since returning.[5]

Starzel's appointment as acting general manager did not become public knowledge until mid-October; a few days later, Cooper announced the board's decision to make him general manager permanently.[6] Starzel had worked for AP for almost twenty years, starting out as head of promotion for its then-new feature service and moving on to positions as night city editor in the New York bureau and Ohio bureau chief before becoming traffic executive in 1942. According to Alan Gould, Starzel was reluctant to take the GM job.[7] The obvious successor was Byron Price, who had previously taken over during Cooper's medical leave of absence in 1939.[8] In 1945, however, when Price's appointment as U.S. chief press censor came to an end, Cooper refused to provide clarity about his own retirement plans, and Price was not prepared to continue as Cooper's deputy indefinitely.[9] Starzel, with his background in different aspects of AP's operations, including relations with members, was the strongest of the internal candidates. There was no doubt about Starzel's "ability and his force," McLean observed, but he wondered whether he had "the necessary imagination and capacity to inspire the staff."[10]

The exact division of responsibility between Cooper and Starzel was unclear. Ben Bassett, who spent twenty-five years as foreign news editor during an AP career of more than forty years, wrote later that many staff members "did not realize [Cooper's] power was gone" after 1948.[11] But Cooper continued to deal directly with McLean and the board on many matters, including the VOA, the establishment of a $250,000 fund to promote closer relations with AP members, and the admission of radio stations as associate members.[12] At the end of 1948, Cooper said that as executive director he retained all the authority he previously had as general manager and had delegated the GM's title to Starzel, "who is immediately responsible to me."[13] Two months later, E. Lansing Ray, publisher of the *St. Louis (MO) Globe-Democrat* and a long-serving AP director, asked whether a dinner for Cooper to mark the transition was in the works and was told there was no need: "He is not retiring at this time."[14]

But there was a distinctly valedictory feeling to many of Cooper's interactions with AP staff. One asked Cooper's secretary to pass on in writing something he had not wanted to say with others present: "You made The AP great and also made it a great place for people to work. You are the kindest man I ever worked for."[15] After a celebration in 1949 to mark McLean's twenty-five years as a member of the board of directors, McLean told Cooper that many of the tributes he received gave him credit "for developments for which you are entirely responsible."[16] In a tolerantly retrospective mood, McLean acknowledged the awkwardness of their relationship over the past ten years. But he and Cooper were ultimately able to resolve their differences, and AP "is going to go down in history as your and Melville Stone's accomplishment—not that of its Presidents." (When ending his term as president several years later, McLean addressed Cooper as "a person who sought and constantly reached for my friendship, and yet who felt that there was some invisible web that prevented there ever developing a perfect alloy."[17]) For Cooper, increasingly conscious of how he would be remembered, McLean's praise "lifted up my spirits beyond all powers of description. . . . There is nothing that I have wanted more in these last ten years than the benediction from you that this letter to me gives so adequately."[18]

He was, at least for the time being, inclined to soften the edges of other difficult relationships as well. In a note congratulating Sulzberger on his fifty-eighth birthday, Cooper recalled that Sulzberger's father-in-law, Adolph Ochs, was "the best friend I ever had." If Ochs had lived, "he might have been more tolerant and understanding of my methods and intentions than you have been," but "no matter how far apart we are in our views . . . my affection and admiration for you are on your own account." (Sulzberger replied in verse: "I really don't think that we're so far apart / For we both use our heads and we each use our heart."[19]) Two years after Starzel's promotion, McLean continued to insist for public consumption that Cooper "is now and continues to be the responsible Chief executive in charge of the entire Associated Press operation" while acknowledging that he was delegating more and more responsibility.[20] In fact, by then Cooper had withdrawn from practically all day-to-day activity, skipping the January 1950 board meeting with a manufactured excuse about illness and leaving the preparation of that year's general manager's report entirely to Starzel.[21]

Despite occasional expressions of warmth toward McLean and Sulzberger, Cooper became increasingly dissatisfied about how the transition was being handled. When McLean proposed a commemorative dinner in April 1950 to mark the twenty-fifth anniversary of his appointment as general manager, Cooper demurred. Since he had "turned everything over" to Starzel at McLean's request, there was "no reason now to identify me as the chief executive for twenty-five years because it didn't work out that way. I prefer to avoid the embarrassing contradiction."[22] But he relented when McLean told him it was too late to cancel.[23] The dinner went ahead on April 19 at the Waldorf-Astoria, where

Cooper was presented with a silver plaque etched with all the directors' signatures. Writing in *Editor & Publisher*, McLean praised "the particular quality of genius that makes [Cooper] what he is," citing Cooper's imagination, vision, initiative, boldness, and especially his "human understanding, his dedication to certain ideals and his quick sympathy" for AP employees.[24] An accompanying editorial described AP's history since 1925 as "largely the history of Kent Cooper, the ambitions and ideals he imparted to his fellow workers, his philosophy and his far-sighted planning."[25]

Amid the public tributes, Cooper and McLean had some uncomfortable exchanges about his continuing role at AP. Cooper wanted to be treated as Melville Stone had been when he gave up the general manager's position at the age of seventy-three. Stone continued in the hands-off but still influential role of counselor, with full salary, until his death in 1927, and Cooper, as assistant general manager from 1920 and GM from 1925, had to pay attention to Stone's wishes. Now that he had the elder statesman's role, Cooper argued that AP's character was "made and refined by its chief executive, who himself, in the process of 40 years, has become so much a part of it that death alone should remove him from any connection with it."[26] But if either Starzel or the board did not want Cooper to have a continuing role, his pension should be fixed at fifty thousand dollars a year, the average of his salary since 1930—worth about five hundred thousand dollars today. (The board agreed to pay this amount as of January 1, 1951.[27]) These exchanges also made clear that at times Cooper faced financial difficulties. The insurance policy taken out for him in 1930 after he turned down David Sarnoff's offer to leave AP for NBC eventually made him liable for heavy tax payments, and he was unable to keep up his share of the premiums.[28] Cooper had spent the last twenty-five years in the company of wealthy publishers like McLean, McCormick, and Sulzberger but was not wealthy himself and was especially concerned about providing for Sally after his death.

Cooper's friendship with McCormick, no longer an AP director after 1948, played an important part in his retirement plans. For years Cooper had been spending at least a month every winter in Florida, where he and Sally socialized with McCormick and his wife, Maryland.[29] In the spring of 1949 McCormick agreed to build a house for Cooper and Sally next to his property in Boynton Beach, renting it to him for 5 percent of its cost.[30] Although Cooper was delighted with this plan, the gulf between his financial situation and McCormick's led to some uncomfortable moments, as when he had to remind McCormick that they had agreed on a 5 percent rental rate, not 10 percent.[31] However, "whatever you say will be all right with me. Our friendship can go on from there the same as ever." The rate was indeed 5 percent, and at the end of 1950 Cooper warmly thanked McCormick for "something I never dreamed I would have or that I would ever have time to enjoy as I am enjoying this place."[32]

The board of directors formally stripped Cooper of all operating authority in April 1951. He kept the title of executive director and the large corner office at Rockefeller Center, although he almost never used it.[33] Major challenges such as the arrest in Prague of AP correspondent William Oatis on espionage charges were now handled exclusively by Starzel.[34] A few months later, citing the Oatis case, Cooper asked McLean for a letter stating explicitly that he now had "no responsibility respecting any actions or decisions that are being made on any matters, that obviously I could not have such responsibility any way since I have been neither consulted nor informed."[35] Starzel was puzzled by Cooper's "emotional sensitivity, about whatever it might be," and this request weakened his hope that it would eventually diminish.[36]

Christopher Chancellor of Reuters considered Cooper's new position "most peculiar."[37] But he was still "the grand old man of the news agency world," and in recognition of this Reuters invited him to be the main speaker at a gala in London marking its centenary. Chancellor and Esmond Harmsworth, publisher of the *Daily Mail* and a Reuters director, had first discussed this with Cooper in 1948, and Rothermere delivered the invitation publicly at AP's general meeting that year.[38] But with Cooper's sensitivity to anything that highlighted his uncertain status, misunderstandings were always possible. When Chancellor repeated the invitation in February 1951, Cooper replied that McLean, not he, should rightly be AP's representative. Chancellor was "terribly shocked" by this response but assured Cooper that although the invitation was intended to honor AP, "we want you because you are Kent Cooper and because of your achievements over the years and because we feel you are the leading exponent of the conception of the freedom of news in the international field." There would be more than one thousand guests at the dinner, including the prime minister, Clement Attlee. Cooper quickly reconsidered and gratefully accepted the invitation.[39] He did have one remaining concern, though. On seeing Chancellor in New York in April, he immediately asked, "Is Jones coming to the banquet?"[40] Chancellor replied that Reuters' former managing director—the bête noire of *Barriers Down* and Cooper's nemesis since 1919—obviously had to attend, prompting Cooper to ask whether this foreshadowed Jones's return to Reuters.

(It did not.) This all demonstrated, Chancellor observed, that Cooper had "not yet recovered from the impact of Roderick Jones."

Cooper's toast to Reuters at the gala, vetted in advance by McLean, Sulzberger, and Chancellor, struck familiar notes: the importance of news being controlled by newspaper-owned agencies "rather than by opportunists or by governments" to guarantee truthful news, which was "a groundwork for international peace."[41] He lavishly praised Reuters—now, like AP, a newspaper-owned agency. McLean deliberately stayed away "in order to put the attention entirely on Kent. It is his day."[42] The dinner was the culmination of a weeklong round of cocktail parties, receptions, and luncheons. Cooper and Sally attended them all, and he proudly told McLean that whenever remarks were made, every publisher "insisted on giving me credit for the change in Reuters."[43] Chancellor told an AP colleague afterward that it was "wonderful to see KC on top of the world," and Cooper himself described it as "the greatest honor of my life."[44]

While Cooper was now entirely disconnected from any AP management responsibilities, his public statements and writings could still affect AP's reputation—positively, in the case of the Reuters centenary, or otherwise. A few months after the London festivities, McLean congratulated him for turning down a request to address the International Labor Press of America. "The waters have been made turgid," McLean complained, by a book titled *The First Freedom*, in which Morris Ernst, the American Civil Liberties Union's legal counsel (and the Newspaper Guild's lawyer in AP's unsuccessful effort to have the Wagner Act declared unconstitutional) put forth "a succession of distortions" about AP.[45] Though Cooper was not identified by name in Ernst's book, AP, as "the loudest and most potent shouter for world freedom of thought," was sharply criticized—such "pious and worthy hopes of reforming the world are a trifle ironic when flowing from domestic monopolists."[46] The labor editors persisted, however, and in 1952 Cooper accepted their renewed invitation.[47] This venture into potentially hostile territory ended up yielding a more substantial address than the high-profile Reuters event. One of the reasons for inviting Cooper, the group's president told him, was that the editors of labor publications considered AP and its members "the natural enemies of a free press."[48] In his speech, Cooper cheerfully denied the charge, stressing that he was himself an employee: "a worker, never an owner, and far removed from being a capitalist." Freedom of the press was the people's right and did not exist "solely for the protection of publishers."

Cooper acknowledged that at one time U.S. newspapers were "violently partisan" and sometimes unfair in covering labor news—as the pre-1900 AP itself might have been. But the twentieth-century AP was different. The general manager had "exclusive and autocratic authority to conduct an unbiased news service" that could be used by any newspaper regardless of its political orientation. Carefully avoiding any mention of AP's long struggle against the Newspaper Guild, in which he had a central role, Cooper noted that most of its employees were now union members. He also rejected the characterization of privately owned newspapers as "the kept press." American newspaper readers were so intelligent and demanding that any kept newspaper's advocacy of particular corporate or other narrow interests was futile: "newspapers that thought they could play that game long since lost their subscribers."[49] Invoking the sovereign reader was Cooper's preferred way of arguing that there was no contradiction between private, profit-oriented ownership of newspapers and public service. All two hundred of Cooper's listeners may not have been convinced, but he told McLean that he received a standing ovation.[50] Presented with a subsequent invitation to address the American Civil Liberties Union, however, Cooper and McLean immediately agreed that it was out of the question.[51] Cooper's, and AP's, willingness to engage directly with critics only went so far.

Cooper's friendship with McCormick brought him into the one substantial business activity of his retirement. In 1953 McCormick told Cooper that Hamilton Fish, a former Republican congressman and ally of McCormick, had asked him to help establish a new Republican newspaper in New York.[52] McCormick was unwilling to get personally involved but suggested Cooper as editor of the new publication. Cooper was grateful for the recommendation and raised no objection to the idea of editing a partisan newspaper but said he would prefer to work with McCormick "because I know you and feel you would 'give me my head.'" Perhaps if McCormick bought the *Herald Tribune* in New York, as he had bought the *Washington Times-Herald* in 1949 after the death of its publisher, his cousin Cissy Patterson, Cooper could take over at one of those newspapers.[53]

Nothing came of these suggestions, but a year later Cooper acted as middleman in the sale of the *Times-Herald* to new owners. According to his account of events—delivered to *Tribune* executives after McCormick's death in support of his claim to be paid a commission on the sale—it was his idea that McCormick should sell the *Times-Herald* because the stress of running the Washington paper in addition to the *Tribune* was damaging McCormick's health. Cooper offered to find a buyer willing to pay what McCormick had spent on the *Times-Herald*, keeping the effort a secret. One possible purchaser was Eugene Meyer, publisher of the *Washington Post*. When Cooper contacted Meyer, he was indeed interested and immediately came to see Cooper in Florida. They agreed on the price that McCormick wanted, and McCormick was greatly relieved when the sale went through.

Cooper, who was then living in the house that McCormick had built for him, did not raise the question of compensation for his efforts, but when McCormick sent him a check for $10,000 after the sale went through, he returned it. The ostensible reason was that he was acting strictly out of friendship, did not expect to be paid, and, as executive director of AP (a title he still held, though by now it had no practical meaning), wanted to be able to say that he had not profited personally from the sale. In fact, he considered the amount insultingly low but did not say so to McCormick.[54] (McCormick then had his wife purchase a diamond bracelet for $10,500 at Cartier in New York and give it to Sally as a gift; this was not returned.[55]) Cooper estimated that $240,000 would be a fair commission on a deal of this magnitude, but after McCormick's death, Cooper told *Tribune* executives that $120,000 would be satisfactory.[56] Eventually the *Tribune* paid him $60,000 to write a series of substantial articles about different aspects of McCormick's career and political views, none of which appear to have been published.[57] The long, drawn-out affair underscored Cooper's continuing concern about the amount of money he would leave to Sally after his death and provided another illustration of the uneasiness underlying his friendship with McCormick.

Publication of Cooper's book *The Right to Know* in 1956 brought a flurry of public, and private, attention.[58] McLean was worried about advance publicity promising unspecified revelations and reminded Cooper that if any of these involved discussions at the board of directors or Cooper's own activities before 1951, AP had "a real interest" in making sure that nothing he wrote would involve it in controversy.[59] Subtitled "An Exposition of the Evils of News Suppression and Propaganda," *The Right to Know* was in some ways a more substantial book than *Barriers Down*. Echoing, consciously or not, one of the main themes of the district court's 1943 antitrust judgment against AP, Cooper argued that the term "right to know" should replace "freedom of the press" because it "represents the people's right ... and not merely a selfish right of printers alone." If press freedom was understood "only as a right of the printers of this country to carry their business to more profitable heights without interference," the courts and U.S. government might come to see it the same way, "as a private right instead of a public right."[60]

At the same time, as part of a broad defense of the journalistic status quo in the United States, Cooper continued to insist that private ownership was the only arrangement that allowed journalism to do its job of disseminating truthful information. The idea that a public broadcaster could operate with at least as much independence as a privately owned newspaper or radio station was not worth considering; as in the case of the newly established, government-subsidized French news agency, Agence France-Presse, "obviously it must serve its master."[61] The argument that financial control meant editorial control did not apply, however, to newspapers operated by wealthy publishers and dependent on advertising revenue. The fact that a newspaper's editorial department was subject to the publisher's demands for profitability was not a problem, in Cooper's view, because newspapers only became profitable by giving readers what they wanted. In fact, it was successful business operation that allowed newspapers to do without partisan political financing and control in the first place.

The argument that publishers wanted to associate only with other millionaires and had little real connection to their readers—a mild way of stating the class-based criticism that publishers were members of the ruling elite and mainly served that group's interests—was waved aside by noting that Joseph Patterson of the *New York Daily News* made a habit of eating lunch at soda fountains and seeking the opinion of whomever he happened to be sitting beside—"clerk, stenographer, salesman, truckman or small businessman." Cooper also dismissed growing concern about consolidation of ownership expressed by the Hutchins Commission and other critics. While the number of papers in many U.S. cities was indeed declining, Cooper contended that one well-financed publication would do a better job of providing complete news coverage than two weaker competitors. His brief defense of publishers who took their fight against the right to collective bargaining to the Supreme Court on press-freedom grounds (AP was not mentioned, though it was the most prominent organization to adopt this course) was contradictory and unconvincing. Cooper acknowledged the court's conclusion that labor legislation had no effect on newspapers' ability to print whatever they wanted to print. Still, the appeal was justified because publishers "would have been remiss had they not gone to the highest court for a decision on any point they felt effected a barrier or militated in any way against their right to disclose information that the public wanted." At the same time, this litigation contributed to a public view that publishers "expected freedom of the press to be maintained primarily for the protection and prosperity of their own properties."[62]

The Right to Know restated Cooper's long-standing view that American journalism was a model for the rest of the world. His U.S.-centric account of journalism's historical evolution included some claims that were simply inaccurate—such as his claim that the Zenger trial made the United States the first country in the world to have a free press, setting an example for Britain and other countries to follow.[63] Others were exaggerated or were likely to strike journalists in other countries as patronizing, as when he observed that the best Parisian newspapers had only recently learned that they should rely on U.S. and British agencies rather than French sources "for accuracy and impartiality."[64]

The book included long accounts of how Americans and citizens of other countries were essentially manipulated into participating in both twentieth-century world wars by government propaganda. In the case of the First World War, AP became involved when it published the notorious Zimmerman telegram.[65] With most news agencies that were part of the Reuters-led cartel beholden to or outright controlled by their national governments, the international news system itself was a major conduit of this propaganda. Cooper's criticism of the German and Japanese news agencies in the years leading up to the Second World War, servants of the regimes that controlled them, was withering, but its uncompromising clarity was the product of hindsight. In the 1930s Cooper was well aware of the political control exercised over Rengo in Japan and Deutsches Nachrichtenbüro in Germany but said nothing publicly about it at the time, motivated by competitive concern to maintain AP's connections with both agencies.[66] Ultimately, the book's publication did not cause any substantial problems for AP. Cooper's account of the Edward Kennedy affair—the subject that McLean and others were most worried about—"covers the ground pretty well," McLean concluded.[67]

By the late 1950s, Cooper's pursuit of personal recognition became increasingly complicated. He very much wanted such recognition but insisted on pursuing it indirectly. It was in this vein that Sally wrote, "with Kent's tolerant consent," to Paul Miller—a close personal friend since Miller's days as AP's Washington bureau chief and now executive vice president of the Gannett newspaper chain and an AP director—describing a recent dinner she and Kent had attended with several AP staffers and their wives.[68] Cooper "held forth brilliantly and we heard later that the men told others at The AP office that they were simply enthralled." As Kent and Sally departed, the others insisted that he write a book about his experiences, "as Kent is the only remaining person who knows these things. . . . Unless all of this is told it will be lost forever." She had been urging

Cooper for several years to write an autobiography, but so far unsuccessfully, and now asked Miller to help promote the project.

Miller enthusiastically agreed, offering to present the idea to the board of directors. A few days later Cooper followed up himself, again presenting the autobiography as Sally's idea and repeating that he wanted to be treated as Melville Stone had been treated at the end of his career: Sally "seems to have been wondering, are these 'glorious chapters' to be written about my work since the work of Mr. Stone was so generously recognized in his lifetime in the volume printed in 1918."[69] This was a reference to *M.E.S.—His Book*, a tribute volume commissioned by the board of directors and published to mark Stone's twenty-fifth anniversary as general manager. It was not an autobiography or conventional biography, however, but a collection of written tributes along with a biographical sketch and the text of numerous articles about AP that Stone had written, distributed free to all AP members.[70]

A kind of shadow play was now set in motion. The board established a committee to consider the idea of commissioning Cooper to write an autobiography. One of its members would contact Cooper to see if he was agreeable, at which he was to act surprised.[71] Ben McKelway (editor of the *Washington Star* and one of Noyes's protégés), who had recently replaced McLean as AP's president, had concerns. The board of directors could end up as "the sponsor of a biography that could loose numerous skeletons from the closet and probably end up pleasing nobody."[72] Miller responded that otherwise Cooper might write the book on his own, leaving AP unable to influence it in any way. The board approved the proposal, allocating ten thousand dollars to cover research, editing, and the distribution of complimentary copies.[73]

Cooper's elation about the book project went along with continuing grievances about other aspects of his treatment by AP. McKelway strongly encouraged Cooper to attend the AP annual luncheon in 1958, where McLean was to be honored, and to take part in board meetings "as long as you can do so." A barrier of some kind had developed between Cooper and the board, McKelway wrote, and he wanted to "tell the world that the A.P. thinks of you with deep affection and gratitude."[74] More controversially, he asked Cooper to contact Starzel "and suggest that he move into the corner room"—the large office that Cooper still claimed, although he no longer came to Rockefeller Center. Cooper quickly took offense. He replied that he had once suggested that Starzel move into the larger office, but unsuccessfully. Now McKelway apparently wanted there to be "no place there at all where I can drop in and feel at home like I so felicitously arranged for Mr. Stone."[75] If Cooper was to attend board meetings, McKelway should know that this would upset Starzel: "He has been happier and done better in overcoming his inferiority complex by my not being there." AP had been Cooper's entire life, involving sacrifices that could not be repaid in monetary terms: "Complete severance of the relationship to help Frank get over his complex has been tragic for me, but I have not complained. . . . He has not been responsive to my assurance made when I quit going to Board meetings that I wanted to help him confidentially between the two of us with advice. He has asked me nothing and told me nothing."

What Cooper really wanted, McKelway concluded, was to have him order Starzel to consult Cooper about everything he did. "I realize what you must have gone through," he told McLean ruefully.[76] Cooper eventually did correspond with Starzel, who replied diplomatically, saying Cooper need not be told "that it is extremely difficult, if not impossible, to share the burdens of this post with anyone."[77] The two exchanged a few carefully correct letters after that, but Cooper continued to believe that Starzel was the wrong man for the job. "I must tell you how happy I am with the present management of [AP]," he told Sulzberger after Wes Gallagher took over as GM in 1962. "I was sure Starzel was not temperamentally fitted to lead other men in the spirit of camaraderie necessary and that his lack of experience as a news man would not be a good thing for [AP]."[78]

Kent Cooper and The Associated Press was published in April 1959. Nine months earlier McKelway and Miller—evidently concerned about what Cooper might say—spent a day with him vetting a draft and found no major concerns.[79] Cooper made a point of saying that there were "many many things that I could tell in detail but which I suppressed," such as the Edward Kennedy controversy:[80]

> If I ever did expose all the incidents that aroused acrimonious discussions within The Associated Press in the last fifty years, I could probably write a best seller, but I doubt that it would do [AP] any good. . . . God knows its publication could not be sponsored by The AP Board![81]

While the autobiography was a much more personal book than *Barriers Down* or *The Right to Know*, it included a familiar list of Cooper's successes at AP. In addition to establishing AP as a truly international news organization, these included saving one hundred thousand dollars in telegraph costs; introducing the pension plan; reducing the size of members' locally exclusive zones with a concomitant increase in membership; stimulating members' loyalty;

introducing a broader conception of news and a livelier writing style; allowing bylines and celebrity interviews; establishing news features, news photos, and eventually Wirephoto; and streamlining the administration. He took credit for a remarkable degree of foresight, recalling that when he first convinced the board to approve a news photo service in 1926, he already had in mind the transmission of photos by wire and that he knew as early as 1914 that AP's system of exclusive local franchises would eventually be wiped out on antitrust grounds.[82]

This was Cooper's last opportunity to recount the long struggle with Reuters, and now, more than ten years after Noyes's death, he was more explicit than ever in holding Stone and Noyes responsible for the long delay in freeing AP from the restrictions of the cartel contract. AP willingly accepted these limitations until Cooper arrived on the scene, he wrote, and after Stone's death, Noyes refused as firmly as Stone had to consider a break with Reuters. Not until 1932, when Reuters granted AP a free hand in Japan, did Cooper have "what I needed for my immediate plans." His subsequent negotiation of a contract with Rengo infuriated Jones, who canceled Reuters' contract with AP in retaliation. Until this point, Cooper's account was consistent with the actual events, but he then depicted his own role as more heroic than it was, saying that Jones's action was "a justifiable cause for open warfare" and that he went to London to demand an explanation in person.[83] In fact, Cooper went out of his way in their London conversations to propitiate Jones.[84] This may have been a tactic—above all, Cooper wanted to convince Noyes that he had made every effort to reach agreement with Jones—but he was certainly not aggressive. He claimed implausibly that the capitulation contract Jones was forced to sign in 1934 gave him "no feeling of personal success" but did admit that he regretted "the years of condescending attitude Jones had assumed toward [AP] and toward me ever since I first met him."[85]

The autobiography also gave Cooper one more chance to present his views about journalism's evolution and its future. He recalled telling the board as early as 1914 that since U.S. newspapers—meaning AP's owners—were "the largest and most prosperous group in the world's press," they could make AP into "the instrument that could by its truthful news dissemination make the whole world aware of the intellectual, ethical and material progress developed in this great country of free men."[86] Much as he criticized the government-sponsored nationalism of the cartel agencies, Cooper saw nothing wrong with a private organization like AP promoting American values around the world.

Reviews of the book were mostly favorable, although *Nieman Reports* noted the contrast between Cooper's campaign against limitations on news distribution internationally and his support for exclusive local franchises in the United States.[87] Cooper arranged to have copies sent to all living AP pensioners, and several responded with heartfelt appreciation. A former traffic department employee thanked him for "thirty-eight years of happy employment through the humanitarianism and generosity of Mr. Kent Cooper and [AP]," citing the pension plan, life insurance, and sick benefits.[88] McLean was measured in his praise, saying only that he enjoyed the book, and that in his view Cooper's biggest achievements were worldwide expansion and bringing radio stations into membership. Wirephoto "would have come anyway," but Cooper led the way here too.[89] Cooper, still inordinately sensitive to McLean's opinion, described the letter as "an affectionate benediction to a life dedicated to [AP]" and "one of the most satisfying I have ever received."[90] He also wondered whether a critic of the book, "noticing the long list of accomplishments, might say, 'and on the seventh day he rested,'" but none did. However, one longtime Cooper associate, Alan Gould, did believe that that Cooper had "anoint[ed] himself as God Almighty" in the autobiography. Cooper was "the genius responsible for the modern AP," Gould acknowledged; he "revitalized the organization, stimulated its staff and was responsible, generally speaking, for the expanded operations of the AP at home and abroad." But "for all his accomplishments, he claimed too much credit for himself and exploited his reputation for enterprise and innovation."[91]

Even as the book attracted largely favorable reactions, Cooper's criticism of AP policy and management continued. To an ally on the board, he lamented that he was heartsick about the direction that AP was taking, "but there is nothing I can do in my lonely-isolated position other than . . . to sound the warning."[92] He was invited to attend a board meeting in October 1959, where a resolution was passed praising him as "an inspiration to all who believe that society cannot be secure until its members have not only the right to know but the facilities to permit them to exercise that right."[93] In response, Cooper referred to ominous competition "that may be undermining The AP's strength."[94] He was especially concerned that AP had not attempted to take over the International News Service after Hearst's death in 1951, allowing UP to do so and to become a more formidable competitor as United Press International. McKelway's mild but pointed response was that AP did take competition from the newly created UPI seriously and that an AP-INS merger would probably fall afoul of the Supreme Court's antitrust ruling in 1945.[95] This prompted Cooper to compose a bitter six-page rejoinder, which he (or perhaps Sally) wisely decided not to send. It was a catalog of neglect and marginalization, beginning with McKelway's instruction not to make any substantive comments at the few board meetings he attended and going on to a long and patronizing explanation of why AP should have taken over INS.[96] Cooper was no more restrained in his correspondence with Katherine Graham, publisher of the *Washington Post*, a few years later. It began as an amiable exchange, with Cooper quite unrealistically offering to buy and operate the *Post* after the death of Graham's husband, Philip (Cooper was eighty-four years old at the time and in failing health), and then turned into a request for compensation in recognition of his role in the purchase of the *Times-Herald* by Eugene Meyer, Graham's father. When Graham diplomatically deflected this request, the correspondence ended abruptly when Cooper accused her of ungratefully ignoring his contribution to the *Post*'s subsequent success.[97]

Now in his eighties, Cooper was well known enough to be honored in non-journalism circles. In the summer of 1964, Cooper (along with Roy Howard, among others) was declared a Distinguished Hoosier at Indiana Days at the New York World's Fair.[98] Sally proposed a greater honor, suggesting to Haley that he might follow up on the now-deceased DeWitt Mackenzie's efforts to nominate Cooper for a Nobel Prize. Haley gently demurred, noting that the initiative had to come from the nominee's own country.[99]

By this time many of Cooper's contemporaries had died. When Roderick Jones died in January 1962, Haley commented to Cooper that despite all the past struggles between Reuters and AP, he was grateful to Jones: "If it had not been for him and for the things which had to be put right because of him, I should never have met you."[100] Roy Howard's death in 1964, three months after he and Cooper last met in person at the world's fair, came as a "great shock."[101] He and Howard "were friends long before either of us started on an upward climb, and we remained friends loyally through the years though we were heads of competitive institutions," Cooper told another old friend.[102]

A Christmas card from December 1964 showed Kent and Sally standing in bright sunshine outside their Florida home, with a wide blue sky and a blue ocean in the background.[103] The text was a brief poem by Cooper, based loosely on "The South Country" by the prolific author and conservative Catholic Hilaire Belloc:

A long happy life—and now very old
I've a deep thatched house

To protect me from the cold
Where I live by the sea
With a wonderful wife, glory be!

Despite the cheerful image and message, Cooper was in very poor health. He never fully recovered from an operation to remove his prostate in the summer of 1963.[104] Nine months after the surgery, he disputed his doctor's assessment that his health was improving: "I do not feel any better than I did then, nor as well."[105] On January 22, 1965, Cooper was admitted to Good Samaritan Hospital in Palm Beach after suffering a heart seizure and then developed pneumonia.[106] A tracheotomy eased his breathing, but his condition worsened after that, and he died on January 31. His final, whispered, words, Sally wrote later, were "I'm so grateful."[107]

Cooper's death was reported in hundreds of U.S. and international newspapers. Letters of condolence to Sally, Miller, and Gallagher arrived from the United States and around the world.[108] In a heartfelt note to Sally, Haley wrote that Cooper was "the most shining light in all The A.P.'s history, . . . internationally known and loved," and "the kindest and truest of friends."[109] His meeting with Cooper in 1942 was "a turning point in my life" that "opened up new horizons."

AP's story on Cooper's death described him as "a dominant figure in world journalism for a quarter-century," the "key figure in the modernization and growth of the world's largest press association," and "one of the journalistic giants of his time, and a taboo smasher all the way." He worked and competed with the journalistic titans of his time: Ochs, McCormick, Hearst, and Howard. The highlights of his career were listed: he championed truthfulness, absence of bias in news coverage, and freedom of the press from government influence; he expanded the range of what AP considered to be newsworthy and the geographical scope of its operations; and he pushed for technological innovations like the replacement of Morse telegraphs with teletypes and Wirephoto.[110] By the time he retired, "nobody any longer called The AP 'Grandma.'"

In a detailed and mostly admiring portrait, the *New York Times* described Cooper as "one of the great men of his time" in journalism. Between 1925 and 1948, he "in a very real sense *was* The Associated Press"; like Melville Stone before him, he was "Mr. A.P."[111] With the support of Noyes and other long-serving directors, Cooper "ran the organization as a one-man show," arousing intense feelings of either admiration or dislike among AP staff: "There was never any middle ground." In an editorial, the *Times* observed that while most Americans would not recognize Cooper's name, he was "one of their great educators." By "breathing life" into AP's international coverage, he helped lift readers, as he wrote in his autobiography, "out of their isolation and into an awareness of how large their world is."[112] According to the *Washington Post*, Cooper's leadership had made AP "the greatest news gathering organization in the world" by 1951. Its foreign presence would have expanded in any event, reflecting America's growing role in the world in the twentieth century, but Cooper "gave impetus to that expansion and put a proper emphasis on the independence and integrity" of AP's international news.[113]

The most personal reflection on Cooper's life and death came from Hal Boyle, a Pulitzer Prize–winning war correspondent and for many years AP's popular daily columnist. Cooper, he wrote, was "a tradition-smasher and an applecart-upsetter" who had big dreams and was ready to step on toes to get things done.[114] He was stocky, of medium height; his dark and magnetic eyes "seemed to have fingers in them that reached out and grabbed your mind as he talked." Boyle was well aware of Cooper's volatility and capriciousness: "He could in one instant be as boyish as Tom Sawyer and in the next as imperious as a Turkish sultan"—sometimes sentimental and sometimes "tougher than the foreman of a railroad gang." He was either greatly admired or extravagantly disliked but excelled in inspiring loyalty. After getting a Cooper pep talk before heading overseas during the Second World War, Boyle "felt that 'The Associated Press' was branded on my forehead in neon lights," and he was ready to take on Hitler and the Nazis single-handed, armed only with a pen.

A resolution of the board of directors in April enumerated Cooper's many roles: "creator, innovator, organizer, technician, a writer of both prose and music, a skilled negotiator, a breaker of barriers."[115] Diplomatically glossing over Cooper's dissatisfaction with his post-retirement treatment, it declared that at the end of his life he was grateful for the confidence shown by the board, AP members, and AP employees who had made his many achievements possible. Gallagher praised Cooper for leading "the fight to break up the cartels and bring new techniques into writing and distribution of the news. He was a true genius in his field, and, more than that, the right man in the right place at the right time. World journalism owes him a great debt."[116]

Seen from a greater distance, Cooper stands out as one of the main architects of the global news system in the twentieth century. The first wave of news globalization in the nineteenth century was led by individuals—Julius Reuter, Charles Havas, and Bernard Wolff. In Cooper's era the international economy was shaped more by bureaucratic, multinational corporations run by hired managers.[117] Cooper was one of these: a technocrat, a strategist, a negotiator, and in all those roles a strikingly successful organization man.

* * *

In all the tributes to Cooper's journalistic achievements, competition with United Press was often the unstated context. Emphasizing human interest in the news and expanding AP's international news distribution capacity were necessary to keep AP from being overtaken, and possibly even marginalized, by UP. Cooper certainly succeeded in meeting this challenge; by the time he retired, AP had 4,274 members and subscribers around the world, as compared to around 1,200 in 1925.[118] But beyond AP's institutional imperatives, what did these and other Cooper-era changes mean to the millions of readers of AP news? After all, their right to know, by Cooper's own account, was the point of the whole enterprise. In his autobiography, Cooper asserted that the changes in AP news during his tenure contributed to the "tremendous increase in all newspaper circulation" between 1925 and 1950.[119] But if more readers were attracted by sports or celebrity news, were they necessarily any better informed? Some of the changes Cooper introduced—the expansion of AP's Washington staff to provide more coverage of state and regional interests; the growth of state news coverage generally; and the establishment of science, education, and other beats—did improve the quality of AP news as information. The amount of AP's self-generated international coverage increased greatly as well, most of it directed by American journalists working with local staff. Much of the time, Reuters (or UP) might have covered the same events, but AP's version would always have been written with an American audience in mind—good for American readers, perhaps, but not necessarily for Canadians or Germans.

Particularly in his early years at AP, Cooper played an important part in enlisting more small newspapers as members. This meant that more people in the United States had access to AP news, although this was limited by the wholesale extension of protest rights in 1926. In fact, it was only the antitrust suit that took the opening up of membership to its logical conclusion. While Cooper strongly opposed the suit, he was much in favor of its practical results: making any legitimate newspaper eligible for membership and effectively ending the rule that prevented many afternoon newspaper members from publishing AP news in their Sunday editions.

Was AP news much better than the news provided by UP and INS? Well into the 1920s, AP supporters like Adolph Ochs insisted it was more reliable, but by the 1930s this complaint was heard less often. In its origins, UP was more progressive in its politics and more oriented to working-class readers, but that distinction was also fading somewhat by the 1930s.[120] INS, meanwhile, was strongly associated with the polarizing figure of Hearst, who veered from radicalism in the early years of the twentieth century to red-baiting later on.[121] In any case, U.S. newspapers generally had—within the limits of an oligopolistic system—more choice about the sources of their national and international news in 1950 than in 1915 along with access to a broader array of different kinds of news. But for Cooper, more choice meant the opportunity to choose one of AP's services rather than any of its rivals'. With AP's competitive interests as his lodestar, his strong preference was always to discourage AP members from subscribing to UP, INS, or their subsidiaries and, if possible, to make it mandatory to sign up for initially optional services like news features or Wirephoto.

For technological and organizational reasons, the news agency business always tended toward monopoly or oligopoly. Competition does not inevitably lead to better journalism, but some competition is usually better than none, and for readers in the United States, it was important that there were two strong national/international agencies. While the competition between AP and UP often involved pumped-up claims of superiority or cutthroat sales tactics, it was also about being fast and accurate in news coverage and finding other ways to appeal to readers. Internationally, AP's increasingly strong presence meant that newspapers and radio stations in non-Communist countries could choose among several major international agencies after 1945: AP, UP, Reuters, and AFP. Each of these was nationally based—either in the United States or Europe—and as a UNESCO report in 1953 observed, "However impartial they may be, however strictly they may comply with the professional code of ethics, they will inevitably judge and present news from the viewpoint of the country of which they are citizens."[122] UNESCO's suggestion for reform was the establishment of a truly international cooperative agency. The authors were apparently unaware that Cooper had suggested something very similar in the 1920s[123]—although he eventually adopted a much different approach, where AP operated around the world entirely on its own.

While Cooper strongly identified himself with the idea of unbiased and impartial news, this was an AP tradition that he inherited, not a new creation. In fact, under his leadership AP moved toward allowing more interpretation and, with bylines, acknowledging the individuality of its journalists. Cooper's argument that the availability of AP's impartial and unbiased news outside the United States made future wars less likely was always overstated, not least because Reuters (after the Jones era) and UP had essentially the same approach. Did the increasing use of AP news in Germany and other countries after 1945 and the employment of local journalists in AP bureaus change the understanding in those countries of how journalism should be practiced? Possibly, but as a study tour by a group of German editors to the United States in 1948 amply demonstrated, deep-seated cultural and historical differences stood in the way of any rapid or complete homogenization.[124]

What difference did it make that Cooper, and not someone else, was AP's general manager for the second quarter of the twentieth century? There were some things the board would have insisted on, or refused to accept, no matter who was in charge. The directors would have pushed any general manager toward China and Japan in the early 1920s, but Cooper (unlike his predecessors) took on the assignment with great enthusiasm, persistence, and foresight. Mostly because of Frank Noyes's attachment to the cartel contract, it took Cooper almost fifteen years to bring about the changes in AP's international operations that he identified as necessary in 1920. He could not prevent the board from cutting assessments and salaries in the early 1930s and made no headway in restoring revenue for years afterward. When it came to radio, Cooper was unable for years to act on his clear understanding of the situation that faced AP because of deep divisions among the members—although his views eventually prevailed, and it is hard to imagine any general manager doing much better. In some cases, like that of Edward Kennedy, Cooper was overruled in managing the news service, which he and others considered his central responsibility. And at the end of his career, Cooper was forced to retire when he did not wish to and was not able to carve out the kind of continuing advisory role that Melville Stone had enjoyed.

But there is also a great deal of evidence to show that Cooper successfully led AP, the board, and its members in the directions he thought were necessary. His leadership was especially evident in matters of technology—from the one-hundred-thousand-dollar saving on telegraph costs in 1911 to Wirephoto—and the overall character of the news service, with his emphasis on human interest, celebrity interviews, features, and photos. Would another general manager have gained complete freedom of action for AP everywhere in the world by 1934? It is impossible to say for certain but difficult to imagine anyone pursuing this goal with greater strategic sense and determination than Cooper did. AP's directors would not have agreed to spend heavily on international expansion after 1944 without his and Stratton's forceful recommendation. After the war ended, Cooper's strong opposition to any involvement with the Voice of America was decisive. Cooper may not have run AP entirely as a one-man show or had the board in the palm of his hand, but again and again the directors turned to him when they faced challenges and mostly followed his advice.

It is impossible to write history without an awareness of one's own time. One thing that stands out from the vantage point of today is the unquestioned importance of impartiality and factual accuracy in news for Cooper and everyone around him. Impartiality, as Cooper often explained, applied mainly to political coverage. Treating the two major U.S. political parties evenhandedly—which he and others saw as a defining characteristic of news agency journalism, whose reports had to be acceptable to publications with varying political affiliations—was a reaction against the overt partisanship that characterized much of American journalism in the nineteenth century. This version of impartiality had, and has, definite limits. It is not especially concerned—nor was Cooper—with how adequately or inadequately the dominant political parties represented less powerful groups in society: racial and ethnic minorities, the poor and working class, and women, for example. Oswald Garrison Villard, a former AP director and later publisher of *The Nation*, criticized AP for "its constant omissions of news. . . . The activities of great groups of our citizens are reported not at all or with extreme bias."[125] The boundaries of the "sphere of legitimate controversy," to use Daniel Hallin's term,[126] where the rules of journalistic objectivity applied, were defined by a largely implicit consensus about who, and what, deserved to be taken seriously—a consensus that was very much the product of a particular moment in history and a particular group of people.

U.S. journalism has seen a resurgence of the kind of overt partisanship that Cooper rejected and that professional journalism organizations like AP continue to reject. It is an asymmetrical resurgence, with outlets like Fox News and many Republican voters in particular dismissing fact-based "mainstream" journalism as just another partisan point of view.[127] In an atmosphere of growing political polarization, some audiences believe reports that come from their preferred sources and not otherwise—a reversion to the nineteenth-century idea of politics as a matter of group identity rather than rational, evidence-based choices.[128]

All the available evidence indicates that Cooper was a Republican from the age of sixteen onward, yet where AP's news coverage of politics was concerned, this does not seem to have compromised his commitment to impartiality. When Republican AP publishers and board members demanded in 1928 that AP pay more attention to Sen. William Borah, Cooper's initial inclination was to resist. Eventually he agreed in the face of sustained pressure, but this was hardly an example of his own political sympathies dictating news decisions. Later, despite his personal friendship and obvious political affinity with Robert McCormick, he regularly deflected McCormick's pressure for anti-Roosevelt coverage. There is much evidence of efforts at all levels to ensure and enforce evenhanded political coverage. The limitations of a form of impartiality that applies mainly to electoral politics are clear; the answer, however, is surely not to discard this approach but to extend it to other spheres of life.

Cooper's commitment to impartiality was at times abandoned when AP's corporate interests were involved, even when these overlapped with controversial political issues. During the highly political antitrust case in the 1940s, he was firmly in the anti-Roosevelt camp and actively involved in AP's efforts to defuse the threat. AP's news treatment of the controversy was mainly characterized by an absence of coverage, though if Cooper had his way, a combative tone would have been adopted. AP's coverage of Cooper's free press crusade was clearly promotional and, behind the scenes, involved a good deal of political manipulation. AP news coverage from Germany between 1933 and 1941 was compromised by Cooper's isolationist tendencies and his overriding concern for AP's competitive position.

Journalistic independence—specifically, independence from government control or influence—was perhaps Cooper's greatest concern. Holding governments accountable for their actions, without censorship or punishment, is one of the most basic and important functions of journalism. (It goes without saying that individuals and corporations must equally be held to account.) For much of his career, Cooper dealt with agencies that were, to a greater or lesser degree, compromised by government influence—so he came by this concern honestly. There was one major inconsistency and one major gap in his position, however. The inconsistency was his record in dealing with agencies like Rengo and Wolff/DNB, where AP's corporate interests dictated alliances with organizations that were clearly the agents of fascist regimes.

The gap was his failure to acknowledge that private ownership could impose equally troubling limits on journalistic independence, and that publicly supported broadcasters or other news organizations could—if set up with proper safeguards against interference—also carry out the watchdog role effectively.[129] Cooper did emphasize from time to time that the right to know belonged to readers, not publishers, but he accepted the journalistic status quo, asserting that the market guaranteed that publishers would serve readers adequately and fairly. This was wishful thinking; whether one considers the *Chicago Tribune* in the 1930s and 1940s or Fox News today, it's clear that slanted news coverage can flourish under private ownership and without any formal or financial ties to government. But as with political impartiality, the limitations of Cooper's position on journalistic independence do not mean that it should be discarded entirely. Freedom from government interference or control is a necessary, but not a sufficient, condition if journalism is to fulfill its role in liberal democratic societies.

Cooper also mostly ignored the various ways that he and AP were involved with the U.S. government. AP's expansion into South America during the First World War would not have happened—certainly not at the time—without the government's strong encouragement and practical assistance. As the Second World War came to an end, "AP moved in with the troops as enemy territory was freed" in France, Germany, and other European countries. The growing presence and influence around the world of the American state, broadly conceived, was an essential foundation for AP's international expansion. Cooper's crusade to guarantee news agencies' access to foreign markets in postwar peace settlements involved direct and sustained efforts to marshal political and official support. AP's (and UP's) use of U.S. government transmission facilities in China after the war is one example of the kinds of local assistance that American news agency correspondents received at different times. None of these involvements were as compromising as direct government subsidies in exchange for control of an agency's coverage or direct political censorship, but the picture that Cooper painted of AP as uniquely devoid of any government connections was never entirely accurate.

* * *

Cooper's funeral was held in the Park Avenue Christian Church on February 3, 1965. It was a cold, sunny day in New York—the kind of winter weather he had been trying to avoid for decades. Sally and Jane, the daughter of his first marriage, were among hundreds of mourners, who included senior representatives of UPI, the Hearst organization, Reuters, the *New York Times, New York World-Telegram,* and *New York Daily News.*[130] Miller, Gallagher, McKelway, and David Sarnoff were honorary pallbearers. "Sally had the kind of service she thought Kent would have approved," Miller reported to Robert McLean. "It was sad indeed, but well attended and fortunately we had a beautiful day." His estate was valued at more than one hundred thousand dollars (around eight hundred thousand dollars in 2020), though it was not clear how much more. Most of the money went to Sally, with a thirty-thousand-dollar bequest to Jane.[131]

Just as the funeral service began, AP's wires fell silent for one minute as Sally had requested.[132] Then they roared back to life, sending AP news to thousands of subscribers around the world and in forms that not even Cooper imagined when he walked into Melville Stone's office fifty-four years earlier.

Notes

Abbreviations

APCA	Associated Press Corporate Archives
APD	Associated Press Board of Directors and Annual Meetings
APKC	Associated Press Records of Kent Cooper
APLS	Lloyd Stratton Papers
APRM	Associated Press Papers of Robert McLean
APSU	Associated Press Subject Files
APW	Associated Press Writings about AP
APWS	Associated Press World Services
BP	Byron Price Papers
ER	Elmer Roberts Papers
FDR	Franklin D. Roosevelt Presidential Library and Museum
FDRB	Francis Biddle Papers
LL	Lilly Library Cooper mss.
LL2	Lilly Library Cooper mss. II
NYTO	New York Times Ochs Papers
NYTS	New York Times Sulzberger Papers
PPF	President's Personal File (FDR)
RA	Reuters Archive
RAJ	Roderick Jones Papers
RRM	Robert R. McCormick Papers
RWH	Roy W. Howard Archive

STE   Stephen T. Early Papers

USPA   Records of the Assistant Secretary of State for Public Affairs

Chapter 1. "Fitting Himself for the Newspaper Profession"

1. District Court of the United States for the Southern District of New York, *U.S. v. Associated Press et al.*, 21. 52 F. Supp. 362 (1943)

2. See James L. Baughman, "Decline of Journalism since 1945," in *Making News: The Political Economy of Journalism in Britain and America from the Glorious Revolution to the Internet*, ed. Richard R. John and Jonathan Silberstein-Loeb, 164–95 (New York: Oxford University Press, 2015); District Court of the United States for the Southern District of New York, *U.S. v. Associated Press et al.*, 21.

3. For a recent study that sees Cooper as a key figure in U.S. free-flow-of-information policies generally in the twentieth century, see Diana Lemberg, *Barriers Down: How American Power and Free-Flow Policies Shaped Global Media* (New York: Columbia University Press, 2019).

4. "Kent Cooper," *New York Times*, February 1, 1965, 22.

5. Cooper's role in both of these campaigns has previously been studied by Margaret A. Blanchard, *Exporting the First Amendment: The Press-Government Crusade of 1945–1952* (New York: Longman, 1986).

6. "Kent Cooper Dies; Former A.P. Chief," *New York Times*, January 31, 1965, 1.

7. Alan J. Gould interview, p. 63, Associated Press Oral History Collection, Associated Press Corporate Archives (APCA).

8. Matthew Pressman, "Objectivity and Its Discontents: The Struggle for the Soul of American Journalism in the 1960s and 1970s," in *Media Nation: The Political History of News in Modern America*, ed. Bruce Schulman and Julian Zelizer, 96–113 (Philadelphia: University of Pennsylvania Press, 2017).

9. Nicole Hemmer, "From 'Faith in Facts' to 'Fair and Balanced': Conservative Media, Liberal Bias, and the Origins of Balance," in *Media Nation: The Political History of News in Modern America*, ed. Bruce Schulman and Julian Zelizer, 126–43 (Philadelphia: University of Pennsylvania Press, 2017); Jane Mayer, "Making of the Fox News White House," *New Yorker*, March 11, 2019, 40–53; Jennifer Rubin, "Fox News Has Succeeded—In Misinforming Millions of Americans," *Washington Post*, April 1, 2020.

10. Kent Cooper, *Kent Cooper and the Associated Press: An Autobiography* (New York: Random House, 1959), 313.

11. "Narrow Escape from Drowning," *Indianapolis Journal*, August 2, 1889, 2.

12. "Dug Up Treasure: A Collection of Rare Old Coins Unearthed near Bloomington, Ind.," *Louisville Courier-Journal*, August 21, 1891.

13. Cooper, *Kent Cooper*, 317.

14. Ibid., 319.

15. *Columbus (IN) Evening Republican*, July 29, 1896.

16. "From the High School," *Evening Republican*, May 31, 1897; "Township Commencement," May 30, 1896; "Rathbone Sisters' Social," November 8, 1897; "The Pirates of Penzance," February 8, 1898.

17. "Has Resigned his Position," *Evening Republican*, February 28, 1898.

18. Beth Murphy, "Indianapolis News," in *The Encyclopedia of Indianapolis*, ed. David J. Bodenhamer and Robert G. Barrows, 796–97 (Bloomington: Indiana University Press, 1994).

19. "Those Charges Against Raum," *Indianapolis Journal*, July 16, 1890, 1; "Mr. Cooper On the Stand," *Indianapolis State Sentinel*, April 20, 1892, 3.

20. Kent Cooper, "Discusses Truth and Honesty in the News," *The Ohio Newspaper* 6, no. 7, May 1925.

21. "Cooper, Kent," *Current Biography*, October 1944, 19–22.

22. "How It Was Settled," *Evening Republican*, November 9, 1896.

23. Alan Gould interview, 38, Oral History Collection, APCA.

24. See the further discussion of Cooper's political allegiance later in this chapter.

25. *Evening Republican*, September 16, 1898.

26. Richard G. Groome, "Holliday, John Hampden," in *The Encyclopedia of Indianapolis*, ed. David J. Bodenhamer and Robert G. Barrows, 700–701 (Bloomington: Indiana University Press, 1994).

27. Cooper, *Kent Cooper*, 12–13, 20; "Personal Points," *Evening Republican*, October 23, 1899; John Sherman, "Indianapolis Times," in *The Encyclopedia of Indianapolis*, ed. David J. Bodenhamer and Robert G. Barrows (Bloomington: Indiana University Press, 1994), 811.

28. Richard Allen Schwarzlose, *The Nation's Newsbrokers*, vol. 2. *The Rush to Institution, from 1865 to 1920* (Evanston, IL: Northwestern University Press, 1988), 196–97.

29. Cooper, *Kent Cooper*, 20.

30. Ibid., 25; "New Association," *Evening Republican*, March 14, 1905.

31. "Old Republicans Were Not Permitted to Vote," *Indianapolis Star*, January 9, 1904.

32. Cooper to The Associated Press, April 5, 1905, Indiana University, Lilly Library, Cooper mss II (LL2).

33. Cooper, *Kent Cooper*, 33.

34. Ibid., 32–33; Joe Alex Morris, *Deadline Every Minute: The Story of the United Press* (New York: Greenwood Press, 1968), 33–34.

35. David Hochfelder, *The Telegraph in America* (Baltimore: Johns Hopkins University Press, 2012), 154–55.

36. "Secret Marriage Made Public," *Ohio Democrat* (Logan, OH), May 14, 1892; "General Gleanings," *Salt Lake (UT) Herald*, May 8, 1892.

37. "Approaching Wedding," *Evening Republican*, May 16, 1905; "Starr-Cooper," *Evening Republican*, May 25, 1905; "Social and Personal," *Indianapolis Morning Star*, May 25, 1905; "Cooper-Starr," *Indianapolis News*, May 24, 1905.

38. "Personal Mention," *Waterloo (IN) Press*, March 5, 1908.

39. Cooper, *Kent Cooper*, 35.

40. Terhi Rantanen, "Foreign Dependence and Domestic Monopoly: The European News Cartel and U.S. Associated Presses," *Media History* 12, no. 1 (2006): 21. DOI: 10.1080/13688800600597145/.

41. Schwarzlose, *Nation's Newsbrokers* 2: 177–78.

42. Oliver Gramling, *AP: The Story of News* (New York: Farrar and Rinehart, 1940), 220–27.

43. Schwarzlose, *Nation's Newsbrokers* 2: 177–78.

44. George Seldes, *Freedom of the Press* (New York: Da Capo Press, 1971. First published 1935 by Bobbs-Merrill, New York), 191.

45. Upton Sinclair, *The Brass Check: A Study of American Journalism* (Pasadena, CA: The author, 1920), 147, 150. See also Oswald Garrison Villard, *The Disappearing Daily: Chapters in American Newspaper Evolution* (New York: Alfred A. Knopf, 1944), 48.

46. "GM of AP," *Newsweek*, May 5, 1947, 65–66.

47. Cooper, *Kent Cooper*, 36.

48. Ibid., 42.

49. Ibid., 43.

Chapter 2. Apprenticeship and Ascent

1. L.F.C[urtis].,"Kent Cooper and The Associated Press," *AP World*, Spring 1965, 35.

2. "Directors Honor 'KC' on 25th Anniversary of His Appointment as General Manager," *AP World* 3 (1950); Ben Bassett, "Kent Cooper's Legacy," *AP World* 1 (1980).

3. Kent Cooper, *Kent Cooper and the Associated Press: An Autobiography* (New York: Random House, 1959), 45.

4. Menahem Blondheim, *News over the Wires: The Telegraph and the Flow of Public Information in America, 1844–1897* (Cambridge, MA: Harvard University Press, 1994).

5. Cooper, *Kent Cooper*, 47.

6. Adolph Ochs to Cooper, November 24, 1928, New York Public Library, New York Times Company Records, Adolph S. Ochs Papers (NYTO).

7. Robert McLean interview, p. 23, AP Oral History Collection, APCA.

8. AP *Service Bulletin* 26 (1912): 2, General Order No. 348, January 23, APCA.

9. "The Associated Press, Twenty-Fifth Annual Report of the Board of Directors to the Members," 8, APCA, Records of the Board of Directors and Annual Meetings (APD).

10. Cooper, *Kent Cooper*, 45.

11. Alfred D. Chandler, *The Visible Hand: The Managerial Revolution in American Business* (Cambridge, MA: Belknap Press of Harvard University Press, 1977).

12. AP *Service Bulletin* 27 (1912), APCA Records of the Board and Annual Meetings, Bylaw Amendments, 1915–1960, October 9, 1912, APD.

13. Cooper, *Kent Cooper*, 62–63.

14. "The World's Series," *Traffic Bulletin of The Associated Press*, no. 1, October 25, 1916, APCA.

15. See chapter 8.

16. "Kent Cooper Dies; Former A.P. Chief," *New York Times*, January 31, 1965, 1.

17. Roy Howard to Cooper, Thursday (January 1916), LL2. For an overview of the long rivalry/friendship between the two, see Terhi Rantanen, "After Five O'Clock Friends: Kent Cooper and Roy Howard," *Roy W. Howard Monographs in Journalism and Mass Communication Research*, no. 4 (School of Journalism, Indiana University, 1998).

18. Howard to Cooper, "personal," January 20, 1916, LL2.

19. Cooper to Howard, March 16, 1916, LL2.

20. Howard to Cooper, March 18, 1916, LL2.

21. See chapter 4.

22. Remarks of Adolph S. Ochs at AP Annual Luncheon, April 23, 1918, APCA, Papers of Board President Robert S. McLean (APRM).

23. V. S. McClatchy to Ochs, April 29, 1918, NYTO.

24. Four-party contract, October 9, 1902, APCA, Records of General Manager Kent Cooper (APKC); Board of directors minutes, April 25, 1918, 495–96, APD. For the history of Havas, see Antoine Lefebure, *Havas: Les arcanes du pouvoir* (Paris: Bernard Grasset, 1992).

25. For the late nineteenth-century origins of international news in South America, see Rhoda Desbordes-Vela, "L'information internationale en amerique du Sud: Les agences et les reseaux, circa 1874–1919," *Le temps des medias*, no. 20 (printemps-été 2013): 125–38.

26. Kent Cooper, *Barriers Down: The Story of the News Agency Epoch* (New York: Farrar and Rinehart, 1942), 5.

27. Christopher McKnight Nichols, *Promise and Peril: America at the Dawn of a Global Age* (Cambridge, MA: Harvard University Press, 2011), 5–6.

28. David M. K. Sheinin, *Argentina and the United States: An Alliance Continued* (Athens: University of Georgia Press), 34, 38, 46–47.

29. Heidi Tworek, "Magic Connections: German News Agencies and Global News Networks, 1905–1945" (PhD diss., Harvard University, 2012), 72–73. See also Tworek, *News from Germany: The Competition to Control World Communications, 1900–1945* (Cambridge, MA: Harvard University Press, 2019), 58–63, 68.

30. Board of directors minutes, October 5, 1922, 376, APD.

31. Cooper, *Barriers Down*, 48.

32. James Cane, *The Fourth Enemy: Journalism and Power in the Making of Peronist Argentina, 1930–1955* (University Park: University of Pennsylvania Press, 2011), 33, 47, 53.

33. Michael Palmer, *International News Agencies: A History* (New York: Palgrave Macmillan, 2020), 91–95.

34. Board of directors minutes, April 25, 1918, 497, APD.

35. An unsigned 1941 memorandum in the AP Corporate Archives states that this news service was prepared for La Prensa Asociada and adapted to its "pro-German attitude" ("The Associated Press–Latin America," typescript [1941], APRM). The implication is that *La Prensa* was behind Prensa Asociada. This is difficult to believe, however, since *La Prensa* was known as a supporter of the Allied cause. See Percy Alvin Martin, *Latin America and the War* (Baltimore: Johns Hopkins University Press, 1925), 181; Ronald C. Newton, *German Buenos Aires, 1900–1933: Social Change and Cultural Crisis* (Austin: University of Texas Press, 1977), 32; Maria Inés Tato, "Luring Neutrals: Allied and German Propaganda in Argentina during the First World War," in *World War I and Propaganda*, ed. Troy Paddock (Boston: Brill, 2014), 325. The German-subsidized Buenos Aires daily *La Unión*, described as "Argentina's and South America's biggest propaganda newspaper" (Carla Russ, "Persuasive Identities? German Propaganda in Chile and Argentina during the First World War," *National Identities* 24, no. 1 [2019], 5), or some of its backers may have been involved in redistributing the news delivered by the *La Prensa–New York Herald* combination under the banner of La Prensa Asociada. On *La Unión*, see Tato, "Fighting for a Lost

Cause? The Germanophile Newspaper La Unión in Neutral Argentina, 1914–1918," *War in History* 25, no. 4 (2018): 464–84; Stefan Rinke, "The Reconstruction of National Identity: German Immigrants in Latin America during the First World War," in *Immigration and National Identities in Latin America*, ed. Nicola Foote and Michael Goebel (Gainesville: University Press of Florida, 2014), 172.

36. Cooper, *Barriers Down*, 45, 65; Dwayne R. Winseck and Robert M. Pike, *Communication and Empire: Media, Markets, and Globalization, 1860–1930* (Durham, NC: Duke University Press, 2007), 246, 279; "The Associated Press–Latin America," typescript (1941), APRM; Board of directors minutes, April 25, 1918, 544, APCA; Joe Alex Morris, *Deadline Every Minute: The Story of the United Press* (New York: Greenwood Press, 1968), 102–103.

37. Board of directors minutes, April 25, 1918, 499, APD.

38. Ibid., 590–91.

39. "The Associated Press–Latin America," typescript (1941), APRM.

40. Cooper to Edward House, September 20, 1918, and September 21, 1918. Yale University Library, Manuscripts and Archives, Col. E. M. House Papers.

41. Board of directors minutes, April 25, 1918, 585, 589, APD.

42. Kent Cooper, "Hands across the Equator," AP *Service Bulletin* 50 (1919), 3+, APCA.

43. Board of directors minutes, April 25, 1918, 578, APD; Cooper, *Barriers Down*, 50; Jean-Luc Renaud, "U.S. Government Assistance to AP's World-Wide Expansion," *Journalism and Mass Communication Quarterly* 62, no. 1 (1985): 36.

44. For details of French government subsidies, see Pierre Frédérix, *Un siècle de chasse aux nouvelles*, preface by André Siegfried (Paris: Flammarion, 1959); and Palmer, *International News Agencies*.

45. For Reuters, see Peter Putnis, "Share 999: British Government Control of Reuters during World War I," *Media History* 14, no. 2 (2008): 1410–65.

46. Board of directors minutes, April 25, 1918, 557, APD.

47. Ibid., 583–84.

48. Ibid., 583.

49. Stratton Abstracts, South American services, 1900–1960, APD.

50. "The Associated Press–Latin America," typescript (1941), APRM.

51. For an account of Howard's travels, see Terhi Rantanen, "Mr. Howard Goes to South America: The United Press Associations and Foreign Expansion," *Roy W. Howard Monographs in Journalism and Mass Communication Research*, no. 2 (School of Journalism, Indiana University, 1992).

52. Cooper, *Barriers Down*, 71; Board of directors minutes, October 3, 1918, 270, APD.

53. Cooper, *Barriers Down*, 72.

54. Board of directors minutes, October 3, 1918, 81, APD.

55. Cooper, *Barriers Down*, 73.

56. Board of directors minutes, April 25, 1918, 501, remarks of Stone, APD.

57. Ibid., 548.

58. Board of directors minutes, October 3, 1918, Cooper report on South America, APD.

59. Ibid.

60. Board of directors minutes, April 25, 1918, 563, APD.

61. Ibid., 581.

62. Board of directors minutes, October 3, 1918, 102, APD.

63. Cooper, *Barriers Down*, 79.

64. Board of directors minutes, October 4, 1922, 92–93, APD.

65. Board of directors minutes, October 3, 1918, 101, APD.

66. Ibid., 100–101.

67. "The Associated Press–Latin America," typescript (1941), APRM.

68. Morris, *Deadline Every Minute*, 107.

69. "The Associated Press–Latin America," typescript (1941), APRM; Cooper, *Barriers Down*, 113–14.

70. Morris, *Deadline Every Minute*, 108.

71. Howard to Karl Bickel, May 10, 1931, Indiana University, The Media School, Roy W. Howard Archive (RWH).

72. Lloyd Stratton memorandum, October 15, 1958, APCA.

73. Ibid.

74. "Notes of the Service: The Foreign Field," AP *Service Bulletin* 50, 1919, APCA.

75. Cooper, *Kent Cooper*, 83, 86.

76. See chapters 5, 6, and 9.

77. Christopher McKnight Nichols, *Promise and Peril: America at the Dawn of a Global Age* (Cambridge, MA: Harvard University Press, 2011), 11, 42, 60; Charles A. Kupchan, *Isolationism: A History of America's Efforts to Shield Itself from the World* (New York: Oxford University Press, 2020), 21, 39.

78. Quinn Slobodian, *Globalists: The End of Empire and the Birth of Neoliberalism* (Cambridge, MA: Harvard University Press, 2018), 6, 15, 24.

79. Cooper, *Kent Cooper*, 84, 88.

80. Frédérix, *Un siècle de chasse aux nouvelles*, 339 ff.

81. Tworek, "Creation of European News," 733.

82. Cooper to Melville Stone, September 1, 1919, LL2.

83. *International News Service v. Associated Press*, 248 U.S. 215 (1918). The case and its implications are clearly set out in Will Slauter, *Who Owns the News?: A History of Copyright* (Stanford, CA: Stanford University Press, 2019), chap. 7, "*International News Service v. Associated Press* and Its Legacy."

84. Cooper to Stone, September 1, 1919, LL2.

85. Donald Read, *The Power of News: The History of Reuters*, 2nd ed. (Oxford: Oxford University Press, 1999), 116.

86. Cooper, *Barriers Down*, 93.

87. Bernard Rickatson-Hatt to Roderick Jones, "strictly private and confidential," February 27, 1934, Thomson Reuters Archive (RA), Reuters General 1918–1926.

88. Christopher Chancellor to Lloyd Dumas, May 4, 1951, RA, USA–Associated Press Administration, January 1951–December 1952.

89. Roderick Jones, memorandum of conversation with Cooper and Robert Collins, August 5, 1919, RA.

90. Cooper to Stone, September 1, 1919, LL2.

91. "Funeral of Mrs. Cooper," *Indianapolis News*, January 27, 1920.

92. "Wife of A.P. Chief Passes," *Spokesman-Review* (Spokane, WA), January 27, 1920; *Rochester (NY) Democrat and Chronicle*, January 26, 1920.

93. Cooper to House, n.d. (1920), Yale University Library, Manuscripts and Archives, Col. E. M. House Papers.

94. "Kent Cooper Weds Miss Rothwell," *New York Times*, September 28, 1920.

95. John Frederick Phillips, "A Trip through the New York Office," AP *Service Bulletin* 54 (1920), APCA.

96. AP *Service Bulletin* 61 (1921), APCA; *Editor & Publisher*, April 23, 1921.

97. Cooper to L.F.C.[Curtis], February 28, 1942, LL2.

98. Robert McLean to Paul Miller, May 13, 1965, APRM.

99. Frank Noyes to McLean, November 9, 1943, enclosing undated copy of letter from Noyes to Stone, APRM.

100. Ochs to Cooper, October 18, 1921, NYTO.

101. "Memorandum on Agency Contracts," May 17, 1920, presented to board of directors, January 1922, LL2.

102. Ibid.

103. Ibid.

104. Morris, *Deadline Every Minute*, 102.

Chapter 3. "Very Much the Boss"

1. Kent Cooper to Frederick Roy Martin, February 15, 1922, APKC.

2. Julia Guarneri, *Newsprint Metropolis: City Papers and the Making of Modern Americans* (Chicago: University of Chicago Press, 2017), 6–8, 128–29.

3. Frank Noyes to Adolph Ochs, April 10, 1924, "confidential," NYTO.

4. Miscellaneous Board Resolutions, motions, 1914–1960, April 22, 1914, APD.

5. AP *Service Bulletin* 53 (1920, no. 2), APCA.

6. Frank Noyes to Adolph Ochs, April 10, 1924, "confidential," NYTO.

7. "Martin Resigns from A.P.," *Philadelphia Evening Bulletin*, April 1, 1925, APRM, Clippings (AP), 1924–1925. See also "The Associated Press, Twenty-Sixth Annual Report of the Board of Directors to Members," 1926, March 11, 1926, APD.

8. "Kent Cooper Appointed General Manager," AP *Service Bulletin* (1925), APCA.

9. "Kent Cooper Heads Associated Press," *New York Times*, April 20, 1925.

10. Kent Cooper, *Kent Cooper and the Associated Press: An Autobiography* (New York: Random House, 1959), 92.

11. See Menahem Blondheim, *News over the Wires: The Telegraph and the Flow of Public Information in America, 1844–1897* (Cambridge, MA: Harvard University Press, 1994).

12. Cooper statement to board of directors, n.d. (April 1925), APCA Subject Files (APSU). All quotations in this paragraph are from this source.

13. Byron Price, "Memoir," unpublished, 41, Wisconsin Historical Society, Byron Price Papers (BP).

14. Cooper to members of the Associated Press, June 13, 1925, APSU.

15. Michael Stamm, *Dead Tree Media: Manufacturing the Newspaper in Twentieth-Century North America* (Baltimore: Johns Hopkins University Press, 2018), 42, 48, 50.

16. Richard Kaplan, "From Partisanship to Professionalism: The Transformation of the Daily Press," in *Print in Motion: The Expansion of Publishing and Reading in the United States, 1880–1940*, ed. Karl Kaestle and Janice Radway (Chapel Hill: University of North Carolina Press, 2009), 127.

17. For the Scripps chain, see Gerald Baldasty, *E. W. Scripps and the Business of Newspapers* (Urbana: University of Illinois Press, 1999).

18. Julia Guarneri, *Newsprint Metropolis: City Papers and the Making of Modern Americans* (Chicago: University of Chicago Press, 2017), 6, 100, 128–29, 244.

19. Kent Cooper, "Two Points of View (and a Creed)," AP *Service Bulletin* 30, APCA. All quotations in this paragraph are from this source.

20. Kent Cooper, "Address by Kent Cooper . . . to the American Society of Newspaper Editors," Washington, D.C., January 16, 1926.

21. "New York Close-Up," *New York Herald Tribune*, November 2, 1949.

22. See the section on Cooper's hiring of female journalists later in this chapter.

23. All quotations in this paragraph are from Cooper, "Two Points of View (and a Creed)."

24. Kent Cooper, "Discusses Truth and Honesty in the News," *The Ohio Newspaper*, May 1925.

25. Michael Schudson, *The Good Citizen: A History of American Civic Life* (New York: Martin Kessler Books, 1998), 158–59, 161–62, 190–91; David Goodman, *Radio's Civic Ambition: American Broadcasting and Democracy in the 1930s* (New York: Oxford University Press, 2011), 183–84.

26. Walter Lippmann, *Public Opinion*, preface by Ronald Steel (New York: Free Press Paperbacks, 1997. First published 1922 by Harcourt, Brace [New York]), 226. Thomas Patterson criticizes a "narrow conception" of truth that "boils down to the accuracy of specific facts." See Patterson, *Informing the News: The Need for Knowledge-Based Journalism* (New York: Vintage Books, 2013), 62.

27. Schudson, *Good Citizen*, 192–93; Goodman, *Radio's Civic Ambition*, 183–84.

28. Cooper to the Staff, n.d. [1925], APSU.

29. Price, unpublished memoir, 55; Reporters of the Associated Press, *Breaking News: How the Associated Press Has Covered War, Peace, and Everything Else* (New York: Princeton Architectural Press, 2007), 48–49.

30. See chapter 13.

31. "U.S. Calls Hand in Nicaragua," *Arizona Republican*, November 18, 1926.

32. Kent Cooper, "Address by Kent Cooper . . . to the Association of Life Insurance Presidents," New York, December 9, 1926; "Inquiry Is Sought on A.P. Dispatch," *Baltimore Sun*, December 14, 1926.

33. "Associated Press Reporter Braves Death to Get Amundsen Rescue," *Oakland (CA) Tribune*, July 13, 1925.

34. M. N. Stiles, circular to superintendents, August 3, 1925, APSU.

35. Associated Press, Records of the Board of Directors and annual meetings (APD), Feature service, Mail and Illustrated—1913–1960, APCA.

36. Jackson Elliott to C. E. Honce, November 17, 1930, APSU.

37. Cooper to Price, April 2, 1931, APKC.

38. Jackson Elliott to C. E. Honce, November 17, 1930, APSU.

39. Cooper to Robert McLean, August 11 1926, APKC.

40. Cooper, *Kent Cooper*, 117.

41. Kerry Buckley, "A President for the 'Great Silent Majority': Bruce Barton's Construction of Calvin Coolidge," *New England Quarterly* 76, no. 4 (2003): 593–626.

42. For the interview, see, for example, "Barton Reveals Coolidge as Sympathetic Executive in Exclusive Interview," *Altoona (PA) Tribune*, September 23, 1926.

43. "Coolidge Bid for Popularity Hit," *Louisville Courier-Journal*, September 24, 1926.

44. AP Biographical Service, no. 2821, Cooper biography file, APCA; Cooper to Coolidge, September 14, 1926, quoted in Buckley, "President for the 'Great Silent Majority,'" 620.

45. Cooper to Barton, September 24, 1926, Bruce Barton Papers, Wisconsin Historical Society.

46. Dewey M. Owens, "The Associated Press," *American Mercury* 10, no. 40 (1927): 392.

47. "An A.P. Achievement," *Albuquerque Journal*, September 24, 1926.

48. "Coolidge Bid for Popularity Hit," *Louisville Courier-Journal*, September 24, 1926.

49. Quoted in Owens, "Associated Press," 393.

50. Memorandum enclosed in Martin Creager to Cooper, June 17, 1925, APSU.

51. Unsigned document, September 11, 1925, enclosed in McLean to Cooper, November 10, 1925, APKC.

52. Noyes to Cooper, December 18, 1926, Indiana University, Lilly Library, Cooper mss. (LL).

53. Cooper to Noyes, December 20, 1926, LL.

54. Owens, "Associated Press."

55. Guarneri, *Newsprint Metropolis*, 6–7, 194–233.

56. Board of directors minutes, April 21, 1927, 167, APD.

57. Ibid., 168–69.

58. Ibid., 174–75.

59. Cooper to John Bogart, April 8, 1927, APKC.

60. Cooper to A. L. MacKinnon, April 7, 1927, APKC.

61. Liz Watts, "AP's First Female Reporters," *Journalism History* 39, no. 1 (2013): 15–28.

62. Charles Stevenson Smith, "On the Distaff Side," *FYI*, May 1, 1928, AP 34, APCA.

63. Ochs address to AP members, April 25, 1927, NYTO.

64. Ochs to Noyes, July 29, 1926, NYTO.

65. Noyes to Ochs, August 2, 1926, NYTO.

66. Douglas Williams to Jones, June 10, 1925, RA, Roderick Jones.

67. Noyes to Melville Stone, May 5, 1925 APSU.

68. "Cooper Describes A.P. Developments," *Editor & Publisher*, April 19, 1930.

69. Associated Press, Stratton Abstracts, Feature service, Mail and Illustrated—1913–1960, April 23, 1928, APD; "The Associated Press, Twenty-Ninth Annual Report of the Board of Directors to Members," 1929, 7–8, APD.

70. "News Editors Strategic Correspondents," *FYI*, February 25, 1930, APCA.

71. Records of the Board and Annual Meetings, April 21, 1930, 547–48, APD; "Secretary Talks on Radio," *New York Times*, April 22, 1930.

72. Associated Press, "Address of Kent Cooper . . . at the Thirtieth Annual Luncheon," April 21, 1930.

73. Kaplan, "From Partisanship to Professionalism," 135. Partisanship did not disappear entirely, however, as the success of the *Chicago Tribune*, the Hearst newspapers, and others demonstrated.

74. "The 10 Greatest News Events of 1930," *Des Moines (IA) Register*, December 19, 1930.

75. Associated Press, "Address of Kent Cooper . . . at the Thirtieth Annual Luncheon," April 21, 1930.

76. J.C.D. DeWolf to Elliott, May 16, 1931; S. E. Hudson to Elliott, April 22, 1931, APSU.

77. Ochs to Cooper, November 11, 1931, APKC.

78. Elliott to Ochs, November 12, 1931, APKC.

79. Edwin James to Ochs, April 22, 1932, APKC.

80. Gay Talese, *The Kingdom and the Power: Behind the Scenes at the New York Times* (New York: Random House, 2007; first published 1969, World Publishing Co., [New York]), 17. See also Susan E. Tifft and Alex S. Jones, *The Trust: The Private and Powerful Family behind the New York Times* (New York: Little, Brown, 1999).

81. See chapter 7.

82. Cooper to David Sarnoff, "personal and confidential," October 7, 1930, LL2.

83. Ibid.

84. Cooper to Ochs, "confidential," October 24, 1930, NYTO.

85. Ochs to Cooper, October 31, 1930, NYTO.

86. Noyes to J. R. Youatt, April 23, 1931, LL2.

87. Ben Bassett, "KC's Broom Got Rid of the Cobwebs," *Cleartime* no. 73, September 1978, APCA.

88. See chapter 2.

89. "To Correspondents at Strategic Centers," *FYI*, February 7, 1928, APCA.

90. Cooper to Paul Cowles, Edgar Cutter, and McCall, June 20, 1928, APSU.

91. Cutter to Cooper, October 2, 1928, RRM.

92. Ibid.; L.C. Probert to Elmer Roberts, June 20, 1928, Elmer Roberts Papers, Wilson Library, University of North Carolina.

93. Bernard Rickatson-Hatt to Roderick Jones, September 24, 1931, RA, Roderick Jones.

94. See chapter 5.

95. Board of directors to members, January 14, 1932, APKC; Cooper to Noyes, February 2, 1932; Cooper to Noyes, February 29, 1932; Statement by Board to the Associated Press members, April 25, 1932, APSU.

96. "Alabama A.P. Members Ask Board for Reduction in Assessments," *Editor & Publisher*, April 16, 1932, 12.

97. Cooper to Walter N. Harrison, January 9, 1932, APKC.

98. "A.P. against Economizing on Service, to Restrict News Broadcasting," *Editor & Publisher*, April 30, 1932.

99. "A.P. Aiding Members during Hard Times," *Editor & Publisher*, April 23, 1932.

100. "The Necessary Press," *New York Times*, May 1, 1932.

101. Lloyd Stratton Abstracts of Minutes, 1900–1960, April 26, 1932, APD; Cooper to leased wire members, May 7, 1932, APSU; Board of directors minutes, October 4, 1938, APD.

102. Cooper to news editors and strategic correspondents, n.d. (1932), APKC.

103. Price, unpublished memoir, 177, BP. Walter Lippmann had a similar criticism of journalism in general; see *Liberty and the News* (New Brunswick, NJ: Transaction Publishers, 1995. First published 1920 by Harcourt, Brace, and Howe [New York]).

104. Cooper to Noyes, July 5, 1932, APKC.

105. "A.P. Directors Report on Economy, Service Held at High Level," *Editor & Publisher*, April 30, 1932.

106. See chapter 6.

107. Cooper to L. E. Owens, March 11, 1933, APKC.

108. Cooper to W. J. Pape, March 18, 1933, APKC; Board of directors, verbatim minutes, October 4, 1938, 87, APD.

Chapter 4. The Opposition

1. Roy Howard to Karl Bickel, May 28, 1925, Roy W. Howard Archive, The Media School, Indiana University (RWH).

2. Joe Alex Morris, *Deadline Every Minute: The Story of the United Press* (New York: Greenwood Press, 1968), 145.

3. Jonathan Silberstein-Loeb, *The International Distribution of News: The Associated Press, Press Association, and Reuters, 1848–1947* (New York: Cambridge University Press, 2014).

4. Kent Cooper to E. H. Butler, March 20, 1925, APKC.

5. Cooper, "Address by Kent Cooper . . . to the Association of Life Insurance Presidents," APKC.

6. Cooper to Robert McCormick, March 10, 1925, RRM; Cooper to Frank Noyes, July 31, 1925, APSU.

7. Cooper to Adolph Ochs, December 11, 1925, NYTO.

8. Board of directors minutes, April 20, 1927, 3–4, APD.

9. Howard to Bickel, July 10, 1925, RWH.

10. Ibid.

11. See the discussion below on the Hearst-led challenge to AP's governance structure.

12. Howard to Bickel, July 10, 1925, RWH.

13. Cooper to members of the Associated Press, June 27, 1925, APSU.

14. Cooper to Bickel, June 9, 1925, APSU.

15. Cooper to David E. Town, November 11, 1926, APSU.

16. Jackson Elliott, circulars to superintendents and correspondents, March 12 and March 17, 1925, APRM.

17. Cooper to Adolph S. Ochs and other directors, June 14, 1926, NYTO.

18. Cooper to Howard, "personal," June 22, 1926, APSU. For Baillie's account of the relations between AP and UP, see Baillie, *High Tension: The Recollections of Hugh Baillie* (New York: Harper Brothers, 1959).

19. Hugh Baillie, circular to all business representatives and all bureau managers, June 3, 1926, APSU.

20. Cooper to Ochs, June 14, 1926, NYTO.

21. "Scripps-Howard Purchases Four Newspapers," *Editor & Publisher*, November 27, 1926.

22. Executive committee minutes, November 29, 1926, APKC.

23. Ochs to Cooper, February 12, 1927, NYTO.

24. M. Koenigsberg to William Randolph Hearst, March 18, 1927, William Randolph Hearst Papers, Bancroft Library, University of California–Berkeley.

25. NAH[use] to Cooper, December 22, 1926, APSU.

26. Gerald Baldasty, *E. W. Scripps and the Business of Newspapers* (Urbana: University of Illinois Press, 1999), 4; Price, unpublished memoir, 42, BP.

27. Cooper to Edward T. Clark, February 10, 1927, "strictly personal," NYTO.

28. JSE memorandum to Cooper, November 16, 1926, APSU.

29. W. H. Cowles to Cooper, January 10, 1927, and December 31, 1926, APSU.

30. Cooper to Cowles, January 3, 1927, and January 5, 1927, APSU.

31. Board of directors minutes, January 24, 1927, 34, APD.

32. Ibid., 43–44, APD.

33. Ibid., 34, APD.

34. Milton Garges, memo to Cooper, March 4, 1927, APSU.

35. James MacMullen to Garges, February, 18, 1927, APSU.

36. Jack Wright to Garges, February 25, 1927, APSU.

37. Frank Shutts to Garges, February 11, 1927, APSU.

38. Hilton Brown to Garges, February 24, 1927, APSU. For UP's superior foreign news coverage, see chapter 5.

39. Memo for Mr. Ochs relative to AP dispatches on Chamberlin flight, n.d. (1927), NYTO.

40. UP circular to All Business Representatives and Bureau Managers, June 9, 1927, APSU.

41. Cooper to Noyes, July 20 1927, LL.

42. See chapter 8.

43. Howard "To All editors," June 20, 1927, RWH.

44. Cooper to Noyes, July 20, 1927, APKC.

45. UP story, May 28, 1927, Warsaw, RWH.

46. Howard "To All editors," June 20, 1927, RWH.

47. Harold Turnblad to Paul Cowles, January 11, 1929, APSU.

48. UP asset value contract, n.d., enclosed in David Fernsler to William McCambridge, September 7, 1929, APSU.

49. Paul Cowles to Cooper, January 15, 1929, APSU.

50. Board of directors minutes, October 2, 1929, 111–12, APD; William Cannon to Cooper, September 23, 1929, APSU.

51. See chapter 10.

52. Cannon to Elliott, August 15, 1927, APSU.

53. Board of directors minutes, October 4, 1927, 56, 52–53, APD.

54. Cooper to Paul Cowles, October 18, 1927, APRM.

55. Bickel to Cooper, n.d. but received July 3, 1929, APSU.

56. Cooper to Bickel, December 19, 1929, APKC.

57. Howard to Cooper, June 1, 1929, Roy W. Howard Papers, Library of Congress.

58. W. H. Hawkins to Cooper, February 27, 1931, APKC; "Scripps-Howard Newspapers," May 8, 1934, APRM.

59. Cooper to Noyes, March 14, 1933, APKC.

60. See chapter 10.

61. Board of directors minutes, October 5, 1927, 62, APD.

62. W. F. Brooks to Cooper, October 29, 1934, APSU.

63. W. H. Cowles to Cooper, November 1, 1934, APSU.

64. Stuart Perry to Noyes, November 3, 1934, APSU; see chapter 5.

65. "The Associated Press, Thirtieth Annual Report of the Board of Directors to Members," April 21, 1930, 7, APD; UP memorandum, February 25, 1930, enclosed in Zerbey to Cooper, July 1, 1930, APSU; Elliott to J. H. Snyder, March 16, 1929; Elliott to Robert McLean, June 28, 1935, APRM.

66. David Nasaw, *The Chief: The Life of William Randolph Hearst* (Boston: Houghton Mifflin, 2000), 314.

67. Ibid., 193, 210, 227, 264.

68. See chapter 10.

69. Upton Sinclair, *The Brass Check A Study of American Journalism* (Pasadena, CA: The author, 1920), 409. See also Morris L. Ernst, *The First Freedom* (New York: Macmillan, 1946).

70. Nasaw, *The Chief*, 321.

71. Silberstein-Loeb, *International Distribution of News,* 57.

72. Ibid., 49, 59.

73. "Re-Elect Noyes Head of Associated Press," *New York Times*, April 22, 1926.

74. John Francis Neylan to A. L. Glassman, June 8, 1926, APSU.

75. Ibid.

76. Proxy committee to AP members, n.d., enclosed in Cooper to board of directors, February 16, 1927, APKC.

77. Henry Allen to Cooper, June 14, 1926, APKC.

78. James Thompson to Cooper, June 14, 1926, APKC.

79. Memorandum draft introducing the resolution of the Board of Directors for the reallocation of the bond issue of the Associated Press, n.d. (1926), APKC.

80. Ibid.

81. J. H. Zerbey to Cooper, March 10, 1927, APKC.

82. Zerbey to Associated Press New York, January 28, 1927, APKC.

83. CDW (AP Denver correspondent) to Cooper, February 9, 1927, APKC.

84. Elliott to Moses Strauss, March 15, 1927, APKC; Cooper to members of the board of directors, February 16, 1927, APKC.

85. Cooper to R. C. Hoiles, March 11, 1927, APKC.

86. Noyes circular to AP members, March 31, 1927, APKC.

87. Board of directors minutes, April 25, 1927, 724–25, APD.

88. Neylan to Hearst, May 12, 1927, Hearst Papers.

89. Neylan to Cooper, May 25, 1928, APKC.

90. Cooper to W. D. Little, May 25, 1928, APKC.

91. "The Associated Press, Twenty-Ninth Annual Report of the Board of Directors to Members," 1929, 39–40, APD; "Associated Press Alters Voting Right," *New York Times*, April 24, 1928, 16.

92. Elliott to Ochs, August 20, 1930, NYTO.

93. E. Lansing Ray to Cooper, April 4, 1928, APKC; see chapter 7.

Chapter 5. International Ambitions

1. Jackson Elliot to Frederick Roy Martin, December 1, 1924, APSU.

2. See chapter 2.

3. Roderick Jones to Douglas Williams, December 1, 1924, RAJ.

4. Jones to Williams, "personal and confidential," October 2, 1925, RA.

5. Jones to Williams, "private and confidential," January 5, 1926, RA.

6. Herbert Jeans memo to Jones, June 24, 1925, and June 6, 1925, RAJ.

7. Jones to Williams, "personal and confidential," October 2, 1925, RA.

8. Jones to Frank Noyes, "personal and private," July 14, 1924, RAJ.

9. Kent Cooper to Noyes, "personal," February 2, 1926, APSU.

10. Cooper to Noyes, January 22, 1926, APSU.

11. See chapter 2.

12. Noyes to Cooper, "personal," February 4, 1926, APSU.

13. Cooper to Noyes, January 14, 1926, APKC.

14. Cooper to Noyes, July 30, 1926, APSU.

15. Cooper memo, July 22, 1926, APSU.

16. Cooper to Noyes, March 27, 1926, APSU.

17. Noyes to Cooper, September 4, 1926, APSU.

18. Noyes to Cooper, September 16, 1926, APSU.

19. Noyes, Memorandum on Far Eastern News Conditions, December 13, 1922, APRM. For the development of the Japanese press, see James Huffman, *Creating a Public: People and Press in Meiji Japan* (Honolulu: University of Hawaii Press, 1997).

20. Cooper to Noyes, September 10, 1926, APSU. For background on the international cable network, see Daniel R. Headrick, and Pascal Griset, "Submarine Telegraph Cables: Business and Politics, 1838–1939." *Business History Review* 75 (Autumn 2001): 543–78.

21. See the section on AP's relations with Kokusai/Rengo below.

22. Jones and Noyes memorandum, "private and confidential," October 27, 1926, APSU.

23. Jones memo, "private and confidential," June 25, 1927, RAJ.

24. Board of directors minutes, October 4, 1927, APD.

25. Jones to Cooper, "strictly confidential," August 26, 1927, APSU.

26. See chapter 6.

27. Walter Whiffen to Martin, December 8, 1923; Noyes to Jones, June 13, 1923, APSU; Jones to Noyes, "personal and private," July 14, 1924, RAJ.

28. Victor Eubank to Cooper, October 1, 1925, APKC; see also Eubank to Paul Cowles, July 6, 1925.

29. Eubank to Cooper, September 3, 1925, APKC.

30. Jones to Noyes, "personal and private," July 14, 1924, RAJ.

31. Tomoko Akami, *Japan's News Propaganda and Reuters' News Empire in Northeast Asia, 1870–1934* (Dordrecht, Netherlands: Republic of Letters Publishing, 2012), 3.

32. Ibid., 139, 141, 146.

33. Ibid., 157.

34. Ibid., 177.

35. Kent Cooper, *Barriers Down: The Story of the News Agency Epoch* (New York: Farrar and Rinehart, 1942), 149.

36. Cooper to Noyes, May 19, 1926, LL.

37. Noyes to Cooper, May 18, 1926, LL.

38. Cooper to Noyes, May 19, 1926, LL.

39. Eubank to Cooper, March 31, 1926, LL.

40. Yukichi Iwanaga to Cooper, "personal," March 9, 1926; Cooper to Iwanaga, "personal," February 3, 1926, LL.

41. Iwanaga to Cooper, April 5, 1926, LL.

42. Akami, *Japan's News Propaganda.*

43. Ibid., 78; Iwanaga to Cooper, April 5, 1926, LL; Tomoko Akami, *Soft Power of Japan's Total War State: The Board of Information and Domei News Agency in Foreign Policy, 1934–1945* (Dordrecht, Netherlands: Republic of Letters Publishing, 2014), 65.

44. Akami, *Japan's News Propaganda,* 183.

45. For AP's nineteenth-century origins, see Menahem Blondheim, *News Over the Wires: The Telegraph and the Flow of Public Information in America, 1844–1897* (Cambridge, MA: Harvard University Press, 1994); Cooper to Noyes, "confidential," July 9, 1926, LL.

46. William Turner to Jones, "personal," July 23, 1927, RA.

47. Jones to Turner, "strictly confidential," October 13, 1927, RA.

48. Cooper to Noyes, September 6, 1927, APSU.

49. "A.P. Makes Russian Alliance," *Editor & Publisher,* May 30, 1925.

50. Louis P. Lochner, *Always the Unexpected: A Book of Reminiscences* (New York: Macmillan, 1956), 252.

51. Harold Ickes to Noyes, March 15, 1941, APSU.

52. Board of directors minutes, January 14, 1932, APD.

53. Salvatore Cortesi to Cooper, "confidential," October 27, 1926, APKC.

54. Oliver Gramling, *AP: The Story of News* (New York: Farrar and Rinehart, 1940), 167.

55. John P. Diggins, *Mussolini and Fascism: The View from America* (Princeton, NJ: Princeton University Press, 1972), 44.

56. George Seldes, *Sawdust Caesar: The Untold Story of Mussolini and Fascism* (New York: Harper, 1935), 328, 172.

57. Quoted in Diggins, *Mussolini and Fascism,* 54.

58. Diggins, *Mussolini and Fascism,* 45.

59. Percy Winner, "Memorandum to Mr. Cortesi," February 18, 1927, enclosed in Cortesi to Cooper, February 19, 1927, APKC.

60. Cortesi to Cooper, "confidential," October 27, 1926, APKC.

61. Cortesi to Cooper, February 19, 1927, APKC.

62. See, for example, "Report King Victor Plans to Abdicate," *Philadelphia Inquirer*, September 29, 1928.

63. CSS memo to Cooper, November 1, 1928, APKC.

64. Cooper to Cortesi, October 29, 1928, APKC.

65. Diggins, *Mussolini and Fascism*, 48.

66. Jeans to Cooper, "strictly private & confidential," October 23, 1928, APKC.

67. Giovanni Cappelletto, Report on the service of the special office of the Stefani agency, November 17, 1927, APKC.

68. Cooper to Cortesi, March 5, 1928, APKC.

69. Soon Jin Kim, *EFE: Spain's World News Agency* (New York, Westport, CT: Greenwood Press, 1989)16; Henry F. Schulte, *The Spanish Press, 1470–1966: Print, Power, and Politics* (Urbana: University of Illinois Press, 1968), 230.

70. Kim, *EFE*, 25; Secretary of Prensa Espanola to Cooper, December 30, 1925, APKC.

71. Cooper to Noyes, January 14, 1926, APKC.

72. Cooper to Charles Houssaye, January 19, 1926, APKC.

73. Houssaye to Cooper, February 10, 1926 (author's translation), APKC.

74. Robert Berry to Cooper, February 20, 1926; "Concurrence," Bureau Centrale des agences alliées, Paris, November 23, 1927, APKC.

75. Berry to Cooper, April 7, 1927, APKC.

76. Berry to M. N. Stiles, March 22, 1927, APKC.

77. Elmer Roberts to Cooper, December 14, 1926, APKC.

78. Roberts to Cooper, August 25, 1926, APKC.

79. Roberts to Cooper, October 14, 1926 and November 26, 1926, Elliott to Cooper, Paris, n.d. (ca. August 31, 1925), APKC.

80. Roberts to Cooper, July 10, 1925, APKC; Roberts to Cooper, August 26, 1926, Elmer Roberts Papers (ER), Wilson Library, University of North Carolina.

81. SR [Smith Reavis] to Roberts, n.d., enclosed in Roberts to Cooper, May 25, 1926, APKC.

82. Roberts to Cooper, May 21, 1926, ER.

83. Roberts to Cooper, April 29, 1926, ER.

84. Roberts to Cooper, May 21, 1926, ER.

85. Cooper to Noyes, June 3, 1926, APSU.

86. Cooper to Roberts, "confidential," April 29, 1926, APKC.

87. See chapter 4.

88. "Disabled Zeppelin Landed in France," *Boston Daily Globe*, May 18, 1929.

89. Cooper to Roberts, May 20, 1929, APKC.

90. James Hyde to Roberts, June 5, 1929, ER.

91. Board of directors minutes, October 2, 1929, 22–23, APD.

92. Ibid., 21, APD.

93. Joseph Sharkey to Houssaye, February 11, 1930, APKC.

94. AHU to Sharkey, March 18, 1931, APKC; "F. G. Nixon-Nirdlinger Slain by Shot at Home in France; Wife, Pageant Beauty, Held," *Philadelphia Inquirer*, March 12, 1931; Sharkey to Cooper, April 3, 1931, APKC.

95. John Custis to Cooper, March 20, 1931, APKC.

96. Cooper to Sharkey, May 25, 1932, APKC.

97. Board of directors minutes, April 17, 1929, 251, APD.

98. Ibid., 252, APD.

99. See chapter 6.

100. Board of directors minutes, April 17, 1929, 425–26, APD.

101. Board of directors minutes, September 30, 1930, 49–73, APD.

102. Board of directors minutes, October 1, 1930, 404, APD.

103. Ibid., 415, APD.

104. Board of directors minutes, September 30, 1930, 78, APD.

105. Ibid., 84, APD.

106. Glenn Babb to Cooper, November 29, 1929, APKC.

107. Babb, Memorandum on the trans-Pacific service, May 22, 1931, LL.

108. Cooper to Noyes, December 23, 1930, LL.

109. Noyes to Cooper, December 26, 1930, LL.

110. Cooper to Jones, "confidential," February 15, 1930, RAJ.

111. Board of directors minutes, April 17 1930, 74, APD.

112. Ibid., 91, APD.

113. Reuters board of directors minutes, April 8, 1930, RAJ.

114. Board of directors minutes, April 17, 1929, 251, APD.

115. Ibid., 66–67, APD.

116. Jones to Cooper, "private," August 16, 1930, RAJ; Board of directors minutes, September 30, 1930, 35–37, APD.

117. Board of directors minutes, September 30, 1930, 44–45, APD.

118. Noyes to Jones, September 18, 1930, APKC.

119. Cooper to Jones, October 9, 1930, APKC.

120. Jones to Noyes, November 17, 1930, LL.

121. Noyes to Jones, December 26, 1930, LL.

122. See chapter 2.

123. Marginal notes on Noyes to Jones, December 26, 1930, RAJ.

124. Jones to Robert Webber, March 31, 1931, RAJ.

125. Jones to Noyes, February 14, 1931, RAJ.

126. Board of directors minutes, January 14, 1932, 417, APD.

127. Board of directors minutes, October 7, 1931, 222, APD.

128. Cooper to Noyes, March 17, 1931; Cooper, "Confidential. A Guide for the Foreign Service," n.d. (1932), APKC.

129. Board of directors minutes, April 17, 1930, 71–72, APD.

130. Charles Stephenson Smith to Cooper, March 23, 1931, LL.

131. See, for example, DeWitt Mackenzie to Cooper, November 27, 1931, APKC.

132. Jones memorandum, April 8, 1931, RAJ.

133. Ibid.

134. Reuters board of directors minutes, June 30, 1931, RAJ.

135. Noyes to Jones, confidential, March 31, 1931, APKC.

136. Board of directors minutes, January 14, 1932, 419, 432, APD.

137. Cooper to Noyes, March 23, 1932, APKC; Board of directors minutes, January 14, 1932, 432, APD.

Chapter 6. The Japanese Gambit

1. Kent Cooper to Frank Noyes, May 6, 1933, LL.

2. Roy Howard to Karl Bickel, May 5, 1933, RWH.

3. Cooper to Noyes, May 15, 1933, LL.

4. Ibid.

5. Cooper memorandum on Far Eastern news situation, May 30, 1933, LL. *Editor & Publisher* reported Cooper's trip but not its purpose. "Howard, Cooper to Orient," May 6, 1933.

6. Cooper memorandum on Far Eastern news situation, May 30, 1933, LL.

7. Cooper to Roderick Jones, May 30, 1933, LL.

8. AP-Rengo contract, May 1933, LL.

9. Reuters board of directors, May 30, 1933, RA.

10. Cooper to Jones, June 11, 1933, LL.

11. Reuters board minutes, June 20, 1933, RA.

12. Ibid.

13. Reuters board minutes, July 4, 1933, RA.

14. Jones memorandum, July 27, 1933, RAJ.

15. Cooper to Noyes, July 30, 1933, LL.

16. Cooper to Noyes, "personal," August 23, 1933, LL; "Rengo Director Visits N.Y.," *Editor & Publisher*, August 26, 1933.

17. Reuters-Rengo contract, September 12, 1933; and Commercial Service Contract, September 12, 1933, LL.

18. Reuters board of directors, October 3, 1933, RAJ.

19. Yukichi Iwanaga to Jones, September 27, 1933; AP-Rengo contract, September 27, 1933, LL.

20. Cooper to Iwanaga, September 27, 1933, RAJ.

21. DeWitt Mackenzie to Cooper, "private & confidential," September 18, 1933, LL.

22. George Turner to Jones, August 2, 1933, RAJ.

23. Four Party Treaty, November 21, 1933, enclosed in Jones to Cooper, "private and confidential," November 21, 1933, LL.

24. Noyes to Jones, December 20, 1933, LL.

25. William McCambridge to Cooper, September 25, 1933, and October 6, 1933, APSU; same to same, September 29, 1933, APKC.

26. Mackenzie to Cooper, December 18, 1933, LL.

27. Cooper to Frank King, December 21, 1933, LL.

28. King to Cooper, January 9, 1934, LL.

29. Noyes to Jones, January 12, 1934, LL.

30. "The Associated Press, Thirty-Fourth Annual Report of the Board of Directors to Members," 1934, Minutes of the board of directors for January 10, 1934, 65, APD.

31. Cooper to Hans Mejer, January 12, 1934; Cooper to Charles Houssaye, January 12, 1934; Cooper to H. C. Robbins, January 12, 1934, LL.

32. Cooper to Houssaye, December 26, 1933, LL.

33. Cooper to Noyes, January 8, 1934, LL.

34. Cooper to John Evans, January 12, 1934, LL.

35. Cooper to Mejer, January 12, 1934, LL.

36. "News Services Treaty," enclosed in Cooper to Mejer, January 12, 1934; Cooper to Lochner, January 12, 1934, LL.

37. For the establishment of DNB, see Heidi Tworek, *News from Germany: The Competition to Control World Communications, 1900–1945* (Cambridge, MA: Harvard University Press, 2019), chapter 7.

38. Louis Lochner to Cooper, February 1, 1934, LL.

39. Robbins to Cooper, January 30, 1934, LL.

40. Mejer to Cooper, January 31, 1934; Houssaye to Cooper, January 20, 1934, LL.

41. Cooper to Noyes, February 7, 1934, LL.

42. Cooper to Noyes, January 24, 1934, LL; Jones memorandum, "private and confidential," January 24, 1934, RAJ.

43. Jones memoranda, January 25, 1934, and February 1, 1934, RAJ.

44. Cooper to J. F. B. Livesay, January 23, 1934, LL.

45. Jones to Noyes, January 31, 1934, LL.

46. Cooper to Noyes, "confidential," February 1, 1934, LL.

47. Xavier Baron, *Le monde en direct: De Charles-Louis Havas à AFP, deux siècles d'histoire* (Paris: Editions La Découverte, 2014), 57; Pierre Frédérix, *Un siècle de chasse aux nouvelles,* preface by André Siegfried. (Paris: Flammarion, 1959), 383–84.

48. Cooper to Noyes, January 31, 1934, LL.

49. Noyes to Cooper, February 1, 1934, LL.

50. Cooper to Noyes, February 2, 1934, LL.

51. Manager, New York Bureau, TASS to J. G. Doletsky, February 2, 1934, LL; Terhi Rantanen, "Howard Interviews Stalin," *Roy W. Howard Monographs in Journalism and Mass Communication Research* no. 3., School of Journalism, Indiana University, 1994,16–17.

52. See also "TASS Director Sails for Moscow; Has Exchange Hook-Up with U.P.," *Editor & Publisher,* December 1, 1934; "Americans Dined by Soviet Official," *New York Times,* March 22, 1934, 12.

53. Draft of contract between AP and UP, n.d. (1934), APSU.

54. Cooper to John Francis Neylan, February 10, 1934, LL.

55. AP-UP contract, February 8, 1934, APRM.

56. Howard to Cooper, received February 10, 1934, LL.

57. Cooper to Livesay, "personal and confidential," February 10, 1934, LL. For Cooper's relationship with Livesay and the AP-Canadian Press relationship generally, see Gene Allen, *Making National News: A History of Canadian Press* (Toronto: University of Toronto Press, 2013).

58. Cooper to Livesay, "personal and confidential," February 10, 1934, LL.

59. AP-Reuters contract, March 29, 1934, APKC; Cooper memorandum, February 12, 1934, LL.

60. Livesay to Cooper, "personal," February 14, 1934, LL.

61. Donald Read, *The Power of News: The History of Reuters*, 2nd ed. (Oxford: Oxford University Press, 1999), 176.

62. Reuters board of directors minutes, March 6, 1934, RAJ.

63. Bernard Rickatson-Hatt to Jones, February 27, 1934, RAJ.

64. Rickatson-Hatt to Jones, "private and confidential," April 7, 1934, RAJ.

65. Ibid.

66. Rantenen, "Howard Interviews Stalin," 29–30.

67. Theodore E. Kruglak, *The Two Faces of TASS* (Westport, CT: Greenwood Press, 1972. First published 1962 by University of Minnesota Press [Minneapolis]) 71.

68. Jones memorandum, March 17, 1934, RAJ.

69. Jones, "Postscriptum," April 5, 1934, RAJ.

70. John Evans to Cooper, February 21, 1934; King memorandum, March 20, 1934; Evans to Cooper, April 6, 1934, LL.

71. Cooper to Houssaye, April 26, 1934, LL; Lloyd Stratton to Camille Lemercier, August 7, 1935, APKC.

72. Cooper to Giovanni Cappelletto, June 11, 1934; Cooper to J. R. Youatt, April 9, 1934, APKC.

73. Lloyd Stratton to Cooper, May 10, 1934, APKC.

74. Stratton to King, May 28, 1934, APKC.

75. Rex Smith to Stratton, November 30, 1933, APKC.

76. Smith to Evans, June 27, 1934, APKC.

77. Smith to Cooper, June 8, 1934, APKC.

78. Stratton to King, May 28, 1934, APKC.

79. Larry Heinzerling, John Daniszewski, and Randy Herschaft, *Covering Tyranny: The AP and Nazi Germany, 1933–1945* (United States: Associated Press, 2017), 22.

80. Lochner to Cooper, March 26, 1933, Wisconsin Historical Society, Louis Lochner Papers (LP).

81. Harriet Scharnberg, "The A and P of Propaganda: Associated Press and Nazi Image Journalism," *Zeithistorische Forschungen / Studies in Contemporary History*, online edition, 13 (2016), http://www.zeithistorische-forschungen.de/1-2016/id=5324; Norman Domeier, "Secret Photos: The Co-operation between Associated Press and the National Socialist Regine, 1942–1945," *Zeithistorische Forschungen/Studies in Contemporary History* 14 (2017): 1–32.

82. Heinzerling, et al., *Covering Tyranny*.

83. Ibid., 2.

84. Morrell Heald, ed. *Journalist at the Brink: Louis P. Lochner in Berlin, 1922–1942* (Xlibris, 2007), 22–24.

85. Lochner to Cooper, March 26, 1933, LP.

86. Lochner to Cooper, April 24, 1933, LP.

87. Lloyd Stratton to Lochner, May 21, 1931, AP Germany documents, APCA.

88. Oron J. Hale, *The Captive Press in the Third Reich* (Princeton, NJ: Princeton University Press, 1964), 86.

89. See, for example, Lochner to Cooper, August 12, 1935, LP.

90. Heinzerling et al., *Covering Tyranny*, 3.

91. Cooper to Lochner, October 13, 1933, LP.

92. Lochner to Cooper, October 29, 1933, LP.

93. Cooper to Lochner, October 31, 1933, LP.

94. Heidi Tworek, "Magic Connections: German News Agencies and Global News Networks, 1905–1945" (PhD diss., Harvard University, 2012), 99, 307; Tworek, *News from Germany*, 186.

95. Tworek, "Magic Connections," 326; Tworek, *News from Germany*, 21, 171.

96. Lochner to Cooper, November 2, 1933, APCA.

97. Tworek, *News from Germany*, 187.

98. See the section on Cooper's negotiation of new contracts with Havas and Wolff/DNB earlier in this chapter.

99. Lochner to Cooper, October 22, 1933, LP.

100. Lochner to Betty, November 12, 1933, quoted in Heald, *Journalist at the Brink*, 139.

101. Lochner to Cooper, October 22, 1933, LP.

102. Lochner to Mackenzie, November 11, 1933, LP.

103. Lochner to Cooper, August 12, 1935, LP.

104. Tworek, "Magic Connections," 344, 347, 351; Tworek, *News from Germany*, 191.

105. Lochner to Cooper, August 12, 1935, LP.

106. Lochner to Betty, November 28, 1938, quoted in Heald, *Journalist at the Brink*, 328.

107. "Nations Can't Afford War Says Cooper," *Editor & Publisher*, September 15, 1934.

108. See chapter 9.

109. Gideon Seymour to Cooper, "confidential," August 30, 1934, September 12, 1934, October 1, 1934, APKC.

110. Jones to Christopher Chancellor, July 25, 1934, RAJ. For AP's presence in Australia after 1940, see Peter Putnis, "International News Agencies, News-Flow, and the USA-Australia Relationship from the 1920s till the End of the Second World War," *Media History* 18, nos. 3–4 (2012): 423–41.

111. Jones to Cooper, June 22, 1934, RAJ.

112. Jones to Chancellor, July 25, 1934, RAJ.

113. Iwanaga to Cooper, "personal," February 5, 1934, LL.

114. Babb to Cooper, February 6, 1934, LL.

115. Howard to Cooper, "private," December 3, 1935, RWH.

116. Akami, *Soft Power*, 50, 58, 64.

117. Ibid., 65; "Domei Unites News Agencies in Japan," *Editor & Publisher*, June 6, 1936.

Chapter 7. New Media

1. Michael Stamm, *Sound Business: Newspapers, Radio, and the Politics of New Media* (Philadelphia: University of Pennsylvania Press, 2011); Gwyneth Jackaway, *Media at War: Radio's Challenge to the Newspapers, 1924–1939* (Westport, CT: Praeger, 1995).

2. John Aspinwall, "AP Broadcast News Service," *AP World*, Winter 1964–1965, 9.

3. "A.P. Forbids Broadcasting of Its News Dispatches," *Editor & Publisher*, February 25, 1922.

4. Ibid.

5. List of papers reported as broadcasting by wireless, April 18, 1922, APKC.

6. "Associated Press Order to Be Tested," *St. Louis Post-Dispatch*, October 22, 1924.

7. Like AP, and unlike NBC and CBS, Mutual was a nonprofit cooperative; see James R. Schiffman, "Undervaluing Mutual: The FCC's Missed Opportunity to Restructure Radio Broadcasting in the New Deal Era," *Journal of Radio and Audio Media* 24, no. 2 (2017): 302–319.

8. For the 1927 controversy, see chapter 4; for news photos, see the discussion of Wirephoto later in this chapter.

9. "To Test Rule against News Broadcasting," *New York Times*, October 22, 1922.

10. Harry Chandler to Frank Noyes, December 6, 1924, APKC.

11. "Chicago Tribune Defies Associated Press Rule to Radio Election Returns," *Editor & Publisher*, October 25, 1924.

12. Ibid.

13. "Press Radiocasting of Election Returns Gives Journalism New Ally," *Editor & Publisher*, November 8, 1924.

14. Frederick Roy Martin to John C. Eastman, January 17, 1925, APKC.

15. Kent Cooper to Superintendents, January 22, 1925, LL.

16. Cooper to Noyes, March 16, 1925, LL.

17. Associated Press, minutes of 1925 annual meeting, 700–701, APD.

18. Ibid., 699, 707, 712.

19. For a discussion of AP's efforts to prevent "piracy" of its news by radio stations, see Will Slauter, *Who Owns the News?: A History of Copyright* (Stanford, CA: Stanford University Press, 2019), 256–61.

20. Associated Press, minutes of 1925 annual meeting, APD.

21. Associated Press, minutes of 1925 annual meeting, 729, 732, APD.

22. Ibid., 748, 740.

23. "Survey of Newspaper Broadcasting," enclosed in Walter Strong to Edgar Cutter, July 15, 1925, APKC.

24. George Miller to Cooper, August 10, 1925, LL.

25. Cooper to Noyes, August 13, 1925, LL.

26. MG [Garges] memorandum, October 6, 1925, LL.

27. Paul Cowles to Cooper, October 7, 1925, LL; U. L. McCall to Cooper, October 8, 1925, LL; Jas C. White to Ray Baumgardner, September 16, 1925, APKC; C. S. Coleman to Cowles, October 7, 1925, APKC; W. C. Eastland to H. W. Blakeslee, October 24, 1925, APKC.

28. Cooper, Note to Members, October 10, 1925, LL.

29. E. Lansing Ray to Cooper, December 31, 1925, LL.

30. Cooper to Ray, January 4, 1926, LL; Cooper to Ray, January 11, 1926, LL.

31. "Chimes of London to Ring in Million U.S. Homes in Great New Year Program Exchange," *Brooklyn (NY) Daily Eagle*, December 27, 1925.

32. H. F. Wheeler to Cooper, June 7, 1926, APKC.

33. Cooper, circular to Members of the Associated Press and the Associated Press staff, October 17, 1927, LL.

34. Cooper to Noyes, May 7, 1926; Charles B. Popenoe to Cooper, May 5, 1926, APKC.

35. F. A. Walker to Cooper, June 17, 1926, APKC.

36. Cooper to Popenoe, June 25, 1926, APKC.

37. Walker to Edward McKernon, December 7, 1926; McKernon to Elliott, May 23, 1927, APKC.

38. Jackson Elliott to Cooper, December 20, 1927, APSU.

39. M. H. Aylesworth to Cooper, October 9, 1928, APKC.

40. Cooper to Aylesworth, October 15, 1928, APKC.

41. C. B. Blethen to Cooper, October 16, 1928, APKC.

42. J. Earl Langdon to Cooper, October 17, 1928, APKC.

43. Cooper to Langdon, October 22, 1928, APKC.

44. See chapter 3.

45. Stamm, *Sound Business*, introduction; Robert McChesney, "Press-Radio Relations and the Emergence of Network, Commercial Broadcasting in the United States, 1930–1935," *Historical Journal of Film, Radio and Television* 11, no. 1 (1991): 41–57. See also McChesney, *Telecommunications, Mass Media, and Democracy: The Battle for the Control of U.S. Broadcasting, 1928–1935* (New York: Oxford University Press, 1994).

46. Robert McLean to Cooper, November 1, 1928, APKC.

47. Cooper to Noyes, October 29, 1928, APKC.

48. Cooper to Noyes, November 10, 1928, APKC.

49. Aylesworth to Cooper, November 6, 1928, APKC.

50. "Digest of Complaints re Broadcasting," n.d. (April 1929), APD.

51. JSE to Cooper, December 13, 1928, APKC.

52. Cooper, circular To Members of The Associated Press, February 1, 1929, APKC.

53. "All Very Quiet on the A.P. Front," *Editor & Publisher*, April 26, 1930.

54. "Publishers Warned of Radio Danger," *Editor & Publisher*, April 25, 1931.

55. "A.P. Suggests Conference with A.N.P.A. for Ban on News Broadcasting," *Editor & Publisher*, April 25, 1931.

56. Cooper to Noyes, November 12, 1931, APSU.

57. Elliott to Cooper, November 17, 1931, APSU.

58. J. V. Connolly to S. E. Thomason, January 18, 1932, APSU.

59. "Press Service Policies Differ on Giving News to Radio," *Editor & Publisher*, March 26, 1932.

60. Ibid.

61. "A.P. against Economizing on Service, to Restrict News Broadcasting," *Editor & Publisher*, April 30, 1932; Associated Press, 1932 annual meeting, comments of Howard, APSU.

62. Aylesworth to Cooper, October 20, 1932, APSU.

63. "A.P. Gives Radio Election Data: U.P. and I.N.S. Off the Air," *Editor & Publisher*, November 12, 1932.

64. Cooper to Sevellon Brown, November 7, 1932, APRM.

65. Cooper to Clark Howell, November 8, 1932, APKC.

66. "A.P. Gives Radio Election Data," *Editor & Publisher*, November 12, 1932; "First Test," *TIDE*, March 1933, clipping in APRM.

67. Cooper to news editors, bureau chiefs, correspondents, November 9, 1932, APKC.

68. "Memorandum," November 14, 1932, APKC.

69. Will Campbell to Cooper, December 8, 1932, APSU.

70. Jerome Barnum to Cooper, February 1, 1933; Cooper to Noyes, February 3, 1933, APSU.

71. Cooper to Barnum, February 2,1933, APSU.

72. "A.N.P.A. Acts to Frame Radio Policy," *Editor & Publisher*, November 19, 1932.

73. Leased-wire message to members, December 6, 1932, APSU.

74. "Showdown on Radio Problem Expected as A.N.P.A., A.P. Act on Protests," *Editor & Publisher*, December 10, 1932.

75. Elliott, "Radio questionnaire analysis," enclosed in Elliott to Noyes, March 23, 1933, APSU.

76. Elliott, memorandum for Mr. (Josh) Horne, April 18, 1933, APSU.

77. Noyes to members of the Associated Press, April 11, 1933, APRM.

78. "A.P. News Is Barred from Radio Chains; Members' Use Held to Brief Bulletins," *Editor & Publisher*, April 29, 1933.

79. Cooper to Frank Gannett, September 25, 1933, RRM.

80. Elliott, Memorandum for Mr. Cooper, October 2, 1933, APSU.

81. "Radio News: Broadcasters and Newspapers Make Peace," *News-Week*, December 23, 1933; Stamm, *Sound Business*, 69.

82. Elliott to Noyes, March 17, 1934, APKC.

83. "Radio News Agencies Make Big Claims," *Editor & Publisher*, May 19, 1934.

84. "New Plan," *TIDE*, May 1935, clipping in APRM.

85. "U.P.-I.N.S. Take Lead in Effort to Retain Control of Radio News," *Editor & Publisher*, May 4, 1935.

86. Elliott to Cooper, September 18, 1935, APRM.

87. WWH (Hawkins) to Howard, December 20, 1934, RWH.

88. "'Newscasts' Supplied by Newspaper Agencies Take Definite Form," *Editor & Publisher*, May 18, 1935; "A.P. Clarifies Radio Newscasting Situation by Board Ruling," *Editor & Publisher*, January 18, 1936.

89. Noyes to members of the Associated Press, March 14, 1938, APRM.

90. Transcript of Associated Press Annual Meeting, April 25, 1938, 69, APD.

91. "A.P. Honors Noyes, Its Departing Chief," *New York Times*, April 26, 1938.

92. Oliver Gramling to Cooper, June 30, 1938, APRM.

93. "Truce of Radio and Press Endangered as Bureau Slips," *Newsdom*, December 31, 1938; "NBC Begins Use of AP Reports, Supplied Free by News Service," *Newsdom*, February 18, 1939.

94. Cooper to Board of directors, February 20, 1939, APRM.

95. Paul Bellamy to McLean, March 6, 1939, APRM.

96. McLean to Cooper, April 13, 1939, APRM.

97. Cooper to members of the Associated Press, April 28, 1939, APRM.

98. "Information for the Benefit of the Board of Directors" and "Members' Comment on Radio," n.d. (1939), APRM.

99. Cooper to members of the Associated Press, May 29, 1939, APRM.

100. "AP Allows Sponsorship of News Broadcasts," *Editor & Publisher*, June 3, 1939.

101. "The Associated Press, New York Corporation, Fortieth Annual Volume for the Fiscal Year 1939," 1940, Report of the General Manager, December 31, 1939, 61, APD.

102. James Stahlman to Cooper, March 1940, APRM.

103. William McCambridge to bureau chiefs, July 25, 1940; McCambridge, revenue and expense of service to radio stations, January 9, 1941, APSU.

104. "AP Launches Subsidiary to Sell By-Products of Newsgathering," *Editor & Publisher*, January 25, 1941; "Associated Press in Reverse: PA, Inc., Goes Out for Profit," *Newsweek*, February 3, 1941; Minutes of annual meeting of the stockholders of Press Association, April 22, 1941; Minutes of board of directors meeting, April 23, 1941, APRM.

105. Minutes of board of directors meeting, October 6, 1944, APRM; Cooper to department heads, news editors, bureau chiefs, July 27, 1945, APSU.

106. "Summary of AP and Radio," n.d. (1960); "Radio General, 1925–1960," n.d. (1960), APRM.

107. John P. Hightower, "The Chief Single Source of News," chapter 43, "Shaping the Future," unpublished manuscript, 1976, APCA, Writings about the Associated Press (APWR). See also Jonathan Coopersmith, "From Lemons to Lemonade: The Development of AP Wirephoto," *American Journalism* 17, no. 4 (2000): 55–72.

108. Milton Garges to Cooper, May 22, 1926, APKC

109. Minutes of the board of directors, January 27, 1927, 454, APD.

110. Norris Huse to Ochs, June 15, 1927, NYTO.

111. Julian Mason to Cooper, March 1, 1927, LL.

112. Cooper to Mason, March 2, 1927, LL.

113. "The Associated Press, Thirtieth Annual Report of the Board of Directors to Members," April 21, 1930, Report of the General Manager, 9, APD.

114. "Pictures Keeping Pace with Wire News," *Editor & Publisher*, March 26, 1932.

115. "The Associated Press, Thirty-Third Annual Report of the Board of Directors to Members," April 24, 1933, Minutes of the Board of Directors, April 26, 1932, 62, APD.

116. "In the Beginning: The Creation of the AP Wirephoto Network," *AP World*, Spring 1985, 5.

117. Cooper, *Kent Cooper*, 213.

118. Ibid., 214.

119. R. C. Hollis to AP, January 19, 1934, APKC.

120. On Wirephoto generally, see also Coopersmith, "From Lemons to Lemonade.

121. Arthur Sulzberger, memorandum, February 28, 1934, NYTO.

122. Robert McLean interview, February 1973, 224, APCA, Oral history collection.

123. Minutes of the Board of Directors, April 23, 1934, 20–21, APD.

124. Associated Press, Verbatim minutes of the annual meeting, April 23, 1934, 11, APD.

125. See chapter 4.

126. Associated Press, Verbatim minutes of the annual meeting, April 23, 1934, 16–17, 74, 75, 80–81, APD.

127. David Nasaw, *The Chief: The Life of William Randolph Hearst* (Boston: Houghton Mifflin, 2000), 426, 515, 524, 532.

128. Cooper to members of the executive committee, June 1, 1934, NYTO.

129. Associated Press, Verbatim minutes of the annual meeting, April 23, 1934, 104, 111, 129, APD.

130. Sulzberger memorandum, April 24, 1934, NYTO.

131. Sulzberger, "Memorandum for Mr. Ochs," March 14, 1935, NYTO.

132. Sulzberger memo, April 30, 1934, NYTS.

133. AHS, memorandum, June 6, 1934, NYTO; "Hearst, Scripps-Howard Ban A.P. Plan," *Editor & Publisher*, June 9, 1934.

134. See chapter 4.

135. "Neylan Organizing War on Telephoto," *Editor & Publisher*, June 16, 1934.

136. Charles Graves to Sulzberger, August 21, 1934, NYTS.

137. "Comment by publishers and managing editors of WIREPHOTO Newspapers," January 3, 1935, APRM.

138. Frank Knox to W. J. Pape, April 1, 1935, APKC.

139. Frederik Murphy to Cooper, April 14, 1935, APKC.

140. "A.P. Wirephotos Flash across Nation," *Editor & Publisher*, January 5, 1935.

141. Will Mari, *The American Newsroom: A History, 1920–1960* (Columbia: University of Missouri Press, 2021), 41–42.

142. "Neylan Renews Fight on Wire Photo," *Editor & Publisher*, February 16, 1935.

143. Noyes to members of proxy committee, March 9, 1935, APKC.

144. Cooper to William O. Dapping, June 12, 1934, APKC.

145. Ray to Cooper, March 29, 1935, APKC; Cooper to Ray, April 1, 1935; Leon Durst to Cooper, March 16, 1935; Pape to Cooper, March 25, 1935; Chandler to Noyes, April 13, 1935; Murphy to Cooper, April 14, 1935; Lawrence W. Hager to Cooper, April 16, 1935; Houston Harte to Cooper, April 15, 1935; J. L. Horne Jr., to Cooper, April 16, 1935; R. A. Reeder to Cooper, April 16, 1935—all in APKC.

146. Pape to J. H. Dickey, March 28, 1935. Pape sent similar letters to around one hundred smaller papers. Pape to Cooper, March 28, 1935, APKC.

147. "Supplemental report of the Board of Directors on the operations of the Wirephoto service," April 22, 1935, APRM.

148. Wilson Hicks, circular letter, n.d. (1935), APKC.

149. "A.P. Directors Sustained on Wirephoto: Will Consider Small Dailies' Request," *Editor & Publisher*, April 27, 1935; "The Press: Wirephoto War," *Time*, April 29, 1935.

150. Roy Howard to Karl Bickel, January 12, 1953, RWH.

151. Cooper to Roy Hollis, September 18,1935, RRM.

152. Kent Cooper, Letters from the Correspondence of the General Manager, no. 8., September 20, 1935, APSU.

153. McCormick to Cooper, June 10, 1935, APKC.

154. Minutes of the Board of directors, October 7, 1938, 159, APD.

155. Minutes of the Board of directors, October 7, 1937, APD.

156. Minutes of the Board of directors, October 7, 1938, 134, 164–65, APD.

157. Stratton Abstracts, "Newsphoto—Wirephoto—1920–1960," resolution of April 22, 1939, 6, APD.

158. Cooper to members of the Board of directors, September 21, 1939; Houston Harte to Cooper, September 21, 1939, APRM.

159. "Dailies to Be 50% Pictorial in Future, Kent Cooper Says," *Editor & Publisher*, October 22, 1937, 7, 20; Barbie Zelizer, "Words against Images: Positioning Newswork in the Age of Photography," in *Newsworkers: Toward a History of the Rank and File*, ed. Bonnie Brennen and Hanno Hardt (Minneapolis: University of Minnesota Press, 1995), 143.

160. For a discussion of the cultural barriers in newsrooms that prevented photographs from being treated as seriously as textual accounts, see Zelizer, "Words against Images."

161. Cooper to Board of directors, April 1, 1940, APKC.

162. Godfrey Nelson to Sulzberger, July 10, 1940, NYTS.

163. Nelson to Sulzberger, July 1, 1941, NYTS; "Associated Press Buys Wide World," *Editor & Publisher*, August 2, 1941.

164. Minutes of the board of directors, October 3, 1941, 29–30, APD.

Chapter 8. Politics, External and Otherwise

1. Upton Sinclair, *The Brass Check: A Study of American Journalism* (Pasadena, CA: The author, 1920); George Seldes, *Freedom of the Press* (New York: Da Capo Press, 1971); Morris L. Ernst, *The First Freedom* (New York: Macmillan, 1946); Harold L. Ickes, *America's House of Lords: An Inquiry into Freedom of the Press* (New York: Harcourt Brace, 1939). See also Margaret A. Blanchard, "Press Criticism and National Reform Movements: The Progressive Era and the New Deal," *Journalism History* 5, no. 2 (1978): 33–55; Marion Tuttle Marzolf, *Civilizing Voices: American Press Criticism, 1889–1950* (New York: Longman, 1991); Victor Pickard, *America's Battle for Media Democracy: The Triumph of Corporate Libertarianism and the Future of Media Reform* (New York: Cambridge University Press, 2015); Sam Lebovic, *Free Speech and Unfree News: The Paradox of Press Freedom in America* (Cambridge, MA: Harvard University Press, 2016); and Lebovic, "When the 'Mainstream Media' Was Conservative: Media Criticism in the Age of Reform," in *Media Nation: The Political History of News in Modern America*, ed. Bruce Schulman and Julian Zelizer, 63–76 (Philadelphia: University of Pennsylvania Press, 2017).

2. Alan Gould interview, 38, APCA, Oral history collection.

3. Byron Price, unpublished memoir, 180, BP.

4. J. L. Williams to Kent Cooper, September 6, 1928, APKC.

5. Cooper to Williams, September 4, 1928; Cooper to Herbert Hoover, "personal," September 12, 1928, APKC.

6. Cooper to Edward Butler, "personal," September 20, 1928, APKC.

7. Williams to Cooper, "personal," October 8,1928, APKC.

8. Cooper to W. H. Cowles, September 29, 1928, APKC.

9. "Borah Electrifies Crowd of 25,000 by Indictment of Smith, Tammany," *Minneapolis Morning Tribune*, October 2, 1928.

10. Cooper to Williams, October 6, 1928, APKC.

11. Henry Allen to Cooper, October 6, 1928, APKC.

12. Cooper to Frank Gannett, October 5, 1928, APKC.

13. Frank Noyes to Cooper, October 9, 1928; Cooper to Williams, October 11, 1928, APKC.

14. Williams to Cooper, October 10, 1928, APKC.

15. "Borah and Ex Com," unsigned memorandum, October 12, 1928, APKC.

16. Cooper to Williams, October 9, 1928, APKC.

17. Cooper to J. C. Stark, November 5, 1928; Cooper to James L. West, November 5, 1928; AP story, November 6, 1928, APKC.

18. John P. Hightower, "The Chief Single Source of News," unpublished manuscript, 1976, chapter 28, 28–29, APCA.

19. "Bingham Protests 'Bias' in A.P. Reports of Political Speeches," *Editor & Publisher*, August 27, 1932.

20. Carl Hanton to Cooper, August 20, 1932, APKC.

21. F. A. Miller to Cooper, August 20, 1932, APKC.

22. Donald Sterling to Cooper, August 26, 1932, APKC.

23. Cooper to C. E. Pigford, August 30, 1932, APKC.

24. Lessis S. Read, *Fayetteville Daily Democrat*, to Cooper, August 20 [1932], APKC.

25. Alfred Harrell to R. W. Bingham, August 29, 1932, APKC.

26. Cooper to Pigford, August 30, 1932, APKC.

27. Board of directors minute, adopted October 6, 1932, APKC.

28. Adolph Ochs to Cooper, September 1, 1932, NYTO.

29. Bingham to Noyes, October 7, 1932, APKC.

30. Cooper, Special Notice: To the Staff, August 16, 1932, APSU.

31. Cooper to Price, August 29, 1932, APSU.

32. Price to Cooper August 31, 1932, APSU.

33. Houston Harte to Bingham, n.d. (1932), APKC.

34. Cooper to Price, September 19, 1932, APSU.

35. Steven E. Shoenherr, "Selling the New Deal: Stephen T. Early's Role as Press Secretary to Franklin D. Roosevelt" (PhD diss., University of Delaware, 1976), 87–88. On Roosevelt's relationship with the press, see also Richard W. Steele, *Propaganda in an Open Society: The Roosevelt Administration and the Media* (Westport, CT: Greenwood Press, 1985); and Graham J. White, *FDR and the Press* (Chicago: University of Chicago Press, 1979).

36. Betty Winfield, *FDR and the News Media* (Urbana: University of Illinois Press, 1990), 11, 42.

37. See the section on AP's legal challenge to the Wagner Act later in this chapter.

38. Price speech, October 1935, 5, BP.

39. Shoenherr, "Selling the New Deal," 166.

40. James L. Baughman, *Henry R. Luce and the Rise of the American News Media* (Boston: Twayne Publishers, 1987), 57–58.

41. Photocopy of clipping from *Daily Oklahoman*, October 21, 1933, Franklin D. Roosevelt Library (FDR), President's secretary's file—Subject file, McCormick, Robert.

42. Robert McCormick to Cooper October 13, 1936, RRM.

43. Cooper to McCormick, October 13, 1936, RRM.

44. Cooper to McCormick, October 24, 1936, RRM.

45. McCormick to Cooper, October 24, 1936, RRM.

46. Cooper to McCormick, October 27, 1936, RRM.

47. Price speech, November 1936, 4, BP.

48. File memorandum, May 20, 1937, FDR OF 171–Associated Press, 1933–1945. On Stephen Early, see Linda Lottridge Levin, *The Making of FDR: The Story of Stephen T. Early, America's First Modern Press Secretary* (Amherst, NY: Prometheus Books, 2008); and Diana Knott Martinelli and Jeff Mucciarone, "New Deal Public Relations: A Glimpse into FDR Press Secretary Stephen Early's Work." *Public Relations Review* 33 (2007): 49–57.

49. "Associated Press—News stories showing distinct bias against the President and the Administration, 1936–1938," FDR, Papers of Stephen T. Early (STE).

50. Robert McLean to Franklin Delano Roosevelt, October 10, 1938, FDR.

51. McLean memorandum of meeting with Early, November 1, 1938, APRM.

52. "Chief Executive Calls Statement Regarding Rhine 'Deliberate Lie,'" *Rocky Mount (NC) Evening Telegram*, February 3, 1939.

53. Cooper to Brian Bell, February 9, 1939, APRM.

54. See Philip Glende, "Labor Reporting and Its Critics in the CIO Years," *Journalism Monographs* 22, no. 1 (2020): 11, citing Sinclair's comment in *The Brass Check*: "The greatest single agency in America for making it appear that strikers are violent is The Associated Press." Other articles by Glende provide useful background to the conflict between publishers and the ANG: "Trouble on the Right, Trouble on the Left: The Early History of the American Newspaper Guild," *Journalism History* 38, no. 3 (2012): 142–55; "'We Used Every Effort to Be Impartial': The Complicated Response of Newspaper Publishers to Unions," *American Journalism* 29, no. 2 (2012): 37–65.

55. Roger Daniels, *Franklin D. Roosevelt: Road to the New Deal, 1882–1939* (Urbana: University of Illinois Press, 2015), 154, 233.

56. "National Guild Asks A.P for Meeting," *Editor & Publisher*, August 11, 1934. See also Dale Benjamin Scott, "Labor's New Deal for Journalism—The Newspaper Guild in the 1930s" (PhD diss., University of Illinois at Urbana-Champaign, 2009); and Van B. Dawson, "The American Newspaper Guild and The Associated Press: A Study of Collective Bargaining Relations" (MBA thesis, Columbia University, 1950).

57. "Watson Fired by A.P.; Guild Protests," *Editor & Publisher*, October 26, 1935.

58. "AP Answers Labor Board Complaint," *Editor & Publisher*, December 21, 1935.

59. "A.P., Guild Case Heard by Court; Law Called Invalid," *Editor & Publisher*, January 25, 1936.

60. "Labor Board Orders AP Employee Vote," *Editor & Publisher*, May 9, 1936; "AP Must Reinstate Morris Watson, Says Labor Relations Board," *Editor & Publisher*, May 23, 1936.

61. Cooper to officers and directors of AP, May 5, 1936, APSU.

62. "Circuit Court Upholds Labor Act; Says A.P. in Interstate Commerce," *Editor & Publisher*, July 18, 1936.

63. "AP Rejects Guild Plea," *Editor & Publisher*, August 1, 1936.

64. "The A.P.–Watson Decision," *Editor & Publisher*, July 18, 1936.

65. "ANPA Joins AP in Watson Case," *Editor & Publisher*, February 6, 1937.

66. "Freedom Jeopardized by Ruling of NLRB, Says AP in Appeal," *Editor & Publisher*, September 19, 1936.

67. Cooper, "Letters from the Correspondence of the General Manager," no. 48, December 29, 1936, APSU.

68. "Wagner Act Upheld in AP Case," *Editor & Publisher*, April 17, 1937.

69. "Majority Opinion in Brief," *New York Times*, April 13, 1937.

70. "Text of the Majority and Minority Opinions in the Case of the Associated Press," *New York Times*, April 13, 1937.

71. Board of directors minutes, October 7, 1937, in "The Associated Press: Thirty-Eighth Annual Report of the Board of Directors to Members," April 25, 1938, 47–49, APD.

72. "Guild-AP Hearing Begins in New York," *Editor & Publisher*, January 8, 1938.

73. Herrick, Elinore, Regional Director, National Labor Relations Board, New York, January 10, 1938, FDR OF 171, Associated Press, 1933–1945, Cross Refs.

74. "About-Face by AP Hinted by Cooper; Open to Guild Shop," *Guild Reporter*, January 10, 1938.

75. National Labor Relations Board, testimony of Kent Cooper, "Direct examination, January 5, 1938," and "Cross-examination, January 6, 1938," copies in APRM.

76. McLean to Frank Noyes, February 7, 1938, APRM.

77. James Stahlman to J. L. Van Horne, February 2, 1938, APRM.

78. Adolph Shelby Ochs to Arthur Sulzberger, February 3, 1938, NYTS.

79. McLean to Howard Davis, February 3, 1938, APRM.

80. Eugene McKinnon to "Dear. Mr. M." (McLean), February 4, 1938, RRM.

81. Paul Bellamy to McLean, February 21, 1938, APRM.

82. Ibid.

83. McCormick to W. E. Macfarlane, February 9, 1938, RRM.

84. Stahlman to Sulzberger, February 7, 1938, NYTS.

85. McLean to Bellamy, February 8, 1938, APRM.

86. Noyes to John B. Ewing, February 8, 1938, APRM.

87. Bellamy to McLean, February 21, 1938, APRM.

88. Cooper to Noyes, "confidential," February 15, 1938; Cooper to Noyes, "personal," February 15, 1938, APRM; Cooper to Houston Harte, February 15, 1938, LL.

89. John V. Spielmans, "The Dilemma of the Closed Shop," *Journal of Political Economy* 51, no. 2 (1943): 113, https://www-jstor-org.myaccess.library.utoronto.ca/stable/1824756/; Sam Lebovic, *Free Speech and Unfree News: The Paradox of Press Freedom in America* (Cambridge, MA: Harvard University Press, 2016), 101.

90. Cooper to bureau chiefs, February 16, 1938, LL.

91. "Urge AP Men Join for Bargaining," *Guild Reporter*, February 7, 1938; "Guild Elected at AP," *Editor & Publisher*, February 19, 1938.

92. Cooper to Pat McGrady, February 21, 1938, APRM.

93. Cooper to Stuart Perry, draft, February 24, 1938, LL.

94. "AP Board against Closed Shop Says Kent Cooper," *Editor & Publisher*, February 26, 1938.

95. Walter Lippmann, *Liberty and the News* (New Brunswick, NJ: Transaction Publishers, 1995. First published 1920 by Harcourt, Brace, and Howe [New York]).

96. Price, unpublished memoir, 180, BP.

97. Board of directors minutes, October 7, 1938, 167 ff, APD.

98. Cooper to McLean, March 29, 1940; AP-Guild contract, April 1, 1940, APRM; "A.P. Agrees to Guild Pact," *Guild Reporter*, March 15, 1940.

99. Malcolm Bingay to "Gentlemen of The Associated Press," n.d. (1933), Circular Letters Gould—January to December 1950, APCA 15, no. 3.

100. "Associated Press Guards Freedom of Printed Word," *Detroit Free Press*, November 5, 1933.

101. Alan Gould interview, 68. Oral history collection, APCA.

102. See chapter 3.

103. Robert McLean interview, 39, APCA, Oral history collection.

104. Associated Press, *FYI*, July 23, 1934, APSU.

105. Jackson Elliott to Robert Martin, May 13, 1933, APKC; L. F. Curtis to Morris Hadley, August 14, 1942, APRM; "Gov't Questions, AP Answers Disclose Exchange Agreements," *Editor & Publisher*," April 3, 1943.

106. See chapter 6.

107. Bernard Rickatson-Hatt to Roderick Jones, "strictly private and confidential," February 27, 1934, RAJ; "Highlights of Kent Cooper's Testimony," *Guild Reporter*, January 10, 1938.

108. "Ben Bassett, Ex-Editor of A.P. Foreign News," *New York Times*, October 17, 1987; Ben Bassett, "KC's Broom Got Rid of the Cobwebs," *Cleartime*, no. 73, September 1978.

109. Alan Gould interview, 36, 53, APCA, Oral history collection.

110. Will Mari, *The American Newsroom: A History, 1920–1960* (Columbia: University of Missouri Press, 2021), 127–66.

111. Cooper to news editors and bureau chiefs, December 18, 1939, APRM.

112. Cooper memorandum to news editors, chiefs of bureaus, New York executives, November 17, 1939, APSU.

113. Reid Montfort to Cooper, November 19, 1939, APSU.

114. Cooper to Montfort, January 3, 1940, APSU.

115. W. N. Paxton to Cooper, November 22, 1939; Cooper to Paxton, November 24, 1939, APSU.

116. Harry Montgomery to Cooper, November 22, 1939, APSU.

117. Cooper to McCormick, August 24, 1931, RRM.

118. McCormick to Cooper, January 26, 1937, RRM.

119. Edward Stanelty to McCormick, March 11, 1937, RRM.

120. See discussion of the 1936 campaign earlier in this chapter.

121. McCormick to Cooper, July 18, 1936; Cooper to McCormick, July 20, 1936, RRM.

122. Cooper to McLean, November 21, 1938, APRM.

123. McCormick to Cooper, January 20, 1939; Cooper to McCormick, January 23, 1939, APSU.

124. Cooper, memorandum to Board of directors, October 1935, LL.

125. See chapter 7.

126. Cooper to Noyes, n.d., enclosed in Noyes to McCormick, November 11, 1935, RRM.

127. "A.P. Directors Sustained on Wirephoto; Will Consider Small Dailies' Request," *Editor & Publisher*, April 27, 1935.

128. "Public Avid for News of Trial," *Editor & Publisher*, January 12, 1935.

129. "A.P. Says Unauthorized Equipment and Methods Responsible for Error," *Editor & Publisher*, March 2, 1935.

130. "Dailies' Sales Soar with Trial Climax; A.P. Mars Coverage by Error," *Editor & Publisher*, February 16, 1935.

131. Roy Howard to William Hawkins, February 14, 1935, RWH.

132. See, for example, "Extras and Radios Give Wrong Verdict to Nation: Pittsburgh Press Is Only Local Newspaper to Print Correct Verdict in Its First Extra," *Pittsburgh (PA) Press*, February 14, 1935.

133. Cooper to All Employees, February 25, 1935, U.S. National Archives (USNA) RG 173, Federal Communications Commission, General Correspondence, 1927–46, 44–3, Alburtys–Norman Baker, box 190.

134. See, for example, "New Deal Law Holds on Private Contracts but U.S. Must Pay in Gold," *Wasau (WI) Daily Herald*, February 18, 1935.

135. Price speech, October 1935, 2, BP.

136. Price, unpublished memoir, 115.

137. Edwin James, "Memorandum for Mr. Ochs—Subject: Associated Press Service," March 5, 1935, NYTO.

138. "McLean Succeeded Father as Publisher," *Editor & Publisher*, April 30, 1938.

139. "M'Lean Is Elected President of A.P."; "The New A.P. President," *New York Times*, April 27, 1938.

140. McLean to B. M. McKelway, April 29, 1965, APRM.

141. Robert McLean interview, 22, APCA, Oral history collection.

142. Cooper to McLean, May 18, 1939; Cooper to William McCambridge, "personal and confidential," May 17, 1939, APRM.

143. McLean to Cooper, May 15, 1939, APRM.

144. Cooper to McLean, May 17, 1939, APRM.

145. McLean to Noyes, "personal," June 13, 1939, APRM.

146. McLean to Noyes, June 28, 1939, APRM.

147. McLean to Noyes, July 6, 1939, APRM.

148. Cooper to McLean, May 29, 1939, APRM.

149. Cooper to McLean, June 5, 1939, APRM.

150. Cooper to Noyes, "personal," June 13, 1939, APRM.

Chapter 9. The Shadow of War

1. Associated Press, Report of the Annual Meeting 1943, Report of the General Manager, 54, APD.

2. Richard Pyle, "War II: Soldiers of the Press," in Reporters of the Associated Press, *Breaking News*, 214–53 (New York: Princeton Architectural Press, 2007).

3. See chapter 8.

4. The antitrust suit and Cooper's international expansion efforts are discussed in chapters 10 and 11, respectively.

5. Kent Cooper to J. C. Stark, September 22, 1939, APRM. For the British censorship system, see Phillip Knightley, *The First Casualty: From the Crimea to Vietnam: The War Correspondent as Hero, Propagandist, and Myth Maker* (London: Harcourt, Brace, Jovanovich, 1975), 218–20; and Charles Edward Lysagh, *Brendan Bracken* (London: Allen Lane, 1979), 191, 193–94.

6. See chapter 6.

7. Cooper to John Lloyd, May 21, 1940, APRM.

8. Louis Lochner to Cooper, draft, early 1941, LP.

9. Lochner to Alan Gould, late 1941, LP.

10. Cooper to M. E. Nichols, October 7, 1940, APRM.

11. Cooper to Robert Bates, September 20, 1939, APRM.

12. Cooper to Arthur Treanor, September 22, 1939, APRM.

13. Cooper to Hans Thomsen, May 28, 1940, APRM.

14. Cooper to Paul Scott Mowrer, July 11, 1941, APRM.

15. For a useful recent survey of U.S. isolationism during this period, see Charles A. Kupchan, *Isolationism: A History of America's Efforts to Shield Itself from the World* (New York: Oxford University Press, 2020), 269–98.

16. Cooper to news editors, June 3, 1940, APSU.

17. Cooper to Lewis Randolph, September 16, 1940, APRM.

18. "Address by Kent Cooper to The A.P. Managing Editors . . . October 17, 1941," LL2.

19. "AP Correspondent Sees Mighty German Forces in Action," *Wasau (WI) Daily Record Herald*, May 20, 1940; "German Held Areas Seen by Lochner," *Muscatine (IA) Journal*, May 24, 1940; "Louis Lochner, Associated Press Writer, Says Nazi Attacks Brilliant; Watches Allies Retire," *Murfreesboro (TN) Daily News*, May 22, 1940; "Nazi Right Wing Poised for Attack on 500,000 Allies," *Oakland (CA) Tribune*, May 22, 1940; "Louis Lochner Says Nazis Have Reached the Channel," *Wilmington (DE) Journal*, May 23, 1940.

20. Cooper to Walter Harrison, June 10, 1940, APRM; Minutes of Chesapeake association of AP, September 14, 1940, AP Germany documents, APCA.

21. Quoted in Ray Moseley, *Reporting War: How Foreign Correspondents Risked Capture, Torture, and Death to Cover World War Two* (New Haven, CT: Yale University Press, 2017), 353.

22. Cooper to D. K. Rogers, June 10, 1940, APRM.

23. "The Associated Press, New York Corporation, Forty-First Annual Volume for the Year of 1940," 1941, minutes of the board of directors, 40, APD.

24. Lochner to Bobby, May [12?], 1940, cited in Morrell Heald, ed., *Journalist at the Brink: Louis P. Lochner in Berlin, 1922–1942* (Xlibris, 2007), 427.

25. Lochner to Betty, June 23, 1941, cited in Heald, *Journalist at the Brink*, 493.

26. Heald, *Journalist at the Brink*, 377.

27. Alan Gould interview, 38, APCA, Oral history collection.

28. Walton Cole to Christopher Chancellor, September 5, 1944, RA.

29. Cooper to Brian Bell, November 20, 1940, APRM.

30. Cooper to Harold Turnblad, January 21, 1941, APRM.

31. Lochner to Cooper, draft, [1941], LP.

32. Harriet Scharnberg, "The A and P of Propaganda: Associated Press and Nazi Image Journalism," *Zeithistorische Forschungen / Studies in Contemporary History*, Online edition, 13 (2016). http://www.zeithistorische-forschungen.de/1-2016/id=5324/; Norman Domeier, "Secret Photos: The Co-operation between Associated Press and the National Socialist Regime, 1942–1945," *Zeithistorische Forschungen / Studies in Contemporary History* 14 (2017): 1–32.

33. Harold Ickes, *America's House of Lords: An Inquiry into Freedom of the Press* (New York: Harcourt Brace, 1939).

34. Ickes to Frank Noyes, March 15, 1941, APSU.

35. Report, n.d., enclosed in Robert McLean to Noyes, May 9, 1941, APSU.

36. Scharnberg, "A and P of Propaganda," 20.

37. Noyes to Ickes, March 29 1941, APSU.

38. Cooper to Noyes, April 1, 1941, APSU.

39. Lloyd Stratton to Noyes, April 30, 1941, APSU.

40. McLean to Noyes, May 9, 1941, APSU.

41. Lochner, *What about Germany?* (New York: Dodd Mead, 1942), 369.

42. Ibid., 307.

43. Doris Kearns Goodwin, *No Ordinary Time: Franklin and Eleanor Roosevelt: The Home Front in World War II* (New York: Simon and Schuster, 1994), 61.

44. Larry Heinzerling, John Daniszewski, and Randy Herschaft, *Covering Tyranny: The AP and Nazi Germany, 1933–1945* (United States: Associated Press, 2017), 8.

45. [John Evans], Memorandum on war coverage, n.d. (1940), APSU.

46. Cooper to Milo Thompson, September 18, 1939, APSU.

47. Byron Price to European bureau chiefs, November 1, 1939, APSU.

48. Cooper to board of directors, May 15 and May 16, 1940, APRM.

49. Cooper to board of directors, May 16, 1940, APRM.

50. Cooper to board of directors, January 7, 1941, LL2.

51. "The Associated Press, New York Corporation, Forty-Second Annual Volume for the Fiscal Year of 1941," 1942, Report of the Board of Directors, 26, APD.

52. "Address by Kent Cooper to The A.P. Managing Editors . . . October 17, 1941," LL2.

53. Alan Gould interview, 62, APCA, Oral history collection.

54. McLean to Cooper, April 2, 1943, APRM.

55. Cooper to McLean, June 21, 1945, APRM.

56. Cooper, circular to department heads, news editors, chiefs of bureaus, September 21, 1944, APRM.

57. Cooper to Noyes, October 20, 1941, APRM.

58. "The Associated Press, New York Corporation, Forty-Fourth Annual Volume for the Fiscal Year of 1943," 1944, Report of the Executive Director, 66, APD.

59. "More Legal Moves by U.S. Delay Start of A.P. Trial," *Editor & Publisher*, January 30, 1943.

60. Cooper to Hugh Baillie, January 12, 1945, APRM.

61. Cooper, Special notice, December 16, 1941, APRM; Cooper to Stephen Early, December 22, 1941, FDR.

62. Alan Gould interview, 51–52, APCA Oral history collection.

63. "Wife Wins Divorce from Kent Cooper," *Bakersfield Californian*, May 11, 1940; "Milestones," *Time*, May 20, 1940; Ben Bassett, "KC's Broom Got Rid of the Cobwebs," *Cleartime* no. 73, September 1978; Alan Gould interview, 50, APCA, Oral history collection.

64. Cooper to L. F. Curtis, February 28, 1942, LL2.

65. Sally Cooper to Stratton, March 11, (1942), APCA Lloyd Stratton papers (APLS).

66. Cooper to McLean, March 19, 1942, APRM.

67. Another oddity from this period of Cooper's life is *Anna Zenger, Mother of Freedom* (New York: Farrar, Straus, 1946), a highly speculative novelized biography of the wife of Peter Zenger, the New York colonial printer whose acquittal on charges of libel brought by the colony's governor is a milestone in the history of American press freedom. The book was researched by Sally and apparently written by Cooper in his spare time, but its depiction of a beautiful and intelligent but unheralded woman who was the real power behind a dull and stolid spouse suggests it may have been something of a joke between them, with Sally possibly the co-author. See also Vincent Buranelli, "The Myth of Anna Zenger," *William and Mary Quarterly* 13, no. 2 (1956): 157–68.

68. "W-G-N to Carry New Operetta, 'About the Girl,'" *Chicago Tribune*, September 11, 1943.

69. Associated Press story, September 11, 1943, APRM.

70. Cooper to McCormick, "personal," August 23, 1943, RRM.

71. Cooper to McCormick, October 16, 1940, APRM; "Wythe Williams to Aid Roosevelt in National Defense Radio Shows," *Jacksonville (FL) Sun*, September 23, 1940; "Studio Static," *Newport News (VA) Daily Press*, November 10, 1940.

72. "Col. M'Cormick Says U.S. Army Unfit for War," *Chicago Tribune*, August 17, 1941.

73. Cooper to McCormick, "personal," August 18, 1941, RRM.

74. Cooper to McCormick, January 28, 1941, RRM.

75. Cooper to McCormick, July 31, 1944, RRM.

76. Cooper to McCormick, March 18, 1942, RRM.

77. McCormick to Cooper, December 24, 1943, RRM.

78. McCormick to Paul Patterson, "personal," March 30, 1943, RRM.

79. "Nazis Surrender Unconditionally," *Decatur (IL) Daily Review*, May 7, 1945.

80. John P. Hightower, "The Chief Single Source of News" (Unpublished manuscript, 1976), 115. APCA, Writings about the Associated Press (APW).

81. Cooper to Dwight Eisenhower, May 7, 1945, APRM.

82. "Kennedy V-E 'Beat' Stirs Three-Point Controversy," *Editor & Publisher*, May 12, 1945.

83. AP story, "Night Lead Kennedy-Allen," Paris, May 9, 1945, APRM.

84. "Kennedy V-E 'Beat' Stirs Three-Point Controversy," *Editor & Publisher*, May 12, 1945; Julia Kennedy Cochran, ed., *Ed Kennedy's War* (Baton Rouge: Louisiana State University Press, 2012), 157.

85. Cochran, *Ed Kennedy's War*, 161.

86. AP story, "Night Lead Kennedy-Allen," May 9, 1945, APRM.

87. Cochran, *Ed Kennedy's War*, 162.

88. Ibid., 163.

89. Ibid., 164.

90. Alan Gould interview, 43, APCA, Oral history collection; Gallagher quoted in Tom Curley and John Maxwell Hamilton, introduction to *Ed Kennedy's War*, xviii.

91. AP story, "Night Lead Kennedy-Allen," Paris, May 9, 1945, APRM.

92. Cochran, *Ed Kennedy's War*, 166.

93. Hightower, "Chief Single Source of News," 113.

94. Ibid., 111–12, 119.

95. Cooper to Edward Kennedy, May 7, 1945, APRM.

96. Hightower, "Chief Single Source of News," 121–22. A slightly different version of this statement, dated June 1945, appears in Kent Cooper, *The Right to Know* (New York: Farrar, Straus, and Cudahy, 1956), 211.

97. Cooper to Gen. A. D. Surles, May 8, 1945, APRM.

98. Cooper to William Shepherd, May 8, 1945, APRM.

99. AP story A208, New York, May, 9 1945, APRM.

100. "Statements by AP Officials," *Editor & Publisher*, May 12, 1945; Cooper to Eisenhower, May 10, 1945, APRM.

101. C. S. Miley to Cooper, May 11, 1945; Nelson Poynter to McLean, May 11, 1945; Cooper to McLean, May 10, 1945; Charles Guy to Cooper, May 21, 1945, APRM.

102. Cooper to Wes Gallagher, May 14, 1945, APRM.

103. Arthur Sulzberger to McLean, "strictly personal," May 10, 1945; Noyes to McLean, May 19, 1945, APRM.

104. McLean to Cooper, May 18, 1945, APRM.

105. Noyes to McLean, May 19, 1945; McLean to Noyes, May 21, 1945; McLean to Cooper, May 22, 1945, APRM; McCormick to Cooper, May 14, 1945, RRM; Roy Roberts to Cooper, June 14, 1945, APRM.

106. Cooper to McLean, May 21, 1945, APRM.

107. McLean to Charles Guy, May 24, 1945, APRM.

108. Cooper to McLean, May 22, 1945, APRM.

109. McLean to Cooper, "personal," May 23, 1945, APRM.

110. Cooper to McLean, May 24, 1945, APRM.

111. "Because a Reporter Broke Faith," *Philadelphia Inquirer*, May 11, 1945.

112. Cooper to Sulzberger, "personal," May 25, 1945, APRM.

113. Hugh Wagnon to Cooper, May 20, 1945; Stratton to Wagnon, May 23, 1945, APSU.

114. "Kennedy Details Incidents before His Surrender Flash," *Editor & Publisher*, June 9, 1945.

115. "Reporter Who Told V-E Day News First Is Back in America," *Chicago Tribune*, June 5, 1945; AP story, New York, June 8, 1945, APRM.

116. Cooper to McLean, July 14, 1947, APRM.

117. Board of directors minutes, October 5, 1945, APD.

118. Cooper to McLean, October 17, 1945, APRM.

119. "AP Man Restored as Army Writer," *New York Times,* July 23, 1946.

120. "Eisenhower Restores Ed Kennedy's Rights," *Editor & Publisher,* July 27, 1946.

121. AP story, "Kennedy," Washington, July 22, 1946, APSU.

122. Harris to Cooper, July 23, 1946, APRM; Bernhart to Gould, June 23, 1946, APRM.

123. "Story of A.P.-Kennedy," *Editor & Publisher,* July 27, 1946.

124. "Kennedy Cleared," *Editor & Publisher,* July 12, 1947.

125. McLean to Cooper, July 12, 1947, APRM.

126. McLean to Sulzberger, July 22, 1947, APRM.

127. Edward Kennedy, "I'd Do It Again," *Atlantic Monthly,* July 1948, 36–41.

128. Cooper, *Right to Know,* 230; Cooper to McLean, "personal," May 21, 1945, APRM.

129. Cooper, *Right to Know,* 232, 216.

130. "Statement from A.P. Correspondent on Censor-Banned Surrender Story," North American Newspaper Alliance, April 10, 1956, APCA, AP 21.39, AP Personal Papers Collections, Edward Kennedy.

131. BL to Joe Alex Morris, November 7, 1956, RWH.

132. Frank Starzel to Robert Eunson, June 29, 1956, APRM.

133. Curley and Hamilton, introduction to Cochran, *Ed Kennedy's War,* xviii.

Chapter 10. "The Government Suit"

1. See, for example, Morris L. Ernst, *The First Freedom* (New York: Macmillan, 1946); Oswald Garrison Villard, *The Disappearing Daily: Chapters in American Newspaper Evolution* (New York: Alfred A. Knopf, 1944); Upton Sinclair, *The Brass Check: A Study of American Journalism* (Pasadena, CA: The author, 1920).

2. Jonathan Silberstein-Loeb, *The International Distribution of News: The Associated Press, Press Association, and Reuters, 1848–1947* (New York: Cambridge University Press, 2014), 54–58.

3. Ibid., 65.

4. See chapter 4.

5. Spencer Weber Waller, "The Antitrust Legacy of Thurman Arnold," *St. John's Law Review* 78, no. 3 (2004): 569–613.

6. Lloyd Stratton, "Antitrust suit, other litigation, 1939–1960," APD.

7. Annual Meeting of the Associated Press, April 20, 1942, excerpt, APRM.

8. "AM for Chicago," *TIDE,* October 1, 1941.

9. See chapter 12.

10. Minutes of the board of directors, April 17, 1941, APD; chapter 5.

11. Richard Norton Smith, *Colonel: The Life and Legend of Robert R. McCormick, 1880–1955* (Boston: Houghton Mifflin, 1997), 380, 410.

12. Kent Cooper, "Free Press–Antidote to Atomic Bomb," October 16, 1945, APKC.

13. Robert McCormick to Cooper, November 12, 1942, RRM.

14. "AM for Chicago," *TIDE,* October 1, 1941.

15. "Field's 72-Page *Chicago Sun* Starts with 300 Ad Columns," *Editor & Publisher,* December 6, 1941.

16. Marshall Field to Cooper, October 24, 1941, APKC.

17. Field to Franklin Delano Roosevelt, October 22, 1940; Edwin Watson to Field, November 8, 1940, FDR; Stephen Becker, *Marshall Field III: A Biography* (New York: Simon and Schuster, 1964), 177.

18. Roosevelt to Stephen Early, September 18, 1941; Early to L. B. Sherman, September 20, 1941, FDR.

19. Field to Cooper, October 24, 1941, APKC.

20. Louis B. Weiss to Silliman Evans, October 23, 1941, APKC.

21. McLean to Cooper, October 30, 1941, APRM; "The Associated Press, New York Corporation, Forty-Second Annual Volume for the Fiscal Year of 1940," 1941, minutes of the board of directors, November 7, 1941, 48–49, APD.

22. J. D. Gortatowsky to Marshall Field, November 27, 1941, U.S. National Archives RG 267, U.S. Supreme Court, Appellate Case files, 57 O.T. 1944; "US vs AP–Mr. McLean (9984)," APRM.

23. See chapter 7.

24. Field to Robert McLean, December 3, 1941, APRM.

25. "US vs AP–Mr. McLean (9984)," APRM.

26. Ibid.

27. Annual meeting of the Associated Press, Monday, April 20, 1942–April 22, 1942, 46, APD.

28. Ibid., 24, APD.

29. Board of directors minutes, January 9, 1942, 176, APRM.

30. "A.P. Members to Act on Changes to By-Laws at N.Y. Meeting," *Editor & Publisher*, April 18, 1942.

31. Board of directors minutes, January 9, 1942, 340, APRM.

32. Board of directors minutes, April 15, 1942, 185–86, APD.

33. Board of directors minutes, April 16, 1942, 346, 326; April 15, 1942, 215, APD.

34. Annual meeting of the Associated Press, Monday, April 20, 1942–April 22, 1942, 38, APD.

35. Board of directors minutes, April 17, 1942, 366, APD.

36. Board of directors minutes, April 16, 1942, 316, 319, APD.

37. McCormick to McLean, May 26, 1942, APRM.

38. "AP, Facing U.S. Suit, Drops Right of Protest; Chicago Sun Barred," *Editor & Publisher*, April 25, 1942.

39. "AP Blackball," *Newsweek*, May 4, 1942.

40. Votes on Marshall Field and Eleanor M. Patterson, April 1942, APRM.

41. "Press Freedom: How Gestapo Drive Perils It," *Chicago Tribune*, July 20, 1942.

42. Transcript of record, Supreme Court of the U.S., October Term, 1944, no. 57 [*AP et al. v US*], no. 58 [*Tribune Co. & McCormick v US*], no. 59 [*US v AP et al.*), vol. 1, index, xi, U.S. National Archives, RG 267, US Supreme Court, 57 O.T. 1944.

43. Robert McLean interview, 167, APCA, Oral history collection.

44. Conversation between Morris Hadley, Timothy Pfeiffer, and Noyes, September 25, 1942, 43, APD.

45. McLean to members of the board of directors, June 3, 1942, APRM.

46. McLeish, Hon. Archibald, Librarian of Congress, July 13, 1942, FDR.

47. Field to Roosevelt, March 14, 1942, FDR.

48. Louis Weiss, "Memorandum re The Associated Press," enclosed in Field to Roosevelt, March 14, 1942, FDR.

49. Robert McLean interview, 170, APCA, Oral history collection.

50. Francis Biddle, Notebooks: Attorney General X: The AP Case, 88, FDR Francis Biddle Papers (FDRB).

51. J. J. Strebig to Paul Miller, July 25, 1942, enclosed in Miller to Cooper, "private," October 23, 1942, APRM.

52. Lloyd Stratton to Paul Patterson, July 9, 1942, APRM.

53. McLean to McCormick, July 17, 1942, RRM.

54. McCormick to McLean, July 20, 1942, RRM.

55. Weymouth Kirkland to McCormick, July 21, 1942, RRM.

56. Cooper to McCormick July 22, 1942, RRM.

57. McCormick to Cooper, July 25, 1942, RRM.

58. Cooper to McLean, June 4, 1942, APRM.

59. McCormick memorandum, July 17, 1942, RRM.

60. Cooper to board of directors, "strictly personal and confidential," August 19, 1942, APRM.

61. Cooper to McCormick, "strictly personal," August 19, 1942, RRM.

62. Cooper to Biddle, "confidential," August 19, 1942, LL2.

63. According to Byron Price, Cooper did meet Biddle once to discuss the case. Price, memorandum, August 3, 1945, BP.

64. Alan Gould interview, 62, APCA, Oral history collection.

65. Cooper to McLean, August 25, 1942, APRM.

66. "Digest of U.S. Complaint Charging AP 'Monopoly," *Editor & Publisher*, September 5, 1942.

67. See, for example, Board of directors, Report on Government Suit to AP annual meeting, April 24, 1944, APRM.

68. "Expediting Court Named for Trial of AP Suit," *Editor & Publisher*, January 16, 1943.

69. "U.S. Seeks Summary Judgment in Anti-Trust Suit against AP," *Editor & Publisher*, May 29, 1943.

70. Francis Biddle, memorandum for the president, October 13, 1943, FDRB.

71. "3-Judge Court Hears Opening Argument in Suit against AP," *Editor & Publisher*, July 10, 1943.

72. "Associated Press Members Comment on U.S. Suit," *Editor & Publisher*, November 21, 1942.

73. See chapter 8. The First Amendment arguments in the case are examined in greater detail in Margaret A. Blanchard, "The Associated Press Antitrust Suit: A Philosophical Clash over Ownership of First Amendment Rights," *Business History Review* 61, no. 1 (1987): 43–85.

74. "AP Denies Charge of Monopoly, Hits Political Motive in Suit," *Editor & Publisher*, October 31, 1942; "AP Brief Sees Free Press as Main Issue in Case," *Editor & Publisher*, July 10, 1943.

75. McLean to members of AP, August 28, 1942, APRM.

76. Cooper affidavit, June 18, 1943, APRM.

77. Cooper to Gannett, October 13, 1943, RRM.

78. "AP Affidavits," *Editor & Publisher*, June 26, 1943.

79. Cooper to McLean, July 6, 1943, APRM.

80. "Meet Zilboorg, Who Sells New Minds to Rich," *Chicago Tribune*, June 6, 1943.

81. McCormick statement, August 28, 1942, RRM.

82. McCormick to George Booth, November 12, 1942, RRM.

83. McLean to Cooper, November 15, 1943, APRM.

84. *District Court of the United States for the Southern District of New York, U.S. v Associated Press et al.*, 21. 52 F. Supp. 362 (1943).

85. "No Comment from FDR," *Editor & Publisher*, January 22, 1944.

86. Noyes statement, January 10, 1944, APRM.

87. Cooper to Noyes, January 13, 1944, APRM.

88. Cooper to McLean, July 7, 1944, APRM.

89. McLean to Gordon, February 8, 1944, APRM.

90. AP story, "Night Lead AP," Washington, December 5, 1944.

91. *Supreme Court of the United States, The Associated Press et al. v United States of America*, Oral argument, December 5–6, 1944, 70–71, 326 U.S. 1.

92. Supreme Court of the United States, nos. 57, 58, and 59—October Term, 1944, June 18, 1945; 326 U.S. 1.

93. Supreme Court of the United States, nos. 57, 58 and 59—October Term, 1944, 13, 20, 14, 32, 36.

94. McLean to board of directors, June 30, 1945; Cooper to McLean, July 3, 1945, APRM.

95. Cooper to Arthur Moynihan, August 6, 1945; "The Associated Press, New York Corporation, Forty-Sixth Annual Volume for the Fiscal Year of 1945," 1946, 70, APD; see chapter 7.

96. "Memorandum for discussion, July 17, 1945," APRM.

97. Cooper to John Cowles, November 13, 1945, APRM.

98. Cooper to McLean, November 23, 1945, APRM.

99. George Booth to McLean, December 8, 1945, APRM.

100. Booth to members of special committee on bylaws, September 20, 1945; Cahill to Cooper, November 5, 1945, APRM.

101. "Field Gets Associate Status as AP Votes New By-Laws," *Editor & Publisher*, December 1, 1945.

102. McCormick to Cooper, June 18, 1945, RRM.

103. McLean to board of directors, June 30, 1945, APRM.

104. Cooper to Josh Horne, July 9, 1945, APRM.

105. Louis Levand to George Booth, October 25, 1945, APRM.

106. AP story, February 28, 1946, APRM; McLean memorandum, November 15, 1945, APRM.

107. "McCormick Resolution Backed by Publishers," *Editor & Publisher*, April 27, 1946.

108. "Press Service Bill Is Rejected by House Group," *Chicago Tribune*, May 16, 1947.

109. Cooper to McLean, May 16, 1947, APRM; E. M. Antrim to McCormick, July 2, 1947, RRM.

110. Kent Cooper, *Kent Cooper and The Associated Press: An Autobiography* (New York: Random House, 1959), 282.

111. Robert McLean interview, 189, APCA, Oral history collection.

112. Alan Gould interview, 62, APCA, Oral history collection; John P. Hightower, "The Chief Single Source of News" (Unpublished manuscript, 1976), 23. APCA, Writings about the Associated Press (APWR).

113. Quoted in Hightower, "Chief Single Source of News," 24.

114. Hightower, "Chief Single Source of News," 23.

115. "AP Assessments Up $847,000 over 1943," *Editor & Publisher*, April 21, 1945.

Chapter 11. The Crusade

1. Kent Cooper, *Barriers Down: The Story of the News Agency Epoch* (New York: Farrar and Rinehart, 1942), 6.

2. Ibid., v.

3. Ibid., 320.

4. Christopher McKnight Nichols, *Promise and Peril: America at the Dawn of a Global Age* (Cambridge, MA: Harvard University Press, 2011), 11, 42, 60; Frank A. Ninkovich, *The Diplomacy of Ideas: U.S. Foreign Policy and Cultural Relations, 1938–1950* (Cambridge, UK: Cambridge University Press, 1981), 24.

5. Diana Lemberg, *Barriers Down: How American Power and Free-Flow Policies Shaped Global Media* (New York: Columbia University Press, 2019), 4, 31–32; Charles A. Kupchan, *Isolationism: A History of America's Efforts to Shield Itself from the World* (New York: Oxford University Press, 2020), 21–22, 39; Alan Brinkley, *The Publisher: Henry Luce and His American Century* (New York: Knopf, 2010), 268.

6. Stephen Wertheim, *Tomorrow, the World: The Birth of U.S. Global Supremacy* (Cambridge, MA: Harvard University Press, 2020), 11, 57–62, 72, 85.

7. Quinn Slobodian, *Globalists: The End of Empire and the Birth of Neoliberalism* (Cambridge, MA: Harvard University Press, 2018), 15.

8. John Chamberlain, "Books of the Times," *New York Times*, December 5, 1942; "Kent Cooper Dies; Led A.P. in Changes, *Editor & Publisher*, February 6, 1965.

9. DeWitt Mackenzie, "The Great Barrier," 1941–1942, early draft, AP 28, Writings about the Associated Press (APW).

10. Mackenzie, Notes for early draft, APW.

11. DM to Cooper, January 21, 1942, APW.

12. Associated Press NY to Press Associated, London, received December 4, 1941, APSU.

13. Cooper circular, November 27, 1942, APKC.

14. Ibid.

15. Lloyd Stratton to Philip Hodge (Farrar and Rinehard), January 7, 1943; Farrar and Rinehard, Advertising statement, April 30, 1943; Franklin Spier to Stratton, January 12, 1943, APKC.

16. Cooper, *Barriers Down*, 299.

17. Cooper to Coleman Harwell, February 12, 1959, LL2.

18. *Richmond Times-Dispatch, Pittsburgh Sun Telegraph*, in "Extract of News Comment on Barriers Down," n.d. (1943), APRM.

19. C. G. Douglas to Cooper, June 1, 1943; Jos. Snyder to Hackler, February 25, 1943, APKC.

20. Robert Bunnelle to Cooper, August 3, 1943; Cooper to Bunnelle, "personal," August 16, 1943, APKC.

21. Keith Hutchison, "The Truth about the A.P.: I. Growth of a News Trust," *The Nation*, February 6, 1943, 190–94.

22. Roy Howard to William Hawkins, Karl Bickel, and Hugh Baillie, March 24, 1952, RWH.

23. Stanley M. Rinehart Jr. to Stratton, January 5, 1943, APKC.

24. "World Press Freedom Crusade Urged by Cooper at AP Meeting," *Editor & Publisher*, April 24, 1943.

25. Cooper to Cordell Hull, September 28, 1943, APSU.

26. Cordell Hull to Cooper, November 16, 1943, APSU.

27. Paul Miller to Cooper, January 24, 1944, APSU.

28. William Fulbright to Cooper, February 18, 1944, APSU.

29. Cooper to J. R. Knowland, June 16, 1944, APRM.

30. Cooper to James Chappell, July 5, 1944, APRM.

31. "GOP Endorses Principle of International Free Press," *Editor & Publisher*, July 1, 1944.

32. "Shop Talk at Thirty," *Editor & Publisher*, August 19, 1944.

33. AP story, London, July 7, 1944, APRM; Cooper to Chappell, July 21, 1944, APRM.

34. Quoted in Margaret A. Blanchard, *Exporting the First Amendment: The Press-Government Crusade of 1945–1952* (New York: Longman, 1986), 57.

35. Fulbright to Miller, August 22, 1944; Cooper to Fulbright, September 1, 1944; Cooper to Thomas Connally, September 1, 1944; Cooper to Robert Taft, September 1, 1944. APSU.

36. Department of State, release no. 246, June 21, 1944; Miller memorandum, n.d., enclosed in Miller to Claude Jagger, July 7, 1944, APKC.

37. Miller to Cooper, confidential, August 22, 1944, APSU.

38. AP story, "Night Lead News Freedom," September 7, 1944, APKC.

39. AP story, Washington, September 8, 1944, APKC.

40. Fulbright to Cooper, September 11, 1944, APSU.

41. Cooper to Miller, September 12, 1944, APSU.

42. Cooper to Sol Bloom, September 13, 1944, APSU.

43. Senate Concurrent Resolution 53, September 21, 1944.

44. Miller, "Strictly confidential memorandum," n.d., (October 1944), APSU.

45. Cooper to Arthur Vandenberg, September 28, 1944, APSU; Cooper to Guy Gillette, James Tunnell, Tom Connally, September 28, 1944, APRM; Cooper to Alben Barkley, September 28, 1944, APSU.

46. WDH, memorandum for Mr. Early, October 10, 1944, FDR.

47. STE [Early], memorandum for Roosevelt, October 13, 1944, FDR; AP story, October 13, 1944, APKC.

48. Roosevelt, memorandum for STE, October 24, 1944, FDR.

49. Blanchard, *Exporting the First Amendment.*

50. Cooper to Gen. Douglas MacArthur, September 26, 1945, APRM; Lindesay Parrott, "All Japanese Trade Frozen, Free Press Ordered by Allies," *New York Times,* September 25, 1945.

51. Cooper to J. R. Knowland, June 16, 1944, APRM.

52. "Freedom of Information: Head of Associated Press Calls for Unhampered Flow of World News," *Life,* November 13, 1944.

53. See chapter 4.

54. "Free Exchange of News Vital in Postwar World," *The Quill,* May-June 1944, 11.

55. Jagger to bureau chiefs in Lisbon, London, Rome, Madrid, Cairo, India, South Africa, Stockholm, November 22, 1944, APSU.

56. *Free World,* September 1944; speech to National Editorial Association, Chicago, October 21, 1944; "Freedom of Information: Head of Associated Press Calls for Unhampered Flow of World News," *Life,* November 13, 1944; AP Inter-Office, November 1944, APSU; speech delivered to English-Speaking Union, November 28, 1944, APKC; speech to National Association of Manufacturers, December 8, 1944, APKC.

57. "Freedom of Information: Head of Associated Press Calls for Unhampered Flow of World News," *Life,* November 13, 1944.

58. Rafael Hayes, radio adaptation of *Barriers Down,* transcript, November 21, 1944, 6, APKC.

59. AP story, London, December 1, 1944, APKC.

60. AP story, London, December 7, 1944, APKC.

61. "Crusade for Truth: Kent Cooper Heads a Uniquely American Campaign for Worldwide Freedom of the Press. Meaning What?," *Fortune,* April 1945.

62. Ibid.

63. L. S. Frank to *Life,* n.d., enclosed in Dorothy Westphal to Cooper, December 22, 1944, APSU.

64. Cooper, "The Right to Know: Toward World Press Freedom," *Free World,* September 1945.

65. Cooper, "Associated Press World News Objectives," April 25, 1946, APKC.

66. Blanchard, *Exporting the First Amendment,* 129.

67. AP story, April 11, 1947, APKC.

68. "Sevellon Brown to U.S. Press: Don't Highhat Task of World Freedom," *Editor & Publisher,* April 17, 1948.

69. Cooper to bureau chiefs, February 10, 1939, APSU.

70. Stratton memorandum, October 15, 1958, APRM.

71. Cooper to Milo Thompson, May 24, 1939, APRM.

72. Stratton to Cooper, February 22, 1943, APRM.

73. Stratton to Cooper September 30, 1944, LL2; Stratton to Cooper, November 6, 1943, APCA 2.01.

74. Stratton to J. J. Wurzel, August 17, 1943, APRM.

75. "Stratton Returns after World Tour," *Editor & Publisher*, April 8, 1944; AP Inter-Office, November 1943, vol. 2, no. 1, APKC; Stratton to Cooper, November 14, 1943; December 5, 1943; January 25, 1944, APCA 2.01; AP story, New York, October 31, 1944, APKC.

76. Stratton to Cooper, September 30, 1944; Cooper to board of directors, October 4, 1944, LL2.

77. Ibid.

78. Cooper to board of directors, October 4, 1944, LL2.

79. Ibid.

80. Stratton to Cooper, October 16, 1956, LL2.

81. Cooper to James Chappell, October 9, 1944, APRM.

82. Donald Read, *The Power of News: The History of Reuters*, 2nd ed. (Oxford: Oxford University Press, 1999), 238.

83. Ibid., 180–93.

84. Ibid., 241, 244.

85. Ibid.; see chapter 6.

86. Haley, "Reuters and Associated Press of America," July 1, 1942, 1, RA.

87. William Haley, Report for the Reuters board by William J. Haley on his mission to the United States, April-June 1942, dated July 1, 1942, RA.

88. Ibid.

89. Haley memorandum, July 16, 1942, RA.

90. Cooper to Reuters Board of directors, June 26, 1942; Cooper to Bunnelle, June 29, 1942, APRM.

91. Bunnelle to Philip Dunn, May 7, 1945, NYTS.

92. Memorandum, "The Associated Press," May 11, 1945, RA.

93. "How the Nation Got Its False Peace Report," *PM*, April 30, 1946.

94. Chancellor to Kimpton Rogers, May 15, 1945, RA.

95. Chancellor to J. H. Scott and Malcolm Graham, July 31, 1945; Chancellor to Geoffrey Kork, May 18, 1945, "personal," RA.

96. Chancellor to H. M. Heywood, "personal," January 25, 1945, RA.

97. Arthur Sulzberger to McLean, July 6, 1945, RA.

98. Telegram, Sulzberger to McLean, n.d. (July 1945), NYTS.

99. Sulzberger memoranda, July 8 and July 10, 1945, NYTS.

100. Chancellor to Walton Cole, "personal," July 13, 1945, RA.

101. Chancellor to Cole, "confidential," July 18, 1945, RA.

102. Sulzberger to McLean, July 23, 1945, NYTS.

103. Chancellor to Cooper, July 17, 1945, NYTS.

104. Chancellor to Sulzberger, August 7, 1945, NYTS.

105. Chancellor to Reuters board of directors, September 6, 1946, RA; Reuters-AP contract, January 1, 1947, APCA, AP World Services (APWS).

106. Cooper to John Lloyd, October 8, 1946, APWS.

107. Stratton to Cooper, March 12, 1946, APWS

108. Jonathan Silberstein-Loeb, *The International Distribution of News: The Associated Press, Press Association, and Reuters, 1848–1947* (New York: Cambridge University Press, 2014).

109. "The Associated Press, New York Corporation, Forty-Fifth Annual Volume for the Fiscal Year of 1944," 1945, Report of the Executive Director, December 31, 1944, 59, APD; Blanchard, *Exporting the First Amendment*, 168.

110. Heidi Tworek, "Magic Connections: German News Agencies and Global News Networks, 1905–1945" (PhD diss., Harvard University, 2012), 395; Xavier Baron, *Le monde en direct: De Charles-Louis Havas à AFP, deux siècles d'histoire* (Paris: Editions La Découverte, 2014), 80, 110–11; Pierre Frédérix, *Un siècle de chasse aux nouvelles.* Preface by André Siegfried. (Paris: Flammarion, 1959), 420.

111. "The Associated Press, New York Corporation, Forty-Sixth Annual Volume for the Fiscal Year 1945," 1946, Report of the Executive Director, December 31, 1945, 91, APD; AP story, New York, April 6, 1946, APKC.

112. Stratton to Cooper, April 10, 1946, APRM.

113. Stratton to Cooper, April 12, 1946, APRM.

114. "Inside–Associated Press," *Frontpage*, October 1946.

115. McLean to Sulzberger, "confidential," October 15, 1946, NYTS.

116. Cooper to McLean, November 17, 1948, APRM.

117. Richard O'Regan to Cooper, August 10, 1959, LL2; Wes Gallagher to Cooper, October 3, 1947; Cooper to Milt Kelly, September 2, 1947, APRM.

118. John Dunning to Jack McDermott, May 22, 1947; Dunning to McDermott, June 8, 1947, U.S. National Archives College Park, RG 0306, U.S. Information Agency Advisory Commission on Information, Entry #P 216: Records relating to the International Press service: 1946–1954 (USIA).

119. Cooper to Arthur Vandenberg, November 5, 1945, APRM.

120. Christopher Chancellor to Harold King, April 22, 1947, RA. AFP depended on state funds until 1957. Michael Palmer, *International News Agencies: A History* (New York: Palgrave Macmillan, 2020),132.

121. Cooper to Pat Morin, April 2, 1947, APRM.

122. Cooper to Dan DeLuce, "confidential," June 6, 1947, APRM.

123. AP-TASS contract, January 1, 1947, APRM.

124. Cooper to Chiefs of Bureau Abroad, September 23, 1947, APSU.

125. "Another U.S. Newsman Ousted by Soviet-Bloc Nation," *Baltimore Sun*, November 4, 1947.

126. Cooper to Matyas Rakosi, November 3, 1947, APRM.

127. Stratton to McLean, May 13, 1948; Stratton to McLean, April 26, 1951; Stratton memorandum, October 15, 1958, APRM.

Chapter 12. The Voice of America

1. For an earlier account of this conflict, see Margaret A. Blanchard, *Exporting the First Amendment: The Press-Government Crusade of 1945–1952* (New York: Longman, 1986), chapter 3.

2. Cooper to Brian Bell, October 6, 1941, APRM.

3. Press Association, minutes of board of directors meeting, October 4, 1941; Stratton to J. J. Wurzel, September 14, 1942, APRM.

4. Cooper to Bell, October 31, 1941, APRM.

5. Paul Miller to Cooper, November 9, 1942, APSU.

6. Cooper to Miller, "personal and confidential," November 10, 1942, APRM.

7. Cooper to Miller, December 1, 1942, APSU; Miller to Lloyd Stratton, March 13, 1943, APSU; Stratton to Miller, April 26, 1943, APRM.

8. Cooper to Henry Stimson, May 20, 1943, APSU; Cooper to Robert Sherwood, June 22, 1943, APRM.

9. Frank Starzel to Cooper, February 8, 1944, APSU.

10. Cooper to Louis Lochner, September 19, 1945, APSU.

11. Cooper to Noel Macy, November 27, 1944, APSU.

12. Cooper to Miller, December 1, 1944, APSU.

13. AP story, Mount Vernon, NY, December 16, 1944, APKC.

14. David F. Krugler, *The Voice of America and the Domestic Propaganda Battles, 1945–1953* (Columbia: University of Missouri Press, 2000), 34. On the VOA generally, see also Nicholas J. Cull, *The Cold War and the United States Information Agency: American Propaganda and Public Diplomacy, 1945–1989* (Cambridge, UK: Cambridge University Press, 2008); Shawn J. Parry-Giles, "Exporting America's Cold War Message: The Debate over America's First Peacetime Propaganda Program, 1947–1954" (PhD diss., Indiana University, 1992); Robert William Pirsein, *The Voice of America: A History of the International Broadcasting Activities of the United States Government, 1940–1962* (New York: Arno Press, 1979).

15. "Truman Abolishes O.W.I.; Byrnes to Run Job Abroad," *Louisville (KY) Courier-Journal*, September 1, 1945

16. Sydney Hyman, *The Lives of William Benton* (Chicago: University of Chicago Press, 1969), 307.

17. Ibid., 314, 315, 332.

18. Cooper to Robert McLean, November 23, 1945; McLean to Cooper, January 24, 1946; Macy to William Benton, January 17, 1946, APRM.

19. Macy to Benton, January 17, 1946; Stratton to Macy, December 6, 1945, APRM.

20. Macy to Stratton, December 28, 1945, APRM.

21. Resolution adopted by the board of directors, January 9, 1946, APRM.

22. "AP Shuts Off News for Use Abroad by State Department Service," *New York Times*, January 15, 1946.

23. Benton to McLean, January 16, 1946, U.S. National Archives College Park, RG 59, State Department records, Records of the Assistant Secretary of State for Public Affairs (USPA).

24. Arthur Sulzberger to McLean, January 17, 1946, NYTS.

25. McLean to Cooper, January 19, 1946, APRM.

26. Stratton to Robert Bunnelle, January 14, 1946, APRM.

27. "Statement by the Honorable William Benton," January 18, 1946, APRM.

28. James Byrnes to McLean, January 26, 1946, APRM.

29. McLean to Sulzberger, December 20, 1948, and April 4, 1949, APRM.

30. Asa Briggs, *The War of Words: The History of Broadcasting in the United Kingdom,* vol. 3 (Oxford: Oxford University Press, 1995), 19. See also Michael Stamm, "Broadcasting News in the Interwar Period," in *Making News: The Political Economy of Journalism in Britain and America from the Glorious Revolution to the Internet,* ed. Richard R. John and Jonathan Silberstein-Loeb (New York: Oxford University Press, 2015), 152–53.

31. Cooper to board of directors, February 18, 1946, APRM.

32. David Goodman, *Radio's Civic Ambition: American Broadcasting and Democracy in the 1930s* (New York: Oxford University Press, 2011), 14.

33. Memorandum, "Background data–INP," n.d., enclosed in Benton to Stewart Brown, January 2, 1947, USPA.

34. Benton statement, January 18, 1946, APRM.

35. Stratton to Cooper, January 31, 1946, APRM.

36. Stratton to Cooper, January 31, 1946, APRM.

37. McLean to Byrnes, January 28, 1946, APRM.

38. Cooper to board of directors, February 18, 1946, APRM.

39. Roy Howard to Benton, January 17, 1946, USPA.

40. "Statement by the Honorable William Benton," January 28, 1946, APRM.

41. Seymour Berkson to Benton, February 5, 1946; Jesse MacKnight to George Allen, April 12, 1948, USPA.

42. Macy to Stratton, February 11, 1946, APRM.

43. Cooper to Gerald Lyons, March 21, 1946, APRM.

44. Krugler, *Voice of America*, 2.

45. Ibid., 39; Benton to McLean, April 24, 1946, USPA.

46. Cooper to board of directors, February 18, 1946, APRM.

47. Cooper to McLean, March 8, 1946, APRM.

48. Benton to McLean, March 22, 1946, APRM; John Howe to Benton, March 1, 1946, USPA.

49. Allan Murray to Benton, March 26, 1946, USPA.

50. William Benton, "The American Press Associations: An Opportunity and Responsibility," speech to New York Women's Newspaper Club, March 31, 1946, USPA.

51. "Excerpt from address by Arthur Hays Sulzberger," March 31, 1946, NYTS.

52. Sulzberger to Edwin James, April 1, 1946, NYTS; "Benton Assails AP as Failing in Duty," *New York Times*, April 1, 1946.

53. Sulzberger to Frank Noyes, February 6, 1946, "confidential," NYTS.

54. McLean to Sulzberger, April 11, 1946, NYTS.

55. Krugler, *Voice of America*, 39; AP story, "With appropriations," Washington, April 9, 1946, APKC.

56. Krugler, *Voice of America*, 42.

57. "AP Members Hear Cooper in 'News Exchange' Plea," *Editor & Publisher*, April 27, 1946.

58. Cooper, "Associated Press World News Objectives," April 25, 1946, APKC.

59. AP story, "With AP," New York, April 22, 1946, APKC.

60. Board of directors minutes, April 22, 1946, APKC.

61. AP story, New York, April 24, 1946, APKC; McLean to Benton, April 25, 1946, APRM.

62. "What Happens Now?" *Editor & Publisher*, February 2, 1946.

63. "President, Editors Talk Off-Record," *Miami Herald*, April 19, 1946; "Editors to Study Problem of World News Dissemination," *Boston Globe*, April 21, 1946.

64. American Society of Newspaper Editors, "Report of Special Committee Appointed to Investigate World News Dissemination," October 1, 1946.

65. James to Sulzberger, July 4, 1946, NYTS; N. R. Howard to Benton, August 23, 1946, USPA; Cooper to Sulzberger, August 19, 1946, APSU.

66. Sulzberger to Cooper, August 20, 1946, APSU.

67. Howard to Cooper, September 25, 1946, APSU.

68. Cooper to Howard, September 30, 1946, APSU.

69. Stephen Bates, *An Aristocracy of Critics: Luce, Neibuhr, and the Committee That Redefined Freedom of the Press* (New Haven, CT: Yale University Press, 2020), 172, 174. See also Margaret A. Blanchard, "Reclaiming Freedom of the Press: A Hutchins Commission Dream or Nightmare?," *Communication Law and Policy* 371 (1998): 1–59.

70. Cooper to McLean, October 29, 1945. APRM.

71. Llewellyn White and Robert D. Leigh, *Peoples Speaking to Peoples* (New York: Arno Press, 1972; first published 1946), 103–104, 112.

72. "Controlled Press Opposed by Cooper," *New York Times*, August 2, 1947. For journalists' response generally, see Bates, *Aristocracy of Critics*, chapter 17; Blanchard, "The Hutchins Commission"; Frank Hughes, *Prejudice and the Press: A Restatement of the Principle of Freedom of the Press with Specific Reference to the Hutchins-Luce Commission* (New York: Devin-Adair, 1950).

73. Blanchard, "Hutchins Commission," 39.

74. Excerpts from Marshall news conference, February 7, 1947, enclosed in Stratton to McLean, April 29, 1947, APRM; Hyman, *Benton*, 372.

75. Krugler, *Voice of America*, 39, 58.

76. Cooper to McLean, May 6, 1947, APRM.

77. McLean to Cooper, May 8, 1947, APRM.

78. Cooper to McLean, May 9, 1947, APRM.

79. Cooper to Arthur Krock, May 12, 1947, APRM.

80. McLean to Cooper, May 16, 1947, APRM.

81. Sulzberger to McLean, May 16, 1947, APRM.

82. "Marshall Insists 'Voice' Must Go On," *New York Times*, May 17, 1947.

83. Cooper to McLean, May 19, 1947, APRM.

84. McLean to Cooper, May 21, 1947, APRM.

85. Address of Kent Cooper on "Government and News" before the Inland Press Association, May 26, 1947, APRM.

86. Ibid.

87. Ibid.

88. Quinn Slobodian, *Globalists: The End of Empire and the Birth of Neoliberalism* (Cambridge, MA: Harvard University Press, 2018).

89. AP story, advance for AMs of Tuesday, May 27, [1947], Chicago, NYTS; "'Disguised News' Plan Denounced by Cooper," *Editor & Publisher*, May 31, 1947.

90. Sulzberger to McLean, May 26, 1947, NYTS.

91. Cooper to McLean, June 3, 1947, APRM.

92. "VOA Questions Attack by Cooper," *New York Times*, June 15, 1947.

93. Krugler, *Voice of America*, 63, 66–70.

94. Ibid., 71; Hyman, *Benton*, 372–75.

95. MacKnight to Allen, April 12, 1948, USPA.

96. Allen to Sulzberger, April 13, 1948, NYTS.

97. "ASNE Committee Endorses Government Newscasts," *Editor & Publisher*, April 17, 1948; "ASNE Urges AP, UP Service for Government Newscasts," *Editor & Publisher*, April 24, 1948.

98. Allen to Cooper, May 26, 1948, APRM.

99. Cooper to McLean, June 2, 1948, APRM.

100. Lloyd Lehrbas to Allen, June 3, 1948, USPA.

101. Lehrbas to Allen, December 20, 1948, USPA.

102. McLean to Sulzberger, December 20, 1948, APRM; Lehrbas to H. H. Sargeant, December 20, 1948, USPA.

103. McLean to Sulzberger, April 4, 1949, APRM.

104. Cooper to Wes Gallagher, Lemkow, and Charles Guptill, November 19, 1948; Cooper to chiefs of foreign bureaus, November 24, 1948, APRM.

105. Cooper to McLean, December 17, 1948, APRM.

106. Cooper to McLean, December 8, 1948, APRM.

107. McLean to Sulzberger, April 4, 1949, APRM.

108. Cooper to McLean, March 9, 1949, APRM.

109. Lehrbas to Cooper, March 5, 1949, APRM.

110. McLean to Sulzberger, April 4, 1949, APRM.

111. McLean to Ben McKelway, May 11, 1949, APRM.

112. Memorandum, n.d., with notation "Authorized by board 4/22/49 should question arise in annual meeting," APRM.

113. Lehrbas to Cooper, March 5, 1949, APRM.

114. Cooper to Lehrbas, June 3, 1949, APRM.

115. Cooper to Lehrbas, June 20, 1949, APRM.

116. McLean to Cooper, July 7, 1949, APRM; Frank Starzel to McKelway, February 16, 1950, APRM.

117. Memorandum of Conversation, Subject: AP UP Wire service, June 5, 1950, USPA; McLean to Barrett, January 26, 1951, APRM.

118. McLean to Starzel, January 6, 1950, APRM.

119. Cooper to Gallagher, Lemkow, Guptill, November 19, 1948, APRM; "Sevellon Brown to U.S. Press: Don't Highhat Task of World Freedom," *Editor & Publisher*, April 17, 1948.

120. Richard O'Regan to Cooper, August 10, 1959, LL2.

Chapter 13. "Mr. Associated Press"

1. "AP Re-Elects McLean; Knight Goes on Board"; "100-Year-Old AP Renews Truth Pledge"; "Lord Rothermere Proposes AP-Reuters 'Truth Team'," all in *Editor & Publisher*, April 24, 1948.

2. Robert McLean to Frank Noyes, May 8, 1948; Stratton to Ben McKelway, "private," April 10, 1958, APRM.

3. McLean to Noyes, May 8, 1948, APRM.

4. Alan Gould to Harold Turnblad, June 2, 1948, APSU.

5. Frank Starzel to McLean, August 4, 1948, APSU; Walton Cole to Christopher Chancellor, "private," September 3, 1948, RA.

6. "Starzel Steered AP While Cooper Travelled," *Editor & Publisher*, October 16, 1948; AP story, October 21, 1948, APSU.

7. Alan Gould interview, 51, APCA, Oral history collection.

8. See chapter 8.

9. Gould interview, 50–51.

10. McLean to Noyes, May 8, 1948, APRM.

11. Ben Bassett, "KC's Broom Got Rid of the Cobwebs," *Cleartime: The AP Alumni Newsletter* no. 73, September 1978.

12. Kent Cooper to McLean, July 5, 1949, APRM; Cooper to McLean, December 21, 1948, APSU.

13. Cooper to W.H.B. Fowler, December 20, 1948, APKC.

14. Arthur Sulzberger to E. Lansing Ray, February 14, 1949, NYTS.

15. MM [Mary Murray] to Cooper, March 29, 1949, APRM.

16. McLean to Cooper, June 22, 1949, APRM.

17. McLean to Cooper, October 16, 1957, LL2.

18. Cooper to McLean, June 24, 1949, APRM.

19. Cooper to Sulzberger, September 9, 1949; Sulzberger to Cooper, September 12, 1949, NYTS.

20. McLean to Robert Brown, March 16, 1950, APRM.

21. Cooper to Robert McCormick, January 4, 1950, RRM; "The Associated Press Annual Report," board of directors minutes, January 10, 1950, 3, APD.

22. Cooper to McLean, April 5, 1950, APRM.

23. McLean to Cooper, April 10, 1950, APRM.

24. Robert McLean, "KC–AP's Chief Executive for 25 Years"; "'I Shall Do the Best I Can' Were Cooper's Words—They Were Not Idle Ones," both in *Editor & Publisher*, April 22, 1950.

25. "Tribute to K.C.," *Editor & Publisher*, April 22, 1950.

26. Cooper to McLean, September 19, 1950, APRM.

27. McLean to Robert Booth, October 11, 1950, APRM.

28. See chapter 3; McLean to Cooper, September 20, 1950, APRM.

29. McCormick to Cooper, January 20, 1945; Cooper to McCormick, April 26, 1945, RRM.

30. McCormick to Willis Nance, May 2, 1949, RRM.

31. Cooper to McCormick, June 8, 1949, RRM.

32. Cooper to McCormick, December 13, 1950, RRM.

33. Board of directors resolution, April 1, 1951, Lloyd Stratton Abstracts of Minutes, 1900–1960, APD.

34. AP story, April 26, 1951, APRM. See also Edward Alwood, "The Spy Case of AP Correspondent William Oatis: A Muddled Victim/Hero Myth of the Cold War," *Journalism and Mass Communication Quarterly* 87, no. 2 (2010): 263–80.

35. Cooper to McLean, July 19, 1951, APRM.

36. Starzel to McLean, "personal," July 24, 1951, APRM.

37. Chancellor to Lloyd Dumas May 4, 1951, RA.

38. Chancellor to Cooper, March 14, 1951, RA.

39. Cooper to Chancellor, March 14, 1951; Cooper to Chancellor, March 19, 1951, RA.

40. Chancellor to Dumas, May 4, 1951, RA.

41. "K.C. Toasts Reuters," *Editor & Publisher*, July 14, 1951.

42. McLean to Paul Miller, June 22, 1951, APRM.

43. Cooper to McLean, July 19, 1951, APRM.

44. Chancellor to Relman (Pat) Morin, September 10, 1951; Cooper to Chancellor, June 30, 1952, APRM.

45. McLean to Cooper, October 16, 1951, APRM.

46. Morris L. Ernst, *The First Freedom* (New York: Macmillan, 1946), 23, 86.

47. Cooper to McLean, October 13, 1952, APRM.

48. Cooper speech to labor editors, September 14, 1952, APRM.

49. Ibid.

50. Cooper to McLean October 13, 1952, APRM.

51. Cooper to McLean, September 18, 1952; McLean to Cooper, September 19, 1952, APRM.

52. McCormick to Cooper, January 12, 1953, RRM; "Hamilton Fish Announces Group to Fight 'Internationalism,'" *Richmond (IN) Palladium-Item and Sun-Telegram*, November 27, 1953.

53. Cooper to McCormick, January 14, 1953, RRM; "Col. McCormick Buys Washington Times-Herald," *Editor & Publisher*, July 23, 1949.

54. Cooper to McCormick, March 20, 1954, LL2; Cooper to Howard Wood, March 23, 1954, LL2; Cooper to Wood, February 1, 1956, Tribune Company Archives, Tribune Company (TRIB).

55. Bill from Cartier, New York, to Mrs. Robert R. McCormick, April 30, 1954, RRM.

56. Cooper to Weymouth Kirkland, June 25, 1955; Cooper to Kirkland, October 12, 1955, TRIB.

57. Cooper to W. D. Maxwell, May 4, 1956, LL2.

58. Kent Cooper, *The Right to Know: An Exposition of the Evils of News Suppression and Propaganda* (New York: Farrar, Straus, and Cudahy, 1956). More than sixty years later, the phrase still has resonance; see, for example, Michael Schudson, *The Rise of the Right to Know* (Cambridge, MA: Harvard University Press, 2015).

59. McLean to Cooper, September 19, 1955, APRM.

60. Cooper, *Right to Know*, 16–17.

61. Ibid., 51. Until 1957, reliance on government funds did limit AFP's independence; it was seen as "quasi-official." Michael B. Palmer, *International News Agencies: A History* (New York: Palgrave Macmillan, 2020), 153–55.

62. Cooper, *Right to Know*, 42, 45, 55, 51–52, 59.

63. Ibid., 11–12. John Peter Zenger, a printer and publisher of the *New York Weekly Journal*, was charged with seditious libel in 1734 for criticizing the colonial governor of New York. His acquittal by a jury is seen as an important milestone in the evolution of journalistic freedom in the United States. See, for example, Paul Finkelman, "Zenger Trial," *The Oxford Encyclopedia of American Political and Legal History* (New York: Oxford University Press, 2012), https://www.oxfordreference.com/view/10.1093/acref/9780199754618.001.0001/acref-9780199754618-e-0565/.

64. Cooper, *Right to Know*, 51. French journalism after the war was indeed highly politicized. Palmer, *International News Agencies*, 134.

65. See Reporters of the Associated Press, *Breaking News: How the Associated Press Has Covered War, Peace, and Everything Else* (New York: Princeton Architectural Press, 2007), 48–49. This was a fairly common view in the 1920s; see David Greenberg, "The Ominous Clang: Fears of Propaganda from World War I to World War II," in *Media Nation: The Political History of News in Modern America*, ed. Bruce Schulman and Julian Zelizer (Philadelphia: University of Pennsylvania Press, 2017), 59.

66. Cooper's prewar involvement with the German and Japanese news agencies is discussed in chapters 5, 6, and 9.

67. D. LaSpaluto, memorandum to Mr. Wheeler, May 1, 1956, APKC; McLean to Gould, March 27, 1956, APRM. For Cooper's account of the Kennedy affair in *Right to Know*, see chapter 10.

68. Sally Cooper to Paul Miller, September 14, 1957, LL2.

69. Cooper to Miller, September 25, 1957, LL2.

70. *"M.E.S."—His Book: A Tribute and a Souvenir of the Twenty-Five Years 1893–1918 of the Service of Melville E. Stone as General Manager of the Associated Press* (New York: Harper, 1918).

71. Miller to Dear KC and Sally, Thursday, 4 p.m. (October 1957), LL2.

72. McKelway to McLean, October 13, 1957, APRM.

73. Board of directors minutes, January 15, 1958, APD; McKelway to Cooper, January 21, 1958; McKelway to Cooper, April 23, 1958, LL2.

74. McKelway to Cooper, April 1, 1958, LL2.

75. Cooper to McKelway, n.d. (April 1958), APRM.

76. McKelway to McLean, April 8, 1958, APRM.

77. Cooper to Starzel, March 23, 1959; Starzel to Cooper, March 26, 1959, LL2.

78. Cooper to Sulzberger, January 4, 1965, LL2.

79. McKelway to Cooper, August 1, 1958, LL2.

80. Cooper to McKelway, April 24, 1959, LL2.

81. Ibid.

82. Kent Cooper, *Kent Cooper and The Associated Press: An Autobiography* (New York: Random House, 1959), 138–39, 188, 212.

83. Ibid., 264.

84. See chapter 6.

85. For the awkward first meeting between Cooper and Jones, see chapter 2. Cooper, *Kent Cooper,* 266.

86. Cooper, *Kent Cooper,* 270.

87. "Kent Cooper's Career," *Nieman Reports,* Fall 1959, 36–37.

88. Joe Miller to Cooper, June 15, 1959, APRM.

89. McLean to Cooper, September 25, 1959, APRM.

90. Cooper to McLean, October 1, 1959, APRM.

91. Alan Gould interview, 52, APCA, Oral history collection.

92. Cooper to R. A. Spangler, May 15, 1959, LL2.

93. Board of directors minutes, October 13, 1959, APD.

94. McKelway to Cooper, December 29, 1959, LL2.

95. McKelway to Cooper, January 8, 1960, LL2.

96. Cooper to McKelway, January 29, 1960 (not sent), LL2.

97. Cooper to Mrs. Philip L. Graham, February 3, 1964; Graham to Cooper, February 6, 1964; Cooper to Graham, February 27, 1964; Graham to Cooper, March 17, 1964; Cooper to Graham, April 28, 1964, LL2.

98. Matthew Welsh to Cooper, June 11, 1964; "McKinney 'Not Serious,'" *Columbus (IN) Evening Republican,* August 18, 1964.

99. Sally Cooper to Haley, October 22, 1964; Haley to Sally Cooper, October 26, 1964, LL2.

100. Haley to Cooper, January 31, 1962, LL2.

101. Cooper to Wilbur Forrest, December 19, 1964, LL2.

102. Cooper to Wheeler, November 23, 1964, LL2.

103. Christmas card, 1964, LL2.

104. WGvS to Saul D. Rotter MD, n.d., (1963), LL2; Cooper to Charles Stephenson Smith, December 12, 1963; Cooper to Dear Lloyd (Dumas), June 3, 1964, LL2.

105. Cooper to Miller, May 21, 1964, LL2.

106. AP story, A214 to A217, West Palm Beach FL, January 31, 1965, LL.

107. Sally Cooper to Gramling, June 17, 1966, LL2.

108. See letters of condolence to Gallagher from J. Santiago Castillo (*El Telegrafo,* Guayaquil, Ecuador), February 3, 1965; Philip D. Adler (Lee Enterprises, Davenport, IA), February 1, 1965; Luis Miro Quesada (*El Comercio,* Lima), February 1, 1965; and Sen. George A. Smathers, February 3, 1965. Also see letters to Paul Miller from John L. Burgess (Reuters), February 4, 1965; David Friedmann (South African Press Association), February 4, 1965; Grayson Kirk (Columbia University), February 10, 1965; John Knight, February 2, 1965; Robert McLean, February 8, 1965; Gerald Long (Reuters), January 31, 1965; Esmond Rothermere (n.d.); David Sarnoff and Robert Sarnoff (received February 1, 1965); Frank Starzel, February 3, 1965; and Arthur Sulzberger, February 1, 1965, LL2.

109. Haley to Sally, n.d. (1965), LL2.

110. AP story "Cooper Bjt," by Relman Morin, January 31, 1965, LL.

111. "Kent Cooper Dies; Former A.P. Chief," *New York Times,* January 31, 1965. In the *New York Herald Tribune,* he was "Mr. Associated Press"; see "Kent Cooper dead at 84, Was AP General Manager," *Herald Tribune,* February 1, 1965.

112. "Kent Cooper," *New York Times*, February 1, 1965.

113. "Kent Cooper," *Washington Post*, February 3, 1965.

114. Hal Boyle, "A Man Called 'K.C.'—He Changed the World of Journalism," AP News-features, February 4, 1965.

115. Board of directors resolution, April 12, 1965, LL2.

116. Statement by Wes Gallagher, April 16, 1965, LL2.

117. Alfred D. Chandler and Bruce Mazlish, *Leviathans: Multinational Corporations and the New Global History* (Cambridge, UK: Cambridge University Press, 2005).

118. *AP World* 17, no. 3, 3; "The Associated Press, Twenty-Fifth Annual Report of the Board of Directors," 1925, 9, APD.

119. Cooper, *Kent Cooper*, 283.

120. See chapter 4. For the evolution of UP's and Howard's approach to politics, see A. J. Leibling, "The Boy in the Pistachio Shirt," in Liebling, *The Telephone Booth Indian* (New York: Broadway Books 2004. First published 1942 by Penguin [New York]), 166–228; Patricia Beard, *Newsmaker: Roy W. Howard: The Mastermind behind the Scripps-Howard News Empire from the Gilded Age to the Atomic Age* (Guilford, CT: Lyons Press, 2016), xxiii; Donald A. Ritchie, *Reporting from Washington: The History of the Washington Press Corps* (Oxford: Oxford University Press, 2005), 115, 117. Philip Glende notes that Scripps-Howard papers supported news unions in the 1930s. Glende, "Labor Reporting and Its Critics in the CIO Years," *Journalism Monographs* 22, no. 1 (2020):10. See also George Seldes, *Lords of the Press* (New York: Messner, 1939), 80–81.

121. David Nasaw, *The Chief: The Life of William Randolph Hearst* (Boston: Houghton Mifflin, 2000), 330–31, 517, 522.

122. UNESCO, *News Agencies: Their Structure and Operation* (Paris: UNESCO, 1953), 200.

123. See chapter 2.

124. William S. Kirkpatrick, "Showing German Editors a Free Press at Work," *Journalism Quarterly* 26, no. 1 (1949): 29–35. See also Jessica Gienow-Hecht, *Transmission Impossible: American Journalism as Cultural Diplomacy in Post-War Germany, 1945–1955* (Baton Rouge: Louisiana State University Press, 1999).

125. Oswald Garrison Villard, *The Disappearing Daily: Chapters in American Newspaper Evolution* (New York: Alfred A. Knopf, 1944), 41.

126. Daniel Hallin, *The "Uncensored War": The Media and Vietnam* (New York: Oxford University Press, 1986),116–18.

127. Pew Research Center, "U.S. Media Polarization and the 2020 Election: A Nation Divided," January 2020.

128. See Richard Kaplan, *Politics and the American Press: The Rise of Objectivity* (Cambridge, UK: Cambridge University Press, 2002), 2, 12, 14.

129. For the importance of public support for journalism in northern European countries, see Daniel Hallin and Paolo Mancini, *Comparing Media Systems: Three Models of Media and Politics* (Cambridge, UK: Cambridge University Press, 2004), 160–65.

130. "Hundreds Mourn A.P.'s Kent Cooper," *New York Times*, February 4, 1965.

131. "Kent Cooper's Will Filed; Estate Exceeds $100,000," *New York Times*, February 17, 1965.

132. Daniel DeLuce to Sally Cooper, February 3, 1965, LL2.

Bibliography

Manuscript Collections

Associated Press Corporate Archives (APCA)
  AP01.1   Records of the Board of Directors and Annual Meetings (APD)
  AP01.4B   Papers of Board President Robert McLean (APRM)
  AP02.1   Records of General Manager Kent Cooper (APKC)
  AP02A.3   Subject Files (APSU)
  AP12   World Services (APWS)
  AP20.01   AP Oral History Collection
  AP 21.9   Lloyd Stratton Papers (APLS)
  AP 21.39   Edward Kennedy Papers
  AP28   Writings about The Associated Press (APW)
  AP34   AP Publications [Service Bulletin and FYI are in AP 34]
Bancroft Library, University of California Berkeley
  William Randolph Hearst Papers
Col. Robert R. McCormick Research Center (Cantigny, IL)
  Robert R. McCormick Papers (RRM)
  Tribune Company Files
  Howard Wood Papers
Franklin D. Roosevelt Presidential Library and Museum (FDR)
  Franklin D. Roosevelt, Papers as President
      OF 171—Associated Press, 1933–1945
      OF 253—Early, Stephen T., 1933–1939
      OF 4054—Field, Marshall, 1940–1943

Franklin D. Roosevelt, President's Personal File
   PPF 273—Associated Press
   PPF 426—McCormick, Col. Robert R.
   PPF 5476—Early, Stephen T.
   PPF 5940—Noyes, Frank Brett
   PPF 6095—Field, Marshall
   PPF 8319—Arnold, Thurman W.
The President's Secretary's File, 1933–1945
   McCormick, Robert
Stephen T. Early Papers (STE)
Francis Biddle Papers (FDRB)
Library of Congress, Manuscript Division
   Roy W. Howard Papers
Lilly Library, Indiana University
   Kent Cooper Papers, 1905–1985
     Cooper mss. (LL)
     Cooper mss. II (LL2)
The Media School, Indiana University
   Roy W. Howard Archive (RWH)
National Archives of the United States
   RG 0306, U.S. Information Agency
   RG 59, State Department records, Records of the Assistant Secretary of State for Public Affairs (USPA)
   RG 173, Federal Communications Commission
   RG 267, U.S. Supreme Court, Appellate Case files
New York Public Library
   New York Times Company Records
     Adolph S. Ochs Papers, 1853–2006 MssCol 17781 (NYTO)
     Arthur Hays Sulzberger Papers 1823–1999 MssCol 17782 (NYTS)
Reuters Archive, London
   Reuters news agency files (RA)
   Roderick Jones Papers (RAJ)
Special Collections Research Center, Lauinger Library, Georgetown University
   Francis Biddle Papers GTM, Gamms251
Special Collections Research Center, Syracuse University Libraries
   DeWitt Mackenzie Papers
Wilson Library, University of North Carolina, Chapel Hill
   Elmer Roberts Papers 1835–1937 (ER)
Wisconsin Historical Society Library and Archives
   Byron Price papers, 1901–1976 U.S. Mss 142AF (BP)
   Louis Paul Lochner Papers 1903–1972 U.S. Mss 21AF (LP)
   Bruce Barton Papers 1881–1967 U.S. Mss 44AF
Yale University Library
   Col. Edward M. House papers, MS 466

Newspapers

Editor & Publisher
Newspapers.com (online)

Secondary Sources

Akami, Tomoko. *Japan's News Propaganda and Reuters' News Empire in Northeast Asia, 1870–1934*. Dordrecht, Netherlands: Republic of Letters Publishing, 2012.

———. *Soft Power of Japan's Total War State: The Board of Information and Domei News Agency in Foreign Policy, 1934–1945*. Dordrecht, Netherlands: Republic of Letters Publishing, 2014.

Allen, Gene. *Making National News: A History of Canadian Press*. Toronto: University of Toronto Press, 2013.

Alwood, Edward. "The Spy Case of AP Correspondent William Oatis: A Muddled Victim/Hero Myth of the Cold War." *Journalism and Mass Communication Quarterly* 87, no. 2 (2010): 263–80.

Aspinwall, John. "AP Broadcast News Service." *AP World*, Winter 1964–1965, 3–17.

Baillie, Hugh. *High Tension: The Recollections of Hugh Baillie*. New York: Harper Brothers, 1959.

Baldasty, Gerald. *E. W. Scripps and the Business of Newspapers*. Urbana: University of Illinois Press, 1999.

Baron, Xavier. *Le monde en direct: De Charles-Louis Havas à AFP, deux siècles d'histoire*. Paris: Éditions La Découverte, 2014.

Bassett, Ben. "Kent Cooper's Legacy." *AP World* 1 (1980). *Associated Press Collections Online*. http://tinyurl.galegroup.com/tinyurl/GfGf3/.

Bates, Stephen. *An Aristocracy of Critics: Luce, Neibuhr, and the Committee That Redefined Freedom of the Press*. New Haven, CT: Yale University Press, 2020.

Baughman, James L. "The Decline of Journalism since 1945." In *Making News: The Political Economy of Journalism in Britain and America from the Glorious Revolution to the Internet*, edited by Richard R. John and Jonathan Silberstein-Loeb, 164–95. New York: Oxford University Press, 2015.

———. *Henry R. Luce and the Rise of the American News Media*. Boston: Twayne Publishers, 1987.

Beard, Patricia. *Newsmaker: Roy W. Howard: The Mastermind behind the Scripps-Howard News Empire from the Gilded Age to the Atomic Age*. Guilford, CT: Lyons Press, 2016.

Becker, Stephen. *Marshall Field III: A Biography*. New York: Simon and Schuster, 1964.

Belmonte, Laura Ann. "Defending a Way of Life: American Propaganda and the Cold War, 1945–1959." PhD diss., University of Virginia, 1996.

Blanchard, Margaret A. "The Associated Press Antitrust Suit: A Philosophical Clash over Ownership of First Amendment Rights." *Business History Review* 61, no. 1 (1987): 43–85.

———. *Exporting the First Amendment: The Press-Government Crusade of 1945–1952*. New York: Longman, 1986.

———. "The Hutchins Commission, the Press, and the Responsibility Concept." *Journalism Monographs* 49 (May 1977): 1–59.

———. "Press Criticism and National Reform Movements: The Progressive Era and the New Deal." *Journalism History* 5, no. 2 (1978): 33–36, 54–55.

Blanchard, Margaret. "Reclaiming Freedom of the Press: A Hutchins Commission Dream or Nightmare?" *Communication Law and Policy* 371 (1998): 1–59.

Blondheim, Menahem. *News over the Wires: The Telegraph and the Flow of Public Information in America, 1844–1897*. Cambridge, MA: Harvard University Press, 1994.

Briggs, Asa. *The War of Words: The History of Broadcasting in the United Kingdom*. Vol. 3. Oxford: Oxford University Press, 1995.

Brinkley, Alan. *The Publisher: Henry Luce and His American Century*. New York: Knopf, 2010.

Buckley, Kerry W. "A President for the 'Great Silent Majority': Bruce Barton's Construction of Calvin Coolidge." *New England Quarterly* 76, no. 4 (2003): 593–626.

Buranelli, Vincent. "The Myth of Anna Zenger." *William and Mary Quarterly* 13, no. 2 (1956): 157–68.

Cane, James. *The Fourth Enemy: Journalism and Power in the Making of Peronist Argentina, 1930–1955*. University Park: University of Pennsylvania Press, 2011.

Chandler, Alfred D. *The Visible Hand: The Managerial Revolution in American Business*. Cambridge, MA: Belknap Press of Harvard University Press, 1977.

Chandler, Alfred D., and Bruce Mazlish. *Leviathans: Multinational Corporations and the New Global History*. Cambridge, UK: Cambridge University Press, 2005.

Cochran, Julia Kennedy, ed. *Ed Kennedy's War*. Baton Rouge: Louisiana State University Press, 2012.

Cooper, Kent. *Anna Zenger, Mother of Freedom*. New York: Farrar, Straus, 1946.

———. *Barriers Down: The Story of the News Agency Epoch*. New York: Farrar and Rinehart, 1942.

———. *Kent Cooper and the Associated Press: An Autobiography*. New York: Random House, 1959.

———. *The Right to Know: An Exposition of the Evils of News Suppression and Propaganda*. New York: Farrar, Straus, and Cudahy, 1956.

"Cooper, Kent." *Current Biography*, October 1944, 19–22. Available at https://www.hwwilson inprint.com/current_bio.php/.

Coopersmith, Jonathan. "From Lemons to Lemonade: The Development of AP Wirephoto." *American Journalism* 17, no. 4 (2000): 55–72.

Cull, Nicholas J. *The Cold War and the United States Information Agency: American Propaganda and Public Diplomacy, 1945–1989*. Cambridge, UK: Cambridge University Press, 2008.

Curley, Tom, and John Maxwell Hamilton. Introduction to Cochran, *Ed Kennedy's War*, vii–xxi.

C.[urtis], L. F. "Kent Cooper and The Associated Press." *AP World*, Spring 1965, 29–36.

Daniels, Roger. *Franklin D. Roosevelt: Road to the New Deal, 1882–1939*. Urbana: University of Illinois Press, 2015.

Dawson, Van B. "The American Newspaper Guild and The Associated Press: A Study of Collective Bargaining Relations." MBA thesis, Columbia University, 1950.

Desbordes-Vela, Rhoda. "L'information internationale en amerique du Sud: Les agences et les réseaux, circa 1874–1919." *Le temps des médias*, no. 20 (printemps-été 2013): 125–38.

Diggins, John P. *Mussolini and Fascism: The View from America*. Princeton, NJ: Princeton University Press, 1972.

"Directors Honor 'KC' on 25th Anniversary of His Appointment as General Manager." *AP World* 3 (1950).

District Court of the United States for the Southern District of New York. *U.S. v Associated Press et al*. 52 F. Supp. 362 (1943).

Domeier, Norman. "Secret Photos: The Co-operation between Associated Press and the National Socialist Regime, 1942–1945." *Zeithistorische Forschungen / Studies in Contemporary History* 14 (2017): 1–32.

Ernst, Morris L. *The First Freedom*. New York: Macmillan, 1946.

Fine, Richard. "Edward Kennedy's Long Road to Reims: The Media and the Military in World War II." *American Journalism* 33, no. 3 (2016): 317–39.

Finkelman, Paul. "Zenger Trial." *The Oxford Encyclopedia of American Political and Legal History*. Oxford University Press, 2012. https://www.oxfordreference.com/view/10.1093/acref/9780199754618.001.0001/acref-9780199754618-e-0565/.

Frédérix, Pierre. *Un siècle de chasse aux nouvelles*. Preface by André Siegfried. Paris: Flammarion, 1959.

Gienow-Hecht, Jessica. *Transmission Impossible: American Journalism as Cultural Diplomacy in Post-War Germany, 1945–1955*. Baton Rouge: Louisiana State University Press, 1999.

Glende, Philip M. "Labor Reporting and Its Critics in the CIO Years." *Journalism Monographs* 22, no. 1 (2020): 4–75.

———. "Trouble on the Right, Trouble on the Left: The Early History of the American Newspaper Guild." *Journalism History* 38, no. 3 (2012): 142–55.

———. "'We Used Every Effort to be Impartial': The Complicated Response of Newspaper Publishers to Unions." *American Journalism* 29, no. 2 (2012): 37–65. DOI: 10.1080/0882 1127.2012.10677825/.

"GM of AP." *Newsweek*, May 5, 1947, 65–66.

Goodman, David. *Radio's Civic Ambition: American Broadcasting and Democracy in the 1930s*. New York: Oxford University Press, 2011.

Goodwin, Doris Kearns. *No Ordinary Time: Franklin and Eleanor Roosevelt: The Home Front in World War II*. New York: Simon and Schuster, 1994.

Gramling, Oliver. *AP: The Story of News*. New York: Farrar and Rinehart, 1940.

Greenberg, David. "The Ominous Clang: Fears of Propaganda from World War I to World War II." In Schulman and Zelizer, *Media Nation*, 50–62.

Groome, Richard G. "Holliday, John Hampden." In Sherman, *The Encyclopedia of Indianapolis*, edited by David J. Bodenhamer and Robert G. Barrows, 700–701. Bloomington: Indiana University Press, 1994.

Guarneri, Julia. *Newsprint Metropolis: City Papers and the Making of Modern Americans*. Chicago: University of Chicago Press, 2017.

Hale, Oron J. *The Captive Press in the Third Reich*. Princeton, NJ: Princeton University Press, 1964.

Hallin, Daniel. *The "Uncensored War": The Media and Vietnam*. New York: Oxford University Press, 1986.

Hallin, Daniel, and Paolo Mancini. *Comparing Media Systems: Three Models of Media and Politics.* Cambridge, UK: Cambridge University Press, 2004.

Headrick, Daniel R., and Pascal Griset. "Submarine Telegraph Cables: Business and Politics, 1838–1939." *Business History Review* 75 (Autumn 2001): 543–78.

Heald, Morrell, ed. *Journalist at the Brink: Louis P. Lochner in Berlin, 1922–1942.* Xlibris, 2007.

Heinzerling, Larry, John Daniszewski, and Randy Herschaft. *Covering Tyranny: The AP and Nazi Germany, 1933–1945.* United States: Associated Press, 2017.

Hemmer, Nicole. "From 'Faith in Facts' to 'Fair and Balanced': Conservative Media, Liberal Bias, and the Origins of Balance." In Schulman and Zelizer, *Media Nation*, 126–43.

Hightower, John. P. "The Chief Single Source of News." Unpublished manuscript, 1976. APCA, Writings about the Associated Press (APWR).

Hochfelder, David. *The Telegraph in America.* Baltimore: Johns Hopkins University Press, 2012.

Huffman, James. *Creating a Public: People and Press in Meiji Japan.* Honolulu: University of Hawaii Press, 1997.

Hughes, Frank. *Prejudice and the Press: A Restatement of the Principle of Freedom of the Press with Specific Reference to the Hutchins-Luce Commission.* New York: Devin-Adair, 1950.

Hutchison, Keith. "The Truth about the A.P.: I. Growth of a News Trust." *The Nation*, February 6, 1943, 190–94.

Hyman, Sydney. *The Lives of William Benton.* Chicago: University of Chicago Press, 1969.

Ickes, Harold L. *America's House of Lords: An Inquiry into Freedom of the Press.* New York: Harcourt Brace, 1939.

"In the Beginning: The Creation of the AP Wirephoto Network." *AP World*, Spring 1985, 3–8.

Jackaway, Gwyneth. *Media at War: Radio's Challenge to the Newspapers, 1924–1939.* Westport, CT: Praeger, 1995.

Kaplan, Richard. "From Partisanship to Professionalism: The Transformation of the Daily Press." In *Print in Motion: The Expansion of Publishing and Reading in the United States, 1880–1940*, edited by Karl Kaestle and Janice Radway, 116–39. Chapel Hill: University of North Carolina Press, 2009.

——. *Politics and the American Press: The Rise of Objectivity.* Cambridge, UK: Cambridge University Press, 2002.

Kim, Soon Jin. *EFE: Spain's World News Agency.* New York, Westport, CT: Greenwood Press, 1989.

Kirkpatrick, William S. "Showing German Editors a Free Press at Work." *Journalism Quarterly* 26, no. 1 (1949): 29–35.

Knightley, Phillip. *The First Casualty: From the Crimea to Vietnam: The War Correspondent as Hero, Propagandist, and Myth Maker.* London: Harcourt, Brace, Jovanovich, 1975.

Kruglak, Theodore E. *The Two Faces of TASS.* Westport, CT: Greenwood Press, 1972. First published 1962 by University of Minnesota Press (Minneapolis).

Krugler, David F. *The Voice of America and the Domestic Propaganda Battles, 1945–1953.* Columbia: University of Missouri Press, 2000.

Kupchan, Charles A. *Isolationism: A History of America's Efforts to Shield Itself from the World.* New York: Oxford University Press, 2020.

Lebovic, Sam. *Free Speech and Unfree News: The Paradox of Press Freedom in America.* Cambridge, MA: Harvard University Press, 2016.

———. "When the 'Mainstream Media' Was Conservative: Media Criticism in the Age of Reform." In Schulman and Zelizer, *Media Nation*, 63–76.

Lefebure, Antoine. *Havas: Les arcanes du pouvoir.* Paris: Bernard Grasset, 1992.

Leibling, A. J. "The Boy in the Pistachio Shirt." In Liebling, *The Telephone Booth Indian*, 166–228. New York: Broadway Books, 2004. First published 1942 by Penguin (New York).

Lemberg, Diana. *Barriers Down: How American Power and Free-Flow Policies Shaped Global Media.* New York: Columbia University Press, 2019.

Levin, Linda Lottridge. *The Making of FDR: The Story of Stephen T. Early, America's First Modern Press Secretary.* Amherst, NY: Prometheus Books, 2008.

Lippmann, Walter. *Liberty and the News.* New Brunswick, NJ: Transaction Publishers, 1995. First published 1920 by Harcourt, Brace, and Howe (New York).

———. *Public Opinion.* Preface by Ronald Steel. New York: Free Press Paperbacks, 1997. First published 1922 by Harcourt, Brace (New York).

Lochner, Louis. *What about Germany?* New York: Dodd Mead, 1942.

Lochner, Louis P. *Always the Unexpected: A Book of Reminiscences.* New York: Macmillan, 1956.

Lysagh, Charles Edward. *Brendan Bracken.* London: Allen Lane, 1979.

Mari, Will. *The American Newsroom: A History, 1920–1960.* Columbia: University of Missouri Press, 2021.

Martin, Percy Alvin. *Latin America and the War.* Baltimore. Johns Hopkins University Press, 1925.

Martinelli, Diana Knott, and Jeff Mucciarone. "New Deal Public Relations: A Glimpse into FDR Press Secretary Stephen Early's Work." *Public Relations Review* 33 (2007): 49–57.

Marzolf, Marion Tuttle. *Civilizing Voices: American Press Criticism, 1889–1950.* New York: Longman, 1991.

Mayer, Jane. "The Making of the Fox News White House." *New Yorker*, March 4, 2019, 40–53.

McChesney, Robert. "Press-Radio Relations and the Emergence of Network, Commercial Broadcasting in the United States, 1930–1935." *Historical Journal of Film, Radio, and Television* 11, no. 1 (1991): 41–57.

———. *Telecommunications, Mass Media, and Democracy: The Battle for the Control of U.S. Broadcasting, 1928–1935.* New York: Oxford University Press, 1994.

"M.E.S."—*His Book: A Tribute and a Souvenir of the Twenty-Five Years 1893–1918 of the Service of Melville E. Stone as General Manager of the Associated Press.* New York: Harper, 1918.

Morris, Joe Alex. *Deadline Every Minute: The Story of the United Press.* New York: Greenwood Press, 1968.

Moseley, Ray. *Reporting War: How Foreign Correspondents Risked Capture, Torture, and Death to Cover World War Two.* New Haven, CT: Yale University Press, 2017.

Murphy, Beth. "Indianapolis News." In *The Encyclopedia of Indianapolis*, edited by David J. Bodenhamer and Robert G. Barrows, 796–97. Bloomington: Indiana University Press, 1994.

Nasaw, David. *The Chief: The Life of William Randolph Hearst.* Boston: Houghton Mifflin, 2000.

Newton, Ronald C. *German Buenos Aires, 1900–1933: Social Change and Cultural Crisis*. Austin: University of Texas Press, 1977.

Nichols, Christopher McKnight. *Promise and Peril: America at the Dawn of a Global Age*. Cambridge, MA: Harvard University Press, 2011.

Ninkovich, Frank A. *The Diplomacy of Ideas: U.S. Foreign Policy and Cultural Relations, 1938–1950*. Cambridge, UK: Cambridge University Press, 1981.

Owens, Dewey M. "The Associated Press." *American Mercury* 10, no. 40 (1927): 385–93.

Palmer, Michael B. *International News Agencies: A History*. New York: Palgrave Macmillan, 2020.

Parry-Giles, Shawn J. "Exporting America's Cold War Message: The Debate over America's First Peacetime Propaganda Program, 1947–1954." PhD diss., Indiana University, 1992.

Patterson, Thomas. *Informing the News: The Need for Knowledge-Based Journalism*. New York: Vintage Books, 2013.

Pickard, Victor. *America's Battle for Media Democracy: The Triumph of Corporate Libertarianism and the Future of Media Reform*. New York: Cambridge University Press, 2015.

Pirsein, Robert William. *The Voice of America: A History of the International Broadcasting Activities of the United States Government, 1940–1962*. New York: Arno Press, 1979.

Pressman, Matthew. "Objectivity and Its Discontents: The Struggle for the Soul of American Journalism in the 1960s and 1970s." In Schulman and Zelizer, *Media Nation*, 96–113.

Putnis, Peter. "International News Agencies, News-Flow, and the USA-Australia Relationship from the 1920s till the End of the Second World War." *Media History* 18, nos. 3–4 (2012): 423–41.

———. "Share 999: British Government Control of Reuters during World War I." *Media History* 14, no. 2 (2008): 1410–65.

Pyle, Richard. "War II: Soldiers of the Press." In Reporters of the Associated Press, *Breaking News*, 214–53. New York: Princeton Architectural Press, 2007.

Rantanen, Terhi. "After Five O'Clock Friends: Kent Cooper and Roy Howard." *Roy W. Howard Monographs in Journalism and Mass Communication Research*, No. 4. School of Journalism, Indiana University, 1998.

———. "The End of the Electronic News Cartel, 1927–1934." In *International Communication and Global News Networks: Historical Perspectives*, edited by Peter Putnis, Chandrika Kaul, and Jürgen Wilke, 167–87. New York: Hampton Press, 2011.

———. "Foreign Dependence and Domestic Monopoly: The European News Cartel and U.S. Associated Presses." *Media History* 12, no. 1 (2006): 19–35. DOI: 10.1080/13688800600597145/.

———. "Howard Interviews Stalin." *Roy W. Howard Monographs in Journalism and Mass Communication Research* No. 3. School of Journalism, Indiana University, 1994.

———. "Mr. Howard Goes to South America: The United Press Associations and Foreign Expansion." *Roy W. Howard Monographs in Journalism and Mass Communication Research* No. 2. School of Journalism, Indiana University, 1992.

Read, Donald. *The Power of News: The History of Reuters*, 2nd ed. Oxford: Oxford University Press, 1999.

Renaud, Jean-Luc. "U.S. Government Assistance to AP's World-Wide Expansion." *Journalism and Mass Communication Quarterly* 62, no. 1 (1985): 10–16, 36.

Reporters of the Associated Press. *Breaking News: How the Associated Press Has Covered War, Peace, and Everything Else.* New York: Princeton Architectural Press, 2007.

Rinke, Stefan. "The Reconstruction of National Identity: German Immigrants in Latin America during the First World War." In *Immigration and National Identities in Latin America,* edited by Nicola Foote and Michael Goebel, 160–81. Gainesville: University Press of Florida, 2014.

Ritchie, Donald A. *Reporting from Washington: The History of the Washington Press Corps.* Oxford: Oxford University Press, 2005.

Russ, Carla. "Persuasive Identities? German Propaganda in Chile and Argentina during the First World War." *National Identities* 24, no. 1 (2019): 1–15.

Scharnberg, Harriet. "The A and P of Propaganda: Associated Press and Nazi Image Journalism." *Zeithistorische Forschungen / Studies in Contemporary History,* online edition, 13 (2016). http://www.zeithistorische-forschungen.de/1-2016/id=5324/.

Schiffman, James R. "Undervaluing Mutual: The FCC's Missed Opportunity to Restructure Radio Broadcasting in the New Deal Era." *Journal of Radio and Audio Media* 24, no. 2 (2017): 302–319.

Schoenherr, Steven E. "Selling the New Deal: Stephen T. Early's Role as Press Secretary to Franklin D. Roosevelt." PhD diss., University of Delaware, 1976.

Schudson, Michael. *The Good Citizen: A History of American Civic Life.* New York: Martin Kessler Books, 1998.

———. *The Rise of the Right to Know.* Cambridge, MA: Harvard University Press, 2015.

Schulman, Bruce, and Julian Zelizer. *Media Nation: The Political History of News in Modern America.* Philadelphia: University of Pennsylvania Press, 2017.

Schulte, Henry F. *The Spanish Press, 1470–1966: Print, Power, and Politics.* Urbana: University of Illinois Press, 1968.

Schwarzlose, Richard Allen. *The Nation's Newsbrokers.* Vol. 2. *The Rush to Institution, from 1865 to 1920.* Evanston, IL: Northwestern University Press, 1988.

Scott, Dale Benjamin. "Labor's New Deal for Journalism—The Newspaper Guild in the 1930s." PhD diss., University of Illinois at Urbana-Champaign, 2009.

Seldes, George. *Freedom of the Press.* New York: Da Capo Press, 1971. First published 1935 by Bobbs-Merrill (New York).

———. *Lords of the Press.* New York: Messner, 1939.

———. *Sawdust Caesar: The Untold Story of Mussolini and Fascism.* New York: Harper, 1935.

Sheinin, David M. K. *Argentina and the United States: An Alliance Continued.* Athens: University of Georgia Press, 2006.

Sherman, John. "*Indianapolis Times.*" In *The Encyclopedia of Indianapolis,* edited by David J. Bodenhamer and Robert G. Barrows, 811. Bloomington: Indiana University Press, 1994.

Silberstein-Loeb, Jonathan. *The International Distribution of News: The Associated Press, Press Association, and Reuters, 1848–1947.* New York: Cambridge University Press, 2014.

Sinclair, Upton. *The Brass Check: A Study of American Journalism.* Pasadena, CA: The author, 1920.

Slauter, Will. *Who Owns the News? A History of Copyright.* Stanford, CA: Stanford University Press, 2019.

Slobodian, Quinn. *Globalists: The End of Empire and the Birth of Neoliberalism*. Cambridge, MA: Harvard University Press, 2018.

Smith, Richard Norton. *The Colonel: The Life and Legend of Robert R. McCormick, 1880–1955*. Boston: Houghton Mifflin, 1997.

Spielmans, John V. "The Dilemma of the Closed Shop." *Journal of Political Economy* 51, no. 2 (1943): 113–34. https://www-jstor-org.myaccess.library.utoronto.ca/stable/1824756/.

Stamm, Michael. "Broadcasting News in the Interwar Period." In *Making News: The Political Economy of Journalism in Britain and America from the Glorious Revolution to the Internet*, edited by Richard R. John and Jonathan Silberstein-Loeb, 133–63. New York: Oxford University Press, 2015.

———. *Dead Tree Media: Manufacturing the Newspaper in Twentieth-Century North America*. Baltimore: Johns Hopkins University Press, 2018.

———. *Sound Business: Newspapers, Radio, and the Politics of New Media*. Philadelphia: University of Pennsylvania Press, 2011.

Steele, Richard W. *Propaganda in an Open Society: The Roosevelt Administration and the Media*. Westport, CT: Greenwood Press, 1985.

Talese, Gay. *The Kingdom and the Power: Behind the Scenes at the New York Times*. New York: Random House, 2007. First published 1969, World Publishing Co. (New York).

Tato, Maria Inés. "Fighting for a Lost Cause? The Germanophile Newspaper La Unión in Neutral Argentina, 1914–1918." *War in History* 25, no. 4 (2018): 464–84.

———. "Luring Neutrals: Allied and German Propaganda in Argentina during the First World War." In *World War I and Propaganda*, edited by Troy Paddock, 322–44. Boston: Brill, 2014.

Tifft, Susan E., and Alex S. Jones. *The Trust: The Private and Powerful Family behind* The New York Times. New York: Little, Brown, 1999.

Tworek, Heidi. "The Creation of European News: News Agency Cooperation in Interwar Europe." *Journalism Studies* 14, no. 5 (2013): 730–42.

———. "Magic Connections: German News Agencies and Global News Networks, 1905–1945." PhD diss., Harvard University, 2012.

———. *News from Germany: The Competition to Control World Communications, 1900–1945*. Cambridge, MA: Harvard University Press, 2019.

UNESCO. *News Agencies: Their Structure and Operation*. Paris: UNESCO, 1953.

Villard, Oswald Garrison. *The Disappearing Daily: Chapters in American Newspaper Evolution*. New York: Alfred A. Knopf, 1944.

Waller, Spencer Weber. "The Antitrust Legacy of Thurman Arnold." *St. John's Law Review* 78, no. 3 (2004): 569–613.

Watts, Liz. "AP's First Female Reporters." *Journalism History* 39, no. 1 (2013): 15–28.

Wertheim, Stephen. *Tomorrow, the World: The Birth of U.S. Global Supremacy*. Cambridge, MA: Harvard University Press, 2020.

White, Graham J. *FDR and the Press*. Chicago: University of Chicago Press, 1979.

White, Llewellyn, and Robert D. Leigh. *Peoples Speaking to Peoples*. New York: Arno Press, 1972. First published 1946.

Winfield, Betty. *FDR and the News Media*. Urbana: University of Illinois Press, 1990.

Winseck, Dwayne R., and Robert M. Pike. *Communication and Empire: Media, Markets, and Globalization, 1860–1930.* Durham, NC: Duke University Press, 2007.

Zelizer, Barbie. "Words against Images: Positioning Newswork in the Age of Photography." In *Newsworkers: Toward a History of the Rank and File,* edited by Bonnie Brennen and Hanno Hardt, 135–59. Minneapolis: University of Minnesota Press, 1995.

Index

Voice of America); nature of, 254; Nazi, 117–18, 190–94, 261; postwar Soviet Union and, 260, 261, 264; Reuters-Havas-Wolff cartel and, 19–22, 24–25, 29, 80, 81–82, 90; during World War I, 104, 190–91
Propaganda Kompanie, 191
Providence Journal, 18
Providence Journal-Bulletin, 234

Radio Agency (Havas), 89
radio broadcasting, 122, 123–38, 165–66; advertising/sponsorship revenue from, 127, 129–31, 134, 136 38, 195; AP member and board debates concerning, 123, 124–38, 148–49, 284; of *Barriers Down*, 232; Biltmore Agreement, 134–35; bulletin broadcasting and, 127–29, 132, 134, 135; election coverage and, 123–26, 128–30, 132–33; INS/Hearst and, 127–30, 131, 135–37; K.C. musical creativity and, *179*, 198–99; PRB and, 135–36, 170; radio stations as AP associate members, 138, 169, 220 21, 222, 266; sports and, 123, 127–28; as threat to print media, 123–29; Transradio and, 135–38, 259, 260; UP/Scripps and, 125, 127–33, 135–37; Voice of America and (*see* Voice of America)
Rathom, John, 18
Ray, E. Lansing, 90, 127–28, 266
RCA, 128
Read, Donald, 111
Read, Lessis S., 155
Rengo/Nippon Shimbun Rengo (Japan): AP expansion into Japan and, 76–83, 93–96, 98, 99–106, 120, 243, 274, 284, 286; Domei as successor, 81–82, 120; financial difficulties of, 100–102; government subsidies of, 81–82, 100, 101, 120; Kokusai as predecessor, 77, 79–81; merger plans for, 100, 101; as nonprofit cooperative news agency, 80–82, 93
Republican National Committee, 152–53, 217
Reuter, Julius, 282
Reuters (UK), 9, 15, 26–29, 32, 47–48, 57, 64, 74–79; AP expansion into Japan and, 99–106, 120–21; AP post-1945 expansion into Europe, 235, 236–43; AP renegotiation with (1942), 236–39, 240; AP renegotiation with (1946), 239–40; AP-Rengo contract in Japan and, 76–77, 79–83, 93–96, 99–106; as cooperative news agency, 270;

K.C. as speaker at centenary gala, 28, *183*, 269–70; news provided to VOA, 259, 260; Press Association (UK) and, 27, 29, 74, 75, 91, 97, 107, 109–11, 236–38. *See also* Jones, Roderick; Reuters-Havas-Wolff cartel
Reuters-Havas-Wolff cartel, 9–10; *agences alliées* system and, 25–26, 64, 84–85, 96, 242; AP expansion into China and, 76–78, 90, 93, 94; AP expansion into Europe and, 24–30, 51, 64–65, 87–89; AP expansion into Japan and, 76–83, 90, 93–96, 98, 99; AP expansion into South America and, 15–24; AP fees paid to, 31, 33; AP original contract with, 9, 24–30, 38–39, 69, 70, 77, 78, 91, 106; AP renegotiation/separation from, 99, 106–13, 119–20, 166–67, 169, 234, 236–37, 277; AP renegotiation with (1926–1927), 74–79, 93–94, 96, 98, 102, 106; AP renegotiation with (1931–1932), 90–98; censorship in Europe and, 83–84; competition with United Press (Scripps), 17–18; exclusive agreements, 57; K.C. resists AP reliance on cartel system, 19–22, 31–33, 73–75, 90–98; members, described, 9, 15; propaganda resistance and, 19–22, 24–25, 29, 80, 81–82; territorial restrictions of, 15–16
Rickatson-Hatt, Bernard, 53, 111–12, 166–67
Right to Know, The (Cooper), 205–6, 272 74
Robbins, H. C., 108
Roberts, Elmer, 88–89
Roberts, Owen, 220
Roberts, Roy, 143, 222
Rochester Times-Union, 68, 69
Rogers, Will, 146
Roosevelt, Eleanor, 47, 209, 252
Roosevelt, Franklin D., 83; AP antitrust litigation and, 207, 213–14, 215–16, 219, 229; censorship during World War II and, 197, 245–46, 266; claims of AP pro-Republican/anti-Roosevelt bias and, 10, 44–45, 150, 153–58, 168–69, 198–99; "court-packing" plan, 158; K.C. press freedom campaign and, 229–31; New Deal programs (*see* New Deal); presidential elections of 1944 and, 228–29
Roth, Franz, 191

Sacramento Bee, 12–13, 129
San Antonio Light, 71
San Antonio Standard Times, 156

GENE ALLEN is a professor emeritus of journalism at Toronto Metropolitan University. He is the author of *Making National News: A History of Canadian Press.*

The History of Communication